Juvenal and the Satiric Emotions

Juvenal and the Satiric Emotions

CATHERINE KEANE

OXFORD
UNIVERSITY PRESS

OXFORD
UNIVERSITY PRESS

Oxford University Press is a department of the University of
Oxford. It furthers the University's objective of excellence in research,
scholarship, and education by publishing worldwide.

Oxford   New York
Auckland   Cape Town   Dar es Salaam   Hong Kong   Karachi
Kuala Lumpur   Madrid   Melbourne   Mexico City   Nairobi
New Delhi   Shanghai   Taipei   Toronto

With offices in
Argentina   Austria   Brazil   Chile   Czech Republic   France   Greece
Guatemala   Hungary   Italy   Japan   Poland   Portugal   Singapore
South Korea   Switzerland   Thailand   Turkey   Ukraine   Vietnam

Oxford is a registered trademark of Oxford University Press
in the UK and certain other countries.

Published in the United States of America by
Oxford University Press
198 Madison Avenue, New York, NY 10016

Cataloging-in-Publication Data is on file at the Library of Congress.
ISBN 978–0–19–998189–2

9 8 7 6 5 4 3 2 1
Printed in the United States of America
on acid-free paper

CONTENTS

ACKNOWLEDGMENTS

This book has been long in the making, and I finish it in debt to many people. Over the past decade, my colleagues and students at Washington University were willing to listen to me talk about Juvenal again and again, keeping me focused on the project even as other responsibilities kept progress slow. Proto-chapters and overviews were also shared at conferences and colloquia in Columbia, Missouri; San Francisco; Oxford; Urbana-Champaign; Tucson; Ithaca; Austin; and Miami, Ohio, and on each occasion my audience taught me a great deal. During a luxurious year's leave in 2012–13, I benefited from the help of my summer research assistant, Jacob Emmett (and from research funds provided by my department and administration); from Washington University's Center for the Humanities, where I spent the fall as a Faculty Fellow; and from the University of Cincinnati Department of Classics, where I was a spring Tytus Fellow. As I peruse parts of the book in the future, I will be visited with visions of the different offices and desks where they were created. I will also remember the many individuals who helped make these experiences possible and useful, including George Pepe, Tim Moore, Caroline Bishop, Joe Loewenstein, Erin McGlothlin, Steve Zwicker, Dan Hooley, John Henderson, Susanna Braund, Barbara Gold, Susan Prince, Daniel Markovic, and Lauren Ginsburg.

I have been unbelievably lucky in other mentors, supporters, friends, and readers; quite a few have left marks on this project through conversations, invitations, careful evaluations, and/or other forms of inspiration. Their interventions and encouragement helped me go in new directions and solve nagging problems, and any flaws that remain in the book are my own doing. I particularly thank Ralph Rosen, Joe Farrell, Jen Ebbeler, Amanda Wilcox, Carlos Noreña, Allen Miller, David Larmour, Brian Hook, Henry Dyson, Bryce Walker, Heather Elomaa, Eric Brown, Christine Johnson, Denise McCoskey, Kirk Freudenburg (special thanks for reading a big chunk of the manuscript at a pivotal stage), and John Henderson (again). Two scholars in particular have oriented and inspired me many times over with their work and, even more important, welcomed me warmly into the field. I feel I owe as much to W. S. Anderson and Susanna Braund as Juvenal does (and that's an awful lot). Finally, I must also single out Dan Hooley again because I have been so lucky to have him as a neighbor and to benefit from his hospitality and professional wisdom. He has given an enormous amount of the greatest gift in our line of work, time, in reading and commenting on this and other manuscripts for me.

Stefan Vranka has given solid and patient support for several years now, assisted by Sarah Pirovitz, who efficiently and cheerfully shepherded my manuscript back and forth across the country and the Internet. It has been an honor to work with Oxford University Press again. The production process has been smooth and reassuring, thanks to the professionalism of Pete Mavrikis and Susan Ecklund. Chris Lovell provided valuable advice and assistance on the indices. I thank my parents, Barry and Clare, whose sense of humor has sustained us all for forty-odd years and made it inevitable that I would be drawn to ancient comic literature. More thanks to the rest of our family—John, Angela, Dave —for cheering me on as I completed the book, and to our new joy Elizabeth for special inspiration these last few months. Finally, and for always, I am most grateful to David Scheu, who gave practical help and moral support from the proposal stage up through the proofing and indexing, and who with his matchless optimism has helped the good and civilized emotions prevail in our life.

October 2014

NOTE ON TEXTS AND TRANSLATIONS

For quotations, I use the Oxford texts of ancient authors wherever possible (Juvenal and Persius: Clausen, 1992; Horace: Wickham and Garrod, 1912; Seneca's dialogues: Reynolds, 1977). All exceptions are cited. Translations are my own except where others' are quoted or adapted, with citations.

Juvenal and the Satiric Emotions

Introduction

IS A SATIRIST SUPPOSED to express emotion? Should satire engage its audience's emotions as well as its intellect and appetite for play? Precisely what feeling or feelings are appropriate to express, or to elicit, in the practice of mockery and social criticism? Any student of literature who volunteers answers to these questions has been influenced, directly or indirectly, by one Roman satiric poet. Juvenal's sixteen *Satires*, written in the early second century C.E., offer memorable commentary on the role of emotion in satire. Juvenal did not simply suggest answers to the questions I pose above, but prompted the questions themselves, thus helping to shape the reception of his work and his genre. In this way as in others, "Juvenal's satiric perspective has become completely ours."[1] In this book, I argue that my opening questions about emotion were central to Juvenal's definition of the satirist's role. They inspired the first pose he struck and guided his subsequent creation of satiric verse.

Juvenal connects the matter of emotion's role in satire to a broader idea that dominates satiric theory from antiquity to the present: namely, the notion that there are a variety of ways to *do* satire. This idea affects even the relatively narrowly defined Roman verse genre, which consists largely of monologues on moral topics or social ills. It is not simply that satire was seen as a genre "not bound, either in form or matter, by rigid rules."[2] It is more accurate to say that *varietas* was a definitive feature of the genre, "staged as a problem of writing . . . by the ancient satirists themselves" and replicated in satiric

---

[1.] Winkler, "Media Age," 542.
[2.] Duff, *Iuvenalis Saturae XIV*, xxx–xxxi.

theory.[3] It is inevitable that this generic theme would permeate the work of the most prolific extant Roman satirist. The corpus of Juvenal, despite the accident of transmission that severed off part of the last poem, totals nearly four thousand lines of hexameter and would originally have filled five book rolls. This is close to twice Horace's satiric output, and more than five times that of Persius. It could only have been surpassed by the prodigious thirty books of the genre's "inventor," Lucilius, now almost entirely lost. Juvenal was a career satirist. He spent at least a dozen years (by some accounts, closer to thirty) producing his poems and left no other works.[4] By comparison, Horace wrote satire only during the first decade of a long and generically diverse poetic career, while Persius had not even finished his single book when he died. Juvenal's poetic career was devoted to thinking about satire's nature, and to trying new and different things with the genre.[5] His *Satires* should be a focal point for any scholar who aims to theorize satire, ancient or other.

From the beginning of this corpus, emotion is a principal theme. Like previous Roman verse satire, Juvenal's poetry is generally dominated by a first-person speaker who insists on being the center of satiric discourse, posing as the chief commentator on the state of the world. This fact greatly influences the theoretical debate, since the speaker of satire essentially embodies his genre—often defending it polemically. The generic theory is inevitably bound up in this "I." Juvenal's particular approach to inventing his "I" is a move so swift, smooth, and deceptively natural in appearance that its novelty can easily go unnoticed. The *Satires* introduce the satirist's personality, or persona—to use the established critical term—by describing his emotional state. In the series of poems that follows, the dazzlingly varied subjects and settings are matched by a persona that, despite its own changeability, creates unity in the corpus.

This book is neither particularly humorous nor particularly concerned with the humor of satire, a perennially popular subject in literary studies. Humor is certainly always entangled in satire's emotional dynamics. The laughter of a reader or viewer can be connected to many emotions and take

---

[3] The quote is from Freudenburg, *Satires of Rome*, 2; see also Classen, "Satire—The Elusive Genre"; Griffin, *Satire: A Critical Reintroduction*, 6–34; and the essays in Connery and Combe, *Theorizing Satire*.
[4] The most conservative *termini* assigned to Juvenal's career, going by references in the individual books, are about 117 and 130 C.E.; see Syme, "Juvenal, Pliny, Tacitus," 259–60, and *Tacitus*, 2:774–78; cf. Courtney, *Satires*, 1–10; and Coffey, *Roman Satire*, 119–23. Hardie, "Name-Repetitions" and "Juvenal, Domitian, and Hadrian," offers additional evidence on a date after 117 for Book 1. Arguments for an earlier start date were advanced by Friedländer (*Roman Life and Manners*, 310–18); a new case is made in Uden, *Invisible Satirist* (appendix).
[5] "We are struck by Juvenal's persistent tendency to innovation" (Jones, *Juvenal*, 144).

many forms: superior mockery (of the satirist's targets or even the satirist himself), a scandalized frisson at obscenity, a hasty means of avoiding darker and discomfiting thoughts. We modern consumers of "satire" (by a much broader definition that includes all manner of media, such as viral Internet memes and partisan journalism) are familiar with all of these experiences; we may even seek them out routinely from an ever-growing menu of options. But ancient Roman satire, and particularly Juvenal's, has a peculiar way of packaging emotions so as to mask the fact of our participation. When there is a prominent satirist figure constantly doing the talking, it can seem as though the only emotions in the air are his. Everything that he tells us—about private injuries, conflicts in social life, national moral crises, episodes in history and myth, and goings-on in the emperor's court, Roman streets, and barbarian villages—is supposedly a product of his observing, thinking, and feeling mind. Then too, just taking in the narrative and thematic variety of what he has to say can keep us from noticing or admitting the provocations he is throwing our way. But this book proceeds from the assumption that Juvenal does not mean for his audience to have an easy or purely anodyne experience of satiric humor. The performer exploits the audience. Although I concentrate on the original cultural and literary context of the *Satires*, it is worth reflecting throughout on the ways these ancient poems can still engage our feelings and our conscience.

Generalizing about Juvenal

Though it has much to offer, Juvenal's work is underutilized in scholarly discussions of the workings of ancient satire. Typically, the early *Satires*—particularly Books 1 and 2 (*Satires* 1 through 6)—are disproportionately represented, and the rest are often mentioned only in "hasty generalizations."[6] There are exceptions in recent studies that take a systematic, anatomizing approach, classifying strategies of humor, allusion, and the like. But while these give deserved space to the complex later *Satires*, by eschewing the poem-by-poem or book-by-book format, they make it difficult to see how each text or series might be working as a whole.[7]

---

[6] Stramaglia, *Giovenale*, 7. The pattern is evident even in recent works on Roman satire: see Braund and Osgood, *Persius and Juvenal*; Freudenburg, *Companion to Roman Satire* (excepting Rimell's fairly wide-ranging "Poor Man's Feast"); and Freudenburg, *Satires of Rome*, 209–77.
[7] Schmitz, *Satirische in Juvenals Satiren*; Plaza, *Function of Humour*; and Jones, *Juvenal*. Cf. the fairly even coverage in Rudd, *Themes in Roman Satire*. Romano, *Irony in Juvenal*, does proceed

In genre studies, from the theoretical to the thematic, one most often sees Juvenal summed up as a *type* of satirist. Imitators and critics since the Renaissance have pinned him to one end of a spectrum of possible rhetorical styles of satire—or in a simpler scheme seen just as frequently, one of two opposite poles. The "Juvenalian" style is vehement, scathing, intensely negative, and loudly provocative; it is characterized by "fiery indignation," rhetorical "violence," and "outrage" (note the blend of rhetorical and emotional terminology, which is also seen in ancient rhetorical theory). The "Horatian" foil to this is a style that conveys "easy laughter."[8] A convenient analogy of dramatic genres suggests itself: Juvenal, being the grander stylist, approaches a "tragic" style, while the pedestrian Horace is "comic."[9] It is as if these two poets consciously worked out Roman satire's stylistic and affective parameters between them. Persius, the third wheel in an otherwise neat dichotomy, is dealt with in various ways—sometimes likened to one or the other "extreme" type, at other times idealized or criticized for resisting both poles.[10] And Lucilius, although his work is lost, is conveniently portrayed by all three of his successors as fearless and profuse; he can thus be confidently attached to the Juvenalian end of the spectrum and credited with its invention. Of course this scheme has its weaknesses (Juvenal's stylistic range proves quite broad on close technical analysis)[11] and its paradoxes (scholars have called portions of Juvenal's oeuvre "Horatian" and "Lucilian," citing not just rhetorical style but themes and moral attitudes).[12] Taking a step further back, we must also appreciate that the evaluative terms that have been used so regularly

---

book by book and concludes that the "early" and "late" poems use irony in similar ways (but also endorses others' impressions of declining force and topicality).

[8.]For these terms see Kernan, *Cankered Muse*, 25 and 28–29. Cf. Anderson's comparison of Juvenal and Martial in "*Lascivia* vs. *ira.*"

[9.]The distinction that eighteenth-century English critics made between Horace and Juvenal "became an elaborate schema which organized a number of specific qualities in opposition around the central dichotomy between comedy and tragedy"; this language legitimized the practice of both types of satire (Weber, "Comic Humor," 277). Cf. Dryden's remark that "Juvenal excels in the tragical satire, as Horace does in the comical" in his "Discourse Concerning the Original and Progress of Satire" (Ker, *Essays of John Dryden*, 2:96). The model of the dramatic genres persisted in twentieth-century criticism; see, e.g., Kernan, *Cankered Muse*, 29: satires in the Juvenalian manner "seem always to be on the threshold of tragedy."

[10.]Kernan, *Cankered Muse*, 29: "Horace and Juvenal . . . provide us with the two extremes of the satirist." Griffin, *Satire: A Critical Reintroduction*, 10–28, surveys comparisons of the pair (and the slippery Persius) in satiric theory from the Elizabethan era to the eighteenth century. Nisbet, "Revoicing Imperial Satire," considers the effects of the binary scheme on translations.

[11.]Powell, "Stylistic Registers in Juvenal."

[12.]See Singleton, "Juvenal's Fifteenth Satire," 198 (on the contemplative, "Horatian" later Juvenal); and Braund, *Beyond Anger*, 189–96 (characterizing Book 4 as "Horatian" and Book 5 more cautiously as "Lucilian").

are first suggested by the satirists themselves—for example, in Horace's comparison of his work to comedy in *Satire* 1.4, and Juvenal's parallel invocation of tragedy in his *Satire* 6. Again, how well their poetry fits these handy characterizations is another question. But the poets' tendentious cues have worked their way into their own reception,[13] much as their representation of Lucilius came to stand for the real thing after his poems were lost.

The view that there is a distinct "Juvenalian" kind of satire took a particularly radical form in one nineteenth-century monograph. Responding to differences between the earlier and later *Satires*, Ribbeck made the argument that most of the latter are not Juvenal's at all, but the work of a skilled declaimer and imitator.[14] Ribbeck's thesis is now cited only as a curiosity, for most scholars are perfectly ready to believe that Juvenal tried out various satiric modes. Still, the idea of "two Juvenals" remained as a refrain in commentaries and studies, with virtually all the poems Ribbeck marked as spurious repeatedly lumped together as the "later" work. Duff stresses the "remarkable difference between the earlier and later satires," suggesting that if one "read[s] the fifteenth satire after the first . . . the difference will seem astonishing" because of their "different object" and style.[15] A more subtle "Analyst" than Ribbeck, de Decker proposes that there was "un Juvénal vrai et un Juvénal factice." He means not that the poet was succeeded by an imitator, but that Juvenal himself embodied both "un poète et un rhéteur." These two sides of the author, one more adventurous in ideas, the other more interested in systematically exhibiting his rhetorical talent, take turns controlling the poems.[16] As the author of a very thorough rhetorical study of Juvenal, de Decker has nothing in principle against the "rhéteur," but he reaffirms Ribbeck's vision of the authentic and the artificial.

The "two Juvenals" idea has endured in a fuzzy but consequential form: the lukewarm reception of the later *Satires*. These poems have frequently been compared unfavorably to their earlier counterparts, even moved to a marginal category. One scholar sums up the critical reception with deliberate irony: "Juvenal's last two books are curiously un-Juvenalian."[17] Behind the criticisms is a vision of the poet's creative

[13.]On other manifestations of this process, see Keane, "Critical Contexts."

[14.]Ribbeck, *Echte und unechte Juvenal*, identifies *Satires* 10 and 12–15 as imitations.

[15.]Duff, *Iuvenalis Saturae XIV*, xxix and xxx. The two-part career model is also accepted in Harris, *Restraining Rage*, 226; and Cucchiarelli, *Satira e il poeta*, 213–14.

[16.]De Decker, *Juvenalis declamans*, 66–67.

[17.]Singleton, "Juvenal's Fifteenth Satire," 198.

decline, his failing capacity for economy, and his increasing dependence on a rhetorical toolkit. The language of the later *Satires* has been called "feeble, diffuse, clumsy, and commonplace," their comparatively clear organization evidence that the aging Juvenal began treating satire as a "routine."[18] Scholars stop short of accusations of senility, but there is certainly an insinuation that Juvenal's reconception of satire represented a decline from the genre's telos and coincided with a loss of mental energy and purpose. Descriptions of the later *Satires* as more contemplative and "philosophical" are not intended purely as compliments.[19]

Despite his initial self-presentation as belated, Juvenal's debut was not the final chapter in the tradition; it was a beginning, for this poet and for the genre. By the same token, the variation in his work is best viewed as chapters in a literary career featuring, and exploiting, various changes and shifts. For many other ancient authors and their readers, the notion of the career provided a meaningful framework for literary production and reception. Readers had notions of what a proper career trajectory could look like—for instance, what genres and subjects a young poet should take up, or what sort of work represented the acme of a career. These ideas can even be seen influencing the forgery of famous authors' youthful works.[20] (Sadly, although we have tantalizing epigrams of Martial that seem to depict the pre-*Satires* Juvenal, no ancient forgers have left us any *juvenilia Iuvenalis* to enjoy.) Roman authors built their careers, and their audiences processed them, with the familiar trajectory of the typical elite political career in mind—although a self-conscious poetic career could follow other paths than the rise to "high" genres. If the relative grandeur of genres is used as a measure, Vergil and Ovid represent contrasting career models (one linear and ascending to epic, the other almost defiantly twisting and turning until its self-reflective end). Political engagement (or lack thereof) is another career theme, with Cicero and Pliny visibly

---

[18.]The first quote is from Friedländer, *Essays on Juvenal*, 44; the second from Townend, "Literary Substrata to Juvenal," 159. Cf. Highet's claim that the later poems lack topical interest, vividness, and variety (*Juvenal the Satirist*, 138–39). Henke collects these and similar judgments ("Elefanten, Tochtermörder und Erbschleicher," 202–3). Lindo, collecting characterizations of the later *Satires*, points out that they are actually quite diverse—the lack of consensus being an effect of overall lack of attention ("Evolution of Later Satires," 17). Uniquely, Williams (*Change and Decline*, 287) suggests that Juvenal's abandonment of his early style reflects his growing "confidence" as a poet.

[19.]See Zarini, "Indignation chez Juvénal," 454: "il n'est pas interdit . . . de préférer l'ardeur de la première manière à la sagesse de la dernière." Highet believes that Juvenal turned toward Epicureanism in old age ("Philosophy of Juvenal").

[20.]See Peirano, *Rhetoric of Roman Fake*.

self-conscious about how their sequencing of works reflects their changing public status. In love elegy the career narrative is explicitly entwined with a personal story of *amor* and inspiration, but as the love object persists in unattainability, or mutates, or multiplies, the story can come to look parodically repetitive or cyclical.[21]

Where verse satire is concerned, Juvenal's predecessors are understood to offer significant food for thought about careers. Horace, because he went on to compose lyrics and verse letters after the *Satires*, exemplifies a kind of generic ascent (linked to his relationships with Maecenas and Augustus).[22] The *Satires* alone also tell stories about Horace's emergence and experience as a poet. There was a time when mapping Horace's early career narrative meant identifying which poems in the collection were written first (i.e., the nugatory and obscene ones).[23] But the two books of *Satires* are now commonly viewed as coherent texts in their own right, which can also be read as deliberate, dynamic, and multilayered narratives. A large and still-growing body of Horatian scholarship unpacks the intricate design of these narratives, exploring suggestive groupings of poems, subtle patterns of imagery, and development of key ideas.[24] The status and purpose of satire itself is always a rich theme in Horace, so that it is no surprise that Persius's single book has been read as containing its own story about the production and sharing of satire. As in Horace, the story has both linear and cyclical dimensions, inviting rereading even as it hints at movement toward closure.[25] Juvenal's two predecessors may well have wished their work to dramatize their own explorations of the genre's possibilities; satiric production is, by these precedents, a meditation on satire.

It makes sense to look for the same kind of story in Juvenal, open-mindedly and deliberately.[26] Perhaps it is the critic who "decides

---

[21.]These examples are revisited throughout the essays in Hardie and Moore, *Classical Literary Careers*.

[22.]Harrison, "There and Back Again."

[23.]*Satires* 1.2, 1.5, and 1.7–9 have been labeled youthful efforts or minor experiments; see Fraenkel, *Horace*, 76,124; cf. Rudd, *Satires of Horace*, 54–85.

[24.]On Book 1 alone, see Zetzel, "Horace's *Liber Sermonum*"; Gowers, "Fragments of Autobiography" and *Horace: Satires Book I*, especially 15–20; on the two books, see Oliensis, *Rhetoric of Authority*, 17–63; and Gowers, "Restless Companion."

[25.]See Henderson, "Persius' Didactic Satire"; Malamud, "Out of Circulation"; and Freudenburg, *Satires of Rome*, 195–208.

[26.]I find "satiric career" applied to Juvenal first in Bellandi (*Etica diatribica*, 8); cf. the use of the term "itinerario" throughout Stramaglia, *Giovenale*. Pertinent but low-profile discussions are Lindo, "Evolution of Later Satires"; and Coffey, "Indignant Satirist" (a brief review of Anderson's "Anger in Juvenal"). In the present chapter I draw on Keane, "Persona and Satiric Career."

whether a poet has a career"[27]—whether patterns and changes add up to a narrative that is worth thinking about and that may have something to teach us about genre. For further inspiration, we may look to satire's purported inventor. Lucilius represents an unprecedented sort of self-assertion by a "gentleman poet"; he self-consciously substituted literary activity for a traditional career in politics. And instead of playing the patron to literary professionals as he might have, he produced an oeuvre that in volume and fame rivaled the output of the great professionals of early Roman literature.[28] Indeed, the case of Lucilius gives us a good reason not to give short shrift to a satirist's "later" work: it was only after he had written a collection of five books in a variety of meters that Lucilius settled exclusively on dactylic hexameter. It is hard to know what meanings the various meters, and his permanent shift to hexameter, held for Lucilius. But as his ultimate choice became the standard for the genre, it is fair to say that Lucilius's successors saw "phase two" of his career as a key stage in the formal coalescence of satire.[29] This is just one more precedent Juvenal would have considered as he articulated his own career—with Lucilius's entire oeuvre available to consult—and one more reason to read his five books as a story of different approaches to satire.

Satire and Affect

Tradition notwithstanding, Juvenal's first move marks him as an innovator. He begins by connecting his creation of poetry to his emotions—a claim that naturalizes a poetic process dependent on extensive learning and labor. *Satire* 1 opens with a performed explosion of anger, the satirist claiming he has been holding back his feelings as long as he can bear ("Will I always just have to listen? Will I never get revenge?," *semper ego auditor tantum? numquamne reponam . . . ?*, 1.1). The causes of his rage—posers, criminals, and deviants running rampant in Rome—are the subject of this colorful and fast-paced poem. But an equally important subject is the rage itself; Juvenal describes its physical and emotional symptoms (all

---

[27.]Hardie and Moore, "Introduction: Literary Careers," 2.
[28.]Farrell, "Greek Lives," 41–42.
[29.]The original book chronology of Lucilius's *Satires* was muddled when the corpus was posthumously rearranged, so that it is the hexameter Books 1–21 and 30 that represent his "later" work. Lucilius's "decision to use hexameter was momentous for the establishment of the genre and its nature" (Muecke, "Rome's First Satirists," 41). On chronology, meters, and the ancient transmission, see also Warmington, *Remains of Old Latin*, 3:xx–xxiv; and Hooley, *Roman Satire*, 20.

passages to be revisited in chapter 1) and claims that the proper therapy is to scribble. The conceit, then, is that satire is motivated by, and produced in a state of, anger. This represents a striking transformation of the claims that Horace and Persius make as they launch their satiric careers. Both of those poets claim to laugh at human folly: Horace "telling the truth with a laugh" (*ridentem dicere verum, S.* 1.1.24), and Persius, with his "petulant spleen," "cackling" at the world around him (*sum petulanti splene—cachinno,* 1.12). While there is plenty of humor in Juvenal's *Satires*—indeed, woven into the vitriol from the beginning—there is nothing like a programmatic statement acknowledging a role for humor or laughter. Moreover, his profession of anger is unparalleled. Authorial satiric anger is virtually invisible in Horace's *Satires,* seemingly relegated to the *Epodes.*[30] When the satiric Horace does mention anger, he is usually discussing the feelings of satire's victims and critics (see 1.4.24–38 and Horace's own irritated response to being a target in 2.3 and 2.7). Persius's splenetic cackle might hint at underlying indignation, but as Persius emphasizes the rejecting gesture more than the motivating emotion, this tantalizing half-line is only a prelude to Juvenal's more methodical self-diagnosis.[31]

The Horatian idea that satire is emotionally provocative reappears in Juvenal: in *Satire* 1 the anxious interlocutor warns the poet that the most outspoken kind of satire can make other people angry and resentful. "From [strong satire] come anger and tears" (*hinc ira et lacrimae,* 1.168). Whether the "tears" refer to the angry audience or to the satirist on whom it takes revenge in turn,[32] the quip suggests a cycle of emotional expression and engagement. Nor are *ira et lacrimae* the only emotional options for satire's audience, if the summary of Juvenal's most ardent English reader has any worth. Dryden, who lavishly praises both Horace and Juvenal in an elaboration of the binary satiric theory, explains his ultimate choice of a favorite this way: "Juvenal gives me as much Pleasure as I can bear: He fully satisfies my Expectation, he Treats his Subject home: His Spleen is rais'd, and he raises mine: I have the Pleasure of Concernment in all he says."[33] For Dryden the Juvenalian recipe—which includes in varying

---

[30] See Cucchiarelli, *Satira e il poeta* on the generic boundary-drawing of *Satires* I and the *Epodes.*
[31] Anderson, "Rejection of Society."
[32] Braund (*Satires Book I*, 110) and Rosen ("Satire in the Republic," 39) understand the latter.
[33] Ker, *Essays of John Dryden,* 2:84. In Dryden, the term "concernment" is typically connected to the effects of "great art, especially high tragedy," including the Aristotelian mixture of audience emotions (Jensen, *Dryden's Critical Terms,* 32–33). Evidence of another critic's deep pleasure in Juvenalian outrageousness is Ramsay's ten-page rhapsody on the "brilliant" *Satire* 6 in the introduction to his Loeb edition (*Juvenal and Persius,* lii–lxii). See Nisbet, "Revoicing Imperial Satire," 506 for more comments.

combination indignant rhetoric, outlandish claims about human behavior, and cutting mockery—adds up to pleasure. Although he separates pleasure from instruction (citing the latter as Horace's special gift), Dryden's explanation is otherwise reminiscent of Aristotle's explanation of how tragedy works: mimesis of suffering is converted to catharsis and audience pleasure. And Dryden does write, echoing his words on tragedy elsewhere, that "the end or scope of satire [at least in Juvenal and Persius] is to purge the passions."[34]

We must take Dryden's evaluation of Juvenal with a grain of salt, as his critical posture is a strategy for participating in contemporary political and literary debates.[35] But even if his profession of emotional engagement is interested and forced, he has chosen a suitable author to champion; Dryden's evaluation brings to mind plenty of qualities intrinsic to Juvenal's work, such as the lurid colors in which the poet paints the world and his borrowing from other genres both high and low. A more recent but similarly adventurous evaluation of Juvenal's style holds that this poet "deepened [satire's] tendency toward the immediately human and emotional, and made it a keystone of his satires," and that he achieved this by representing ordinary suffering in the world from a closer distance than his predecessors: in his work "the poet is part of the existential subject matter" as well as an observer.[36] As I will discuss shortly, Juvenal's ability to express and arouse emotions is a function of his rhetorical training and rhetorical approach to satire. But the dominance of emotional terms in critical treatments of Juvenal, and of satire generally, reflects something else: Juvenal's success at convincing readers that the genre's business is emotional expression and engagement. Juvenal's emotional debut reorients the conventions of satiric self-presentation, creating an interpretive context for later gestures to laughter and freedom from passions. It is no surprise that this series of moves has had a strong influence on criticism. Juvenal prods his audience to "type" satire according to its emotional flavor on a scale that runs from detached to engaged.[37]

[34.]Ker, *Essays of John Dryden*, 2:101 (where Dryden is engaging with Heinsius's inadequate definition of satire). On his use of "purge" to mean "cleanse, purify, rectify," see Jensen, *Dryden's Critical Terms*, 96. Hopkins, *Conversing with Antiquity*, 145–46, further discusses the intersection of poetic pleasure, laughter, and anger in Dryden.

[35.]Hokpins, *Conversing with Antiquity*, 130–36, reviews political and literary interpretations of Dryden's satiric theory; Hooley sketches an argument of the first type in "Imperial Satire Reiterated," 348–50.

[36.]Witke, *Latin Satire*, 150 and 151.

[37.]Braund, *Masks*, classifies works by the three extant Roman satirists as "angry," "mocking," or "smiling."

In this emotional formula, the Juvenalian satirist is not an isolated observer. The emotional theory of the genre—that is, the conceit that satire is an affective reaction—implies a symbiotic relationship between the satirist and the world he is moved to describe. In satire's generic recipe, subject matter is no less important than the satirist figure. Moreover, satire's content is not an inert element, as it were, but plays a dynamic role. To explain, when we are trying to analyze the satirist's emotional rhetoric at every turn, we must consider this in connection with *what* he happens to be treating; what a satirist chooses to write about surely already says a great deal about his agenda.[38] A consistent persona may appear to "impose a unity on widely scattered material,"[39] but on the fictional level, the reverse is operating: satire is the creation of a speaker who has been provoked by what he sees or hears. Content influences style, and changes in content over time tell a story.

Where this story begins—that is, following Juvenal's initial outburst and introduction of his material—is a much-quoted claim about the content and motivation of *Satires* Book 1. At *Satire* 1.85–86, Juvenal sums up his book this way: "whatever people do—their prayers, fears, anger, pleasures, joys, diversions—is the fodder of my little book" (*quidquid agunt homines, votum timor ira voluptas/gaudia discursus, nostri farrago libelli est*). This is a definition of the satirist's field that blurs the line between human activity (*quidquid agunt homines*) and the various emotions that motivate and color it. This catchy couplet represents a way of seeing the genre, a way that hooks satire up to a kind of communal emotional pulse. It seems that Juvenal has led many readers to believe that this is the true nature of satire.

Satiric Emotions as Subjects and Tools

Why would Juvenal choose to reinvent satire as an emotionally engaged and engaging genre—and not just an angry genre, but one that can travel around a sort of affective spectrum? How, moreover, are we to read the

---

[38] So Henderson has argued about the male satirist's interest in women and gender ("Satire Writes Woman"). Cf. Gold's exploratory discussion of thematic continuity in "Idea of the Book," and the remarks of Fruelund Jensen: Juvenal's "ethos" should be seen as linked to his "fictional structure"; he "suit[s] his emotional colouring to his fictional scheme" ("Crime, Vice, and Retribution," 166–67; cf. 156–57). Hardie, "Condition of Letters," 152 (on *Satire* 7), seems to adopt a similar principle.

[39] Williams, *Change and Decline*, 287.

evident changes in his satire's particular emotional flavoring over his career? One interpretation is that the early *Satires* show bottled-up feelings coming out in the wake of Domitian's death, and that Juvenal's approach becomes more relaxed when these feelings run their course.[40] But this explanation reads a lot into the role of Domitian in Book 1 (in the grand scheme of things, not a substantial one) and implies that Juvenal had held his breath for an improbably long period. Another argument holds that the emotional style of the *Satires* reflects a more general cultural and literary trend: imperial authors, conscious that they lived in a radically different world than their predecessors, sought a "retreat into exploitation of irrationality." Thus, in its application of rhetorical devices, imperial literature aimed at "moving" rather than "persuading."[41] As hard as this argument is to prove, it admittedly has some appeal in light of recent scholarship highlighting imperial Latin literature's visible interest in emotions. In pursuing the "why" and "how" questions above, I propose to consider the *Satires* alongside examples of Greco-Roman literature—narrative, rhetorical, and philosophical—and particularly works that highlight social and literary meanings of the emotions. Throughout the *Satires*, Juvenal can be seen creatively exploiting the ideas they explore.

Juvenal recognized that emotions are interesting literary fodder, and not just because "the personal" is an appealing theme; recent studies of ancient concepts of the emotions have certainly traversed much broader territory. To point to the most obvious imperial context, emotions figure in the rules and the reception of rhetoric. Juvenal lived during an era when rhetorical performance and persuasion were a form of entertainment. Moreover, ancient literature acknowledges that emotions have many forms and functions. They were not simply experienced privately by individuals but could be evaluative or normative tools, socially useful or destructive, and politically interested.[42] Like other ancient writers, Juvenal understood emotion to be a potential source of conflict and tool of manipulation as well as a sign of humanity.

---

[40] Hardy, *Juvenalis Saturae*, lii.

[41] Williams, *Change and Decline*, 153 and 277. Cf. Witke, *Latin Satire*, 150: satire's new "tendency toward the immediately human and emotional" "had great importance for literature of the time of Hadrian and onwards."

[42] See Nussbaum, *Therapy of Desire* and *Upheavals of Thought* (dealing with philosophical perspectives on aspects of private life); Fitzgerald, *Passions and Moral Progress* (emphasizing philosophical discussions of the morality of the emotions); Toohey, *Melancholy, Love, and Time* (on the experience of depression and similar states), and several other studies cited below.

I have so far casually referred to the way emotions "flavor" Juvenal's satire. In fact, the complexity of emotions and their entanglement in social practice make it difficult to imagine that they could serve merely as a "flavoring" element. Anger, for example, is simply not stable or monolithic enough to function in this way—as we will see, it has too many different associations to have one guaranteed and clear effect on an audience. For this reason, I propose that when Juvenal weaves a particular emotion into his satire by rhetorically expressing it or by otherwise making it seem relevant to his work, we should see him as writing "about" that emotion rather than just *conveying* it. To put it another way, what have been called the "angry satires" might be better called the "anger satires"—since they are a space for the satirist to play with all the possibilities and associations of the emotion that he has invoked as his fundamental inspiration. This is just an extension of the conceit that the subject matter programs the persona's emotional state; by the same logic, the persona's emotion also becomes part of what the satire is *about*. This should be easy to accept in the case of the early *Satires*, which open with such loud self-assertion. The satirist is programming his audience to pay attention to anger as a force. In subsequent books, he finds other ways to call attention to emotions. Hence this study does not set out to diagnose methodically the emotional condition of each of Juvenal's discrete personae but instead to listen for the different ways he makes emotion relevant to the satiric project. We may now take a page from Caston's study of elegy: that genre uses the emotion of jealousy not simply as an object of representation but as fuel that "creates and structures . . . generic features."[43] The emotions of Juvenalian satire are endowed with an analogous power.

Contemporary and earlier literature would have offered Juvenal plenty of inspiration. As studies in the relatively new field of "ancient emotions" have shown, all kinds of prose and verse texts explore facets of the emotions. Moral criticism or approval of certain emotions (anger, pity) are of course familiar strains; anger, being one of the stronger passions, has a whole discourse of disapproval and control surrounding it, extending from the earliest Greek literature to late antiquity.[44] But this does not establish anger (to stay with this particularly rich example) as a "bad" force or trait in all Greco-Roman literature from the *Iliad* on; many texts certainly carry memories of the destruction caused by Achilles's *mēnis*, but these

---

[43] Caston, *Elegiac Passion*, 19.
[44] See Harris, *Restraining Rage*.

are mixed with other ideas and intertexts. Few of us would accept the notion that all the literary works that thematize anger or other passions aim to be ethically normative and nothing else; many authors are demonstrably familiar with, and exploit, more than one perspective on a given emotion.[45] Even the discourse of anger control, as Kalimtzsis has recently shown, can exhibit a tolerant and nuanced view of that passion, recognizing its origins, contexts, and purposes and the consequent difficulties that individuals may have in controlling it.[46] Subtler emotions such as shame and resentment—which have recently joined the "passions" as objects of study—are perhaps easier to see as tools that societies shape, manipulate, and use for social control.[47]

In this examination of Juvenal's *Satires*, it will prove useful to take a holistic approach to ancient emotions that does not assume Juvenal's anger is meant to look morally "bad" or ridiculously misguided. While these ideas may well reflect the perspective of dogmatic works like Seneca's *On Anger*, they are not universal ancient views. Greeks and Romans surely lived within multiple "emotional communities," as Rosenwein calls them, each prescribing particular behaviors and responses.[48] Just as ancient people did not simply experience more "primitive" emotions or lack a concept of emotional control, so too they did not all live according to the dogma of the Stoics (to name the philosophy that is most frequently cited in connection to Juvenal's representation of anger). And the conventional "grand narrative" that Rosenwein criticizes, which holds that "the history of the West is the history of increasing emotional restraint,"[49] might have surprised many ancient thinkers. One well-known ancient myth, highlighted by Kaster, points to the existence of a very different conception of emotions in history. In the Golden Age, emotions like shame, fear, and respect supposedly performed the work of "civilization," preventing crime—until the race degenerated and the comparatively crude substitutes of laws and

---

[45] See the essays in Braund and Gill, *Passions in Roman Thought*, and Braund and Most, *Ancient Anger*. An underlying theme of both essay collections is that ancient authors seem aware of two basic philosophical views on the emotions, or more specifically on the strong passions: a "therapeutic" view that advocates their suppression, and an "Aristotelian" view that, insisting on the cognitive and sometimes beneficial nature of emotions, recommends moderation.

[46] Kalimtzsis, *Taming Anger*.

[47] Kaster, *Emotion, Restraint, and Community*, explores the way Romans deployed and interpreted such emotions in order to shape their own public images and judge one another.

[48] Rosenwein, "Worrying about Emotions," 842.

[49] Rosenwein, "Worrying about Emotions," 827. Rosenwein identifies in this grand narrative a "hydraulic view" of emotions as controlling forces with a life of their own, a view that has long been discounted in science and is also undermined by recent scholarship on ancient emotions (834–37; cf. 827 n. 31). Cf. Nussbaum, *Upheavals of Thought*, 24–26.

the state had to be invented.[50] These and other ancient literary perspectives indicate that there was room for variety and even inconsistency when it came to views on the emotions.

Modern discussions of Juvenalian emotion have been dominated by two interpretive frameworks. There is the rhetorical framework, in which Juvenal's various emotional postures (e.g., the *indignatio* he declares at 1.79) are read as elements of a multifaceted rhetorical performance designed to entertain. Rhetorical theory teaches the speaker to perform emotions with the goal of arousing the audience; emotions are a speaker's instrument of power. Juvenal's ancient audience, then, may have accepted his expression of emotion as enhancing their enjoyment of the *Satires'* content. Alternatively, there is the philosophical or moral framework, in which Juvenal's emotional performances are seen as inviting moral evaluation (and specifically a Stoic-informed evaluation). Philosophers, while certainly interested in the "physics" of emotional processes, offer something more relevant to the satirist in their moral analyses of emotion as a response to circumstances and a guide of action.[51] In different cases, this might mean identifying the pernicious effects emotions can have on an individual or community, or lauding certain emotions as responses proper for a human being. An audience that approached Juvenal's *Satires* this way would have judged the words of the satirist by the soundness and seemliness of his emotional perspective.

These frameworks represent two different "emotional communities" with different values and priorities. But it would not be easy either to choose between them or to reconcile them when we try to reconstruct the original production and reception of the *Satires*. A third and better option allows for conflict and interplay between multiple paradigms. Concluding a study of grief and anger in Juvenal's thirteenth *Satire*, Braund comments that while "anger in Juvenal has been much studied in recent years, [it] has not been widely considered as a passion in relation to (Greco-)Roman philosophical discourse on the passions."[52] This can be interpreted as a call to read the *Satires* not as reflections of one paradigm of thought or other but as a contribution to the wide-ranging and often messy ancient discourse about the emotions. The satirist has a say in what emotions are, what they do to us, and how they relate to our conceptions of humanity and

---

[50] Kaster, *Emotion, Restraint, and Community*, 3–4.
[51] For the most recent comprehensive study of ancient philosophical treatments of the various dimensions of emotions, see Knuuttila, *Emotions*.
[52] Braund, "Passion Unconsoled," 87.

civilization. Nor is he merely a commentator or a behind-the-scenes engineer of dramas involving "masks." Juvenal claims to participate in emotional life himself, a move that grants him special authority.

Themes in Roman Satire Studies

Our best evidence on how the Greeks and Romans perceived and analyzed emotions is rhetorical theory, since it was a central concern of the orator—as for the student of declamation, and the actor—to represent emotion convincingly and to engage his audience's emotions in turn.[53] As will be discussed in the next chapter, Juvenal claims that he studied declamation in his youth, and his *Satires* advertise his knowledge of rhetorical conventions at every turn.[54] Juvenal's work has also proved fertile ground for the modern rhetorical interpretation of satire, the "persona theory" that regards the satiric speaker as a fictionally constructed performer.[55] Moreover, since virtually no biographical information about Juvenal has survived, his *Satires* are that much more easily read alone as pure satiric performance; in this way they made a special contribution to the shaping of persona theory itself. Once the subject of biographical speculation—his criticisms of women, foreigners, and patrons interpreted as reflections of personal disappointments—Juvenal became the poster satirist, the quintessential actor, in persona studies.[56] He even offered a five-book oeuvre that shows satirists, like actors and orators, can play different parts at different times. Braund's study of *Satires* Book 3 took up Anderson's suggestion that Juvenal used each book to explore a different way of performing criticism. With his wide-ranging rhetorical talent, Juvenal was not confined to the signature "angry mode" of Books 1 and 2. He was also capable of performing as an ironist (Book 3), as unruffled and amused (4), and as a merciless cynic, devoid of anger but full of disgust for his fellow humans (5).[57]

[53.] Aristotle's *Rhetoric* provides "the most sophisticated and detailed account of the emotions" found in any ancient author (Konstan, *Emotions of the Greeks*, 41).

[54.] De Decker, *Juvenalis declamans*; cf. Kenney, "Satirist or Rhetorician."

[55.] The seminal works by Mack ("Muse of Satire") and Kernan (*Cankered Muse*) inspired Anderson's series of studies on the Roman satirists in the 1960s (later collected in *Essays*). For general remarks on this period in the field, see Anderson's "Roman Satirists and Criticism."

[56.] Juvenal is the subject of more than half of Anderson's collection of essays (see *Essays*, 115–50 passim and 197–486), and of the equally important monograph by Braund (*Beyond Anger*).

[57.] Besides Braund's *Beyond Anger*, the key studies are Anderson, "Programs of Later Books" and "Anger in Juvenal"; Corn, "Persona in the Fifth Book"; and Winkler, *Persona in Three Satires*. Although Bellandi, *Etica diatribica*, rejects Anderson's version of persona theory, it does lean

The readings that produced these conclusions acknowledge that like earlier Roman and Hellenistic poets, Juvenal used the boundaries set by the physical poetry book to create poetry collections with definition, coherence, and an impression of narrative.[58] We may likewise refer to the two satiric books of Juvenal's predecessor Horace, which feature performances by two discrete satiric personae that assert and efface themselves to different degrees; they may be read as meditations on the different challenges that face a satirist at different stages of his career.[59] In satire as in other genres, individual poems or books can represent discrete performances of a particular persona, even attempts to redefine program and push generic boundaries. In its best forms, then, persona theory does not constrict the idea of what satire is and does—or what constitutes an author's "definitive" work—but reflects the mutability of satiric theory.

But could persona theory plausibly answer the question of *why* Juvenal's satire changed? On the one hand, persona scholars started on more solid ground than the purely biographical reading. Highet, who was Juvenal's greatest champion in the age of burgeoning Latin literary scholarship, saw in the sequence of books a reflection of the poet's aging process. At first a vigorous and bitter moralist, Juvenal withdrew from society, let his views mellow and his rhetoric weaken, and then experienced episodes of renewed vigor and bile in his old age.[60] This is the kind of thinking that made Highet the persona school's straw man. Yet in persona studies, too, the phases of Juvenal's career are characterized according to the rhetorical and emotional tone that dominates the verse. Only the personal *causes* for change are removed from the picture. The only cause that (implicitly) remains is Juvenal's own desire to experiment in multiple emotional modes in order to put his full talent to use.[61]

This is not the usual objection made to the persona approach, which has certainly had its critics. Some scholars continued to object to the implication that the poet's personal disposition or experiences are not relevant to

---

on a concept of the satiric mask to express the differences between earlier and later Juvenal (see chapter 4 below).

[58] In many of the cases of this kind studied in Hutchinson, *Talking Books*, coherence and narrative are created by recurrent emphasis on the experience of the narrator. Also on practical matters and poetic conventions, see Van Sickle, "Book-Roll."

[59] Readings in this vein include Anderson, "Roman Socrates"; Freudenburg, *Satires of Rome*, 15–124; Oliensis, *Rhetoric of Authority*; and Gowers, "Restless Companion" (cf. n. 24 above).

[60] See Highet, *Juvenal the Satirist*.

[61] A recent summary of persona studies reflects just how far the discussion of this question has (not) gone: Juvenal essentially exhausts the possibilities of *indignatio* and has to choose another mode (Zarini, "Indignation chez Juvénal," 451–54).

his art.[62] Others have found the persona scholars' insistence on the distinction between author and speaker overstated, and point out that ancient audiences may have been comfortable thinking with the biographical veneer of "personal" poetry.[63] Still others detect a disappointing implication that the reader's work is merely to distinguish between poet and persona. The payoff in that case is insubstantial—the satire becomes an empty joke, "an exercise in sublime irony on the part of an omniscient author."[64] Indeed, intentionalism of the most traditional stripe works its way back into the picture in one persona study that argues that the ranting, conservative Juvenal is at heart a liberal preacher, parodying the opposite position in order to demolish it.[65] The mask is pulled off only to reveal an imagined historical Juvenal.

The persona-theory account of Juvenal's full career—admittedly, an account that is adumbrated rather than deliberately reconstructed—has its own problematic intentionalist strain. It arises in cues given by the poet: in *Satire* 10, in Book 4, he appears to dismiss tears in favor of laughter; in *Satires* 13 and 15, in Book 5, he condemns anger. Hence it is concluded that "the farther he gets away from *Satire* 1, the more outspoken does the satirist grow against his once cherished *indignatio*." Other readings speak of "clear rejection of the angry mask adopted in the early satires" and the "increasingly ironic or negative presentation" of *indignatio*.[66] In a nutshell, moral and aesthetic judgments are being read into these apparent turning points in the poet's career. Besides implying that our poet is a moralist

---

[62.] See, e.g., Highet, "Masks and Faces"; McCabe, "Was Juvenal a Structuralist"; and Rudd, *Common Spring*, 84 (where Rudd challenges the notion that "we have only the mask and know nothing of the man" from his satire; cf. 86: Juvenal's style comes from his unique "disposition").

[63.] See Clay, "Theory of Literary Persona"; and Mayer, "Persona (I) Problems"; both scholars find significant differences in the ancient and modern conceptions of persona. Iddeng, in a multipronged critique of the Andersonian version of persona theory, also questions the applicability of the modern model to ancient poetry ("Juvenal, Satire, and Persona").

[64.] Miller, *Subjecting Verses*, 51—concentrating on applications of persona theory to Roman erotic poetry, but considering the impact of persona theory more generally. Cf. Wray, *Poetics of Roman Manhood*, 163–67; and Freudenburg, "*Horatius Anceps*."

[65.] I.e., Winkler, *Persona in Three Satires*, an application of persona theory as a sort of detective work that is anticipated with strong criticism by Highet ("Masks and Faces," 329–30). Highet puts his finger on some real problems in persona criticism: first, inconsistent claims or tone have been read as evidence of the poet's aim to create a ridiculous persona, yet a real person *can* be inconsistent; second, in judging a persona ridiculous or parodic, we may impose our own tastes (aesthetic and moral) without even knowing it.

[66.] The first quote comes from Anderson, "Programs of Later Books," 158 (=*Essays*, 290), the second from Braund, *Masks*, 22. The last is from a more recent work sympathetic to persona theory: Jones, *Juvenal*, 114 (*Satire* 13 shows *indignatio* "openly being mocked"); cf. 171 n. 66. See also Zarini, "Indignation chez Juvénal," 452–53: there are "germes" of an ironic attitude to indignation in Books 1 and 2, prefiguring total abandonment of the mode.

after all, this promotes the idea that the earlier and later personae are qualitatively different devices—the former a flawed and ridiculous spectacle, the latter a naturally matured voice of reason (which conveniently offers us commentary on the former). It is as if the persona in the later *Satires* need not be objectified to the same degree as the angry one—after all, it is so kindly helping us achieve a critical long view of the whole oeuvre. It has been pointed out that this reflects a double standard;[67] I will add that it imposes a teleological frame and casts the complex "middle" period reductively as "transitional [away from *indignatio*]."[68]

If the Juvenalian satiric persona, in its more appealing later incarnations, has successfully convinced some readers to see things his way, it is not so surprising. This master rhetorical performer's goal *would* be to move and persuade his audience, using convincing fictions and an authoritative voice. Satire is manipulative literature, and even critics may not be immune. What we might regard as our sound analytical interpretation of echoes and differences between the earlier and later *Satires* may actually be a scripted, compliant response. Evaluating angry rhetoric, if we are honest, is a particularly tricky business: we seem to find it easy to objectify and condemn such talk as inflammatory, by imagining it working on other people "out there."[69] This may reflect a reluctance to ever identify with that audience, to contemplate the possibility of our own compliance. If we are prone to insulate ourselves this way, can we in fact ever "get the joke" in satire? Can we be sure that the angry satirist is not reaching us, or by the same token that the more alluring ironist is not manipulating us? And would either one's intentions really be to let us uncover his secret agenda, the joke he is playing on someone else?[70] These questions inspire many parts of the present study.

[67.] See Iddeng, "Juvenal, Satire, and Persona"; and Walker, "Moralizing Discourse," 36.

[68.] Anderson, "Anger in Juvenal," 129 (=*Essays*, 295) applies the term "transitional" to Book 3; Braund, *Beyond Anger*, improved significantly on this noncommittal label (and although the book is usually cited for its thesis that Book 3 showcases an "ironic" persona, it has far more to offer in its revelations about the rich literary play in *Satires* 7 through 9). Stramaglia is the latest to assert that the "ironic" phase fits into a larger trajectory: with Book 3, "L'*indignatio* si attenua, e cede gradualmente il passo a un atteggiamento improntato piuttosto ad ironia" (*Giovenale*, 117).

[69.] A Harris poll conducted in the United States in 2011 showed many respondents believing that political discourse had become angrier than in the past, that this trend was lamentable, and that angry rhetoric had an adverse influence on public behavior; see Taylor, "Very Large Majorities." Helfert's 2012 essay on political rhetoric and violence ("Unfortunately, Anger Works") laments the influence of angry rhetoric generally, but most of his examples involve conservative groups and "their" leaders.

[70.] Freudenburg, *Satires of Rome*, highlights moments that "diagnostically" force us to choose positions of this kind (see, e.g., 240–41 on Juvenal 1). Rudd (*Common Spring*, 75–94) also recognizes that satiric rhetoric can pull us in multiple directions and proposes that we try to read

At the same time, the notion that satire is "personal" is not to be thrown out just because it has the power to mislead. Both the biographical approach and the persona approach are motivated by impulses that reflect how satire works. If the later, mellower speakers of the *Satires* read like mature and reflective (and disapproving) successors of the early, angry ones, perhaps there is something to the idea that the whole series is actually telling a story of one man's personal change and emotional enlightenment. This suggestion might seem to flirt with antiquated scholarly views, but like the persona approach, it is based on verse satire's ostensible message. From Lucilius to Juvenal, Roman satire *is* about a person expressing himself; this is the most cherished fiction of the satiric genre, and of invective literature generally.[71] What would happen if we started seeing the interest in the satirist as a person(a) as a response to Juvenal's own promptings? If we critics started thinking of ourselves as participating readers, being fed a story that cultivates our interest in certain generic issues? And while the study of Juvenal's persona changes has stagnated in recent years, it is now possible to reinvigorate it with newer insights into satire as literary, political, and cultural discourse. The speaking "I" is now appreciated as a generic category or a social agent—a poetic body, a priapic defender of masculine territory, a manipulative social climber, or a resentful loser in the Roman patronage system.[72] There is plenty of room for "personality" in all this.

---

by alternately "standing, as it were, beside Juvenal, entering into his feelings of indignation and disgust," and objectifying him by sympathizing with his victims and recognizing the "extravagance of his satirical wit." In other words, we should try out both positions in order to appreciate Juvenal properly—but are we always able to control these responses in ourselves? Cf. Nadeau, who reads *Satire* 6 for interplay between two aspects of the satirist's persona, "a straight man and a funny man" (*Sixth Satire*, 15)—presumably feeling that it is always possible to distinguish between these voices.

[71.] The latest study of Lucilius concludes that the first satirist invented his genre to express "personality" (Haß, *Lucilius*). Muecke, "Rome's First Satirists," advances similar ideas but includes Ennius's motley and mysterious *Satires* in the picture. On the important role satire's audience has in thinking about the authorial "I," see Rosen and Baines, "I Am." Uden makes the elusiveness of the satiric speaker the theme of *Invisible Satirist*; cf. Hardie, "Condition of Letters," 151, on the "personal" nature of pre-Juvenalian satire and the enigma of the "more reticent" Juvenal.

[72.] On a range of satiric social entanglements, see Henderson, "Satire Writes Woman"; Richlin, *Garden of Priapus*; Oliensis, *Rhetoric of Authority*; Gowers, "Fragments of Autobiography;"; and Keane, *Figuring Genre*. Many of the essays in Freudenburg, *Cambridge Companion*, and Braund and Osgood, *Persius and Juvenal*, emphasize the angle of the satirist as part of his society; see, e.g., Armstrong, "*Juvenalis eques*." On the satiric body, see Keane, "Satiric Memories," and Barchiesi and Cucchiarelli, "Satire and the Poet"—where Juvenal's work is characterized as the point in the tradition where the satirist's body "faded from view" (219–22).

How to Do Things with Feelings

This book recognizes several key features of Juvenal's use of emotions. First, the *Satires* participate in a rich and diverse literary tradition that thematizes emotions and related topics. The comparison texts I highlight in each chapter represent some of the most interesting treatments of these themes; many of these would have been known to the satirist. No single text constitutes a key to understanding any of the *Satires*—for example, there is more behind satiric anger than Seneca's *On Anger*, and more behind the satirist's *senex* persona than Cicero's *On Old Age*. But these comparison texts offer complex treatment of themes that Juvenal takes up, and this can give us an idea of how much complexity we can expect in a satiric treatment.

One premise of this book is that Juvenal used other literature eclectically and creatively. This is certainly the case with his use of philosophical literature, and it has important consequences for his representation of emotions. Far from being doctrinaire or partisan, he seems inspired as much by the literary qualities of philosophical writings as by the moral ideas they present. Nor should we expect philosophy to be the satirist's only source on emotions. Omnivorous in his sampling of the poetic genres, creative in his adaptation of historical themes,[73] Juvenal is interested in using what they have to give in terms of emotional color and theory, not in aligning his satire with a particular moral conception of the passions. And he does not make it easy to distinguish between, for example, legitimate and improper forms of anger.

A second premise is that Juvenal's engagement with ideas about emotions and his engagement with satiric subject matter are not two separate things. *Satire* 1 represents the poet's anger as a reaction to preexisting satiric subjects. Elsewhere, there are variations on the same formula. In *Satire* 10, the satirist's alter ego Democritus laughs at what he sees around him. Juvenal even constructs some poems as documents of or responses to *other* people's emotional responses (e.g., *Satires* 3, 13, and 15). In every case, explicit commentary on emotions is not an external interpretive key but part of the satire's substance and work.[74]

Third, and related, emotions in the *Satires* are not static states of mind but dynamic forces; they play roles in chains of events. Not only are they

---

[73.]On Juvenal as a contributor to a heavily allusive literary and social culture, see Jones, *Juvenal*, 40–47.

[74.]Cf. Bogel's analogous argument about the satirist's apologia (*Difference Satire Makes*, 10).

reactions, but they cause changes, and themselves change. They both work inside the text and reach out to manipulate readers, lay and scholarly. These qualities are all a given in ancient discussions of the emotions, but they are easy to forget when the focus is on static images like caricatures of "the angry man." Rhetoric may seem a familiar and conventional tool to ancient and modern readers alike, but that does not mean it cannot be used to push a reading audience to uncomfortable, even perhaps unfamiliar, places. Another consequence of the dynamism of emotions, in this case "inside" the text, is that poems and books inevitably tell stories around the satiric emotions. It is not a new idea that satiric texts, though they may mimic unscripted commentary on assorted themes, are actually creating narratives about those themes by means of their compositional structure.[75] Potentially the most significant story of all is that of the satirist's experiments with his genre. With each new poem, he affirms that the last one did not bring closure to his project of criticism and complaint, that there are always going to be other ways to do satire. Every reader notices changes in Juvenal's satire from the beginning to the end of his oeuvre. The chapters that follow argue that we have much to gain if we see Juvenal as "owning" these changes and the story that emerges from them.

The first two chapters show how the poet uses anger as a source of power in Books 1 (*Satires* 1 through 5) and 2 (*Satire* 6). It is probably no coincidence that anger is the first item on Aristotle's list of emotions in the *Rhetoric* and was the first specific emotion studied by the Americanists who invented "emotionology."[76] It is the quintessential multifaceted passion, its image of visceral simplicity belying its complex origins and operation. By posing as an angry man as he begins *Satire* 1, Juvenal embroils himself in anger's multiple meanings in contexts from the earliest classical literature ("sing of rage, goddess") to Hellenistic and Roman rhetoric and philosophy. The *Satires* that thematize *indignatio* cannot be read through

---

[75.]On Horace and Persius, see nn. 24 and 25 above and cf. Schlegel, *Threat of Speech*, 12, on the "triads" in Horace's first book. Seeds of the stories in the next Horatian book are identified in Boll, "Anordnung im zweiten Buch." On Juvenal, Henderson sees in Book 3 "complicity between . . . compositions" (via thematic and rhetorical signals) that have a cumulative effect (*Figuring Out Roman Nobility*, 95). Cloud and Braund point out reflections of the careful design of Book 1, including thematic arcs and symmetry in poem lengths ("Juvenal's Libellus," 79). Hardie, "Name-Repetitions," finds unity and a sense of dramatic setting created from prosopographical elements.

[76.]Ari. *Rh.* 2.1.1378a21–22 first lists the emotions this way: "anger, pity, fear, and all such things, and their opposites" (ὀργὴ ἔλεος φόβος καὶ ὅσα ἄλλα τοιαῦτα, καὶ τὰ τούτοις ἐναντία); anger comes first again at 2.2.1378a 29 and in the list at Quint. *Inst.* 3.8.12. Konstan, *Emotions of the Greeks*, follows Aristotle in treating anger first (41–76). On the first steps in the field of "emotionology," see Rosenwein, "Worrying about Emotions," 824.

only one of these lenses, for they reflect how anger can be regarded as destructive or constructive, infectious or ridiculous.

Juvenal writes a whole new history of the satiric genre, one that claims anger was its first and essential mode. From this tendentious beginning, he examines anger from many angles even as he uses it as a rhetorical tool, exposing its tensions, pleasures, and discomforts to create a kind of running story about satiric criticism that centers on his angry persona's fulfillment. Besides relating his own anger's genesis, he writes various mini-dramas featuring characters who act out facets of that emotion, constructing a kind of "anger community." This becomes a way for the satirist to take a position of distance from the emotion's greatest discomforts. Meanwhile, his characters—from the streets of Rome, to private conversations, to Domitian's council chamber—continue to encounter and use anger. Some find moral outrage gratifying and conducive to solidarity, others are disappointed or mocked in that same quest, and a few feel the special pain of righteous anger that must be bottled up in dangerous circumstances.

The "anger games" of Book 1 culminate in the simultaneous encouragement and victimization of the helpless addressee Trebius, who combines the roles of wronged client, satiric target, and compliant audience of angry satire. Juvenal engages in the same kind of game in the single and monumental poem of his second book. In this attack on Roman wives, the prospective husband Postumus is the lone direct recipient of the satirist's anger-mongering rhetoric. The external audience, on the other hand, is treated to a spectacle that illustrates aspects of anger through intimations about Postumus's current discomfort as audience and visions of his future unhappiness.

It has proved difficult to theorize or even describe the change that comes in the third book, Juvenal's purported "period of reassessment."[77] My third chapter makes the case for resisting a teleological approach and listening to the story told in *Satires* 7 through 9 themselves. More telling than any detectable unity of rhetorical style is the fact that these three poems, otherwise seeming to have little connection to one another, are all about change. Book 3 contemplates the various ways people relate to the past and conceive of progress and decline in the world of poetry and letters, in traditional aristocratic morality, and—the most enigmatic case—in the professional experience of an aging prostitute. Each story can be told

---

[77] Lindo, "Evolution of Later Satires," 24.

in more than one way; the resulting tension defines both the book and the very concept of "post-angry" satire. If Book 3 has seemed to some scholars only a tentative step away from *indignatio*, this is understandable. In the poetic world that Juvenal has created so far, where anger is his genre's original mode and his birthright, such a move has high stakes. As I will argue, it is Juvenal's own programming that cultivates readers' nostalgia for anger's power. He plants the idea throughout *Satires* 7 through 9 in the form of *representations* of the angry response to vice and social change. Thus, while the satirist's voice does not show emotional investment in his subjects, his satire is still tapping into anger's riches. It is also inviting judgment of his new, chillier, more indirect mode—not to be confused with a moral rejection of anger—in relation to the touchstone of *indignatio*.

To cultivate (albeit ambivalent) nostalgia for anger is one of Juvenal's "emotional agendas" in the later *Satires*. The other is to reveal, bit by bit, that non-angry satire—while it may not be as wearing on the reader as angry screeds—can be discomfiting and disorienting in its own way. Irony, detached mockery, cynicism—to borrow labels that have been attached to the styles of Books 3 through 5—may be more subtle than *indignatio*, but they have their own surprising and unsettling powers. This applies even to the most cited and imitated of the later *Satires*, the tenth. There, a portrait of the "laughing philosopher" Democritus is set next to a series of conventional ethical topics and exempla. In chapter 4, I first argue that Juvenal is pointing to a clash between nonverbal and antisocial laughter and the worldly values that shape the ethical material of his own satire. He ends up redefining the Democritean model to unearth a more complex, genuine, and ethically informed criticism. In the two remaining poems of Book 4, the story is all about the satirist himself, who becomes a visible character for the first time since *Satire* 1. Tranquility, the philosophical buzzword that appears at the end of *Satire* 10, is not an advertisement of persona but a challenge that Juvenal takes up. *Satires* 11 and 12 dramatize his selection of a satiric identity, using his home as metaphor. The result is anything but monochromatic, tranquil meditation, and the end point defies expectations.

The last two books show the satirist trying on more conventional, culturally entangled roles than before—moral adviser, enlightened friend, transmitter of tradition. All these and still more roles can be associated with old men, and Juvenal exploits the many facets of the *senex* stereotype, juggling different roles to produce satire that can be disorienting and disconcerting to read. In the *Satires* of Book 5, treated in chapter 5, he communicates traditional wisdom and values but also exhibits loquaciousness, callousness, and inconsistency. The most fundamental paradox may be the fact that for all his professed cynical worldliness—expressed, for instance, in mockery of another old man who is upset by humanity's ethical failings (*Satire* 13)—he himself is continuing to identify and speak about new social ills, at home and abroad.

The satirist of Book 5 has been described as an enlightened, if cynical, critic of the destructive passions. But those criticisms do not have a purely moral basis, nor does the satirist convey a mild or appealing perspective on the world's problems. Denial of other people's right to *indignatio* is not equivalent to personal renunciation of anger or other passions. Instead, what we are seeing in this series of poems is a *senex* character who has nothing to lose by criticizing everyone around him. While he identifies with his society's moral ideals and institutions, he is not trying to make friends. In a sense, this role was always waiting for Juvenal to grow into: he makes satire appear to be the natural practice for an old man who combines life experience, a grasp of rhetoric and ethics, and a sense of alienation from the very society that gave him these tools. With this, the Juvenalian career comes to an abrupt end—if not with a feeling of closure, perhaps with a fitting final surge of ambition. The change-filled generic history that Juvenal began writing in *Satire* 1 has been extended in new and provocative ways.

CHAPTER 1 | Anger Games

DRYDEN'S PROFESSION OF A "rais'd Spleen" and "Pleasure of Concernment" aside, most modern critics would probably not describe Juvenal's rhetorical powers with reference to their own emotional responses. But there should be no doubt that the rhetorical display that characterizes imperial literature is a means to an end: the engagement of the audience. In Martial's *Epigrams*, the response of the audience is thematized—indeed, the poet seems to revel in the idea that his poetry will arouse strong and even conflicting feelings. "Look, someone's blushing, growing pale, freezing in shock, yawning, hating [my book]. This is how I want it: now I'm pleased with my poems" (*ecce rubet quidam, pallet, stupet, oscitat, odit;/ hoc volo: nunc nobis carmina nostra placent*, 6.60.3–4).[1] This playful celebration of the complex audience response appears downright straightforward next to Juvenal, who is far less explicit about his affective aims. All the same, in the early *Satires* he does imagine how his angry verse might be received.

The Indignant Performer

"Declamatory rhetoric, the rhetoric of the schools, is Juvenal's *idiom*."[2] This is nowhere more obvious than in Book 1, where the "angry mode" is

---

[1] Cf. Martial's reference to his ability to stimulate complex feelings and conflicts at 1.68, and numerous poems highlighting particular emotions cited in Anderson, "*Absit Malignus Interpres*."
[2] Kenney, "Satirist or Rhetorician," 707. Cf. de Decker, *Juvenalis declamans*; Anderson, "Juvenal and Quintilian"; and, on the larger generic context, Braund, "Declamation and Contestation." Much commentary on rhetorical devices in Book 1 can be found in Braund, *Satires Book I*, but Courtney, *Satires*, 36–48, is still usefully thorough.

championed as proper satire. Juvenal claims that "if talent can't, indignation will make my verse" (*si natura negat, facit indignatio versum*, 1.79). For all its fallacious representation of poetry as personal expression, in one sense this still contains an honest advertisement of Juvenal's training, because *indignatio* can denote a crafted rhetorical performance (technically, part of a speech's peroration).[3] Juvenal's proficiency at rhetorical indignation is well documented. Even in the first twenty lines of *Satire* 1, where he begins to "tell" his anger, he also "shows" it with an array of rhetorical devices. These include the aggressive questions that open the poem: "Will I always just have to listen? Will I never get revenge?" (*semper ego auditor tantum? numquamne reponam?*, 1) "Will that one go unpunished who has recited to me his comedies, and this other one his elegies? Will that enormous *Telephus* go unpunished for wasting my time . . . ? (*inpune ergo mihi recitaverit ille togatas,/hic elegos? inpune diem consumpserit ingens/Telephus . . . ?*, 3–5). Anaphora accents lists of ascending length (suggesting ascending rage): the satirist is tired of hearing "what the winds are engineering, which souls Aeacus tortures, from what place that one guy steals that dumb little golden fleece, how big are the ash trees that Monychus hurls like missiles" (*quid agant venti, quas torqueat umbras/Aeacus, unde alius furtivae devehat aurum/pelliculae, quantas iaculetur Monychus ornos*, 9–11). There is hyperbolic summary: "From the best and the worst poet, you can expect the same result" (*expectes eadem a summo minimoque poeta*, 14).

If the language and phrasing in this passage were not proof enough of Juvenal's rhetorical training, we could also cite the poet's explicit (and anaphoric) claim that he has been through the standard curriculum: "Well, I too have snatched my hand from under the cane; I too have given Sulla the advice to retire as a private citizen" (*et nos ergo manum ferulae subduximus, et nos/consilium dedimus Sullae, privatus ut altum/dormiret*, 15–17). "Giving Sulla advice" refers to the *suasoria*, that exercise practiced by students beginning the standard rhetorical curriculum.[4] Juvenal proffers this as

---

[3.]The standard topics (*loci*) with which one can convey *indignatio* are spelled out at Cic. *Inv.* 1.100–105; see discussion below and cf. very similar instructions on *amplificatio* at *Rhet. Her.* 2.48–49. Craig, "Means and Ends," examines examples from Cicero's courtroom speeches. Anderson, "Juvenal and Quintilian," 19–85 (=*Essays*, 414–80), discusses the relevance of sources closer to Juvenal, while Carey analyzes Greek examples and techniques ("Rhetorical Means of Persuasion," 29–33). De Decker's survey of elements of declamatory style in the *Satires* (*Juvenalis declamans*, 137–98) includes strategies for showing indignation (declarations of inability to restrain oneself, repetition, anaphora, hyperbole, etc.). Greek sophists in Juvenal's age sometimes employed an indignant style, called βαρύτης, "weightiness" (see Rutherford, *Canons of Style*, 28–29).

[4.]On this early exercise in formal rhetorical training, normally tackled under the *rhetor* but evidently also assigned by some *grammatici* in the early empire, see Seneca the Elder's *Suasoriae*

a qualification—perhaps *the* only important qualification—for joining the army of poets in Rome. It is a signal that his own poetry will exhibit his training. All of this unfolds quickly, before Juvenal reaches the poem's main subject of contemporary Roman vice.

As the poem's scope broadens, Juvenal employs more techniques straight from the rhetorical handbooks. At *On Invention* 1.100–105, Cicero enumerates a list of common topics (*loci*) that are conventionally associated with righteous anger; illustrations of these devices throughout *Satire* 1 establish the satirist as not just an angry speaker but a moral conservative who is essentially "prosecuting" the agents of his society's deterioration. Cicero recommends invoking the authority of moral tradition in the form of gods, religion, virtuous ancestors, lawgivers, and so on (*Inv.* 1.101); accordingly, Juvenal imagines the gods' anger at a criminal (*dis iratis*, 1.49–50) and later decries modern luxury by asking "what ancestor of ours built this many villas, or dined alone on seven courses?" (*quis totidem erexit villas, quis fercula septem/secreto cenavit avus?*, 94–95). His sweeping claims that Roman vice has reached a new and unsurpassable peak (87–90, 147–49) also recall Cicero's advice to the prosecutor to make the defendant's acts seem unprecedented (*Inv.* 1.104). Making the crime(s) in question out to be deliberate and premeditated also helps the prosecution (*Inv.* 1.102); in this spirit, Juvenal claims that greed drives husbands to pimp their wives and play dumb: one is "skilled at looking at the ceiling, and at snoring-while-awake over his cup" (*doctus spectare lacunar,/doctus et ad calicem vigilanti stertere naso*, 56–57). The husband is also the last person who should be engaging in such acts (cf. *Inv.* 1.104), just like other bad actors in *Satire* 1: the guardian who defrauds his young ward (46–47), the *matrona* who teaches her neighbors to poison their husbands (69–72). Cicero also notes that it is useful to call attention to the plight of crime's victims (*Inv.* 1.101); thus the satirist uses a combination of personification and apostrophe to lament for the provincial victims of an extortionist governor: "Marius [Priscus], now in exile, starts his drinking in the afternoon and enjoys having the gods angry at him; meanwhile, Province [of Africa], though you've won in court, you weep" (*exsul ab octava Marius bibit et fruitur dis/iratis, at tu victrix, provincia, ploras*, 49–50). In the capital, we see equally pathetic victims: the clients of a patron who never assists them or even acknowledges their morning visit. "Longtime clients,

---

and Quintilian *Inst.* 2.1.2, 3.5.5–16, and 7.1.24; cf. Bloomer, "Roman Declamation"; and Bonner, *Education in Ancient Rome*, 277–87.

worn out, leave the entryway and abandon their hopes, though the hope that dies hardest in a person is the hope for dinner; one has to buy cabbage, and firewood too" (*vestibulis abeunt veteres lassique clientes/votaque deponunt, quamquam longissima cenae/spes homini: caulis miseris atque ignis emendus*, 132–34).

The Contexts of Juvenalian Anger

What agenda is satiric *indignatio* meant to serve, and how might it have been received by Juvenal's contemporaries? Some scholars have pictured the ancient audience performing a fairly "straight" reading of the satirist's anger as a plausible vehicle for the expression of ideology. This idea could be supported by what we know about the traditional conditions for the production and consumption of poetry in Rome—namely, that it was a playground and a tool of self-definition for the socioeconomic elite.[5] Because the moral and social ideas expressed by the "angry Juvenal" are quite conventional (e.g., in *Satire* 1 he complains about foreigners, women, sexual deviants, and social climbers), the satirist's rhetoric could have served a normative and conservative moral function, namely, the policing of the established boundaries between "Normal" and "Other."[6] The implication of this view is that satiric rhetoric looks and functions much like its real-world rhetorical counterpart, playing on and reinforcing audience prejudices to secure support.[7] And for what it is worth, while contemporary sources are virtually silent, many later readers would regard Juvenal as a great moralist.[8]

[5.]For one account of the production and consumption of literature in Rome as guided by elite concerns, see Habinek, *Politics of Latin Literature*. Elsewhere, Habinek includes satire among the genres that were vehicles for the promotion of elite values and construction of male identity, even though the satirist uses unconventional, playful means to do this job, "mim[ing] his opponents even as he ridicules them" ("Satire as Aristocratic Play," 182); he has also argued that the "overwrought tone" of some Juvenalian poems reflects anxiety about maintaining elite identity and values in a changing empire (*World of Roman Song*, 208–9). Corbeill (*Controlling Laughter*) shows that oratorical invective was a vehicle for reinforcement of norms and concepts of deviance.

[6.]On satire's function of identifying "Others," see Richlin (*Garden of Priapus*, 66: the speaker in Roman comic poetry generally "voic[es] and then exaggerat[es] the hostilities of the figure perceived as normal, the middle-aged male Roman citizen"); Henderson, "Satire Writes Woman"; and Bogel, *Difference Satire Makes*, 12. Developing a suggestion of Bakhtin's that satiric laughter is unlike the norm-overturning carnivalesque laughter of comedy, Miller writes: "[Roman satire's] humor does not seek to open up the world to change and the other, as does the Rabelaisian grotesque, but to [picture] the violation of boundaries as leading to death and sterility" ("Bodily Grotesque," 277; cf. "Imperial Satire as Saturnalia").

[7.]On ancient rhetorical theories of humor, see especially Grant, *Ancient Rhetorical Theories*, and (specifically on normative humor in Roman oratory) Corbeill, *Controlling Laughter*.

[8.]The few quotations and mentions of Juvenal we possess from the first few centuries after his death certainly do not illuminate the question of how he made his readers feel, though they hint

Those who regard the persona itself as satire's principal vehicle for entertaining its audience take a different position. Juvenal is said to have designed the early *Satires* to have comic effect, making the persona's indignation look irrational, out of control, and hypocritical.[9] His speaker unabashedly valorizes his own anger, sees threats to his own status in the behavior or success of others (such as his barber-cum-millionaire at 1.24–25), confesses to lack of self-control (the fault of Rome itself, he says at 1.30–31), and admits pleasure in unleashing his anger in verse (scribbling at the very crossroads, 1.63). These attitudes tend to attract the disapproval of ancient moral philosophers, the most vehement and memorable treatment being Seneca's dialogue *On Anger*. In an important chapter in persona studies, Anderson illuminated a strong resemblance between the satirist of Juvenal's first book and the pro-anger speaker that Seneca invents to be his interlocutor.[10] According to Anderson's reading, Juvenal purposely invests his own speaker with serious moral shortcomings that invite mockery of his tirades.

Challenges to this reading can be posed from both formalist and historicist perspectives. We might ask first whether it is really satire's function to espouse or teach "correct" moral positions—or, indeed, whether it is the critic's function to uncover the author's moral agenda. From a historicist angle, it could be pointed out that ancient readers would not have had just one interpretive context (i.e., the particularly rigid views of one philosophical school) for processing the satirist's anger.[11] For one thing, they would have been familiar with the treatment of anger as a given in civic life, and indeed a tool, by rhetoricians and orators. Rhetorical theory—the context for so much of our ancient discussions of the emotions—assumed that the orator's goal was to stir his audience's emotions, including, when it was profitable, anger. According to Cicero, the impassioned peroration called an *indignatio*—a favorite tool of prosecutors—had one clear purpose: to "have the effect of stirring up a great hatred toward someone or a deep aversion toward something" (*indignatio est oratio, per quam conficitur, ut*

———
at his later reputation as a moralist. See Parker, "Manuscripts," 144–45; Hooley, "Imperial Satire Reiterated," 340; and Sogno, "Transformation of Satire," 370–77.

[9] "Irrational": Anderson, "Anger in Juvenal," 145–48 (=*Essays*, 311–14); "unhinged": Braund, *Beyond Anger*, 7–8; "hypocritical" (because he avoids high-profile living targets): Braund, *Satires Book 1*, 120.

[10] Anderson, "Anger in Juvenal," 149–73 (=*Essays*, 315–39).

[11] "There was no single morality of anger in Classical antiquity," notwithstanding a "strong and continuous tradition of both philosophical argument and therapy directed toward [anger's] limitation or . . . elimination" (Harris, "Rage of Women," 129).

in aliquem hominem magnum odium aut in rem gravis offensio concitetur,
Inv. 1.100). The general refrain that it is the orator's obligation to arouse emotions can be seen throughout Cicero's other rhetorical works.[12]

The moral views and tastes of Juvenal's first readers would have ranged beyond the teachings of Stoicism; that includes views on anger's function in life and in literature. While Stoic ideals are certainly celebrated in many instances in Roman narrative literature, we can discern as least as much influence from the Aristotelian notion that *some* kinds of anger were appropriate.[13] In the aristocratic self-image and culture, anger had an important place as a status marker and even a source of pleasure. Upper-class Roman men seem generally to have cherished the right to feel and express anger; the emotion (especially when "performed") was valued as a weapon by elite men in a competitive society who needed to assert their status when affronted.[14] And these men may have felt a certain emotional charge in instances when anger was "properly" deployed.[15] Finally, while the Roman moral tradition recognized anger as a vice (it merits a chapter in Valerius Maximus's collection of exempla),[16] and Roman and Greek literary works had thematized the problems of anger for centuries, it is probably most accurate to say that ancient literature demonstrates a *fascination* with anger that transcends black-and-white moral judgment.[17]

[12.]See, e.g., *Top.* 98, *Part.* 9 and 128; *Orat.* 128 and 131–33; *de Orat.* 1.30, 1.53, 1.87, 1.220–22, 1.245, 2.189–204, 2.214–15, and 3.104–5.

[13.]See Gill, "Emotions in Greco-Roman Philosophy," and many other chapters in Braund and Gill, *Passions in Roman Thought.*

[14.]Mattern-Parkes, "Seneca's Treatise 'On Anger,' " explains that this is the ingrained attitude Seneca was trying to combat in *On Anger*; his advice, compared with Plutarch's in *On Controlling Anger*, is quite dismissive of worldly expectations, as van Hoof shows ("Strategic Differences"). The ancient Greek context is similarly status conscious (see Konstan, "Aristotle on Anger," and, for more extensive social contextualization, Kalimtzis, *Taming Anger*). Medieval aristocrats experienced anger in a similar social context; see White, "Politics of Anger," and Barton, " 'Zealous Anger.' "

[15.]Nussbaum imagines that for a Roman man anger would be "hooked up to a feeling of manly pride, and to a quasi-erotic excitement, as he prepares to smash the adversary" (*Upheavals of Thought*, 160). Cf. the claim of Seneca's straw man that righteous anger affords pleasure (see below on *Ira* 2.32.1 and cf. 2.16.1, 2.17.2, and 2.33.1). Seneca also defines anger as a desire to pay back pain (*Ira* 1.3.2–4), citing Aristotle (cf. *Rh.* 2.2.1378a30–32, b1–2, and *de An.* 1.1.403a29–b3). The role of desire or pleasure is also recognized at Pl. *Phlb.* 47e and Arist. *Rh.* 1.11.1370b9–14 and 2.2.1378b4–9; all three passages cite Homer's reference to rage "sweeter than honey" at *Il.* 18.108–10. Cf. Sorabji, *Emotion*, 80.

[16.]See V. Max. 9.3; on Roman criticisms of anger and their Greek parallels, see Harris, *Restraining Rage*, 201–28.

[17.]Many Roman imperial authors show a vernacular "Aristotelian" (i.e., moderate) perspective on anger, often mixed with a Stoic (critical) perspective; readers who did the same would have found the literature more powerful for its exploration of moral tensions. For readings in this vein, see Fantham, "Envy and Fear"; Wright, "*Ferox Virtus*"; Gill, "Passion as Madness" and "Reactive and Objective Attitudes"; and Brinnehl, "Medusa's Blood."

Juvenal's satiric predecessors certainly acknowledge anger's dangers.[18] Yet Horace wrote two books in different genres that exploited, respectively, the poetic potency of bitter anger and the moral authority conferred by "pedestrian" geniality; this is having one's cake and eating it too.[19] Cicero manipulates a term for resentment ("stomach," *stomachus*) in his *Letters* in a way that allows him to launch political attacks while insulating himself with the term's comic, harmless associations.[20] And the famous declarations by Juvenal's older contemporary Tacitus that anger has no place in a real historian's agenda[21] only underscore the temptation to righteous anger that he suggests could well inspire a senatorial historian writing about the early empire.

In short, anger makes a powerful literary (and metaliterary) theme *because* of its moral ambiguity. Rhetoricians would not use anger if it did not have power, or set guidelines on its expression (e.g., an *indignatio* must only be used when the facts are not in dispute) if to misfire did not entail some risk.[22] Presumptuous use of the technique could incur criticism; simply poor execution might bring on laughter. Both scenarios underscore anger's ambiguous moral status: powerful if justifiably or well performed, offensive if not. One device associated with oratorical anger, the *prosopopoeia* of a dead statesman, may have been designed to lend dignity to a performance that would not be as appealing in the orator's voice.[23] As

---

[18.] See Pers. 3.18 and Hor. *S.* 2.7.44 (cf. the poet's bad temper at the end of the same poem). Cf. Hor. *Ep.* 1.2.59–63 and *C.* 1.16. The classic "angry father" character from New Comedy can be a figure of fun, though his moral attitudes are conventional and often sympathetic; see Duckworth, *Nature of Roman Comedy*, 242–45.

[19.] On the interplay between the *Epodes* and *Satires* Book 1, see Cucchiarelli, *Satira e il poeta*. Horace's association of iambos with anger and invective (cf. the "natural" association of meter with genre at *Ars* 79) reflects a post-Aristotelian characterization; see Rotstein, *Idea of Iambos*, 281–346.

[20.] See Hoffer, "Cicero's Stomach."

[21.] *Hist.* 1.1.3; cf. *Ann.* 1.1.3. These may be differently worded claims that reflect the author's different circumstances vis-à-vis his subjects (see Leeman, "Structure and Meaning," 183), but they may be considered together as statements about generic requirements. Similarly, Pliny, though happy to use *indignatio* in his oratory (*Ep.* 6.33.10), makes an effort to distance himself from the destructive anger that motivated Domitian's opponents in the period just after his assassination (*Ep.* 9.13.4). On the historiographical and moral traditions behind Tacitus's remarks, see Goodyear, *Annals of Tacitus*, 1:100–101.

[22.] See Cic. *Inv.* 2.48, and Craig, "Means and Ends," 77–78. Anderson, "Juvenal and Quintilian," notes that Juvenal occasionally breaks rhetorical rules in expressing anger—for example, by using obscenity. On Juvenal's "proper" techniques, see Braund, *Beyond Anger*, 3–4, and *Masks*, 5–9. A similar concern for propriety governed the use of invective in oratory; see Arena, "Roman Oratorical Invective," 154 and 156–57.

[23.] On the rhetorical and moral advantages Cicero gains (and the problems he avoids) by using a *prosopopoeia* of Appius Claudius Caecus in his speech for Caelius, see Dufallo, "Appius' Indignation" and *Ghosts of the Past*, 13–35. Ancient references to the *prosopopoeia* include Cic.

for the orator's own emotional state, ancient rhetoricians disagree about whether a performer of *indignatio* should actually feel the emotion he is feigning. This may reflect, in some quarters, a moral discomfort with emotional manipulation.[24]

Likewise, philosophers would not criticize anger if it did not have an allure and a privileged social role. Seneca may reject arguments for anger's "usefulness" (especially in high-stakes social relations or combat; see *Ira* 3.3), but he does recognize the appeal of this and similar emotions, both in oratorical performance (2.17.1) and in other literature.[25] It might even be said that *On Anger* itself is enlivened by anger's power. Seneca writes engagingly about the emotion, exploiting the dialogue form to give his discussion shape and momentum. Moreover, he is conversing not just with the straw man who champions the right to be angry but also with those philosophers who have argued that anger is sometimes appropriate. He deploys striking anecdotes and metaphors to illustrate his argument.[26] He describes his text as undergoing a perilous journey through its subject, taking its author, addressee, and audience along for the ride.[27] Perhaps this animated style and approach to composition are partly responsible for

---

Orat. 85 (excluding the device from the "Attic" orator's arsenal) and *de Orat.* 1.245; Quint. *Inst.* 4.1.28 and 12.10.61; and Aquila Romanus 3 (the last two citing Cicero's Appius).

[24.] See Hall, "Delivery and the Emotions," 232–34. For different positions, see Cic. *Tusc.* 4.55 (against genuine anger) and, for the other side, Cic. *de Orat.* 2.189–96 (Antonius's view), Quint. *Inst.* 6.2.26 and 6.2.34–36. Leigh, "Quintilian on the Emotions," finds the hints of moral conflict in our sources to be surprisingly subtle. Cf. Harris, *Restraining Rage*, 111 and 211, on Cicero in particular, and Graver, *Cicero on the Emotions*, xii–xv and 168, on Cicero's emphatic embrace of the Stoic position in the *Tusculans*. See also the exploration of the problem in Kaster, "Passions," 321–25.

[25.] See Schiesaro, "Passion, Reason, and Knowledge," and cf. *Ira* 2.2.3–6 on the power of theatrical performances or written narratives to stir feelings. Seneca appears nevertheless to condone audience enjoyment of the "emotional" rush afforded by literature, for he uses Stoic theory to deny that these "impressions" are technically developed into emotions (*nec adfectus sed principia proludentia adfectibus*, 2.2.5). Wilson asserts that Seneca saw the need for philosophical writing to "engage the emotions—his own and his readers'" ("Subjugation of Grief," 59). On Seneca's sources for the idea that the orator sometimes needs to perform anger, see Fillion-Lahille, *De ira de Sénèque*, 269.

[26.] On Seneca's exempla, see, e.g., Wilcox, "Bad Emperors"; on his heavy reliance on metaphor for instruction, see Bartsch, "Senecan Metaphor."

[27.] From the beginning of Book 2: "Novatus, our first book had quite copious material; for the downward passage to vice is easy. Now, we must proceed to more barren territory; for we're asking whether anger is set off by a decision or an impulse . . . so then the discussion must descend into these matters so that it can rise up again to loftier ones" (*primus liber, Novate, benigniorem habuit materiam; facilis enim in proclivi vitiorum decursus est. nunc ad exiliora veniendum est; quaerimus enim ira utrum iudicio an impetu incipiat . . . debet autem in haec se demittere disputatio ut ad illa quoque altiora possit exsurgere, Ira* 2.1.1–2). Juvenal may have appreciated this visualization; see Keane, "Philosophy into Satire," 37.

Seneca's popularity as a writer among students of Juvenal's generation (see Quint. *Inst.* 10.1.125–31).

While Juvenal was likely to be familiar with *On Anger*, we have no evidence that he was a Stoic, or that he expected his audience to recognize allusions to this particular text. But there are many aspects of *On Anger* beyond its moral precepts—including the quasi-dramatic format, the momentum of Seneca's argument, and the imagery—that could have inspired a poet.[28] Moreover, Seneca's text shares the above features with many literary representations of anger, so we may still appreciate aspects of its argument—as distinct from Seneca's moral agenda—as background for the *Satires*. Even the perennial argument that anger must be controlled or eliminated can be seen as informing the *Satires*, while not necessarily dictating their moral agenda. The anger-control theme provides Juvenal with ways of probing and dramatizing anger's appeal and its problematic associations. Seneca's interlocutor has the job of championing the former, as when he points out that "there's a kind of pleasure in anger—paying back pain is sweet" (*at enim ira habet aliquam voluptatem et dulce est dolorem reddere, Ira* 2.32.1).[29] Even the imagery the Stoic uses for the purpose of criticism makes compelling literary material, moral purpose aside. At different points he compares anger to a force of nature in its variability, an edifice without foundation, a weight that pulls the mind down in free fall, and a madness that grows in scope. He characterizes it a self-exalting uber-emotion that tramples other emotions underfoot. Such imagery has much in common with Latin epic.[30]

In the latest of his collected essays, Anderson suggests that Juvenal meant to "exploit the long moralistic tradition of Roman culture and to utilize the possibilities for ambivalence in the role of the indignant moralist." Creating an angry character for any literary work means tapping into the "complex response which people have to anger. We are never at ease

---

[28.]Plaza (*Function of Humour*, 251) emphasizes that literary borrowing is not the same as ideological endorsement. On evidence of Senecan influence in Juvenal, see Schneider, *Juvenal und Seneca;* Highet, "The Philosophy of Juvenal," 260–64, and "Juvenal's Bookcase," 374–75; and Friedländer, *Essays on Juvenal*, 30–31.

[29.]On the philosophical background of this idea, see Fillion-Lahille, *De ira de Sénèque*, 192. My translations from *On Anger* in this and subsequent chapters borrow from those in Cooper and Procopé, *Seneca.*

[30.]For these metaphors, see *Ira* 1.17.4–7 (anger is like winds, like a snake losing poison, unable to hold strength, capricious; cf. 1.20.1 and 3.1.4), 1.20.2, 1.7.4, 3.28.1, 2.36.6. Cf. 3.1.1–3.4 for another torrent of metaphors, including "angry" sounds. For a survey of similar imagery in epic, see Braund and Gilbert, "ABC of Epic *Ira*," 280–82.

with our own or others' anger, and yet anger is a basic passion."[31] These remarks preface a final iteration of the argument that Juvenal's ancient readers would have taken a morally critical stance on angry speech. But the brief speculation about the audience's "complex response" should remind us that there would be many variables in play in the reception of "angry satire."

The Rhetoric Student at Work

As Juvenal's conception of anger is not restricted to the Stoic view, so his use of anger in the *Satires* is wide-ranging. Juvenal's persona in Book 1 shares as much with the angry orator (or declaimer) as with Seneca's foolish *iratus*. That is not to dispute the implication that the satirist might be a flawed, compromised figure—a convention that permeates Greco-Roman comic genres.[32] But if we think of the satirist not simply as an exhibit but as a rhetorical performer looking for an audience to control, we are in a better position to perceive his strategies—and even to perceive them changing from poem to poem and book to book.

Moreover, Juvenal had been trained to be concerned with other formal elements besides the persona. Equally important components of satiric poetry are the subjects it treats and the stories it tells. It has been observed that *Satires* Book 1 exhibits a kind of narrative continuity with its emphasis on goings-on in the city of Rome, and even a loose plot with its gestures to morning and evening activities in the "bookend" poems.[33] These findings are reminiscent of Kernan's definition of the "satiric plot": a "movement and . . . relationship of parts occurring at different points of time," which shows the influence of the world's disorder and "dullness."[34] The angry persona is a dynamic part of this bigger picture, and it is constructed to conjure various social contexts, power relations, causes and effects, and changes.

[31.]Anderson, "*Lascivia* vs. *ira*," 29–30 (=*Essays*, 390–91). Anderson had earlier noted that in the *iratus* Juvenal has "faced us with an intricate combination of attractive and repellent traits" ("Anger in Juvenal," 148=*Essays*, 314).

[32.]On the idea of the satiric poet as a combination of scurrility and moral heroism, see Rosen, *Making Mockery*; Compton, *Victim of the Muses*; Braund, *Masks*, 40–41; and (regarding Juvenal and his modern critics) Plaza, *Function of Humour*, 254–55.

[33.]Drawing on evidence primarily from Book 1, Bond characterizes the city as "the essential setting of Juvenalian satire and . . . the entity which gives birth and nurture to the vice which it is the satirist's task to explore" ("Urbs Satirica," 91). Cucchiarelli, *Satira e il poeta*, 204–12, connects Juvenal's pedestrian posture at the crossroads to Horace's ambling.

[34.]Kernan, *Plot of Satire*, especially 100–102.

The "angry *Satires*," then, demand to be read as a story, beginning with the satirist's desire to express his anger at 1.1. Considering the way Juvenal orients this inaugural moment, it makes sense to regard *Satires* 1 through 5 not as an "angry book" but as a book *about* anger—how it is born, cultivated, and experienced. The satirist has plenty of rhetorical means for telling this story. His training would have involved far more than impersonation of an *iratus*, and even more than exercises like the *suasoria* he mentions at 1.15–17.[35] Before ever undertaking something like a *suasoria*, a student beginning to learn rhetoric practiced composition in numerous forms. Presented with a theme or idea, he would be directed to treat it in a variety of ways that exercised different rhetorical muscles: expanding or reducing the idea, illustrating it with famous exempla or speeches, structuring it as moral advice, and so on. Even as he advanced through training, the student would need to keep putting these basic skills to work.[36] Book 1 does showcase different rhetorical structures in this spirit: the first two poems are monologues-on-a-theme, delivered by the satirist to an unspecified audience, and both including quoted speech; in the third, Juvenal introduces a friend as "guest satirist," framing his long inset speech as a traveler's farewell (*syntaktikon*);[37] the fourth consists mostly of a long mock-epic narrative; and the fifth is addressed to a specific addressee and contains a narrative. These are all ways of showing what the angry man we meet in *Satire* 1.1 might see, hear, imagine (using the rhetorical technique called *phantasia*, "imagination" or "envisioning"),[38] and try to accomplish.

[35.]Meanwhile, the mention of the Sulla *suasoria* is Juvenal's opportunity to prefigure his future as an antiauthoritarian satirist, according to Henderson ("Pump Up the Volume," 125=*Writing Down Rome*, 269). See also Keane, "Satiric Memories," 225–30, on the generic significance of Juvenal's memory of education.

[36.]Russell, "Rhetoric and Criticism," describes some examples, and stresses (140) that such exercises would have had an even greater impact on the future writer than the more theoretical concepts behind rhetorical education. See also Quint. *Inst.* 2.4.15–26, and Bonner, *Education in Ancient Rome*, 250–76. De Decker (*Juvenalis declamans*, 71–135) illuminates the influence of declamation on Juvenal's composition. Jones (*Juvenal*, 26–27) contemplates genre as a kind(s) of "speech-act" but without discussing Juvenal's debt to rhetoric. Williams (*Change and Decline*, 213 and 266–71) seems to me to overstate the role of "style and treatment" over content in literature of that period; the last element is no less a reflection of rhetorical influence than the rest.

[37.]On the play with the conventional *syntaktikon* in *Satire* 3, see Cairns, *Generic Composition*, 38 and 47–48; cf. Manzella, *Giovenale Satira III*, 5.

[38.]Vivid description (called *enargeia* by rhetoricians, and understood to make *phantasia* happen) is a forte of Juvenal's (Scott, *Grand Style in Juvenal*, 20–24). On *phantasia* as a device for arousing emotion, see Quint. *Inst.* 6.2.29–32 and 8.3.67; Webb, "Imagination and Arousal"; and Zanker, "*Enargeia*."

Viewed as the systematic work of an accomplished rhetoric student, the book exemplifies the "rhetorical" character of imperial literature—not just in its persona but all the way from the variety in its poems' structures down to microscopic features like *loci communes* and embedded speech. Contemporary audiences were trained to admire such virtuosity, a fact that lends support to the reading of Juvenal's angry performance as something more than a curious or laughable exhibit. Ancient literary appreciation was really appreciation of rhetoric—and as an instrument of power, rather than an object to be dissected and observed from a distance.[39] Quintilian's survey of Greek and Roman literature reflects this kind of approach,[40] and both active students of rhetoric and readers with a less practical agenda expected to be *moved* by the "rhetorical" building blocks of literary works, especially elements like embedded speeches.[41] Furthermore, we can infer that readers not only liked rhetoric but liked seeing it work on literary characters, perhaps because these internal audiences allowed them to feel more connected to the action and emotions of the story.[42] It follows that Juvenal's *Satires* were designed to entertain with their rhetorical complexity at least as much as with their moral provocations, and that the angry rhetoric they exemplify would have been recognized—"appreciated"—as an instrument of power, whether or not readers were swayed by the satirist's arguments. Anger is dynamic; it arises from particular conditions and causes new ones.[43]

---

[39] See Tompkins, "Reader in History," 202–6; cf. Abrams, *Mirror and the Lamp*, 14–21 and 26–27.

[40] See Quint. *Inst.* 10.1 on the ideal (i.e., broad and extensive) reading list. Quintilian points out the relation between rhetoric and historiography at *Inst.* 10.1.31–34 and cites specific historians' use of the emotions at 10.1.73 and 101. Cf. the interpretation of Cic. *de Orat.* 2.36 in Cape, "Persuasive History," and on Greek historiography, Fox and Livingstone, "Rhetoric and Historiography."

[41] The pervasive (vernacular) "Aristotelian" view of the emotions holds that appreciation of rhetoric necessarily involves (but is not restricted to) measuring of words' emotional effect; see Konstan, "Rhetoric and Emotion."

[42] The ancient novels are full of trial scenes and speeches, in which internal audiences readily react with strong emotion; Webb recommends against "explain[ing] all the depictions of rhetoric . . . simply as an unconscious reflection of the training received by their authors" and instead considering how they would have affected the ancient audience ("Rhetoric and the Novel," 533; cf. similar remarks about Apuleius in Anderson, "Rhetoric and the Second Sophistic," 347–49). Narrative authors seem to use embedded scenes of performance and response to give cues to their external readers; Tacitus, for example, appears to exploit the possibility of different, conflicting emotional reactions to Vitellius's actions (Levene, "Pity, Fear, and Audience"). On comparable representations of emotions in drama, see also Munteanu, *Tragic Pathos*.

[43] Wright ("*Ferox Virtus*," 176) shows that Aristotle considers anger in a dynamic context, imagining various chains of events that can arise around it (failure to "pay back pain," retaliation on innocent people, self-punishment by the angry person, etc.).

Histories of Anger

At *Satire* 1.1, the potential cure for Juvenal's anger is conjured even before its cause; we are reading it. The satirist here embraces a cathartic anger therapy that is quite unphilosophical.[44] He will eventually merge this view with an appeal to traditional principles of *libertas* (freedom of speech) and *simplicitas* (frankness); the latter is held up as a desideratum for satire by Juvenal's imaginary interlocutor toward the end of the poem. "Where will you get the nerve to suit your subject? Where will you get that famed frankness our ancestors used?" (*'unde/ ingenium par materiae? unde illa priorum . . . simplicitas?,'* 150–53).[45] But it is some time before the satirist's outburst is contextualized in this way.

Juvenal's first complaint looks trivial and comic, like a self-undermining joke. He claims that he has been driven to this outburst not by criminals or sociopaths but by poets. The epics, tragedies, comedies, and elegies that he is hearing recited in private gardens have filled his brain and taxed his patience, and all without facing retaliation (*numquamne reponam?*, 1; *inpune . . . inpune*, 3–4). This sounds like the over-the-top response of a man sensitive to the most trivial irritations and anxious to assert his dignity. A Senecan moral interpretation suggests itself: a man who claims the right to *indignatio* believes he is suffering something undeserved (*indignum*), but he is in fact misunderstanding what is worthy (*dignum*) of a real man (namely, duty; 1.12.2).[46] Despite all this, the opening complaint about interminable poetry recitals sets up connections and patterns that are key to the poem's anger plot. First, the satirist's outburst creates a comical symmetry between the cause of his anger and the means of his relief. Ironically, elegy supplies him with the conceit of personal ventilation (cf. Propertius's desire "to say what my anger wants"), epic with imagery big enough to express his rage.[47] When

---

[44] Most ancient philosophers believe that speaking or acting in anger is damaging and can even make one angrier. See, e.g., Plu. *Mor.* 455c; cf. Harris, *Restraining Rage*, 388–89, on the unique "cathartic" therapy entertained by Iamblichus.

[45] *Simplicitas* and its cognates, when associated with speech, can be read positively (as at Ovid *Am.* 2.4.18, Quint. *Inst.* 4.2.57, and elsewhere) or with a more critical or mocking sense (Sen. *Ben.* 3.26.1, Juv. 2.18 and 13.35; "unsophistication," "naiveté") (see Braund, *Satires Book I*, 107. Knoche reads 1.170–71 as asking "where did [your current] *simplicitas* come from?" and believes Juvenal's implicit answer is that he has no *simplicitas* at all ("Juvenal's Canons," 261).

[46] Seneca's straw man claims (following Theophrastus) that a good man (*vir bonus*) ought to be angry at outrages (1.14.1; cf. 2.6.1). See also Plu. *Mor.* 462e–f and Harris, *Restraining Rage*, 368.

[47] Prop. 1.1.28: *sit modo libertas quae velit ira loqui*. Propertius "writes as a slave who cannot even voice his anger. . . . But the expression is surely *suggested* by the thought of a patient undergoing pain at the doctor's hands; he must at least be allowed the relief of crying out" (Shackleton Bailey, *Propertiana*, 6). The linking of *ira* with the *furor* of love in Propertius is supported by

Juvenal begins to explain his choice of satire at line 19, it emerges that contemporary poetry is just the latest in a series of outrages. His anger at poets is an extension of his anger at the rest of society. In the same way that he finds himself "running into so many poets everywhere" (*tot ubique vatibus occurras*, 17–18), he encounters offensive characters all over Rome—these, too, apparently running to and fro in his field of vision. There is the millionaire ex-barber, the ostentatious Crispinus, the *delatores* on the prowl, the rich young wastrel, the viricidal wives' club, and many more. This account reads like Seneca's description of the challenges faced by the anger-prone man: "every time he leaves his house, he has to walk among men who are criminals, grasping, spendthrift, shameless, and benefiting from it; his eyes cannot look anywhere without finding grounds for indignation" (*quotiens processerit domo, per sceleratos illi avarosque et prodigos et inpudentis et ob ista felices incedendum erit; nusquam oculi eius flectentur, ut non quod indignentur inveniant, Ira* 2.7.2; cf. 3.6.3–5). Even Seneca takes such provocations seriously; he just happens to have an argument against an angry reaction in every case.

For his part, Juvenal justifies his response by claiming that there is an inevitable symmetry between his subjects and himself. In the much-quoted couplet explaining how his satire is created, the poet specifically credits the emotional energy of humanity: "whatever people do—their prayers, fears, anger, pleasures, joys, diversions—is the fodder of my little book" (*quidquid agunt homines, votum timor ira voluptas/gaudia discursus, nostri farrago libelli est*, 85–86). Scholars have paid much attention to the term *farrago*.[48] The metaphor of feeding suggests that satire should be abstractly imagined not as documentation of the world but as a product of engagement with it. Moreover, Juvenal's list of satiric ingredients, which consists mostly of emotions, hints at another relationship that we might describe as duplication or imitation. The highly indignant satirist draws on "whatever people do"—or "are occupied with"—to produce his own emotionally colored verse (cf. *facit indignatio versum*, 79). And although anger is only one item in the "input" list, this emotion does have a reputation for being infectious. Seneca cites this quality of *ira* as a danger: "it's

---

Cairns, "Observations on Propertius 1.1," 106; and Riesenweber, *Uneigentliches Sprechen*, 174. Behind the Propertian idea is a now-discredited "hydraulic" theory of anger; see Introduction and Rosenwein, "Worrying about Emotions," 836. cf. Larmour, "Incurable Wound of Telephus," 69–70, for a comparison of Juvenal's "disease" of enforced silence with the elegiac commonplace of love as disease. On the epic flavor of the opening of *Satire* 1, see Henderson, "Pump Up the Volume."

[48] Gowers, *Loaded Table*, 192. See also Stramaglia, *Giovenale*, 69–70; Powell, "*Farrago* of Juvenal 1.86" (suggesting that the satirist "feeds on vice"); and Itic, "Implications poétiques."

often the case that people rush to anger in a single throng" (*saepe in iram uno agmine itum est*, 3.2.2).[49] The rhetoricians, as I have noted, count on the performed (if not genuine) anger of the orator generating the same feeling in his audience.[50] In Roman epic, most famously in Vergil's account of the beginning of the Trojan-Latin war, anger is passed (in the form of *furor*) from gods to humans.[51]

The *quidquid agunt homines* formula does not reflect Juvenal's focus on vice, but like the assault on poets, it sets up a framework for interpreting his moral and social criticism. Just about any vignette about gender-bending, the vulgar parade of the nouveau riche, the corruption in the courts, and marginalization of the disadvantaged can be read as a representation of emotional *farrago* "out there"—broken down into basic emotional ingredients, so to speak—and an illustration of its ability to inspire the poet. The account of satire's contemporary origins is as simple as it is tendentious: the feelings of Juvenal's entire society are being channeled into his book.

This sounds like a substantial burden for a lone poet. But Juvenal also contextualizes satiric anger historically, giving himself some company. He claims to be following the "nursling of Aurunca" who "steered his chariot through the plain [of satire]" (*decurrere campo/per quem magnus equos Auruncae flexit alumnus*, 19–20). This aristocratic warrior figure, Lucilius, is summoned again just before the poem's ending, again in martial trappings: "Whenever burning Lucilius bellows as if drawing a sword, the listener whose mind is chilly with crimes blushes, and his guts sweat with silent guilt" (*ense velut stricto quotiens Lucilius ardens/infremuit, rubet auditor cui frigida mens est/criminibus, tacita sudant praecordia culpa*, 165–67). Here, Juvenal's satiric ancestor appears to be performing in the angry mode. The fire imagery echoes ancient rhetoricians' descriptions of passionate delivery[52] and Juvenal's own "burning liver" (*siccum*

[49.]Kirk Freudenburg suggests to me (*per litteras*) a parallel in Sen. *Ep.* 7, which describes how bloodlust is spread through audiences at the arena (I think also of Augustine's description of the games' effect on his friend Alypius at *Conf.* 6.8.13). Seneca notes that anger is the underlying cause of bloodlust at *Ira* 2.5.

[50.]See the citations from Cicero in n. 12 above, and cf. Quint. *Inst.* 2.17.26–29, 4.5.6, 5 pref.1–2, 6.1.7, and 6.2 (especially 1, 4–6, 25–26, and 34–36). *Inst.* 12.10.61 describes the grand style as a raging river that can "carry the judge away even if he is resisting" (*torrens iudicem vel nitentem contra feret*).

[51.]Allecto violently plants a version of her own *ira* in Turnus's breast at *A.* 7.445–62 (*iras . . . ira*), a process that seems to transfer rage entirely to the human sphere (Fantham, "Angry Poet," 237).

[52.]See, e.g., Cic. *de Orat.* 2.35.6, 2.189.1, and 2.190.7; *Brut.* 86.10 ("fire" *in dicendo*) and 276.12; *Orat.* 27.2 (on the fiery *verbum*), 99.2 (linked with the adjectives *gravis* and *acer*), and 132.8 ("burning" *oratio*). Cf. Quint. *Inst.* 9.2.8 and 10.1.90 (characterizing Lucan). Horace, or rather his

iecur ardeat ira, 45);[53] Lucilius's "bellowing" also looks like a version of Juvenal's loud debut. Moreover, the republican poet is shown effectively targeting the secretly guilty, and so seems to have lived the fantasy of Seneca's straw man: "anger is useful, because it lets you escape scorn, and it frightens the wicked" (*'utilis est . . . ira, quia contemptum effugit, quia malos terret,'* *Ira* 2.11.1). Lucilius got to *malos terrere* over and over again, as *quotiens* implies. In sum, this portrait of Lucilius—the vivid present tense notwithstanding—provides Juvenal with a model and a mandate associated with antiquity and nobility.

But this is not the real Lucilius—at least, it is an incomplete picture of this multitalented poet. From the surviving fragments of Lucilius's large corpus and the testimonia of his admirers, it is possible to see that he used a variety of styles, including a playful, genial persona that frequently took the spotlight (what Haß terms "Persönlichkeitsdichtung").[54] As far as we can tell from the fragments, Lucilius's fictionalized *ego* is not tonally consistent.[55] It is true that his satiric successors all emphasize his aggression, creating metaphors of physical violence to describe his satire and so creating precedent for Juvenal's martial vignette. The garrulous Lucilius brutally "stripped off the hides" of hypocrites (Hor. *S.* 1.4.7–13, 2.1.68–69) and "cut into" the city with his teeth (Pers. 1.114–15). Yet only Juvenal implies that Lucilius adopted an angry persona in the process. Meanwhile, Lucilius's republican- and imperial-era readers raved not just about his frankness but about his erudition and wit too.[56] These talents certainly helped him mimic anger (such as that of the gladiator Pacideianus at fr. 181 Warmington),[57] but they are not equivalent to an angry satiric persona. Juvenal's skewed history of satire strategically obscures the full variety of Lucilius's poetry, in order to make anger out to be the genre's originary mode.[58]

---

unfriendly interlocutor, describes the stern New Comic father as *ardens* (*S.* 1.4.48); Woodman, "Juvenal 1 and Horace," sees a gesture to this satiric "ancestor" in Juvenal's Lucilius.

[53.] Bertman ("Fire Symbolism") links other fire imagery in *Satire* 1 to Juvenal's anger as well.

[54.] Haß (*Lucilius*; see especially 9–29) credits Lucilius with the invention of this type of poetry; she takes the term from Knoche's discussions of the Neoterics and elegists ("Eine römische Wurzel" and "Erlebnis und dichterischer Ausdruck").

[55.] See Haß, *Lucilius*, 53–54, 94–95, and (on the impact of this on later satire) 193–204.

[56.] Cicero's Crassus calls Lucilius "a little angry [at Scaevola, one of his targets], but still learned and very witty" (*subiratus . . . sed tamen doctus et perurbanus, de Orat.* 1.72). Cf. the description at Quint. *Inst.* 10.1.94: *eruditio in eo mira et libertas atque inde acerbitas et abunde salis.*

[57.] Quoting these lines in a discussion of anger in *Tusculan Disputations*, Cicero cites—and rejects—the Peripatetic view that anger is a valuable tool in combat (*Tusc.* 4.48–50).

[58.] The adjective "Lucilian" has been attached to the terms "aggression" and "indignation," even in discussions that mention the poet's talent for more relaxed comedy; see, e.g., Miller, *Latin Verse Satire*, 13, and Highet, *Juvenal the Satirist*, 230 and 246 n. 9; cf. 174 and 247 n.9. Greater

In *Satire* 1, Lucilius is made to represent both a model and a lost art. The sword passage is part of the poem's famous closing dialogue about the dangers of outspoken satire, which is modeled on similar programmatic exchanges in Horace and Persius but amplifies the satirist's risks.[59] Juvenal implies that in *his* day, the threat of retaliation against an ambitious satirist is far more serious than social ostracism. "Defame Tigellinus, and you'll turn into a burning torch" in the arena (*pone Tigellinum, taeda lucebis*, 155)—a warning that is itself encoded in Neronian references as if to provide additional insulation for our satirist.[60] Juvenal's solution, to take aim at the dead (170–71), looks on one level like an admission of failure or perhaps a searing indictment of contemporary repression of *libertas*.[61] But it also breaks new and interesting ground for satire, which previously concentrated on the (fictional or real) present.[62] A similar "glass-half-full" approach can illuminate the image of Lucilius's *indignatio:* this is the one element of the first satirist's style that it is still safe to imitate. Juvenal's subjects may not be as high-stakes as Lucilius's, but he poses—to compensate?—as a staunch traditionalist on the matter of satire's proper tone.[63]

The promise to revive satiric *indignatio* appears in stark relief against the rest of the narrative about the genre in *Satire* 1. After Lucilius, fiery satiric anger seems to have been reduced to a slender flame: namely, the "Venusine lamp" that Juvenal cites as a worthy vehicle for his documentation of contemporary vice (*haec ego non credam Venusina digna lucerna?*, 1.51). Like the thundering chariot at line 20, this lamp is a symbol of a satirist—the Venusian Horace. While it evokes a range of meanings associated with poetics and moralizing,[64] this modest and private flame is a far cry

---

emphasis on Lucilian variety can be found in Knoche, *Roman Satire*, 49–51; Rudd, *Themes in Roman Satire*, 2; Braund, *Masks*, 11; Coffey, *Roman Satire*, 35–62; and Svarlien, "*Lucilianus Character.*" Exceptionally, Anderson recognizes that "*Lucilius ardens . . .* is created after Juvenal's image" ("*Venusina lucerna,*" 12 n. 25 =*Essays*, 114 n. 25), and Cucchiarelli calls the vignette "la re-invenzione dell' *inventor*" (*Satira e il poeta*, 205).

[59.]Juvenal's programmatic discussion in *Satire* 1 evokes Hor. *S.* 2.1.7–86 and Pers. 1.103–34; on Juvenal's alteration of these models, see Braund, *Satires Book I*, 117–19; Fredricksmeyer, "Observation on Programmatic Satires"; Shero, "Satirist's Apologia"; and Duret, "Juvénal Réplique à Trébatius."

[60.]Bartsch, *Actors in the Audience*, 90–93; cf. Courtney, *Satires*, 116.

[61.]For the latter interpretation, applied to Horace and Persius as well, see Freudenburg, *Satires of Rome*.

[62.]Keane, "Historian and Satirist," 409–10.

[63.]Compare Juvenal's special emphasis on the model of Lucilius as perceived by Griffith, "Ending of First Satire," 70.

[64.]The *lucerna* might connote late-night study of an Alexandrian poet, satirically productive insomnia, or a Diogenes-style lamp shone on human nature; for these meanings, see Braund, *Satires Book I*, 88–89; Cucchiarelli, "*Venusina lucerna,*" 189; Jones, *Juvenal*, 18; and Stramaglia,

from the fire Lucilius breathed in his victims' faces; in this respect alone it resembles Persius's description of Horace as a private sort of satirist, prodding his friends (1.116–17). Horace's role in the anger narrative is to illustrate the waning or suppression of the old burning mode. In fact, while he gets a lamp (not actually mentioned in his *Satires*),[65] he does not get to keep the metaphorical satiric tool that he *did* claim to wield, the "sword" that symbolized his threatening verse (*S.* 2.1.39–42).[66] Finally, the contrast between Lucilian fire and the Horatian lamp could help explain the total removal of Persius—at least by name or epithet—from the landscape in *Satire* 1, despite a noteworthy borrowing near the end of the poem ("death in the bath," discussed below). This would be the inevitable sequel to the first, Horatian chapter in angry satire's disappearance. Juvenal, then, does not just carry the torch but is responsible for reigniting it.

At the same time, Juvenal's claim to take up the Lucilian torch is qualified. While he may be claiming that anger was satire's originary mode, by his own account it did not survive the transitions that also influenced satirists' choice of targets. With only a tantalizing outline to go on, it is difficult to say whether *indignatio* was weakened, suppressed, or outgrown—but something made it diminish. This raises the prospect that Juvenal's own satire, now driven by nostalgia for a satisfyingly angry past, might eventually undergo some alteration too. In fact, as later chapters in this book will discuss, Juvenal's own career will—at least in this small way—echo the history of satire itself. But for now, the poet is relying on anger for power, all the more because of the delay he has endured (*semper . . . numquam*, 1). In this respect, he challenges another Senecan claim, namely, that delay can *calm* anger (*Ira* 2.29.1). Whether his outburst will ultimately lead to satisfaction is uncertain (Seneca would bet against that too, judging from *Ira* 2.32); for now, he will scribble away.

In addition to (his version of) Lucilius, Juvenal indicates that he will also have contemporary allies of a sort. This comes at the end of the long section on the breakdown of traditional patronage (96–146). The generic rich man has been ignoring the appeals of his poor clients, letting them go hungry while he enjoys a huge feast (a declamatory *locus de luxuria*).[67] This leads to the patron's undoing: a postdinner bath proves fatal. Juvenal's

---

Giovenale, 51–52. The Diogenes explanation is first suggested by a scholiast (Wessner, *Scholia in Iuvenalem vetustiora*, 6).

[65.]Thus Anderson ("*Venusina lucerna*") takes Juvenal to be referring to the patriotic and moralistic *Odes*, not the *Satires*.

[66.]Stramaglia, *Giovenale*, 112.

[67.]De Decker, *Juvenalis declamans*, 33.

phantasia ends with the man becoming an exemplum: "Off goes the tale through all the dinner-parties—it's novel, and not sad either—while your funeral procession travels along to the applause of your angry clients" (*it nova nec tristis per cunctas fabula cenas; ducitur iratis plaudendum funus amicis*, 145–46). There is a clear borrowing from Persius here; his unhealthy rich man meets his death too, and his newly freed slaves serve as his pallbearers (*illum/hesterni capite induto subiere Quirites*, 3.105–6). Juvenal's coda takes a cue from Persius's next lines, in which the satirist tries to use the story as a lesson for his interlocutor.[68] But Juvenal prefers to imagine the event's impact on the dead man's community. He shows us two kinds of social mockery: the gossip of dinner parties, and—for those restricted to lowlier social arenas—self-expression in the streets. Both scenes are reminiscent of Juvenal's own satiric attacks, but the latter makes an especially apt parallel. With their frustration at the *salutatio* and afterward (132–34), they replace Persius's silent, expressionless freedmen and share the satirist's own feelings of marginalization and deprivation. While their casual "satire" is more muted than the poet's, it reflects a similar dark humor and willingness to attack the dead if the alternative is impossible. Indeed, in practice Juvenal resembles these *irati amici* more than he does the sword-brandishing Lucilius.

This dark humor marks a relatively uplifting conclusion to the long section on patronage, but the poet does not change his satiric mode just because he has some kindred spirits in Rome. Rather, he has established what will be a major topic of his satire: the plight of neglected *amici*. The clients' mission of punishment may not accomplish much, but their disappointment has now been integrated into the book's anger narrative. Their experience will be paradigmatic. The rest of Book 1 tells a story through interlocking pairs of poems, in a structure reminiscent of Horace's second book of *Satires*.[69]

Suppression, Contestation, Compensation

We readers finish *Satire* 1 having been told that we have an appetite for angry satire—after all, it's "you," Juvenal's invisible interlocutor, who prompted the Lucilius reference with the anxious questions at lines 150 through 153. We are rhetorically implicated, and set up for more of the

---

[68] Both passages appear to develop the brief reference to a sobering funeral at Hor. *S.* 1.4.126–27.
[69] On this structure in Horace *Satires* Book 2, see Boll, "Anordnung im zweiten Buch."

same. And once Juvenal thematizes the very process of choosing subject matter in that final passage, we might expect an illustration of his chosen approach.

Sure enough, the opening indictment in *Satire* 2 of moralists who hide their own sexual deviance confirms that Juvenal has chosen to limit his angry moralizing to nonpolitical figures and ghosts from the past. The satirist's style does seem to reach its grandest heights when he is talking about the most ancient exempla, good or bad.[70] But throughout the poem, whether he is being grand or obscene, Juvenal demonstrates his skill at *phantasia*—from his insinuation that one man is the "most notorious ditch among the pathic philosophers" (*inter Socraticos notissima fossa cinaedos*, 10), to his lurid description of the secret women's rites they have adopted (83–116), to his envisioning of the private marriage ceremony between a priest and a horn player (117–26). Juvenal is still overplaying the outraged orator. His attack on hypocritical moralists—and then, as the poem shifts focus, on men who openly engage in homosexual and effeminate practices—is sarcastic, punctuated with rhetorical questions and invocations of religion, full of censorious vocabulary, and despairing in its tone.[71] The one puzzling formal feature is the shift of Juvenal's attention from secret practices to unconcealed ones. But that shift has been persuasively explained as a reflection of the slippery way that Roman moral thought links different categories of deviance together.[72]

A matter that merits just as much thought is the reason Juvenal launches into his *first* subject, the supremely irritating moralizing of men who secretly "live a life of orgies" (*Bacchanalia vivunt*, 3). This appears to rank as a personal offense against the satirist (recalling the Aristotelian definition of anger), something that makes him want to flee beyond the borders of the empire (*ultra Sauromatas . . . et glacialem/Oceanum*, 1–2). What makes this the appropriate subject to tackle after the panoramic vision of *Satire* 1? Why is *this* particular catalyst for satiric anger the first to bear fruit? The answer, I propose, lies not in the hypocrites' secret activities but in the noise they are making on the surface—and in this way, they are successors to the group that first sets Juvenal off in *Satire* 1, the reciting poets. These new offenders "have the audacity to talk about morals, pretend to be censors," and they "inveigh against [vice] with rugged language" (*de moribus audent . . . Curios simulant*, 2–3; *talia verbis/Herculis invadunt*,

---

[70] See Freudenburg, *Satires of Rome*, 248–52; and Nappa, "*Praetextati Mores*," 95–96.
[71] For the techniques in this poem, see Braund, *Satires Book I*, 168–72.
[72] See Nappa, "*Praetextati Mores*."

19–20). Juvenal's concern is not vice per se—or so he claims when he contrasts the hypocrites with forgivable, open deviants (15–17, 21–22)—but the fact that deviants would pose as censorious moralizers. This is the satirist's job; he is now encountering "rival performers" who he believes are unqualified.[73] It is telling to compare this with the poems of Martial that also mock pseudo-moralists (1.24, 7.58, 9.47): Martial's targets talk about moral paragons (always with a form of *loquor*), but they do not inveigh.

Satire 2, then, begins as an indignant response to someone else's unwarranted *indignatio*. Juvenal gives himself the job of contesting and taking away the pseudo-moralists' "right to rant." Competition for the role of moralist is not a new satiric theme—Horace made dramas of it (*S.* 2.3, 2.7)—but Juvenal turns it into a livelier game, even a team sport. Borrowing a technique of declamation, he introduces quoted speech from two characters who are also tired of hearing moral tirades from hypocrites.[74] Something like the *irati amici* in *Satire* 1, these characters are also victims of Juvenal's targets, and they assert their right to "bite back when attacked" (*castigata remordent*, 35). The pariah Varillus, who evidently advertises his true effeminate nature, snaps, "Am I supposed to be afraid of you, Sextus, you ass-wiggler? How am I worse than you?" ('*ego te ceventem, Sexte, verebor?'/infamis Varillus ait, 'quo deterior te?'*, 21–22). Juvenal's other partner in satire is Laronia, the woman who "couldn't endure [*non tulit*] a certain stern fellow" invoking the neglected law against adultery (36–37). Where Varillus quipped, Laronia delivers a substantial speech embellished with witty epigrams and scathing accusations against the self-appointed moralists. "A third Cato has fallen from heaven!" (*tertius e caelo cecidit Cato*, 40). "Tell me, where did you buy that *parfum* that's wafting from your shaggy neck?" (*sed tamen unde/haec emis, hirsuto spirant opsobalsama collo/quae tibi?*, 40–42). "There's great concord among [secret] effeminates" (*magna inter molles concordia*, 47). "Everyone knows why Hister filled his will with his freedman's name alone, but gave so much to his wife while he was alive. The woman who's willing to be the third wheel sleeping in a rich man's bed will become wealthy" (*notum est cur solo tabulas inpleverit Hister/liberto, dederit vivus cur multa puellae./dives erit magno quae dormit tertia lecto*, 58–60).

With its length and rhetorical flourishes, Laronia's performance expands on that of Varillus and comes closer to resembling Juvenal's

---

[73] Freudenburg, *Satires of Rome*, 250.
[74] On quoted speech as a declamatory technique, see de Decker, *Juvenalis declamans*, 90–107.

practice of satiric anger. Her speech gives us an opportunity to observe, from the outside, the operation of sustained satiric rhetoric. At the same time, it does not resolve the ambiguities associated with satiric anger; in a way, Laronia remains as inscrutable as the satirist himself, the nature of her "anger" just as ambiguous. She is neither clearly morally righteous nor—although many scholars have taken her to be a prostitute or adulteress[75]—scurrilously amoral. Her performance also shows signs of both real and "rhetorical" anger. She smiles as she begins her tirade (*subridens*, 38), hinting at that "pleasure in anger," the "sweet[ness of] paying back pain" that Seneca's interlocutor mentions in *On Anger*. But her verbal revenge exhibits rhetorical elegance and control;[76] for instance, with the alliteration in *caelo cecidit Cato*, sputtering contempt mingles with playfulness. As a proxy satirist, Laronia represents the self-reproducing and dynamic nature of indignant invective—at least in its idealized form. Her encounter with the *Stoicidae* ends up dramatizing a particularly extreme and pure effect of satiric rhetoric: "those fake Stoics fled in fear, for Laronia was uttering the obvious truth" (*fugerunt trepidi vera ac manifesta canentem/Stoicidae; quid enim falsi Laronia?*, 64–65). This fantasy ending echoes Juvenal's earlier claims about Lucilius's successes.

Laronia's efforts bring Juvenal's game of wresting back the "right to rant" to a satisfying end. But to justify continuing with his poem, the satirist needs another cause for anger. This can be found in the reorientation of his poem to target men who *openly* dress like women, *openly* marry one another, *openly* practice women's religious rites, and so on. This group practices a different kind of offensive *libertas* (77, 112) than that of the hypocritical moralists: they behave as they are. And with this we are sent back to the "second beginning" of the previous *Satire*—the announcement, in abstract terms, that human behavior and emotions feed Juvenal's book. The last hundred lines of *Satire* 2 feature plenty of emotional *farrago*, as the satirist's new targets feel no inhibition. Creticus boldly attends court in a translucent dress, "fierce and indomitable, a model of freedom/ forthrightness" (*acer et indomitus libertatisque magister*, 77; cf. *audebis*, 82). Religious fervor grips the men who conduct the rites for Bona Dea (83–116). Guests joyfully attend the marriage of Gracchus and his horn player and cry out their congratulations (119). Joy and urgent prayers give way to grief (*tormentum ingens*, 137) for the newlyweds when they are

---

[75.] For discussion, see Braund, "A Woman's Voice."

[76.] Braund, "A Woman's Voice," 208–11; cf. Freudenburg, *Satires of Rome*, 252.

confronted with the inevitable sterility of their marriage. The list from 1.85–86 is more or less covered, without any sign of the desire to conceal reality that the hypocrites in the first section exhibited. Juvenal claims to know the feelings of the open effeminates so well that they might as well be part of the public parade of vice seen in *Satire* 1.

Adding to the fuel that comes from the satirist's emotive targets is another identifiable cause of anger: the *lack* of righteous anger from quarters that might make a difference. Although Gracchus, the "bride" in the wedding scene, is one of the Salian priests, Mars has not communicated any dismay ("you're not shaking your helmet or striking the earth with your spear or complaining to your father—so get out, leave the acres of that strict field [i.e., the Campus Martius], which you're neglecting," *nec galeam quassas nec terram cuspide pulsas/nec queries patri. vade ergo et cede severi/iugeribus campi, quem neglegis*, 130–32). Neither divine nor state authorities are weighing in on this moral crisis, a factor that is as aggravating as the unwarranted invective of the hypocrites in the first section.[77] These two parallel problems, each applying to a different case of immoral behavior, invite angry rhetoric. And in proper oratorical fashion, there is a climactic peroration. Juvenal's description of the impression his targets will make on Roman ancestors when they arrive in the underworld (149–58) exhibits all the proper techniques of an *indignatio*, including invocation of traditional religion, a lament on behalf of brave ancestors, and (in the next section, 158–63) unfavorable comparison of contemporary Roman and barbarian mores.[78]

In the next poem that features the satirist in monologue mode, *Satire* 4, the theme of the conditions for anger is further developed. Among other parallels between *Satires* 2 and 4 (such as the concern with sexual misbehavior and the citation of past emperors as examples of vice),[79] we may identify an exploration of extreme scenarios of critical speech and its suppression. But this time, the climate is more favorable to angry speech. Indeed, with *Satire* 4 Juvenal pretends to indulge not just his own appetite

---

[77.] In addition to Rome's patron god remaining silent, traditional mechanisms for addressing or preventing vice are not functioning: the censor (Domitian) is not fulfilling his role as he should (29–33), a soothsayer is needed to interpret these horrific occurrences (122), and belief in a judging underworld has virtually disappeared (149–52).

[78.] The shades of great republican leaders and warriors, Juvenal imagines, would want to be ritually purified upon catching sight of the new arrivals (149–58). He goes on to point to an ironic contrast between the customs of remote conquered peoples and the debauchery witnessed in the capital (159–63). Cf. the pertinent instructions at Cic. *Inv.* 1.101–3.

[79.] Cloud and Braund, "Juvenal's Libellus," 81–82.

for anger but an appetite shared by his whole generation. Juvenal here joins in on the de rigueur Domitian-bashing of the post-Flavian era, assailing the dead Domitian and his lackeys. But he demonstrates an extreme version of the *libertas*, freedom of speech, that his contemporaries are celebrating in their lockstep praise of the new dynasty.[80] Juvenal has signed no contract to write without *ira* or *odium*, so he can produce a poem that shows rage feeding itself to produce extreme results.

This project commences with indulgence in hyperbole, focusing on Crispinus, the wealthy Egyptian freedman who attracts the satirist's attention so early in *Satire* 1 (26–29). "Here he comes again" (*ecce iterum Crispinus*, 1), a man who seems to have become a moral cliché ("no wicked man is happy," *nemo malus felix*, 8) since we first saw him waving his purple cloak and gold rings. But vague references to Crispinus's being a *monstrum* and *adulter* (2, 4) give way to a startling specific one: he was "a sex criminal, recently bedded with a beribboned priestess, who ended up being buried underground with her blood still pumping" (*incestus, cum quo nuper vittata iacebat/sanguine adhuc vivo terram subitura sacerdos*, 9–10). That a Vestal found to be unchaste would have faced capital punishment is confirmed by other evidence;[81] Crispinus's involvement in such a case is not. In fact, although the satirist claims Crispinus was a lackey of Domitian himself, we have virtually no evidence of the Egyptian's existence.[82] Thus it is hard to know how to interpret Juvenal's claim. But the more significant moment may be his easy transition in the very next line: "but now let's talk about his more trivial acts" (*sed nunc de factis levioribus*, 11). Can this be the right choice for an angry satirist addressing the crimes of the past? Is the Vestal story not good enough material for righteous anger? Even if the *factum* of interest turns out to be a classic example of *luxuria* deserving of the censor's ire, is the purchase and selfish consumption of an enormous mullet really worth writing about? After all, this is the kind of satiric crime that Juvenal can just as easily pin on generic characters, such as the selfish patron of *Satire* 1.

What is happening, I suggest, is an exploration of how *libertas*—the kind that names names—can sound when it is not just allowed but encouraged.

[80.]On the theme of *libertas* in Trajanic literature, see Ramage, "Juvenal and the Establishment"; Wilson ("After the Silence") is less inclined to read all manifestations of this theme as panegyric for Trajan. See also Freudenburg, *Satires of Rome*, especially 215–42.

[81.]Plin. *Ep.* 4.11.4–10; Suet. *Dom.* 8.

[82.]The only ancient sources to mention Crispinus are Juvenal (as cited above) and Martial (7.99, 8.48), but scholars have still tried to fit him into Domitian's circle—in various roles; see Jones, *Emperor Domitian*, 69–70.

Juvenal's revenge-enacting speech is both weapon and target. The point of Juvenal's odd focus *is* that Crispinus and his ilk are now fair game; consequently, both the risks and the payoff of free speech are diminished. The satirist sketches the Vestal story as if gesturing to a well-known event, then moves on to dig up something new. It is not that the Vestal episode is unimportant—it efficiently conjures an atmosphere of unpunished criminality that Juvenal wants to associate with Domitian's reign throughout the poem. Domitian-the-corrupt-censor is a theme here (11–14) as it was in *Satire* 2 (29–33).[83] But there is a programmatic hint in Juvenal's question "what can you do with a terrible character who's more repulsive than any charge [*sc.* you can think of]?" (*quid agas, cum dira et foedior omni/ crimine persona est?*, 14–15). When there is a mandate to keep telling stories of villains, the satirist's job is to get creative. And in this climate, he implies, no one will stop him from making shocking claims—such as that Crispinus paid a thousand sesterces per pound of fish flesh, "as people say when they're taking big things and making them bigger" (*ut perhibent qui de magnis maiora locuntur*, 17).

By the same token, there is nothing to prevent Juvenal from casting around for something still bigger when he has done what he wanted with the mullet story. The satirist has been dwelling on a trivial item when his contemporaries, Pliny and Tacitus, have made clear that Domitian's reign saw much worse atrocities. As it turns out, he has been preparing to trade up for the subject of the late emperor himself, who has become just as safe a target as an invented nobody. As he puts it, why stop with an imperial lackey, this small fry, Domitian's palace trash, when we could be launching an even bigger attack on the emperor? (28–31):

> qualis tunc epulas ipsum gluttisse putamus
> induperatorem, cum tot sestertia, partem
> exiguam et modicae sumptam de margine cenae,
> purpureus magni ructarit scurra Palati . . .?

What sorts of banquets, then, do we think the emperor himself gobbled down, when so many thousands of sesterces—a paltry portion, a bit of a side dish of an ordinary-sized dinner—were belched up by [Crispinus] the purple-clad clown of the Palatine?

[83.] Stewart ("Domitian and Roman Religion," 323–26) and Luisi (*Rombo e la Vestale*) find *Satire* 4 to be permeated with the theme of Domitian's failed religious authority.

No fear or convention will prevent Juvenal from answering his own question, and with the most outlandish fiction. He has such big plans for the story of Domitian's turbot that he has to invoke the Muses for help in this second proem (34–36). Free angry speech has fed the appetite for more free angry speech, the relatively minor bad actor serving as a steppingstone to the big game. Accordingly, the fish tale concerning Domitian takes on predictably absurd proportions, and not just in the sense that Juvenal only obliquely gestures to the oppression and violence this emperor engineered during his reign. Anything goes when the subject is comparatively trivial and the players all dead. The satirist piles on outrageous details: the humble fisherman who made the incredible catch would have been arrested by palace spies if he had kept it for himself (45–56); he carried the turbot clear across the Apennines and up to Domitian's door at the Alban palace (56–64); the fish was so huge that the emperor had to call his advisory council together to figure out how to prepare it (72–73).[84] For all the symbolic meanings that have been plausibly seen in Domitian's turbot—it is an allegory for the monstrous ruler, for the world he dominated, for the very task of writing about him[85]—the story must still be appreciated in its literal form and for its shock value.

Woven throughout, however, is a contrasting story with a starkly different atmosphere: the suppression of free speech and the tension and misery that such conditions create. The closest Juvenal gets to indicating that he is affected by such conditions is his joke to the Muses: "you can take a seat, no singing necessary; this is a true story. Begin the tale, Pierian girls—and I hope it benefits me to have called you 'girls'" (*licet et considere: non est/cantandum, res vera agitur. narrate, puellae/Pierides, prosit mihi vos dixisse puellas*, 34–36). This joke about the advantages of tempering one's speech before superiors prefigures a much more serious situation in the story about to unfold.[86] Flattery and indirection will dominate the interactions that make up the tale of the turbot. The fisherman is first, presenting his catch to the tyrant: "receive something too great for private hearths . . . [and] consume a turbot that has been kept in reserve for your lifetime. It *wanted* to be caught" (*accipe . . . privatis maiora focis . . . tua servatum*

---

[84] Winkler ("Alogia and Emphasis") views these claims as manifestations of rhetorical emphasis on the "irrational" or "absurd" (*alogon*).

[85] See Sweet, "Juvenal's *Satire* 4," 288–89; Winkler, "Alogia and Emphasis," 75; Gowers, *Loaded Table*, 202–11; and Keane, "Historian and Satirist," 419–20.

[86] "This is precisely the kind of blatant flattery that the characters in the *concilium* will offer all throughout the poem in their praise of the fish and of Domitian himself" (Uden, "Invisibility of Juvenal," 117).

consume saecula rhombum./ipse capi voluit, 65–66, 68–69). The flattery could not be more absurdly obvious—at least, to anyone but the megalo-maniac emperor (69–71), who proceeds to encourage even worse toadying among his council.

The parade of inhibited speech becomes the show in the second half of *Satire* 4, becoming as big a component of this poem as the criticism of the dead emperor.[87] The council members who rush in on command are an anxious lot, marked by "the pallor of unenviable friendship with the great" (*in quorum facie miserae magnaeque sedebat/pallor amici-tiae*, 74–75). Juvenal, being at liberty to do so, tells their true stories—the tragedies of the ineffectually principled, the chilling acts of the sinister and bloodthirsty. In the council, neither type utters a frank word, instead competing in flattery before a vain despot who eats it up. It is the satirist who points out that Pegasus and Crispus brought to their administrative posts talents that went unused or even suppressed (76–93).[88] It is he who cites the brutal execution of one council member, the younger Acilius, as a recipe for indignation (*iuvene indigno quem mors tam saeva maneret*, 95). Turning his attention to the more vicious schemers (105–43), he brings all that is distasteful out into the open: the smell of Crispinus's perfume, the death-dealing whispers of Pompeius the informer, the cold-blooded war planning of Fuscus in his villa, the calculations of Catullus and Veiento, the lechery of Rubrius, and the greed of Montanus. The advisers (with the exception of Crispinus) are known to history, but Juvenal highlights their inadequacy as honest witnesses of their own careers—he will do the job, through his own contrastingly liberal fabrication. Playing on the con-trast between the pained self-censorship of the past and free, angry speech, the satirist even laces his character sketches with the standard rhetorical vocabulary of horror (*monstrum, saevus, dirus*). His language fulfills Cicero's requirements for *indignatio* as much as it resembles the accounts of Domitian's reign in Tacitus and Pliny.[89]

And yet what is crushingly obvious is that Juvenal's speech here is not the kind that benefits the world—any more than the traumatized coun-cil members were capable of the decisive action eventually taken by Domitian's "worker"-assassins (*cerdonibus*, 153). Juvenal's anger is not high-stakes Lucilian sword-waving but downright conformity with the

---

[87.]Ahl, "Art of Safe Criticism," 197–200.
[88.]Van den Berg, "Imperial Satire and Rhetoric," 280.
[89.]*monstrum* (2, 115); *saevus/saevitia* (85, 95, 109, 151); *dirus* (80); cf. Cic. *Inv.* 1.102. On the correspondence with Tacitus and Pliny, see Ramage, "Juvenal and the Establishment," 697–98.

literary theme of the times. In this anti-Domitianic age, this stuff is as old and smelly as the big turbot itself must have been after its cross-country journey.[90] But as Juvenal demonstrates, demonizing the dead can be an obsessive sport if the audience continues willing. He still has passions to feed off, but this time it is not the passions that operate within the story he tells (tyrannical anger or the grief of victims; these are hardly even expressed in the account).[91] Instead, the satire draws on the *ira* and *odium* that color contemporary literature about Domitian. Juvenal shows that anger, that "desire for revenge," is a self-sustaining and to some extent irrational appetite.

Anger between Friends

As a late product of a literary era that has been described broadly as "satiric,"[92] *Satire* 4 may represent Juvenal's ingenious effort to make his genre continue to stand out as unique. But as we have seen, the poem also draws on dominant themes in its literary climate to present itself as a response to audience taste. The remainder of this chapter will return to the broader question of what the satirist of Book 1 aims to accomplish.

Ancient rhetorical theory would suggest that emotional arousal of the audience is the satirist's primary goal, a consequence, or both. The ancient rhetoricians treat audience emotional response as something highly predictable, and therefore manipulable.[93] The implication is that being on the receiving end of rhetoric like this is at least as much an emotional

---

[90.]Winkler ("Alogia and Emphasis," 61) also makes the case for appreciating the story—and the increasingly absurd fish-in-transit—on the literal level.

[91.]The "anger of tyrants" theme appears at *Ira* 3.16.3–19.5; Braund, *De Clementia*, 164, mentions parallels. Pliny's praise of Trajan in the *Panegyricus* includes a contrast between the reasonable Trajan and the terrifyingly irascible Domitian (*Pan.* 48). On accounts of the early emperors' struggles with anger, see Harris, *Restraining Rage*, 247–57. Tyrants' victims could themselves be driven to *rabies* according to Seneca (*Ira* 1.12.4).

[92.]On characterizations of the age from Nero to Hadrian as "satiric," see Hutchinson, *Seneca to Juvenal*, 77, and Furneaux, *Annals of Tacitus*, 1:36.

[93.]See Webb, "Imagination and Arousal," and note the implication in Cic. *Inv.* 1.100: *indignatio est oratio per quam conficitur ut . . . odium aut . . . offensio concitetur.* See also Porter, *Audience and Rhetoric*, 16–17, and "*Divisio* as Em-/De-Powering Topic," 197; cf. Berlin, "Revisionary History," 54. The rhetoricians' assumption that people will respond in predictable ways to conventional devices can feel like a roadblock to understanding how ancient oratory actually worked; we are left to wonder whether Roman verdicts were determined by emotions or facts. For a nuanced analysis, see Riggsby, "Did the Romans Believe." See also Craig, "Audience Expectations" (on the truth value of invective specifically), and cf. Craig, "Survey of Recent Work," 519. Kennerly ("Getting Carried Away") argues that ancient rhetoricians saw a link between emotional "transport" and the process of judgment.

experience as an intellectual one. This, at least, is the premise under which the speaker or writer would operate, and it surely proved accurate for many ancient audiences of oratory and readers of "rhetorical" literature. For this reason we should hesitate to believe that ancient readers of satire would have been mainly primed to respond to the angry satiric speaker with either moral judgment or laughter. Even if Juvenal's satiric indignation can look absurd, this does not necessarily mean that the poet is inviting his readers to pass judgment on anger, joining him, as it were, outside the text. It is more plausible that Juvenal, like other satirists, is playing on his audience's *desire* to seize on the "right" interpretation of his criticisms, namely, as straightforward or ironic.[94] A reader who insists on an ironic reading, for example, taking the "real" Juvenal to be critical of extreme anger or bigotry, is still being manipulated—and specifically, manipulated into ignoring the programmatic relevance of the angry facade itself.

Since the first facade put up in *Satires* Book 1 is, simply put, angry rhetoric, we might look for hints about how Juvenal imagines that rhetoric being received by minds that are willing to be moved—or are simply incapable of resistance. As Quintilian puts it, the most emotionally forceful rhetorical style (the "grand" style, *grande ac robustum*) can "carry the judge away even if he is resisting, inspire anger and pity; it will make the judge go pale and weep and be carried through all the emotions, this way and that, nor will instruction be his concern" (*torrens iudicem vel nitentem contra ferret, hic [modus] iram, hic misericordiam inspirabit; hoc dicente iudex pallebit et flebit et per omnis adfectus tractus huc atque illuc sequetur nec doceri desiderabit, Inst.* 12.10.61–62). Does our satirist envision himself as wielding such power—for example, over the audience whose appetite demanded *Satire* 4? Does he imagine that his angry satire might move someone with its emotional power—whether that someone feels directly affected by the problems the satirist attacks or is merely susceptible to concern for "other people's struggles," as Seneca claims happens to readers of narrative?[95] Or might there be readers who are moved to anger at the satirist himself? Lucilius was able to provoke "anger and tears" (*ira et lacrimae*, 1.168)—and the first term at least has been taken to refer to resentment from parties injured by the satire. But it implies a kind of poetic success as well, characterizing Lucilian satire as provocative speech that engenders a cyclical or reciprocal emotional

---

[94.]See Rosen, *Making Mockery*, 207–42.
[95.]See *Ira* 2.2.3–6 for Seneca's description of how readers respond to "other people's struggles" (*aliena certamina*); to his mind, this is a proto-emotional reaction rather than full-fledged emotion.

process.[96] Rather than avoid such consequences, our new angry satirist may be steering deliberately toward them. At any rate, the only other reference to *any* poetic audiences in *Satire* 1 lends support to the idea that poetry can have a violent impact on listeners. Readings of endless epics, tragedies, comedies, and elegies have driven Juvenal to unleash his anger, and he observes that even inanimate objects subjected to the same performances are showing feeling: "Fronto's plane-trees and dismembered statues and columns, fractured by nonstop readers, constantly cry out [echoing the poetry they've heard]" (*Frontonis platani convolsaque marmora clamant/semper et adsiduo ruptae lectore columnae*, 12–13).[97] This image of literary reception as torture may be comic, but it is still programmatically relevant for a poet using a mode that is meant to move his audience.

Apart from the implication in *Satire* 4 that Juvenal's contemporaries are hungry for some anti-Domitianic anger, we have seen no gestures to an audience. Yet someone with his rhetorical training must surely have an audience on his mind, as he marshals those conventional tools. Similarly, an author of narrative fiction (a category that suits Juvenal) must imagine that there is someone listening to the unrolling story. Though this need only be a notional audience, its existence in the author's imagination is essential. The concerns of orator and narrator are merged in the construction of what Rabinowitz terms the "ideal narrative audience," one of several audience types that the narrative hypothesizes. As Rabinowitz defines it, the ideal narrative audience is purely sympathetic and persuadable: it "believes the narrator, accepts his judgments, sympathizes with his plight, laughs at his jokes even when they are bad."[98] It is not difficult to envision the angry Juvenal positing such an audience from the outset; the rhetorical questions with which he builds his program in *Satire* 1 are one device that suggests he deeply desires one. Somewhere out there, he imagines an *auditor* agreeing with his every complaint and nodding at his every question.

According to Freudenburg, the external audience (whether ancient or modern) of the ranting Juvenal in *Satire* 1 faces a dilemma: "we are given a dubious choice between silent resentment, on the one hand, and letting the satirist's scripted *ego* become ours on the other."[99] But perhaps there

---

[96] Horace's use of the Terentian *hinc illae lacrimae* (*An.* 126) to describe his carping critics (*Ep.* 1.19.41) paves the way for Juvenal's further mutation. Cf. Cucchiarelli, *Satira e il poeta*, 211–12.

[97] On the lifelike effect of the statues, cf. Stramaglia, *Giovenale*, 29. Larmour ("Incurable Wound of Telephus," 57–64) analyzes the references to noise.

[98] Rabinowitz, "Truth in Fiction," 134.

[99] Freudenburg, *Satires of Rome*, 241.

is a third option: to imagine oneself as a spectator to a rhetorical process or processes, but not the intended audience of the intense and provocative rhetoric. This role is filled by a fictional construct trapped inside the text—sometimes invisible, sometimes more clearly defined. We have already seen Juvenal dramatizing a performance of (proxy) "satire" before an implied internal audience, at the dead gourmand's funeral in *Satire* 1. Even this brief sketch of the *irati amici* applauding suggests that there is a bond between performers of angry attack (if not strictly angry rhetoric), and possibly even that such a performance can recruit supporters on the spot (might we imagine the group growing larger and gaining confidence?). This is a fictional "anger community," a visualization of the social and dynamic dimension of performed indignation. As such, it prefigures Juvenal's other experiments in visualizing satire's effects.

In *Satire* 3, Juvenal expands his use of "proxy satirists"—so far exemplified in his own Varillus and Laronia—to a larger-scale ventriloquism that rivals the greatest Horatian examples. By far the longest poem in Book 1, the third *Satire* consists almost entirely of the farewell speech of Umbricius. On the verge of his move south to quieter country, Umbricius paints a colorful, tragicomic picture of life in Rome that, for readers throughout history, has epitomized "Juvenal."[100] This is understandable: the appropriately named "shadow-man"[101] resembles the satiric speaker of the previous two poems in both his moral attitudes and his anger. He is a proud but down-and-out native Roman, nourished on "the Aventine sky [and] the Sabine olive" (*nostra infantia caelum/hausit Aventini baca nutrita Sabina*, 84–85) and bred to accept client status in principle. But his capital's transformation under the influence of foreign immigrants, new wealth, and intensified competition for work and patronage has him incensed. Umbricius is the quintessential disenfranchised client, a fleshed-out version of that generic type first seen suffering in *Satire* 1.[102] Exhausted and

---

[100.]The third "stands out as being one of the best of Juvenal's satires and is well suited as an introduction to his poetry" (Knoche, *Roman Satire*, 148). For assimilation of Umbricius's outlook to Juvenal's, see Highet, *Juvenal the Satirist*, 69; Bellandi, "Naevolus cliens," 293–94, and *Etica diatribica*, 38–58 and 100–101; and Courtney, *Satires*, 153. On the subject of how the two figures compare, Manzella (*Decimo Giunio Giovenale III*, 4–5) is careful to emphasize the contradictions in Juvenal's own persona.

[101.]The root *umbra* brings to mind failure or inferior imitation (in life or in literary production); see Hooley, *Roman Satire*, 117–18; Jones, *Juvenal*, 86; and Hook, "Umbricius *Caligatus*"; for reflection on such arguments, see Moodie, "Bully as Satirist," 103. Nice, "*Persona* of Umbricius," links Juvenal's character to a historical *haruspex*.

[102.]On the theme of patronage in Juvenal, see LaFleur "*Amicus* and *amicitia*" and "*Amicitia* and Unity"; Bellandi, "Naevolus cliens"; and Damon, *Mask of the Parasite*, 172–91.

bitter, now entering old age (*nova canities . . . prima et recta senectus*, 26), he sums up his life experience as deprivation, marginalization, and wasted labor. He has gone without dinner invitations, financial aid, or business opportunities (29–40). He has risen before dawn to greet his patron, only to be snubbed (126–30). While the powerful and well-off ignore him, the undeserving bump him off the socioeconomic ladder (58–125). Umbricius and his kind are not simply neglected but mocked and bullied (147–53, 278–308). Living in a teetering, flammable apartment building is a threat to life and dignity (190–211), as is simply slogging through the streets (239–308). In short, his lot is the very definition of *indignatio* according to Seneca.

Accordingly, Umbricius revives many sentiments and rhetorical techniques we have by now already heard from Juvenal *in propria persona*. The satirist proper sets him up as his proxy with an opening joke about the aggravation caused by reciting poets (9)—echoing the first complaint in *Satire* 1. The setting of Umbricius's tirade, the Porta Capena (11) that marks the starting point of the southbound Via Appia, may even be seen as a version of Juvenal's *quadrivium* (1.64).[103] In his decision to flee, Umbricius is acting out what Juvenal has only done partially so far; for him the declaration "I cannot endure" (*non possum ferre*, 60) must be accompanied by self-saving action.[104] He is abandoning a ruined city where he is vulnerable to literal conflagrations, the seething criminality of his social superiors, and his own burning bile, while the satirist stays behind to continue "shuddering at fires" (*horrere incendia*, 7) and enduring the presence of criminals who are "boiling over" with guilty secrets (*fervens/occultis . . . tacendis*, 49–50). The physiology (of both wrongdoers and speaker) is Juvenalian and Lucilian, although Umbricius feeds it into a mock-epic representation of the entire capital.[105] Seeking a cooler retreat for physical and emotional relief is, Umbricius says, what all the

---

[103.]In addition, the "violated" natural landscape of the artificial grove of Egeria, additionally sullied by its Jewish occupants (12–20), recalls another performance setting embedded in *Satire* 1: Fronto's garden. It also reflects the general degradation of the site of Rome, a theme that Juvenal has himself pushed; see Hardie, "Juvenal, *Phaedrus*, and Truth," 239–41.

[104.]Manzella, *Decimo Giunio Giovenale III*, 4: "attraverso Umbricio, Giovenale realizza, proprio nell'invenzione letteraria, quella desiderio di evasione di fuga dall'Urbe che, violentemente dichiarato in apertura della satira seconda."

[105.]On the epic associations of Umbricius's fire imagery, which constitutes another link with the other mock-epic elements of Book 1, see Baines, "Umbricius' *Bellum Civile*," and Staley, "Juvenal's Third Satire" (the latter arguing that "Umbricius [like the satirist] wishes to be viewed as an epic hero," 98). Winkler ("Function of Epic") argues that Juvenal means to reclaim epic's *indignatio* (diminished and inadequate, as he sees it) for satire.

poor and honest natives of Latium should have done a long time ago (162–63). Before he goes, however, he delivers a tirade that recalls the emotional "infection" dramatized in *Satire* 1. The city's aggravations and dangers create an atmosphere of fear that fuels Umbricius's anger.[106]

Why would Juvenal frame the dazzling centerpiece of his book, which shares so many themes and rhetorical strategies with the other poems, as someone else's speech? Virtually all studies of *Satire* 3 have sought to understand what the *separateness* of Umbricius represents. The answers are varied. By one account, Umbricius is a vehicle through which Juvenal evokes Martial's epigrams, only to subsume this literary model into a more complex narrative structure.[107] Alternatively, he symbolizes an extreme traditionalism that even Juvenal perceives is out of place in the increasingly cosmopolitan Rome.[108] Finally, some see Juvenal using Umbricius as "satirist" in order to make it easier for his audience to view indignant satiric speech more critically.[109] All these interpretations see Juvenal as creating distance between himself and Umbricius; most touch on the topic of the latter's indignation, highlighting its manifest extremism, inconsistency, and self-interest. But a morally oriented evaluation of *Satire* 3 gets us troublingly close to the conclusion that the entire series is one extended, monotonous joke. It also depends on our placing our trust in the "real" satirist who stands watch in *Satire* 3, as if he were an external commentator. These are, to be sure, the sort of traps that are commonly laid by satiric rhetoric.[110]

Meanwhile, we could pay more attention to the fictional scenario of the poem, namely, that Juvenal is parting from a friend (*veteris . . . amici*, 1). The idea of this "friendship" as a metaphor for literary affiliation, while appealing, does not account for all aspects of the story. It is worth reading

---

[106.]Criminals feel fear at 57; cf. the fear of the generic virtuous and/or poor man at 190, 276, and 310. The running about of clients, objects, and criminals (128, 215, 240, 308) also recalls *discursus* at 1.86.

[107.]See Mason, "Is Juvenal a Classic?," 124–35, for the argument subsequently challenged by Anderson in "*Lascivia* vs. *ira.*"

[108.]Motto and Clark, "*Per iter tenebricosum.*"

[109.]For analyses of Umbricius as an unappealing and/or unreliable "satirist figure," see Winkler, *Persona in Three Satires*, 220–23; LaFleur, "Umbricius and Juvenal Three"; Fruelund Jensen, "Martyred and Beleaguered Virtue"; and now (with the most nuance) Moodie, "Juvenal's Third Satire." Braund (*Beyond Anger*, 15) sees Juvenal "paving the way toward future developments in which the angry man is exposed as foolish." Many examples from *Satire* 3 feature in Anderson's examinations of the tensions in indignant satire; see "Anger in Juvenal," 131–48 (=*Essays* 297–314).

[110.]For a pertinent example, see Schlegel's discussion of Horace's "pest" story (*S.* 1.9; *Threat of Speech*, 108–26).

more importance in the outer narrative frame, especially considering that it is upheld at the end of Umbricius's speech (and the poem; 318–22):

> '. . . vale nostri memor, et quotiens te
> Roma tuo refici properantem reddet Aquino,
> me quoque ad Helvinam Cererem vestramque Dianam
> converte a Cumis. saturarum ego, ni pudet illas,
> auditor gelidos veniam caligatus in agros.'

"Farewell and remember me, and whenever Rome sends you back in your haste to be restored at your native Aquinum, invite me along from Cumae to the Helvian temple of Ceres and your Diana. I'll come to that chilly country in my boots—if it doesn't embarrass your *Satires*—to be their audience."

Here we are reminded that Umbricius is just a guest speaker, and his primary audience is the "real" author of *saturae*.[111] The valediction echoes the poem's first nine lines, Juvenal's own mini-satire on Rome that is occasioned by his friend's departure. These brief gestures are propping up a story in progress. In retrospect after the end of Book 1, the poem may look like a foreshadowing of Juvenal's own "retirement" from indignation; but for the moment, it looks like an exchange between friends.

Juvenal's friendship with Umbricius is as important to this poem as is the ritualized Roman patronage that the latter describes as so disappointing. The relationship of the two characters represents the way anger can be shared through speech and how it can in turn take the form of speech. Umbricius, like Horace's Davus, is emerging from a passive position to take the role of satirist ("I've been listening for a long time now, and [want] to say something to you," *iamdudum ausculto et cupiens tibi dicere, S.* 2.7.1).[112] But this satiric proxy, who enjoys a higher status than Horace's slave, performs a different kind of satiric imitation: rather than direct satire back at the author, he presents his performance as part of a reciprocal cycle that is part of friendship. His appetite for satire will continue, and he will play the audience again at Aquinum. Thus, although he may also be seen as a compliant audience of the angry satire that precedes his appearance—taking Juvenal's criticisms of Rome to their logical conclusion by

---

[111.]Sarkissian ("Appreciating Umbricius," 257–58) uniquely emphasizes this point.
[112.]Davus, in turn, is a kind of successor to the less effective proxy satirist Damasippus (*S.* 2.3); both train their lectures on Horace, eliciting his displeasure (see Keane, *Figuring Genre*, 118–19).

moving away—Umbricius is not passive. He joins a gratifying dynamic of satiric imitation.

It may be no accident that Juvenal nestles *ira* and *voluptas* together at the line end of *Satire* 1.85. It is a reasonable proposition that angry satire can form and maintain bonds between the like-minded. At any rate, the ancient rhetorical evidence implies that to persuade someone by using emotionally arousing rhetoric is to generate pleasure for that person, even if the rhetoric in question is stirring up difficult feelings; this much we hear from the usual sources. In the important tripartite formula of Cicero, emotional effect and pleasure are separate elements (oratory should "teach . . . please . . . and move the feelings good and forcefully," *doceatur . . . delectetur . . . moveatur vehementius, Brut.* 185).[113] Quintilian nowhere disagrees on the separateness of these agendas, but he does note that some critics attack orators for overusing emotional appeal, supposedly "seeking to give pleasure to the audience" (*voluptatem audientum petere, Inst.* 5 pref.1).[114] The implication is that pleasure and emotional persuasion are woven together, collaborating to bind the audience to the speaker. And such bond formation seems especially likely in cases where the audience is, due to mutual concerns, predisposed to agree with the speaker. When two parties are united by a feeling that their personal status is at stake, such as when angry satire is performed for a sympathetic audience, emotional pleasure will mingle with the pleasure of collusion, of affirming "shared righteousness."[115] It is nothing new to observe that satirists traditionally aim to win over their audience by manipulating a notion of common ideology. This point has been made with respect to the subtler, more appealing persona of Juvenal's so-called Democritean *Satires*, but not the early, aggressive one.[116] Perhaps Juvenal has had less difficulty being an *auditor* of Umbricius's "poetry" than he does at recitals by nonsatirists, for in addition to echoing his own concerns, this performance affirms his

---

[113.] Cicero also thinks emotion-inducing ornament should have its limits in oratory; see Fjelstad, "Restraint and Emotion."

[114.] Quintilian also recognizes audience pleasure as a separate thing from emotion; he notes that ornament gives *delectatio, Inst.* 8.3.1–11. Quintilian does assert that there are separate rules for poetry and oratory (cf. Dozier, "Poetry, Politics, and Pleasure"), but this distinction is fuzzy in the Juvenalian dramatic scenario.

[115.] Juvenal "marks the boundaries of what was acceptable for a respectable Roman man. This creates a pleasure in which author and audience collude, the pleasure of affirming their own righteousness" (Walters, "Making a Spectacle," 365).

[116.] The "mocking" persona of *Satire* 10 "aims to seduce us into wanting to join an exclusive club," while the "angry" one "attempts to arouse our emotions by its own emotional appeal and to sweep us into agreement" (Braund, *Masks*, 27).

potency as satirist and contains the promise of a later reversal of roles (*auditor . . . veniam*, 322).[117]

In envisioning this bond with his departing *amicus*, Juvenal may also be seen as upholding a Lucilian ideal—this time, one that Horace also explores. At the beginning of his second book, aiming to convince the lawyer Trebatius that his (allegedly private) manner of practicing satire is harmless, Horace cites the example of Lucilius. He basically conflates his predecessor's practice of satire with his social life (*S.* 2.1.71–74):

> quin ubi se a vulgo et scaena in secreta remorant
> virtus Scipiadae et mitis sapientia Laeli,
> nugari cum illo et discincti ludere donec
> decoqueretur holus soliti.

> Surely, when brave Scipio and gentle, wise Laelius took themselves away from the crowd and the stage of public life, they were in the habit of jesting with Lucilius, and playing around, ungirt and relaxed, while they waited for their pot of greens to boil.

There are obvious, and meaningful, differences between this scene and the one in Juvenal 3: namely, in the men's political status and the tone of their satiric (or proto-satiric) speech. But the private setting at a remove from the urban scene, the comfortable equality, the casual dress code, and the pretension to rustic simplicity are all there.[118] Horace, of course, conjures his own version of this community later in Book 2 (*S.* 2.6.60–117). His proxy satirist, however, speaks in abstracts and allegories (cf. the tale of the country and city mice); Umbricius is more direct, and his material is literally and personally relevant. The Lucilian *amicitia* that he aims to practice with Juvenal contrasts directly with the *amicitia* he has been experiencing as a client in Rome. Instead of humiliating power dynamics and

---

[117.] This symmetry depends on *auditor* being the correct reading (for support, see Manzella, *Decimo Giunio Giovenale III*, 420–21), but the alternative reading *adiutor* ("assistant") certainly upholds the theme of Umbricius's participation in a satiric cycle. LaFleur defends the less commonly printed *adiutor* as the *lectio difficilior*, preferring to see Umbricius as a "bumpkin-booted poetaster" contributing to Juvenal's dissatisfaction with Rome ("Umbricius and Juvenal Three," 415).

[118.] On Umbricius's country *caligae* as a rejection of urban pretension, see Manzella, *Decimo Giunio Giovenale III*, 421–22. These are the same boots soldiers wore, a point that for Pasoli ("Chiusa della Satira III") hints at a moral "battle" undertaken by the satirist and his friend. However, farmers are also described as *caligati*, as Courtney notes (*Satires*, 194), and Umbricius is planning a garden of his own at Cumae (3.226–29). On the relevance of the word's various senses, see Hook, "Umbricius *Caligatus*."

wasted gestures, he can experience a kind of symmetry and exchange. The threatening fire of the city is replaced with the cool of the country.

And yet it is reasonable to doubt that, even in this image of equality, Umbricius achieves the same status as Juvenal. The poet's formal introduction of his friend might be read as sarcasm. His silence at the end of Umbricius's speech, while it seems more encouraging than Horace's displeased reaction to Davus, might be intended to indicate something other than approval. The only clear information that the poem gives us is that *Umbricius* approves of *Juvenal*'s satire and echoes the positions expressed in it. Beyond that, there is ambiguity, such as on the matter of what Umbricius will accomplish with his flight. Is he "right" to leave Rome, when Juvenal himself is staying? There may in fact be more than one way to read *his* "reading" of Juvenal. While his move suggests that he may be taking his friend's words as life advice, his expectation of a continuing appetite for satire indicates that he may enjoy it as entertainment. We might conclude that Umbricius accepts both of satire's traditional ruses: namely, that the satirist is a serious moralist aiming to persuade, and that he is scurrilous and disingenuous, aiming only to shock and entertain. At different points, satirists pull their audiences in the direction of each of these interpretations.[119] Umbricius might have been created to represent a combination of the two readings—as if to outsmart the satirist. Alternatively, his conscious or unconscious compliance with both may make him the ultimate dupe. Umbricius may be a friend of the satirist, but that does not make him immune to taking the bait and "getting carried away."

Since his role entails wielding power over his audience, the satirist who poses as angry orator may be destined to remain without an equal. In the last poem of Book 1, a final demonstration of what anger can do, this point is made much more clearly. In *Satire* 3, there is at least an illusion of equality, even a correction of some of the injustices deplored at the beginning of the book. Where Juvenal felt saturated and silenced by other men's poetry, now both he and Umbricius willingly play the listener. As for Umbricius, unlike the poor clients of *Satire* 1 who remained invisible to their patron, he attains a different, more satisfying kind of *amicitia*. But the book and the story of anger are not over yet; there is one more *iratus amicus* to meet, and his fate will be worse than Umbricius's. At first, the signs look good: the premise for the poem is that Trebius, the addressee, finally gets

---

[119.]See Rosen, *Making Mockery* (cf. n. 94 above), and Rosen and Baines, "I Am Whatever."

that coveted invitation to dinner with *his* patron. He also appears to have a friend in the satirist, who takes an interest in his life. Notably no longer solipsistic or passive, Juvenal has taken on a quasi-philosophical role reminiscent of Horace and Persius.[120] Perhaps he is doing so in the name of *libertas*, after the painful stories of self-censorship in *Satire* 4.

But this combination of circumstances turns out to be very unpleasant for the addressee. For one thing, as Juvenal describes it, being fed by Trebius's rich patron in question is anything but satisfying. The dinner—a product of Juvenal's imagination that constitutes the entire narrative of this poem—is a humiliating and enraging experience. When Virro the patron answers Trebius's prayers by saying "let's do dinner" ('*una simus,' ait. votorum summa*, 18), he does not have fellowship in mind. He has designed *two* dinners to be served simultaneously, just to insult and frustrate his lower-status guests. Course by course and cup by cup, the host and his social equals are served elegant fare while his poorer clients receive comically shabby counterparts meant to underscore their inferiority. While the host across the room drinks the finest vintage wine and spring water, his clients are served cheap stuff hardly fit to drink (24–37, 49–52). Instead of lobster, they get a shrimp each (80–85); instead of fragrant fruits, rotten apples (149–55)—and so on.

Like similar treatments in satire and related genres, this meditation on dining, cuisine, and social relations speaks to big issues of *urbs* and empire: class and power, social values, luxury, and consumption itself.[121] But Juvenal's poem stands out in approaching these grand matters with a painfully sharp personal focus. As Freudenburg has shown, *Satire* 5 is very much about appetite—cruelly whetted, then disappointed. This is a motif in the lavish, painfully funny descriptions of the unequal dinner. The clients long for what is being denied them, but they are always let down— with additional dampers put on their yearning for respect, for opportunity, and most of all for the ability to express themselves.[122] They are not trusted with the nicer tableware because they are assumed to have sticky fingers (39–41). If they sneak a hand out to the fine bread being delivered to their host, they are slapped by his slaves and told to settle for the rock-hard rusks assigned to them (72–75). The whole thing is a textbook recipe (so to

---

[120.]See Braund, *Satires Book I*, 276. Even the satirist's harshness has a philosophical background: the Epicureans approved of frank criticism between friends, including when strong emotions are involved (see Armstrong, "Be Angry," 98).

[121.]On numerous parallels and models in Lucilius, Horace, Menippean satire, Martial, and Pliny, see Gowers, *Loaded Table*, and Braund, *Satires Book I*, 304–6.

[122.]Freudenburg, *Satires of Rome*, 275–77.

speak) for indignation, and as Juvenal imagines it, it is working. Early on, the clients are already so worked up that it only takes some cleaning fluid–grade wine to drive them to brawl with one another—as if for the company's entertainment (24–29).[123] As things progress, they end up fighting over their puny territory using bread loaves as swords (*stricto pane*, 169). The pathetic echo of Lucilius's fearsome drawn sword underscores the indignity. Juvenal tells us this is all Virro's deliberate doing, orchestrated to maximize indignation (120). Trebius, in the narrative, is "compelled to pour out bile along with tears, and give a long hiss through clenched teeth" (*per lacrimas effundere bilem/cogaris pressoque diu stridere molari*, 159–60). Even his indignation is scripted; his subordinate role to Virro and his peers could not be made clearer.

Yet Virro is not Trebius's only tormentor; the satirist plays a part. He may not be involved in the "real" dinner—in this sense Horace's absence from Nasidienus's dinner in his own last *Satire* (2.8) is appropriately recalled—but Juvenal plays a more active role than Horace. Where Horace asks for an account of the *cena* from one who was not excluded, Juvenal invents a fiction, telling Trebius how his dinner *will* go. It is as if the addressee is already disregarding the satirist's advice (making him seem a fool),[124] yet absorbing his goading rhetoric on the emotional level (making him look like a more helpless version of Umbricius). The dinner happens essentially in the present, contemporaneous with the delivery of the satire; Virro's cruel "anger game" is absorbed into, and becomes a metaphor for, the satiric lecture. Juvenal does more than just rehearse Trebius's humiliation; he invents this client in order to trap him in a one-sided rhetorical scenario that is inherent even in the mildest satiric sermons.[125]

It is worth noting that if Juvenal's book were a speech, *Satire* 5 would be the peroration—the place where, according to Quintilian and Cicero, an orator is supposed to let out all the stops. As Quintilian puts it, "here [in the *peroratio*, aka the *epilogus*], if anywhere, we must open up the springs of our eloquence in their entirety . . . this is when we must stir up the theater" (*hic, si usquam, totos eloquentiae aperire fontes licet . . . tunc est commovendum theatrum, Inst.* 6.1.51–52).[126] It is appropriate, then,

---

[123.]On Trebius and his peers as entertainers under Virro's direction, see 5.157–58, and Keane, *Figuring Genre*, 30–31 and 66–67; cf. Adamietz, *Untersuchungen zu Juvenal*, 95–96.

[124.]In Kernan's view (*Plot of Satire*, 26), this case exemplifies Juvenal's two-part agenda to attack "knaves" (like Virro) and "fools" (like Trebius).

[125.]On Horace, see Schlegel, *Threat of Speech*, 16–17.

[126.]See also *Inst.* 6.51. Like Quintilian, *Rhet. Her.* 2.47 notes that the peroration is not the *only* suitable place for amplification or indignation; still, this is the speaker's now-or-never moment (cf. Cic. *Top.* 98).

that the handbook instructions on *indignatio* are coming out in full force. With each course there is vivid description—*phantasia* that in the rhetoricians' terminology should "enslave" the listener.[127] There is emphasis on the insults that come on top of injuries. In the end comes the dramatic prediction that Trebius will eventually stoop to voluntary slavery.[128] It may be particularly easy for Juvenal to perform this way in *Satire* 5 because at last he has a clearly defined, and interested, addressee. Not being bound by normal declamatory or theatrical conventions, Juvenal needs no grateful applause, only the rhetorical success he imagines to be manifested in an angry Trebius.

The satirist also has the power to demonstrate his power in the very *cena* that he has invented. "I'd like to have a word with this [Virro], if he'll lend me a willing ear," the satirist digresses (*ipsi pauca velim, facilem si praebeat aurem*, 107). Here is Juvenal's chance to harangue the ungenerous and malicious patron in the name of *libertas*. Appropriately, the address to Virro adopts a nostalgic tone, with its praise of gift-giving ethics in past generations. But the lecture can only have so much impact on its target when it is so brief (108–13):

nemo petit modicis quae mittebantur amicis
a Seneca, quae Piso bonus, quae Cotta solebat
largiri (namque et titulis et fascibus olim
maior habebatur donandi gloria). solum
poscimus ut cenes civiliter. hoc face et esto,
esto, ut nunc multi, dives tibi, pauper amicis.

No one is asking you to give as much as Seneca and good Piso and Cotta used to send as gifts to their ordinary clients—for back then, the honor of giving was just valued more than titles and offices. I only ask for you to dine as if you're with fellow citizens. Do that, and then go ahead and be what so many are these days: rich for your own purposes, a pauper to your clients.

It is not that this sermon, with its direct imperatives and harsh conclusions, lacks the sting of *indignatio;* it is just that it is over so quickly that

---

[127.] Successful *phantasia* will "enslave" (*dominatur*) the audience (Quint. *Inst.* 8.3.62). Cf. similar language at Long. 15.9: ἡ ῥητορικὴ φαντασία . . . τὸν ἀκροατὴν . . . δουλοῦται.

[128.] Compare these to Cicero's recommendations at *Inv.* 1.104 (place outrages before the judges' eyes with vivid description); 105 (point out that *contumelia* is being added to *iniuria*); and 101 (envision the result of inaction).

we are reminded that it is not the main event. Immediately Juvenal drops the confrontational address and resumes his narrative: "the liver of a huge goose is served to the patron . . . " (*anseris ante ipsum magni iecur*, 114; is it coincidence that the liver was cited as the seat of *ira* at 1.45?). Endowed with the right of free speech, the satirist only cares to use it briefly on Trebius's behalf—indeed, only long enough to show that he has a power that Trebius lacks.

This is not a bonding experience between friends; as even the opening of the poem hints, Juvenal ends up washing his hands of Trebius, so that this *amicus* looks like neither his "friend" nor his satiric "client." He had begun by urging Trebius to choose the relative dignity of begging over the guaranteed humiliations of Virro's company: "Is the insult of this dinner worth so much to you?" (*tantine inuria cenae?*, 9). The long narrative of the hypothetical dinner has taken us into a future reality that confirms Trebius's foolishness and passivity. It is time to mock and condemn the client overtly. "If you can endure all this, you deserve to" (*omnia ferre/si potes, et debes*, 170–71), Juvenal tells Trebius before trotting out the final *phantasia* that shows the client embracing the role of slave: "Sooner or later, you'll be shaving your head and offering it up to be beaten, not afraid to suffer the harsh whip—you who are worthy of such a feast, and such a friend" (*pulsandum vertice raso/praebebis quandoque caput nec dura timebis/flagra pati, his epulis et tali dignus amico*, 171–73). So much for the alignment of satire with the oppressed, and so much for the solidarity of anger. Since Trebius can no more talk back to Juvenal than he can to Virro, it is made clear that this is nothing like the *amicitia* shown in *Satire* 3. With his last words, Juvenal designates his addressee for the relationship he deserves: a kind of slavery.

While Trebius is fated to experience boiling rage and eventually a beating, what happens to the satirist who has stoked that rage? Some have proposed that in *Satire* 5 Juvenal demonstrates a movement away from *indignatio* as a satiric mode by highlighting how ineffectual Trebius's own rage is. This reading depends on an interpretation of Juvenal's later *Satires* as a pointed "exposure of the inadequacy" of anger.[129] But our interpretation of the end of *Satire* 5 has to make sense in the context of Book 1 first

---

[129] Jones, *Juvenal*, 90. Cf. other scholars' conclusions that in *Satire* 5 Juvenal acknowledges anger's "inanità" (Bellandi, "Naevolus cliens," 290) and that "Book I ends with an implicit, muted, condemnation of *indignatio*," foreshadowing more explicit later criticisms (Braund, *Beyond Anger*, 18). On the same page, Braund makes the more nuanced observation that by calling Trebius *dignus* of his treatment, Juvenal strips him of the *right* to feel *indignatio*. This is a taste of a struggle that will resurface in the last book of *Satires*.

and foremost; the poem should make a fitting *end*, whatever it might fore-shadow in the future. When he chooses angry rhetoric as his first satiric mode, Juvenal works to arouse an imaginary audience. He ends his book representing a concretized version of this compliant audience. Are there consequences for him? Given Juvenal's not-so-subtle alliance with the patron Virro, it is tempting to imagine him as relatively unruffled by the whole experience of (imagining) the dinner. While Trebius seethes with bile, Virro's stomach, should it burn from rich food and wine, is cooled by the iciest spring water (49–50). Might Juvenal be hinting at the satiric speaker's ability to escape from the cycle of indignation to a privileged state of dispassion?

This would suggest the idea that Juvenal's "advisory" satire to Trebius, clearly not a sharing of anger between friends, is more like a *transfer* of anger. Perhaps we have just watched anger being passed like a hot potato, the rhetorical equivalent of Hercules's deceit of Atlas. Trebius is left hold-ing up the heavens, while Juvenal moves on to other things.

Anger in *Satires* Book 1 is a dynamic force that generates a plot, com-plete with finale. This interpretation may be the best route to understand-ing why Juvenal chose the satiric subjects he did and arranged them in this way. It also does justice to this well-read poet's imaginative engagement with literature, philosophy, and rhetorical theory. Such tools enabled the poet to write a first book of poems touting the power of satire—at least satire by one definition. In the next book, Juvenal will remain in the posi-tion he took to lecture Trebius, but with an addressee who must endure captivity for much longer. This sustained focus on a "you"—a focus that combines interrogation and appropriation into narrative—makes it easier for us to imagine an infectious rhetorical scenario unfolding.

| Monstrous Misogyny and
the End of Anger

IN *SATIRE* 6, A nearly 700-line attack on Roman wives, Juvenal looks to
be staging another performance by his angry persona. With its length, its
parade of lurid vignettes (thirty-one, by one tally),[1] and its tragic flourish
at the end, this poem is even said to be a reductio ad absurdum of angry
satire—a finale and repudiation rolled into one.[2] It certainly revisits the
invective themes that mark the poems of Book 1. We have already seen
Juvenal display an interest in the perversion of sexual roles, for his first
two exempla were a eunuch who married and a matron who took to boar
hunting (1.22–23), and adultery and murder were cited as wifely crimes
in the same poem (1.55–57, 69–72), while the entire second *Satire* was
entirely dedicated to men with feminine qualities and desires. But *Satire* 6,
framed as advice against marriage from one man to another, takes the "bad
matrona" theme to a new level. The poem reads like a parody of centuries
of Greco-Roman misogynistic literature, bringing it plenty of attention
from scholars of rhetoric and gender alike. This level of interest has even
resulted in conflicting interpretations of the poem: it has seemed to some
to represent a gradual implosion by a ridiculous chauvinist, to others a
relentless, priapic violation of women that is essentially a manifestation
of ancient elite values.[3] It is a variation on the problem that has affected

---

[1.]Richlin, *Garden of Priapus*, 203–4.
[2.]With this performance "*indignatio*, as a satiric technique, is played out" (Braund, *Beyond
Anger*, 22); cf. Anderson, "Programs of Later Books," 152–53 (=*Essays*, 284–85); and Zarini,
"L'indignation chez Juvénal," 452 ("[Juvenal] est arrivé là au terme des possibilités de la seule
indignation").
[3.]The poem is a central text in the study of Juvenal's rhetoric and humor: e.g., Winkler, *Persona
in Three Satires*, 146–206; Johnson, "Male Victimology"; Braund, *Beyond Anger*, 18–22; Gold,
"Humor in Juvenal's Sixth"; and Plaza, *Function of Humour*, 127–55 (most of these considering
how the extremist attack generates humor). Cf. Braund, "Misogynist or Misogamist," for the

interpretation of Book 1. It is impossible to ignore either the conventional roots of the overwhelming misogynistic invective or the absurdly exaggerated form that it takes here, and to do so would only make the poem still more difficult to process. A third option has also been proposed, to hear in the poem *two* competing discourses: one comes from a straight "moralist," the other from a disingenuous "wit."[4] But in such an approach the comic reading still prevails; the "wit" functions to destabilize the invective again and again, and it will always be tempting to read that "wit" into moments of tension and unpleasantness. On the other hand, such a puzzling poem, defined by the tensions just described, surely has something to tell us about anger.

As with *Satires* 1 through 5, it will prove useful to resist the poles of parodic and straight readings and to attempt to understand how this noisy text participates in a story. The anger games of Book 1, even with their purposeful finale, do not preclude another chapter in the same vein. But it does not do justice to *Satire* 6 to read it as a farewell to the old (the angry satiric mode, clearly exhausted) or a harbinger of the new (ironizing of anger). Juvenal's supposed self-distancing from anger in the later books is yet to come, and at any rate it is hard to argue that he would have set out to compose, in a poem two-thirds the length of his first book, an extended exercise in rejection. If we wish to map the meaningful background of *Satire* 6, it is more useful to recall the satirist's complex and productive interest in anger's workings, demonstrated throughout Book 1. This second "book" is reminiscent of the earlier stories of anger finding a verbal outlet. It also shows the influence of the same literary, rhetorical, and philosophical traditions that shaped *Satires* 1 through 5. Among other things, it delves back into the matter of anger's perceived origins (and, by association, the origins of misogyny and angry invective). It also highlights the other end of angry rhetoric and the notion of the audience as victim—in this case, the addressee Postumus, who is thinking of taking a wife. Considering how many female victims this poem has, and how

---

argument that *Satire* 6 performs, among other things, a parody of the conventional wedding song or *epithalamium*. Richlin, in contrast, emphasizes the speaker's chauvinist and violating agenda: the poem's female characters "are essentially alone, at the mercy of the author, able to be manipulated, open to a sort of rape" (*Garden of Priapus*, 202; cf. 203–7). Other scholars of ancient gender have mined the poem for insight on ancient discourse and reality alike; see, e.g., Gold, "House I Live In," and Van Abbema, "Autonomy and Influence"; cf. Bellandi, *Giovenale: Contro le donne*, 9–38, and Battisti, *Rhetorica della misoginia*.

[4] Nadeau, *Sixth Satire*, 11–15; cf. introduction, n. 70. The reader most comfortable with the final product may be Ramsey, who provides an unparalleled ten-page paraphrase of this "most brilliant of Juvenal's Satires" in the introduction to his Loeb edition (*Juvenal and Persius*, lii–lxii).

preposterous its refrain of male victimhood is, it may seem perverse to identify one more victim and a male character at that. But Postumus's role enables Juvenal to explore anger's operation in new ways. Both the rhetorical structure and the themes of *Satire* 6 make it a fitting continuation of the story that ended with the overpowering of Trebius.

Bringing It All Back Home

In *Satire* 5, Juvenal exploited the power imbalance between speaker and addressee to put Trebius through a tortuous game of persuasion, dramatizing his achievement of angry rhetoric's goal. Juvenal renews this formula in *Satire* 6, while he draws on a standard subject of first- and second-century rhetorical exercises: the desirability of marriage (always from the male perspective). The theme of marriage, often in connection with that of the faithless wife, appears throughout *controversiae* and *suasoriae*, and the question "should a man marry?" is the standard cited example of a *thesis* or philosophical proposition that could be the core of a basic or advanced rhetorical exercise.[5] Thus Juvenal appears to be taking on a classic declamatory theme. The poem's ambitious length suggests the culmination of a period of training—something like the *suasoriae* that Juvenal mentioned at 1.15–17 as a building block of his poetic training—and the fact that Juvenal addresses the poem to a named individual strengthens that possibility. Of course, although *suasoriae* were one-sided arguments, Juvenal's exaggerated portrayal of women's behavior surely exceeds the required forcefulness—and length—of such an exercise. Nor is *Satire* 6 a philosophical meditation, but an exercise in conveying anger, fear, and disgust.

This is not simply a reflection of the satirist's irrational persona; it is meant to have an impact on the addressee. It is Postumus whom we are to imagine being subjected to angry speech in the present, and who is at the same time being forced to imagine his intolerable future enslavement to a wife. As I will show, Juvenal cues us to pay attention to this cruel *phantasia* involving Postumus. The addressee's part is written to bear the brunt of

---

[5] See Quint. *Inst*. 3.5.11, and the third- or fourth-century *Ars Rhetorica* attributed to Dionysius that remarks (261) that the most popular subject for elementary rhetorical exercises was the desirability of marriage. Cf. Bonner, *Education in Ancient Rome*, 271; Dominik, "Roman Declamation," 301; and Gunderson, *Declamation, Paternity, and Identity*, 105. On the rhetorical sources for *Satire* 6, see Cairns, *Generic Composition*, 75, and the detailed parsing in Braund, "Misogynist or Misogamist," 78–82. Treggiari (*Roman Marriage*, 223) writes that in *Satire* 6, "the anti-marriage tradition [of ancient rhetoric and literature] comes to full flower."

the "serious" message of the poem without the humor; for him, the outsized, outrageous wives are real and oppressive. He also receives the double-edged gift of infectious rhetoric from his supposed ally, the satirist. It is as if Juvenal has settled on the direct address as the ideal vehicle for his anger game; by this means, he can drive an imaginary audience to anger without putting himself in the spotlight as a violated *iratus*. Moreover, Juvenal goads his addressee with the suggestion that his future unhappiness is his own fault, and his anger therefore as unjustified as Trebius's.

Postumus himself is a shadowy addressee, a type that Juvenal will use increasingly in the later books. But in this fictional character there is a hint of the historical palette of many rhetorical exercises. Numerous *suasoriae*, including the one Juvenal mentions in *Satire* 1, are addressed to figures from history and myth. Quintilian mentions a common historical application of the marriage *thesis* ("should Cato marry?"). Juvenal has avoided replaying this old standard with its historical addressee, using a seemingly generic figure instead. At the same time, it would seem that he has taken some inspiration from a real case from half a century ago: the emperor Claudius. One of the earliest, most lurid vignettes in *Satire* 6 concerns the insatiable sexual appetite of Claudius's third wife, Messalina (115–32), while his fourth and last wife, Agrippina, looms large in the treatment of spousal murder that ends the poem (610–26; cf. 651–61). In this final passage, Postumus, the "you" in all the vignettes of *Satire* 6, is transformed into the doddering emperor who was caricatured as a slave to his wives (Suet. *Cl.* 25.5, 29.1; cf. Tac. *Ann.* 11.28.2). Claudius was also notorious for being prone to fits of anger (Suet. *Cl.* 38.1, Sen. *Apoc.* 6), while also being "timid and suspicious" (*timidus ac diffidens*, Suet. *Cl.* 35.1). This combination makes it irresistible to imagine how he might respond in Postumus's place as addressee of the sixth *Satire*.[6] And Postumus, qua addressee and qua doomed husband, represents an excruciating convergence of themes associated with Claudius—making the name of this fictional character appropriate in more ways than one. The famous Postumus Agrippa is presumed to have been a victim of Tacitus's first example of the powerful *matrona*, Livia.[7] But we might also imagine Claudius himself

---

[6.]It was during Claudius's rule that Seneca wrote *On Anger*; see Fillion-Lahille, "Production littéraire de Sénèque," 1616–19, for the argument that the emperor is the work's implicit addressee.
[7.]Tac. *Ann.* 1.6. On the transgressive women of Tacitus, see Joshel, "Female Desire"; Milnor, "Women and Domesticity," 467–73 (highlighting the paradox of women's "impotence" over their desires as the core of their transgressive power); and Späth, "Masculinity and Gender Performance," 440–43. It is difficult to believe that Juvenal could have read *Annals* 11 before writing *Satire* 6, even if we follow Syme's late date for the early *Satires* ("Juvenal, Pliny, Tacitus";

surviving, as it were, to hear Juvenal's tirade. This is not to imply that Claudius's story is the key to understanding *Satire* 6, but it is surely an important subtext—and a reminder that the satirist had plenty of resources besides Seneca's generic *iratus* to dramatize and contextualize anger.

Historical and literary inspiration aside, can we account for Juvenal's selection of the topic of wives now? Furthermore, how might we understand this treatment to be a fitting thematic finale for the poems that revolve around *indignatio*? There are other answers to be found than the old biographical explanation (Juvenal must have "married a lady of superior rank and pretensions, and found her intolerable").[8] Misogyny and obsession with sexual perversion is evident throughout Roman satire, especially Juvenal's. Much of the social criticism performed in Book 1 reflects the point of view of a generic Roman male who is struggling to maintain his *dignitas*, his voice, and his masculinity in an environment that he perceives as constantly challenging his status. This all creates a compelling satiric plot of its own that contributed to the prominence of the early *Satires* on modern reading lists and in scholarly studies.

But thematic correspondence between the disapproval or dismissal of women in Book 1 and the concentrated attack on them in Book 2 is not the only link of interest. There is also dramatic continuity and momentum between Books 1 and 2, particularly with respect to setting. *Satires* 1 through 5 follow a series of trials for the generic Roman male that begin in a more or less public context and end in a private one. In the programmatic opening of Book 1, the satirist pretends to take on a public fight in the streets of Rome, though he already shows interest in private contexts like marriage and the *cena*. In *Satires* 2 and 3 (again, with some exceptions), the urban, public setting is prominent. The poor, angry *cliens* of *Satire* 3 faces a never-ending series of challenges in public places and streets, only to be revived in the character of Trebius and to enter the home of his patron. At the humiliating *cena*, the client is away from his turf, uncomfortable, and powerless. Even the poems that do not play up the role of the downtrodden male protagonist still underscore the satirist's movement from public to private spaces. *Satire* 2 observes scandalous public behavior (with a detour to private scenes of religious rites and a wedding), while

cf. Highet, "Juvenal's Bookcase," 373–74). But Claudius was caricatured as impetuous and impotent before Tacitus; see Seneca's *Apocolocyntosis* and cf. the *Life* of Suetonius, which would have drawn on first-century sources. Cf. Ramage, "Juvenal and the Establishment," 676–79.
[8] Highet, *Juvenal the Satirist*, 103.

Satire 4 takes us from the open space of the Italian seashore into the tense, pressurized atmosphere of Domitian's privy council.

Satire 6 brings this series to its conclusion, for the two books taken together appear to track the disenfranchised man's experience from his public humiliations to his private miseries. The most private and most miserable of all are those of Postumus. This poem takes us all the way not into someone else's private territory but into the home of Postumus, in order to examine his prospective marriage.[9] But rather than being the private dominion or sanctuary of the husband-to-be (the kind that might console the client trapped at his patron's dinner in *Satire* 5), this home is the scene of a nightmare from the husband's perspective. This hypothesized addressee has a significant dramatic role. In the poem, an intimate domestic struggle plays out between man and wife—though there are sometimes witnesses whose presence intensifies the husband's suffering. A wife, we are told, can be counted on to commit such transgressions as prostitute herself, bear illegitimate children, beat slaves who ruin her hairdos, get drunk in front of her husband's guests, fall in with Eastern priests and soothsayers, and murder her own children and spouse. By the time he has finished, Juvenal has made it seem as though Postumus is going to end up married not to one wife but to a massive contingent of perverse females who represent every kind of vice. His identity as paterfamilias is stripped of meaning over and over again. In the meantime, the consoling intimacy that Postumus's presumed relationship with the satirist might represent will hardly turn out to be a consolation or an affirmation of the addressee's masculinity. As we will see, a rhetorical relationship with Juvenal only compounds Postumus's problems.

Farrago and *Phantasia*

The circular fiction of Juvenal's creative process—passions motivate behavior, behavior feeds satire, satire mimics and encourages passions—finds fertile ground in *Satire* 6. The satirist has discovered his most abundant and concentrated fuel yet in the generally overemotional behavior of Roman wives. Plaza describes the link this way: "Juvenal's satire, like Roman satire in general, performs its mission of humour largely by

---

[9.]"On passe avec [Juvenal] des hommes et de la vie publique aux femmes et à la vie privée," Zarini, "L'indignation chez Juvénal," 452. Cf. Braund, *Beyond Anger*, 18: *Satire* 6 makes a theme of domestic "seclusion and even . . . secrecy."

drawing energy from the powers released by inversion and transgression," in this case the outrageous behavior of *matronae*.[10] Postumus does not have access to the poem's humor, but he certainly experiences the "powers released by inversion and transgression." Juvenal makes his potential wives out to be particularly susceptible to strong emotions, and particularly liable to act on them; of course, he selects and distorts to create this effect, with plenty of help from literary tradition. Tragedy and history supply examples of murderous and power-hungry wives and mothers. Lyric, elegy, and mime are full of unfaithful women. Ovid's advice on finding girlfriends (*Ars* 1.89–100) highlights women's predictable vanity and suggestibility. Epic features female figures possessed by passions.[11] Even philosophy has something to offer: "It is a woman's trait to rage in anger" (*muliebre est furere in ira*, Sen. *Cl.* 1.4.5). Oratory deserves special recognition as an influence: there is something of Cicero's *prosopopoieia* of Appius Claudius Caecus (*Cael.* 33–34) in *Satire* 6. Cicero, launching into a high-style attack on Clodia's lustful and vindictive acts, claims to be using the mask of Appius as protection for himself—"lest [Clodia] get angry [back] at me" (*ne mihi forte ista suscenseat*, 33)—and so gets in one more dig at the woman's emotional nature. But Juvenal needs no mask; the women he is attacking are not in front of him. He does not need them there, as long as they fuel his rhetorical passion.

For his part, the Juvenal of *Satire* 6 is quite invisible, evoking the judging persona of *Satire* 5 much more than the *iratus* at the crossroads in *Satire* 1. It is Postumus who occupies the spotlight in his vulnerable position of powerless husband, and so will experience the more debilitating and unattractive effects of emotional infection. Rather, Postumus *does* experience it, in the sense that the rhetorical *phantasia* is playing out now. Juvenal essentially *makes* him marry, and turns his prospective marriage into multiple and equally horrific ones. This "enslaving" rhetoric both depicts and mimics the marital slavery that the satirist foresees, making Postumus's plight resemble Trebius's in *Satire* 5. This time, the addressee is subjected to endless scenarios of private violation (as defined from the perspective of a male head of household).[12] The emotional energy behind these violations makes things worse; Postumus's potential future wives emanate lust,

<hr />

10. Plaza, *Function of Humour*, 154–55.
11. On the generic texture of *Satire* 6, see Jones, *Juvenal*, 21–22 and 90–91. Smith, *Satiric Advice on Women*, surveys similar comic and satiric works. On the stereotype of the angry woman in diverse literary contexts, see Harris, *Restraining Rage*, 264–82, and cf. Harris, "Rage of Women."
12. Richlin, *Garden of Priapus*, 207.

violent rage, religious fervor, pleasure (in extravagance and in deception), and theatrical jealousy. These ramped-up passions and appetites, certainly problematic in the abstract, are especially threatening to a husband. If passions can infect satire composed in the public crossroads, they are bound to kindle rage in a man who is subjected to constant and close-up degradation in his home. This situation of pure victimhood, entrapment inside a sensationalist fantasy, is what Postumus was invented for.

In fact, not only does Juvenal mention the role of the *maritus* or *vir* more than thirty times in his vignettes, but he frequently uses second person forms to place Postumus explicitly in the scenes and to personalize the impact of the wives' behavior. The addressee is the "you" who must put up with the haughtiness of a beautiful wife (178), with the shame that comes from a masculine wife's forays into the arena (258), with the theatrical weeping of an adulteress who defends herself with accusations of her husband (275–76), and with the suspicious-looking child such a woman eventually produces (601). One wife will take charge of the making of "your" will (218), another will let her pathic friends use the cups that "your" own lips (O14) must later touch. As husband, Postumus will also be soiled with vomit (100–101, 432), excessive makeup (463), and a puddle of urine (312–13; "you" again)—this vestige of his wife's late-night carousing will now mark his morning slog to his patron's home, uniting the well-known Juvenalian theme of the client's abjection with that of domestic humiliation.

With lustfulness the most prominent fault of wives in the catalog, the addressee's inner Claudius is bound to feel pain. The historical exemplum of the emperor and his errant wife even serves to enhance the possibilities for Postumus's suffering. First, a broad contrast may be drawn between the emperor and the addressee, unfavorably for the latter. It might be said that Claudius had it comparatively easy in discovering only his wife's final transgression, her marriage to Gaius Silius. Postumus learns about *all* his wife's (or wives') bad acts, in advance, but without the power to stop them from unfolding before him; it is as if all the undiscovered and unpunished doings of Messalina, both the reality and the rumors, were being paraded before her suffering spouse.[13] The well-known description of Messalina (pre-Silius) working in a brothel turns a sordid rumor in the ancient

---

[13.]Tacitus writes that in her boredom, Messalina pursued "uncharted sexual practices" (*incognitas libidines, Ann.* 11.26.1). The claim that she prostituted herself (though not in an actual brothel) is seen at Plin. *Nat.* 10.83.172 and Dio Cass. 61.31.1. Juvenal's passage also shares language with declamations concerned with prostitution; see Battisti, *Rhetorica della misoginia*, 62–65.

sources into vivid *phantasia*; it also turns a figure whom Tacitus describes as a weak-willed pleasure seeker into a calculated nymphomaniac.[14]

Second, we may read Juvenal's passage on Messalina herself as a clue about Postumus's ultimate fate. The adulterous empress is a symbol of something big and abstract—the degradation of the empire itself, reflected in the very seat of imperial power.[15] The fact that Messalina was an emperor's wife does not make this idea any less applicable to Postumus; throughout *Satire* 6, Juvenal stresses the ability of the female body to bring unsavory and pernicious elements into the home. According to Juvenal, Messalina slunk off to the brothel every night, made her body and her insatiability visible to all comers, only returned home under compulsion, and brought the lamp smoke and the stench of the brothel back to the emperor's bed each morning (*lupanaris tulit ad pulvinar odorem*, 132). This example of female shamelessness was endured by a "rival of the gods" (115); the clear implication is that Postumus should not hope for better. Indeed, bigger problems await Postumus, as they did Claudius.

Messalina has plenty of nonimperial counterparts in *Satire* 6. There are the women who swoon over actors, putting themselves on display as if they were living in Ovid's erotic world (60–75). There are the mothers who make their husbands rear the bastards of actors and gladiators (76–81). Other wives, evidently still interested in their own husbands, manage to verbally violate them by using in the bedroom a language that "has fingers"—that is, Greek (185–97). Somehow there is physical power in the language that these women use to "express fear and pour out anger, joy, anxieties, all their hearts' secrets" (*hoc sermone pavent, hoc iram, gaudia, curas,/hoc cuncta effundunt animi secreta*, 189–90). The suggestion is that the proximity to these feminine passions, expressed in an effeminizing tongue, would be discomfiting to a husband who wishes to rule his own bedroom (presumably in Latin). And the woman who summons the powers of Quintilian to defend herself against a charge of adultery is not any better (268–85).

Adultery may be presented as the biggest threat to the prospective husband,[16] but there are other (albeit often related) ways wives can threaten

---

[14.]On the one hand, in Tacitus's account, Messalina's attention to Gaius Silius is the equivalent of an imperial command to devote himself to her (*Ann.* 11.12.2). But although she "craved the name of [Silius'] wife," Tacitus's Messalina was nervous about assenting to the marriage plan (11.26.3–4) and was the more fearful of the two when execution loomed (11.34, 37).

[15.]Joshel, "Female Desire."

[16.]Richlin, *Garden of Priapus*, 205, notes that eleven of the thirty-one sections she identifies (45 percent of the poem in terms of lines) deal with adultery.

male power. Plenty of the wives in *Satire* 6 take on masculine public roles—pleading cases (242–45), practicing to fight in the arena (246–67, recalling Mevia at 1.22), talking politics and gossiping (398–412),[17] and making erudite dinner conversation to her husband's embarrassment (434–37). These examples all seem to fall under the rubric of female usurpation of power, whether inside or outside the household. Marriage, from the point of view of the husband (*especially* if he loves his wife), is slavery: "bend your head, ready your neck to bear the yoke" (*summitte caput cervice parata/ferre iugum*, 207–8). A wife who is conscious of her husband's devotion will act as household tyrant (219–26). This type is reminiscent not just of the influential women of the Julio-Claudian dynasty but also of the bad male rulers and *domini* recalled or hypothesized in *On Anger*.[18] This woman's "subjects" are potentially limitless, including *amici*, the husband she orders around (*imperat ergo viro*, 224), slaves, and the households of the future husbands she will encounter as her affections change. (Tyranny over slaves is shown again at 474–95.)

This is not just a catalog but a story.[19] By the poem's end, the multiple hypothetical annoying marriages have been collapsed into one deadly one, conjuring the memory of Claudius once again. Juvenal uses the second person again to describe the oblivion of the husband who is being poisoned: "and what you don't know is that this, *this* is the source of the murkiness in your mind and the total forgetfulness of things you've just done" (*quod desipis, inde est,/inde animi caligo et magna oblivio rerum/quas modo gessisti*, 612–14). With Claudius, the conventional account goes, there was less damage to be done: he showed senile characteristics even before Agrippina poisoned him (620–23). That said, this kind of wifely invasion takes over a husband's very mind, making it a fitting example for this climactic point in the poem. Both the satirist's rhetoric and women's passions have been hammering Postumus for a long time.

[17.]The gossiping woman even resembles the satirist himself, according to the analysis in Umurhan, "Poetic Projection."

[18.]E.g., *Ira* 2.23.1 and 3.16.2–3.21.5.

[19.]For another reading of the satire as a drama, see Smith, "Husband versus Wife," 328. The idea is developed by Braund, "Misogynist or Misogamist," 85: the anecdotes of humiliation "culminat[e] . . . in the final section [with Postumus's imagined death]. So the poem has a loose storyline." (While I do not share Braund's view that Postumus is silently resisting Juvenal's rhetoric and that this drives the satirist to further rhetorical extremes, this is still an inspiring example of plot detection in the poem.) Battisti gives some space to discussing the imagined suicide of Postumus as an alternative to marriage (*Rhetorica della misoginia*, 58–59, 61) and considers the addressee "annichilito" by the end of the poem (82).

And the subject of murder leads Juvenal to his most sensational image of female emotionality yet, a stunning simile (647–50):

>   facit ira nocentes
> hunc sexum et rabie iecur incendente feruntur
> praecipites, ut saxa iugis abrupta, quibus mons
> subtrahitur clivoque latus pendente recedit.

> . . . anger drives this sex to crime, and when the fury burns their livers they are borne along headlong, like rocks broken from a ridge, where the mountain is giving way, the face of its slope starting to tumble.

A memory of *Satire* 1 is relevant here: Juvenal had claimed there that modern vice was standing on a precipice (*omne in praecipiti vitium stetit*, 1.149). Now, that metaphor is refashioned into a tumbling landslide. In this way, too, *Satire* 6 smacks of a coda or climax.

    Humiliation, fraud, soiling, disempowerment, mortal threats—these are all conditions for *indignatio* in the world of Juvenal's *Satires*. Accordingly, Juvenal conjures Postumus's future emotional state as a married man—scripts his feelings for him, essentially. As a husband, Postumus is condemned to "close his eyes and check his bile" (*oculis bilem substringit opertis*, 433). Trebius, too, bubbled with bile, bringing to *Satire* 5 a feeling of a live performance with a duly indignant—but muzzled—audience. Postumus, Trebius's heir, will dwell with anger in his marriage, locked into a dynamic emotional bond with his passion-driven and aggravating spouse. And since present and future are collapsed in this poem, he is getting a foretaste of that feeling now. The satirist is already serving him some indignation. In a nutshell, Juvenal makes the rhetorical goal of persuasion utterly irrelevant to this poem. His real goal is not to dissuade Postumus from marrying but to succeed at making him embrace anger.[20]

    To be sure, Postumus is offered a consolation prize: the pleasure of male solidarity with the satirist, flavored with justified rage. After all, this kind of "priapic" invective depends on conceptions of in-groups and out-groups; it is generated by and aimed at those who wish to retain their identity as "in."[21] Juvenal's language invites Postumus to join the club of

---

[20.]There are certainly rhetorical examples of failed persuasion, with their own conventions; see Men. Rh. 397.12–399.10, and Cairns, *Generic Composition*, 138–57.

[21.]Though not emphasizing anger in particular, Richlin stresses the importance of author-audience identification in the dynamics of sexual humor (and other mockery, as her citation of Freud's theory of jokes implies; see *Garden of Priapus*, 58 and 60).

beleaguered and disenfranchised men, sustained by the illusion of a shared enemy. The same speaker who causes Postumus's virtual suffering also offers him an emotional salve. Anger, the fruit of Juvenal's rhetoric, promises pleasures of its own, as Juvenal and the philosophical authors have suggested. The rhetoric of anger is coercive, but in a way that appeals to deep desires.

In fact, the brotherhood of satirist and addressee is as flimsy as the pure savagery of women is fictitious. The supposed homosocial bond is no match for the asymmetrical dynamics of *sermo*. Postumus exists to absorb what he is told; he is no Cato or Sulla in a *suasoria*, but the satirist's social equal at best.[22] It is worth remembering that Juvenal represented himself as being infected by the emotions of the world in *Satire* 1. This process is potentially feminizing, according to the same rules that make Postumus's experience so miserable, but the satirist's infection has a byproduct that mitigates this condition. The practice of rhetoric traditionally confers power on the speaker; he is hypermasculine and dominant over his enthralled audience.[23] The existence of an addressee, and one whose response has already been scripted, anchors Juvenal's own masculinity. We see him push Postumus into experiencing the worst of both worlds: the trials of a man who is married, and the rage of a man who hates women. As the poem nears its end, it becomes clear that Postumus will soon be left to fend for himself as a husband and the "carrier" of *indignatio*. Like Trebius (and unlike Umbricius), he is given no outlet for its expression.

A Look in the Mirror

The degradation of Postumus's masculinity is accentuated by a parallel between his predicament and a passage from Seneca's *On Anger*. We have already noted the resemblance of the satirist's initial angry persona to Seneca's straw man, who insistently points out anger's natural force, its social value, and its concomitant pleasures. But the Senecan model still has more to give readers of *Satire* 6. In particular, *On Anger* provides a lens through which we may view the poem's colorful female subjects and interpret the ordeal through which they are imagined to put Postumus. As we have seen, the passion-driven wives provoke emotions in men and

---

[22] Cairns (*Generic Composition*, 235–40) notes that in poems giving advice, the speaker is implied to have a higher status than the addressee (cf. Men. Rh. 395.5–12).
[23] Cf. Connolly, "Virile Tongues," 95.

so threaten their self-control. Similar claims in *On Anger*, which is written from and for a male perspective, conjure the same dual connection between women and anger that Juvenal makes. Seneca claims that women are especially susceptible to anger (1.12.1; cf. *Cl.* 1.5.5), and that their anger is sharp and gains intensity with time (2.19.4). Elsewhere in the dialogue, he also mentions wives as potential *causes* of male anger—though not with the emphasis we might expect from an author who is treating anger control as a subject mainly of interest to men. Wives are grouped with old parents, children, and slaves as potential objects of forgiveness for a man who is trying to master his emotion (e.g., 2.30.1, 3.24.3; cf. 3.5.4, where Seneca notes that one casualty of men's anger is divorce). It is, however, no surprise that he orients the domestic picture in this general way, pitting the paterfamilias (or at least the man in his prime) against all the other people with whom he lives. This is the natural result of an intimacy that entails power differences.[24]

This problem is expressed in a fascinating passage in *On Anger* that illustrates the effects of anger on a male subject in order to point the addressee toward a therapy. In this passage, there is no general grouping of aggravating household members; anger is decidedly gendered as feminine, but symbolically rather than literally. In the climax of the second book, Seneca encourages his addressee to imagine anger's hold on him as a kind of possession by mythical female monsters, the Furies, Discord, and Bellona—all conventional symbols of anger in ancient literature.[25] Seneca is telling the man-at-risk to go beyond abstraction and visualize anger's effects—particularly its effects on himself (2.35.5–6):

> quales sunt hostium vel ferarum caede madentium aut ad caedem euntium aspectus, qualia poetae inferna monstra finxerunt succincta serpentibus et igneo flatu, quales ad bella excitanda discordiamque in populos dividendam pacemque lacerandam deae taeterrimae inferum exeunt, talem nobis iram figuremus, flamma lumina ardentia, sibilo mugituque et gemitu et stridore et si qua his invisior vox est perstrepentem, tela

---

[24.] See Harris, *Restraining Rage*, 285–336, on the "intimate rage" of the ancient household. Perhaps this problem was a theme of the lost treatise on marriage that Jerome (*Adv. Iov.* 1.49) attributes to Seneca. The tone of the lost work is a matter of confusion and debate; see Bickel, *Diatribe in Senecae fragmenta*, 1:288–372; and Lausberg, *Untersuchungen zu Senecas Fragmente*, 1.

[25.] On the motif of the female deity defined by anger, see Harris, "Rage of Women," 131. Of the many manifestations of this topos, perhaps the best known are found in Vergil's *Aeneid* Books 7–8; for instructive discussions, see Heinze, *Vergil's Epic Technique*, 148–55; and Oliensis, "Sons and Lovers," 303–10.

manu utraque quatientem (neque enim illi se tegere curae est), torvam cruentamque et cicatricosam et verberibus suis lividam, incessus vesani, offusam multa caligine, incursitantem vastantem fugantemque et omnium odio laborantem, sui maxime, si aliter nocere non possit, terras maria caelum ruere cupientem, infestam pariter invisamque. vel, si videtur, sit qualis apud vates nostros est 'sanguineum quatiens dextra Bellona flagellum' aut 'scissa gaudens vadit Discordia palla' aut si qua magis dira facies excogitari diri adfectus potest.

Imagine the appearance of enemies or wild animals dripping with slaughter or heading for the kill; imagine the monsters of hell, as the poets have portrayed them, wreathed in serpents and fiery breath; imagine the most hideous goddesses of the underworld emerging to stir up war, sow discord, and tear apart the peace between peoples—this is how we should visualize anger. With eyes flashing with fire, making loud noises of hissing, bellowing, groaning, grating and any other sound that is still more hateful, brandishing spears in both hands (and it has no concern to shield itself), fierce, bloody, scarred, black and blue from its own lashes, with a crazy way of walking, wrapped in a great darkness, attacking, laying waste, putting to flight, consumed with hatred of all things, especially of itself, if it can find no other way to do harm, ready to confound earth, sea, and sky, equally hating and hated. Or, if you will, let it be as our poets say: "Bellona, shaking a blood-stained whip in her right hand" or "Discord, joyful, goes forth in her torn mantle" or in any more terrible form that can be thought up for this terrible emotion.[26]

According to Seneca, the man who succumbs to anger is allowing these monsters to control and disfigure him. This intimate viewing of anger's internal workings stands out among Seneca's many illustrations of the emotion's power. Most of the negative exempla Seneca cites are men (especially tyrants and heads of household),[27] but this one—elaborate and placed at a climactic point in the dialogue—figures anger as female. In this regard Seneca is in good company; as his poetically inspired vignette reminds us, the angry Fury is a commonplace of epic.[28] But the passage

---

[26.] Seneca's verse quotations are adaptations of Verg. A. 8.702–3; the first also resembles Luc. 7.568.
[27.] "Given the length of De ira we might have expected more" assertions of women's irascibility; but "not one of his numerous exempla of evil temper is female" (Harris, "Rage of Women," 137).
[28.] Schiesaro ("Passion, Reason, and Knowledge," 100–101) cites the passage as a reflection of Seneca's association of poetic inspiration and chthonic "terrors"; cf. Marc. 19.4.

makes for an interesting contrast with philosophical descriptions of the signs of anger, which tend to emphasize the way a *man's* face is distorted by symptoms such as wild eyes and flushed skin.[29]

Somewhat fallaciously, the philosopher compares this visualization exercise to looking into a mirror: "it has benefited some angry men, Sextius [the Augustan-era philosopher] says, to look in a mirror. The great transformation [they saw in themselves] came as a shock" (*quibusdam, ut ait Sextius, iratis profuit aspexisse speculum. perturbavit illos tanta mutatio sui*, 2.36.1). The exercise, in combination with the demonic imagery, allows the subject to objectify his anger as an external force that possesses him.[30] Seneca's therapy is designed to force the subject to admit his intimacy with anger while also giving him a handle on fending it off—by encouraging him to see it as an Other, as feminine. The message is that passion takes up intimate residence within us (men), but its source is external and can be resented as such. Seneca makes anger seem especially alien by employing conventional mythical and literary images of female beasts. Juvenal uses a similar strategy in *Satire* 6 but gives his husband-addressee a double curse. First, the husband lives in intimacy with a female demon that goads him—or rather a host of them. Second, he rages alone, with neither outlet nor therapist.

The end of *On Anger* Book 2 thus offers a special model for the misogynistic theme of *Satire* 6 (and especially *its* ending—coincidentally, in Juvenal's own second book). The Stoic encourages his addressee to imagine himself as being taken over by female monsters when he is angry. These symbols of destructive passion are embodied—albeit slightly domesticated—in the outsized, outrageous women of *Satire* 6. Seneca's mirror image becomes Juvenal's vision of intimate domestic space, in the present and the future. To figure anger as an Other is an ambiguous business, since in reality rage surely involves both external and internal forces;

[29.]Seneca introduces anger as the "most hideous of all [the emotions]" (*maxime ex omnibus taetrum, Ira* 1.1.1) and outlines the outward signs (*indicia*, covering appearance, sound, and movement) that a man is angry (1.1.3–5). See also Harris, *Restraining Rage*, 103 (discussing Phld. *Ir.* fr. 6); Cic. *Tusc.* 4.52 (where anger is said to impart a peculiar *color, vox, oculi, spiritus*, and *impotentia dictorum ac factorum*); and Plin. *Pan.* 48 (asserting that the menacing Domitian exhibited a "womanish pallor"). Cf. Plu. *Mor.* 455e–f and the (ungendered) snake imagery at 457a. See the comparison with Seneca in van Hoof, "Strategic Differences," 72–74.

[30.]The paraphrase of Sorabji, *Emotion and Peace*, 162 ("anger makes you ugly") only scratches the surface of Seneca's elaborate picture. See Ker, "Seneca on Self-Examination," 180–82, for connection of this passage to *Ira* 3.36, where the subject is urged to engage in less literal self-observation or *speculatio*. Fillion-Lahille, *De ira de Sénèque*, 265, notes other references to the mirror strategy.

Juvenal exploits this ambiguity when he conjures an intimate and frightening partnership between the husband and his distinctly female enemy. Postumus is placed in an even more vulnerable position than the one that the angry satirist himself occupies—he is trapped in front of the mirror that shows his fate for as long as he gives the satirist his ear. Man and hypothetical, multifaceted bad wife will be joined for life—and this appropriately named husband is even shown scenes of his poisoning and death at the climax of the poem. The jam-packed narrative of marriage, linear only in the sense that it ends with the husband's death, could never be effective therapy for the addressee. Rather, the satirist invites Postumus to share in the most intense and perversely gratifying of infectious emotions, he concocts a quasi-Senecan fiction that a third party is to blame, and he ultimately leaves his addressee to his own devices. The satirist's show of sympathy actually baits Postumus to become a mirror image of his archenemy.

Passing On the Burden

Juvenal's abuse of Postumus comes to a head in the self-consciously tragic passage on murderous wives (634–46), which hints at a deadly conclusion to the marriage and invites intense and fearful rage. But the satirist has yet to really pull the rug out from under his addressee. The clincher comes in the strange, even surprising, final lines of the poem. Up to this point, Juvenal has cultivated the fiction that the husband's unconstructive and unseemly anger is a response to the infectious passions of his bad wife (or wives!). The "landslide" passage reinforces this idea by representing murderous wives as inspired by *ira*. This is an understandable phenomenon to the satirist: "we should not wonder at those extreme monstrosities, whenever anger drives this sex to crime" (*minor admiratio summis/ debetur monstris, quotiens facit ira nocentes/hunc sexum*, 646–47). But then he swerves away to make a new revelation, one that turns the tables on the reactive husband. There is a type of woman that he claims repulses him far more (651–61):

illam ego non tulerim quae conputat et scelus ingens
sana facit. spectant subeuntem fata mariti
Alcestim et, similis si permutatio detur,
morte viri cupiant animam servare catellae.
occurrent multae tibi Belides atque Eriphylae
mane, Clytemestram nullus non vicus habebit.

hoc tantum refert, quod Tyndaris illa bipennem
insulsam et fatuam dextra laevaque tenebat;
at nunc res agitur tenui pulmone rubetae,
sed tamen et ferro, si praegustarit Atrides
Pontica ter victi cautus medicamina regis.

I can't stand the type who calculates and commits an enormous crime
with a clear head. These women watch Alcestis undergoing death in her
husband's place and then, if offered a similar exchange, they'd want to
buy a puppy's life with their husband's death. Plenty of Danaids and
Eriphylas will bump into you any morning; no district will be found
to lack a Clytemnestra. This is the only difference: the daughter of
Tyndareus grasped an inelegant and unwieldy ax with both hands; now
the deed is plotted with the delicate lung of a toad, but then it *could*
be done with a sword too, if Atreus's son has taken precautions and
ingested in advance the Pontic antidotes of the thrice-conquered king.

In this passage the famous comparison of satire to tragedy turns into a
contrast between the cold-blooded killers of today and their mythological
counterparts who acted on emotion. No matter that most of the satire to
this point has been fueled by the stereotype of women as emotional; at the
climax Juvenal takes a sharp turn. The old-fashioned ax, which suggests
rage-induced strength, is discarded in favor of the modern and clinical
murder weapon, poison. Even the very last twist—the claim that a modern
wife will certainly use the sword if poison proves fruitless—is significant
for Juvenal's argument. The image of violent, dramatic death is converted
to something practical and hurried, stripped of symbolism and of emotion
alike.[31]

The idea of a calculating wife is not entirely at odds with the rest of the
poem, of course; Juvenal has on occasion expressed disapproval at wom-
en's scheming and learning. But the abrupt turn that the ancient-modern
contrast effects does change the rhetorical rules of the poem. It is not the
Senecan image of passionate monsters but the coolheaded murderess, ulti-
mately successful no matter what weapon she uses, that Juvenal leaves
Postumus to face. What is the purpose of this last-minute shift of attention
from the "landslide woman"—the Bellona type who seems at first glance

---

[31] Juvenal conveys this idea even as he imports associations of high tragedy by making the
mythological comparison in the first place; see Schmitz, *Satirische in Juvenals Satiren*, 257–58, on
the convention and the Senecan comparanda (*Thy.* 56–57 and 272–77, and *Phaed.* 688–90).

to sum up all the wives that have been cataloged—to the cold-blooded type who ends up dominating the poem's conclusion? Why is the description of the angry woman, which seems so climactic, abruptly replaced by a new type that Juvenal now warns is Postumus's most dangerous enemy?

The reading I have performed in this chapter suggests this explanation: the poem's closing image of levelheaded murderesses underscores the contrasting emotional state of Juvenal's "ideal narrative audience," the prospective husband. If Postumus has listened compliantly to the satirist, he will have taken on the infectious, burning rage and *odium* that his rhetoric aims to transmit. And when the subject turns to murder, the addressee and future husband may be consumed by an even more righteous anger than he has felt until now, one based on the perception of danger or outrage. This is no protection at all, at least according to a strict Stoic view: he will be the weaker and more vulnerable for his uncontrolled emotion.[32] Meanwhile, he will find his murderous spouse dispassionate and even flexible in her mission. Postumus is thus doomed to be left alone without the satirist's male companionship, and vulnerable to his wife's practical approach to murder. Worst of all, though pumped up with his own anger, he will now lack even a mirror image to blame. Ironically, his treacherous wife shows a quality of the ideal *non*-angry subject of moral philosophy: *she* has avoided the grip of mind-addling passions and become able to focus completely on her (albeit criminal) goal. This scenario denies Postumus even the possibility of attributing his feelings to an infectious female. He becomes a spectacle in his own right, a male (but impotent) version of the angry force of nature.

With this, any germs of Stoic therapy in the poem are fully distorted into satiric victimization. The satirist deprives Postumus of Seneca's/Sextus's mirror therapy, and turns him (or any reader who identifies with him), in effect, into an *iratus* without a cause. Postumus's final torment happens all at once, leaving him no time to adjust to this new threat by becoming a Mithridates (the *ter victi . . . regis* at 661), matching his wife's scheming nature, and building up an immunity to poison.[33] That model is out of his reach, as his death is a foregone conclusion. As the poem's dramatic time rolls to an end, Postumus appropriately becomes a witness to his own

---

[32.] According to Sen. *Ira* 11.1–12.5, in such a situation one must master his anger before confronting the external enemy. Nussbaum, *Therapy of Desire*, 419–26, thinks that Seneca is here concerned mainly for the state of the angry subject's soul. Cf. Sorabji, *Emotion and Peace*, 191–92.

[33.] I thank Joe Loewenstein for remarking to me that Mithridates and the scheming woman mirror one another.

murder; as addressee, he lives on with Juvenal's text, while as husband he must be pronounced dead.

Juvenal participates in the violation of his addressee not just by envisioning his death but by luring him into a disfiguring, destructive, and even isolating emotion. This is the price of compliance with the satiric speaker. Postumus is invented to play Atlas to the satirist's Hercules, willingly and unwittingly shouldering the burden of rage. We readers also have a role: we are allowed to watch—or, more properly, to imagine—the impact of Juvenal's rhetoric on someone other than ourselves. Postumus is a buffer between the *indignatio* and us, donning the mask of naive listener so that we do not have to. To be sure, we stand at a circumstantial and most likely ideological distance from the supposedly beleaguered Roman *vir*. But this does not mean we should view the rhetorical process of this *Satire* as pure comedy. What happens to this addressee is a reflection of what might hypothetically happen to any audience of angry satire. It is in order to drive this message home that Juvenal helps us visualize that audience and its compulsory response.

These two chapters have shown that Juvenal was capable of using moral philosophy in deeper ways than parroting or parody, and that the satiric anger he cultivates is partly legitimized and influenced by rhetorical theory. We must take both these frameworks into consideration when we attempt to understand his play with emotions. Anger is not simply a satiric mode in one phase of Juvenal's career; it is also at the center of a plot about the dynamics of satire. But when that plot reaches the fulfillment of a fundamental rhetorical goal, the satirist may want to move on to other things. It is this momentous step away from the framework of rhetorical anger that I will turn to next.

CHAPTER 3 | Change, Decline, and the Progress of Satire

LUIGI VERCOTTI: . . . a week later they called again and told me the check had bounced and said . . . I had to see Doug.

INTERVIEWER: Doug?

VERCOTTI: Doug. (*Emotional pause; drinks.*) Well, I was terrified of him. Everyone was terrified of Doug. I've seen grown men pull their own heads off rather than see Doug. Even Dinsdale was frightened of Doug.

INTERVIEWER: What did he do?

VERCOTTI: (*Another pause.*) He used sarcasm. He knew all the tricks: dramatic irony, metaphor, bathos, puns, parody, litotes, and satire.[1]

THE *MONTY PYTHON* MOCKUMENTARY on the gangster Piranha brothers provides a useful analogy for the impression made by contrasting satiric methods. The two Piranhas worked their will in London's underworld using two complementary methods of intimidation. Dinsdale's modus operandi was to nail his visitors' heads to the floor; the punch line is that Doug was the real terror. The implication that sarcasm can be more fearsome than violence is relevant to our consideration of all the "later" *Satires*—that is, everything from the third book on. Indignation is by no means the only oppressive satiric mode; even subtle satiric rhetoric can work in unsettling ways.

These points are well illustrated in the third and last poem of Book 3, *Satire* 9, an exchange between the satirist and the disgruntled prostitute

---

[1] Chapman et al., "Piranha Brothers."

Naevolus. The dialogue, the only one in Juvenal's oeuvre, allows us to "look" simultaneously at two speakers, each displaying a particular world-view and brand of wit.[2] Aging, anxious, and bitter—though also capable of searing mockery—Naevolus complains that the ingratitude of long-time clients is endangering his welfare—evoking memories of the angry speakers of *Satires* 1 and 3. His interlocutor, in about half as many lines, responds with sympathetic but cooler musings about human folly. Though he adds his own social criticism to the poem, the satirist's accusations are vague and cryptic; in contrast, Naevolus names his star target (another Virro; 35) and provides numerous lurid descriptions of their interactions. Meanwhile, Juvenal appears to subtly tease his unhappy interlocutor by lacing his show of sympathy with wit and literary allusion. This contrast between the two speakers is outlined in Braund's seminal monograph on Book 3, a work that gave a clearer definition to the book's little-understood persona and program.[3]

For Braund, the term that captures the satirist's method both in *Satire* 9 and throughout the book is irony—meaning not just the passive-aggressive dryness of the Socratic *eiron* but also a whole gamut of verbal and dramatic devices, such as literary allusions that work in subtle but penetrating ways (*Satires* 7–9 teem with literary memories from Homer to Martial). The third book's odd collection of poems on various topics (life in the literary professions, aristocratic degeneracy, and of course Naevolus's crisis) is reimagined as a purposeful new chapter in Juvenal's satiric path, united by consistent rhetorical strategies and qualitatively different from what comes before and after. In this larger scheme, *Satire* 9 functions as a kind of programmatic end piece and an escort to the "laughing" poems that follow.

The dialogue with Naevolus also makes a useful starting point for a reconsideration of Book 3, for even the "ironic reading" of the poem still leaves open several questions about the nature of the satiric persona and program. What does it mean for a poem to have two speakers that sound like satirists, and how does this fact relate to *what* is being said? If Juvenal really sets up this dialogue as a contest of perspectives, must it only have one "winner"? If we readers find Naevolus to be a crude slanderer and a comical *iratus*, to what extent has this impression been influenced by the

---

[2]De Decker cites *Satire* 9 as the only "dialogue naturel" Juvenal composed, despite his frequent use of the more declamatory "adversaire fictif" (*Juvenalis declamans*, 98–99). On the different styles exposed in the dialogue, see most recently Uden, *Invisible Satirist*, 83–85.
[3]See Braund, *Beyond Anger*; pages 130–77 treat *Satire* 9.

other speaker? Should that speaker be scrutinized as carefully? Finally, what does it mean that the most likely "program" poem in the book is placed at the end? Are we meant to be puzzled for two poems until we "see" Juvenal in relief in the dialogue? To these questions can be added a broader one worth asking: Why might Juvenal have followed up an "angry phase" with irony? That he was tired of *indignatio* and capable of doing something else will not suffice as an explanation. The shift has caused enough surprise and puzzlement that we may assume he knew it would be noticed, at least by readers who let themselves be conditioned to enjoy *indignatio* in Books 1 and 2. But this atmosphere of contrast and change is our key to understanding the new book, not an obstacle.

The Janus View

The pose Juvenal strikes in Book 3 is nowhere near as concretely expressed as the scene of indignant, open-air, and dangerous scribbling in *Satire* 1. With the disappearance of the angry Lucilian model comes a new relative invisibility (accentuated by, though not restricted to, the dialogue with the angry Naevolus).[4] Does Juvenal fade from view because "irony" cannot be embodied, or because the shedding of anger represents a sort of loss of identity? However we choose to interpret this detail, any comparison between the articulations of program in the first and third books must take into account the fact that, in the latter, the evidence is simply of a different nature. As *Satire* 7 opens, instead of drawing attention to himself as author or authority, the satirist advises other poets. That he calls them "young men" (*iuvenes*, 20) is just one tantalizing hint at changes in himself; whether it is meant to sound like an older man's speech or a more constructive satiric rhetoric, it seems clear that we are hearing from a different persona.

As he tells us, the satirist's environment is also changing. All three poems in Book 3 begin with a premise that the world has changed in some way (*omnia nunc contra*, as Juvenal observes of his decrepit interlocutor at 9.12). This was also the claim made in *Satire* 1 and its companion poems, of course—Rome has been filled to the brim with foreign upstarts, deviants, crooks, and pushy women, and satire must respond—but the introduction of the theme has a different ring in Book 3. In the framework of

---

[4.]"The invisibility of the satirist takes on a sinister cast [in *Satire* 9]: he may know you, but you cannot know him" (Uden, *Invisible Satirist*, 78)

Juvenal's oeuvre, Book 3—its Flavian accents notwithstanding[5]—must be telling us that conditions have transformed still more *since* Book 1. What is more, the "plot" of the book is change itself. Juvenal thematizes transitions of several kinds: from one patronage model to another, from ancient virtue to modern decadence, from prosperity to privation. This theme is necessarily entangled in the construction of Juvenal's persona.

While he forged a connection with the satiric past in *Satire* 1, here Juvenal explicitly situates his work in the present—a new present. Thus, in a parallel move, the satirist vacillates between ostensible optimism and pessimism. Here, too, he has taken a page from recent literature: Tacitus's *Dialogue on Orators*, echoed so strikingly in *Satire* 7, parades opposed viewpoints and communicates an ambivalence about the truth of literary (and political) change. In the *Dialogue*, gestures to an alternative view destabilize the initial and repeated claim that oratory has declined; in *Satire* 7, we can recognize a discernible competition between a vision of progress—quite a new element in Juvenal!—and a pessimistic or nostalgic undercutting of that vision.[6] The tension is one source of irony. Hutcheon's definition of this term is here as useful as any ancient construction: irony presents different options for interpretation, offering no firm evaluation of subject matter but pushing the audience to engage and impose interpretations.[7]

So, too, the book's representation of anger and the passions is more ambivalent than the "retrospective programmatic" reading of its closing dialogue would suggest. This should come as no surprise, since after the claim in *Satire* 1 that *indignatio* was the satiric genre's original mode, a step away from that would have high stakes. The satirist as we see him in that first performance would surely view the fading of *indignatio* as a loss, and he would be joined by quite a few modern readers of Juvenal. By taking this perspective seriously instead of responding with a defense of the neglected *Satires*, we can get closer to understanding how Juvenal has structured his career and why. I propose that readers who are disappointed in the later *Satires* are feeling the effects of the "training" they

---

[5] Book 3 appears to share much material with Tacitus's *Dialogue on Orators* (see especially *Satire* 7) and with Martial's early books (*Satire* 9). *Satire* 7 highlights the career of Statius (82–90).
[6] "The thought of the *Dialogus* accords well with that of a historian who wavers between nostalgia for the past and realistic acceptance of the present" (Goodyear, *Tacitus*, 16); cf. Luce, "Reading and Response," and Goldberg, "Appreciating Aper" (237: the *Dialogue* presents a "nuanced view of decline"). On the competition of visions (reflected in "doublespeak"), see Bartsch, *Actors in the Audience*, 98–147.
[7] Hutcheon, *Irony's Edge*, especially 9–56.

have undergone in recognizing the conditions for *indignatio* throughout *Satires* 1 through 6.

At the same time, as I will show, those same conditions are kept alive in the stories told in *Satires* 7, 8, and 9, although the satirist now distances himself from the indignant response per se. Instead, his audience witnesses the indignant suffering of other characters in the poems, disabled versions of the early Juvenal, who bear the burden of anger without reaping any of its gratifying results. Thus (looking at it one way) readers are deprived both of the satisfaction that might be gained from the satirist's moral attacks and of the peculiar pleasure that *shared* anger can bring. More optimistically, we could surmise that Juvenal's satire is undergoing an aesthetic and perhaps even philosophical maturation, and our poet is shedding his inner "Naevolus" to achieve greater peace and balance. Either interpretation is possible. The tension thereby created is not a side effect but an important part of the story of Juvenal's career. In a book that constantly encourages contemplation of change, progress, and decline, satire itself seems to be not in "transition" but in limbo.

Anger without Eloquence

The opening of *Satire* 7 heralds changes both in the satirist and in his literary world. "Hope and inducement to writing lie in Caesar alone, for he's the only one now who has given attention to the dejected Muses" (*et spes et ratio studiorum in Caesare tantum;/solus enim tristes hac tempestate Camenas/respexit*, 1–3). A shift has occurred in imperial patronage of letters (*studia*), and specifically poetry.[8] Without revealing his own position or the relevance of this subject to his own career, Juvenal evokes a couple of possibilities for the fiction behind this *Satire*: that he himself has just been the beneficiary of patronage, or that something has prompted him to adopt a positive tone on the subjects of poetic activity and imperial patronage. It is difficult not to think of Pliny's *Panegyric* for Trajan, a text that conveys personal gratitude (for success in a *political* career) in the form of a full account of the new emperor's greatness.[9] But it is also worth remembering that Horace began his second book of *Satires*, set in the aftermath

---

[8] For discussions of the likely dramatic date of this announcement, see LaBriolle, "La 7ᵉ satire," 367–68; Pepe, "Questioni adrianee"; Rudd, *Lines of Enquiry*, 87–88; and Hardie, "Condition of Letters," 204 n. 143.

[9] On Pliny's representation of his intertwined literary and political paths, see Gibson and Steele, "Indistinct Literary Careers," 125–37.

of Actium, musing about (but quickly defying) Trebatius's recommendation to write panegyric poetry. The dialogue in that poem about Horace's poetic future is supposed to have been prompted by diverse criticisms from readers of *Satires* Book 1, specifically concerning whether Horace is "too fierce" (*nimis acer*, 1) or not enough. The Horatian poem also gestures to a new political regime that may prove helpful to the poet. As Juvenal sets about staging a change in his own satiric ways, the memory of the early Augustan poem is relevant.[10]

Juvenal has been playing with the role of adviser in his last two *Satires*. But it constitutes a new twist for him to give advice to poets, indeed encourage them to write. In *Satire* 1, he expressed antipathy to other poets and a desire to drown them out; now he appears as a senior poet supporting younger members of a literary community ("get to work, young men," *hoc agite, o iuvenes*, 20). Superficially at least, Juvenal has changed the way he represents the literary life; this fact alone has made his persona hard to pin down.[11] But the endeavor soon becomes still more complicated after a destabilizing twist in the satirist's theme. The optimistic occasion—the promised support of Caesar (*indulgentia ducis*, 21)—gives way to a dreary portrait of the alternatives to imperial patronage, the reality poets have known recently. As becomes quickly apparent, the poet is far more interested in the suffering of starving poets than in their potential success under a beneficent patron. The old theme of the neglectful patron returns and becomes a vehicle for misanthropic meditation.[12] In retrospect, a single word at the end of line 1 (*in Caesare tantum*) can be seen to hint at this outcome.[13]

Satire 7 rapidly becomes so focused on the poet's recent difficulties and wasted efforts that its original hopeful occasion is entirely eclipsed. While the "doublespeak" connects the poem to Tacitus's *Dialogue on Orators*, there are many points of contact with this and other model texts. The

---

[10.]Hardie finds a meaningful touchstone for *Satire* 7 in the Horatian phrase "tranquil old age" (*tranquilla senectus, S.* 2.1.57); he argues that Juvenal is playing an older man who fails to be *tranquillus* ("Condition of Letters," 156–58).

[11.]Registering this change in stance are Lindo, "Evolution of Later Satires," 25; Wiesen, "Juvenal and the Intellectuals"; Rudd, *Lines of Enquiry*, 84–118; and Freudenburg, *Satires of Rome*, 11. To be sure, the starving professional poets of *Satire* 7 may not be in the same category as the poetasters of *Satire* 1, who sound like wealthy amateurs with plentiful opportunities to recite.

[12.]"Accents de misanthropie" is LaBriolle's term for what replaces the "accents de colère" of the previous poems ("La 7ᵉ satire," 367).

[13.]See Hardie, "Condition of Letters," 147–51. For Anderson, "Programs of Later Books," 154–55 (=*Essays*, 286–87), the optimistic tag *spes et ratio* in line 1 expresses the "dominant mood" of this new book. Others, anticipating the complaints to come, read this line as subtly sarcastic; e.g., Helmbold and O'Neil ("Juvenal's Seventh *Satire*") see an attack on Caesar as an unfair patron.

depiction of the generous *princeps* evokes not just encomiastic prose and verse works such as Statius's most lavishly encomiastic *Silvae*, but also more skeptical reflections on the value and potential of imperial patronage. These include Horace's gentle mockery of contemporary poets who wish that Augustus would "forbid them to be poor, and compel them to write" (*Ep.* 2.1.228), the speech of Tacitus's Aper questioning the value of Vespasian's patronage (*Dial.* 9), and Martial's quip that the existence of "Vergils" depends on a plentiful supply of "Maecenases" (8.55).

The poem makes a theme of trial and failure, beginning with the careers of poets. Juvenal conjures scenarios of poetic labor under private patronage that have for many a poet resulted not in profit but in disappointment and catastrophe. Toil in a cramped garret (28), praise from a patron who thinks his praise is support enough (30–32), the hiring of a hall for a recital (39–47)—all these ingredients lead to meager rewards or actual humiliation. The collective fantasy of a truly special poet (*vates egregius*, 53) turns into a cruel contrast: ideal poetic production means no mundane worries like an empty belly, but poets without a "Maecenas" live in a different reality. Indeed, the historical examples Juvenal cites in this first section of the poem progress chronologically from the successful Horace and Vergil, who enjoyed Maecenas's patronage (62, 69–71); to Lucan, whose inherited wealth was his safety net (79–81—to be sure, he ran into problems greater than debt); and finally Statius, who experienced qualified success in humiliating conditions (82–90, the longest treatment). The ideal *vates egregius* cannot exist in Juvenal's day.

The false starts toward success go on and on. As it turns out, poetry is only the first subject of the satire, and poets only the first category of *diserti* ("intellectuals," 31) to consider. From scenarios of trial and failure within one literary profession, Juvenal widens his scope to imagine failed efforts in one literary profession after another. He considers alternatives to the poetic career, going from history writing (in lines 98–104) to case pleading (105–49) to teaching rhetoric (150–214) and literature (215–43); each prospect is shot down with a grim and mocking portrait of the realities of the profession in question. Worse still, as the poet implies and as would seem to be confirmed by contemporary views of the literary professions, the search moves from professions with greater *dignitas* attached to them toward those with less.[14] Juvenal is speaking, of course, not to one jack-of-all-trades but to a different group of *diserti* in each section of the

---

[14.]See Keane, *Figuring Genre*, 132–33, drawing on Townend, "Literary Substrata to Juvenal."

poem. Nevertheless, the sense of failure increases with each section, as if—in the spirit of *Satire* 6—the accumulated disappointments were coming down on the head of one accursed protagonist.

The poem's theme, the search for security in a literary career, may be represented with exaggerated pessimism and dependent on examples from the past, yet its relevance to this satirist is undeniable. As a *disertus* taking a step into new territory himself, Juvenal has something in common with his struggling subjects. Despite this, as Braund has meticulously documented, Juvenal's advocacy of the *diserti* is double-edged.[15] The satirist does not restore the lost *dignitas* of his subjects but dramatizes its destruction. He puts on display the public and private pain that results from literary effort, public rejection, and professional compromise. As with the addresses to Trebius and Postumus, this *Satire* seems designed to expose, dwell on, and even intensify suffering rather than to avenge it. Victims of society are invented only to become victims of satire.

A particularly cruel contrast emerges in this poem between these victims and their supposed advocate. Juvenal's subjects are all men who make their living, or try to make their living, with words. Speaking, reciting, composing, declaiming, and elucidating others' texts are their means of survival.[16] But in this poem, they do not send out a single word. The financial constraints of their "real" world have much to do with this, but the nature of Juvenal's one-way *sermo* replicates this condition in the text. The early, cynical exhortation to an overconfident poet says it all: "break your pen, wretch, and destroy the battles you worked on late at night, you who write sublime poems in your little room just so you can come out having earned an ivy wreath and a skinny statue" (*frange miser calamum vigilataque proelia dele,/qui facis in parva sublimia carmina cella,/ut dignus venias hederis et imagine macra*, 27–29). This aspiring epicist composes *sublimia carmina* only to be essentially converted into an inarticulate facsimile of himself.[17]

This pattern continues throughout the poem's anecdotes of the literary life. One poet's burning excitement about an upcoming recital is eventually doused when he faces the mundane inconveniences of the venue (39–44):

---

[15] Braund, *Beyond Anger*, 24–68.
[16] The poem's marked "emphasis upon vocal performance . . . allows us to see that . . . all the *diserti* featured at length are permutations of a single type"; Braund, *Beyond Anger*, 49–50.
[17] Contrast this with the statue that Tacitus's Maternus desires to have over his tomb: "not gloomy and harsh-looking, but cheerful and garlanded" (*non maestus et atrox, sed hilaris et coronatus, Dial.* 13.6).

si dulcedine famae

succensus recites, maculosas commodat aedes.
haec longe ferrata domus servire iubetur
in qua sollicitas imitatur ianua porcas.
scit dare libertos extrema in parte sedentis
ordinis et magnas comitum disponere voces.

> . . . if you give a recital, all ablaze with the sweetness of fame, [your patron] lends you a dingy hall. This is the building that's made to serve you: far-off, iron-clad, with doors that sound like frightened pigs. Your patron knows how to supply freedmen to sit at the ends of rows, how to distribute the loud voices of his retinue.

The actual recitation, represented only in the abstract *dulcedine famae*, is elided by other sounds that drown out the poet: squeaking doors (are these latecomers, or early escapees?)[18] and the clamor of the hired claque in their seats.

A few lines later, Juvenal attributes poets' voicelessness to poverty (59–62):

neque enim cantare sub antro

Pierio thyrsumque potest contingere maesta
paupertas atque aeris inops, quo nocte dieque
corpus eget: satur est cum dicit Horatius 'euhoe.'

> Wretched poverty can't sing in the Pierian cave or grasp the thyrsus, for lack of the cash that the body needs night and day; Horace was full when he cried "Evoë!"

Even Vergil needed proper maintenance in order to produce his *Aeneid*. Juvenal hints at the possibility that one of that poem's most compelling passages might have been silenced: if Vergil had not had a slave boy and decent lodgings, "all the snakes would have fallen from the Fury's hair, and the war trumpet would be silent, making no fearsome blast" (*caderent omnes a crinibus hydri,/surda nihil gemeret grave bucina*, 70–71). More recently, Statius's glorious public recital of the *Thebaid* "broke the benches" with powerful verse (*fregit subsellia*, 86), but subsequently the

---

[18.]I thank Kirk Freudenburg for suggesting these meanings (*per litteras*).

poet had to sell a play to the actor Paris so that he could eat (87). Now the actor gets to speak the poet's words, and no doubt to a larger audience.

In the descriptions of other professions centered around speech and writing, it is repeatedly revealed that "poverty can't sing"—either in life or in satire. The historian's career looks promising in that Juvenal describes the copious pages that he turns out, but it turns out that this work yields no financial "harvest" (*seges*, 103); a news-reader (*acta legenti*, 104) is better off, and no doubt better heard. No more pleasant is the situation of the *causidici*, hired advocates who put their voices (and perhaps their principles) on the line for litigants. These men seem full of noise and bluster—they "talk big" (*magna sonant*, 108); their voices in court are like enormous bellows blowing out lies (111). But this exertion has a cost: "break your strained liver, wretch, so that when you're exhausted you can pin up the green palms of victory, the glory of your staircase" (*rumpe miser tensum iecur, ut tibi lasso/figantur virides, scalarum gloria, palmae*, 117–18). The "broken liver" echoes the poet's broken pen (27), and the lonely garret reappears, now ironically adorned with symbols of success.

Teachers may have it the worst in this satire, speech-wise and other-wise. The teachers of declamation, the *rhetores*, are supposed to train their charges to speak—which brings about repetitive droning that "kills the poor teachers" (*occidit miseros . . . magistros*, 154).[19] This effect recalls Juvenal's own trials as a soon-to-be angry satirist sitting through torturous recitals (1.1–13). Both cases involve exaggeration, to be sure, but by these claims satirist and teachers share a vulnerability to metaphorical violence. For his part, the typical *rhetor* of this poem has evidently not made power-ful noise since babyhood, when he was "just beginning to emit [his] first squalls, still red from [his] mother's womb" (*primos incipientem/edere vagitus et adhuc a matre rubentem*, 195–96). Though it is an image of *libertas* of sorts, this hardly dignifies the teacher of rhetoric.

As for the *grammatici*, in their instruction of language and literature they are reduced to disciplinarians and storehouses of mythological trivia. In a parallel loss, their talking tools are damaged. The very Vergil and Horace whom we saw doing relatively well in earlier "flashbacks" are here represented by their texts, living on in the classroom but blackened with soot and rough handling: "your Horace becomes stained all over and soot

---

[19]On this classroom practice, see Allen, "Ovid's *Cantare* and Cicero" 4; Clarke, "Juvenal 7.150–53"; and Wiesen, "*Classis Numerosa.*"

clings to your blackened Vergil" (*totus decolor esset/Flaccus et haereret nigro fuligo Maroni*, 226–27). Even the written word is obscured in the end. Texts are demeaned and confined, destined to remain in the garret, be sold to unworthy buyers, or—in an image that recalls the consequences of free speech in *Satire 1*—immolated in despair and cynicism: "ask quickly for some wood and offer up what you're composing to Venus's husband, Telesinus" (*lignorum aliquid posce ocius et quae/componis dona Veneris, Telesine, marito*, 24–25). The bonfire of poems for "Venus's husband" (as is fitting for an epic poet's grand style and grand expectations)[20] is painted as a quasi-religious ceremony that, ironically, stands to acquire a certain dignity or at least to act out the burning bitterness that the author must feel but cannot express. Yet, being all too literal and effective in its specific task, the fire is far from being the metaphorical weapon that Lucilius was said to wield in *Satire 1*. It even falls short of the spectacular symbolic effect of Juvenal's own imagined execution. While the transgressive satirist is united with his inflammatory texts in a final fiery performance, the failed poet in *Satire 7* will carry the memory of watching his bonfire burn out.

Like the disappointed "flame" felt by the ambitious poet in line 40, the bonfire epitomizes the internalized and unarticulated feelings of the *diserti* throughout the poem. It is also a reminder of their physical vulnerability. Just as sublime poetry is diminished by Juvenal's emphasis on its humble materiality, the *diserti* themselves are reduced to bodies. The teachers of literature, for example, get beaten by their disrespectful young students (213). The poets are burdened with inadequately fed and clothed bodies,[21] an unromantic condition their very Muse is imagined to share (*esuriens . . . Clio*, 7). Nor is there any shortage of metaphorical discomforts in the trade to which they cling against their better judgment (48–52):

> nos tamen hoc agimus tenuique in pulvere sulcos
> ducimus et litus sterili versamus aratro.
> nam si discedas, tenet insanabile multos
> scribendi cacoethes et aegro in corde senescit.

But we keep doing our thing, drawing furrows in the thin dust and turning the seashore with a sterile plow. For if you try to pull away, the

---

[20.] While it is not clear what genre is "Telesinus'" specialty, Juvenal's language suggests a failed epicist; cf. Jones, *Juvenal*, 92.
[21.] See 7.29, 35, 61–62, 66, 87, and 93; cf. the sarcastic conjecture that a would-be patron prefers a pet lion because its belly is easier to fill than a poet's (77–78).

incurable itch of writing holds many men fast, and grows old in their sick hearts.[22]

Such hardships resemble the experiences of the clients and paupers in *Satires* 1 and 3, who were cast aside by patrons and society. But when men of letters suffer this way in *Satire* 7, their inability to perform contrasts with the desire that defines them. Instead, they are trapped as the audience of a description of their own humiliation. Meanwhile, everyone else gets to express themselves—this includes patrons who write their own bad poetry, audience members hired to vocalize, dissatisfied litigants, ungrateful students and parents, and of course the satirist. The writers' and scholars' own passions are kept inside, where, as the angry Juvenal knew, they hurt the most.

It is becoming clear that, despite the satirist's apparently detached stance, anger actually plays quite a significant role in this new phase of Juvenal's oeuvre. Readers familiar with the first book cannot fail to recognize, in the experiences of the *diserti*, all the conditions for *indignatio*. Not only insults and injustices but also a protracted inability to speak out about them prompted Juvenal's indignant debut: *semper ego auditor tantum?* This formula allows Juvenal to make a case against the bad patrons in *Satire* 7—fueled in this case not by his own *indignatio*, which is absent, but from the patent discomfort (anger, resentment, physical suffering) of his subjects. The *diserti* are poetic material—*materia*—for the satirist just as they would have been patronage material for Caesar. But they offer more than a satiric subject; it is the way they remind Juvenal's larger audience of the "angry option," and its limits, that makes this dry poem such an unsettling read. The *diserti* can access neither their dignifying literary speech nor therapeutic speech against those who wrong them; the satirist exposes the need for it, but does not deliver it himself. Thus Juvenal manages to have it both ways. In turn, so does his external audience, which may still be cultivating a taste for anger's ambivalent pleasures.

Ante Ora Parentum

The tension between optimism and pessimism is maintained as the book continues. In *Satire* 8, Juvenal once again contemplates societal change.

[22.]The numbering reflects deletion of the suspect line 51. The passage represents "an extravagant mixture of metaphors taken from the realms of disease and trapping" (Braund, "Juvenal 7.50–52," 166). Cf. Wiesen, "Juvenal and the Intellectuals," 49–50.

Simultaneously, this central and longest poem of Book 3 underscores the changes in the satirist's own work by presenting a fresh treatment of one of his oldest themes: moral decline. On the one hand, this theme suits the indignant mode, and Juvenal's approach uses some standard tricks for performing *indignatio*. In keeping with Cicero's instructions (*Inv.* 1.101), he invokes virtuous ancestors and imagines their judgment of the degenerate present. His opening words, *stemmata quid faciunt?* (What do family trees do?, 8.1), recall the angry rhetorical questions of Books 1 and 2. He also makes as if to take refuge in visions of Rome's virtuous past—enacting, as Braund puts it, a "chronological retrogression" from an imperial context back through republican history, the period of the kings, and Rome's foundation.[23] On the other hand, these devices are not exactly presented in an indignant satiric voice, so that the treatment of the traditional theme reads ironically. Juvenal comes across not as an observer of daily outrages on the streets but as a more distanced, learned, and even cynical chronicler both of moral decline and of the Roman institutions that aimed to prevent it. He suggests that the past does not deserve reverence alone, by highlighting some bad or dubious exempla from earlier Roman history (Catiline and Cethegus, the sons of Brutus, and Romulus's undistinguished first Romans).[24] And while he certainly criticizes the corrupt character of modern-day nobles, Juvenal interweaves arguments from morality with arguments from expediency, shows off his literary learning, and gives as much attention to prurient description of negative exempla as to positive moral advice.[25] As Henderson has argued, this poem interrogates and satirizes Roman moral discourse and moral education themselves, making the satirist out to be something rather different from an indignant witness of decline.[26]

In sum, the lecture to a young noble supposedly poised to begin his own career in degeneracy exploits many opportunities for satire. Yet the traditional theme of living up to one's origins serves as a reminder that satire, too, is part of a story about change—and ambivalent change.

[23.]Braund, *Beyond Anger*, 76.

[24.]Catiline and Cethegus: 231–44; the sons of Brutus: 261–68; and Romulus's motley crowd of runaways: 273–75.

[25.]These are identified as strategies of the ironic persona in Braund, *Beyond Anger*, 94–122; cf. Fredericks, "Rhetoric and Morality." De Decker, *Juvenalis declamans*, 107–10, discusses the display of exempla as a declamatory technique.

[26.]Juvenal makes readers "bore into the system of conceptual images through which Roman reality, not just their names, was negotiated, imposed and contested" (Henderson, *Figuring Out Roman Nobility*, 2).

Just as the poem produces a double vision of Rome's past, interweaving harsh revelations with nostalgic hints, it also illustrates both the advantages of emotionally detached mockery and the allure of pure *indignatio*. Once again, the former satiric mode is illustrated by the words of an invisible satirist, and the latter by a visible group of silent and frustrated victims.

This time, however, the victims are not humans. In fact, apart from a glimpse of provincials mistreated by corrupt governors (98–124), we see virtually no human suffering in *Satire* 8. Instead, Juvenal dramatizes the impact of degeneracy through a different kind of spectacle: the static parade of portraits, statues, and masks of venerable Roman ancestors that opens the poem (1–20):

> Stemmata quid faciunt? quid prodest, Pontice, longo
> sanguine censeri, pictos ostendere vultus
> maiorum et stantis in curribus Aemilianos
> et Curios iam dimidios umeroque minorem
> Corvinum et Galbam auriculis nasoque carentem,   5
> quis fructus generis tabula iactare capaci
> censorem, posthac multa contingere virga
> fumosos equitum cum dictatore magistros,
> si coram Lepidis male vivitur? effigies quo
> tot bellatorum, si luditur alea pernox   10
> ante Numantinos, si dormire incipis ortu
> luciferi, quo signa duces et castra movebant?
> cur Allobrogicis et magna gaudeat ara
> natus in Herculeo Fabius lare, si cupidus, si
> vanus et Euganea quantumvis mollior agna,   15
> si tenerum attritus Catinensi pumice lumbum
> squalentis traducit avos emptorque veneni
> frangenda miseram funestat imagine gentem?
> tota licet veteres exornent undique cerae
> atria, nobilitas sola est atque unica virtus.   20

What do bloodlines do? Ponticus, what good is it to be ranked by your long pedigree—to display painted faces of ancestors, Aemiliani standing in chariots, Curii now broken in half, Corvinus missing a shoulder, Galba minus ears and nose? What's the benefit of boasting of a censor in your extensive family tree, of connecting through many branches with smoke-covered masters of the cavalry and a dictator, if you live shamefully right in front of Lepidi? What good are so many images of warriors, if your all-night dice game goes on before Numantini, if you go to sleep when the morning star rises, right when generals used to move their standards and camps? Why does Fabius, born in the house of Hercules, exult in Allobrogici and the Great Altar, if he's lustful and empty-headed and softer than a Venetian lamb, if with his groin rubbed smooth with Sicilian pumice he makes a mockery of his hairy ancestors—that dealer in poison—and pollutes his wretched clan with his own image, which ought to be shattered? Wax ancestors can decorate atria on all sides, but the one and only nobility is virtue.

Moral decline gets its first representation in the tragically obvious contrast between the painted and sculpted representations of virtuous ancestors and the living, degenerate aristocrats whose homes they fill. Oblivious to the hypocrisy of their pride and the irony of the combined spectacle they create, the depraved descendants of military and civic leaders draw attention to the very examples they are defying.[27] This opening theme brings to mind Seneca's condemnation of the same phenomenon (*Ben.* 3.28.2; cf. *Ep.* 44.5 and 76.12), and the images of ancestor portraits and statues exemplifies a Roman topos in which family *imagines* represent spectators of their descendants' actions. For Cicero the *imagines* can be seen as stern judges of the living (*Planc.* 51, *Cael.* 34; cf. *de Orat.* 2.225) or as sorrowful witnesses to their tragedies (*Mur.* 88).[28] Tellingly, Pliny the Elder complains that the ancestor "portraits" being produced in his time show no regard for accurate representation of individuals but are valued for their costly materials and general symbolism of status (*Nat.* 35.2). His point is that the very idea of supervised emulation embodied in the images has been forgotten.

Juvenal's lecture performs certain twists on the old topos of the observing ancestors and makes a comparison between past and present more complex. As Henderson has shown, the names the satirist chooses to

---

[27.]Flower, *Ancestor Masks*, traces the story of the *imagines* in Roman aristocratic culture; on the display of images in homes, see especially 185–222.

[28.]See Bartsch, *Mirror of the Self*, 124–25. A number of surviving togate statues appear to represent orators speaking or about to speak (see Davies, "Togate Statues"); this makes it easier to imagine them casting judgment on those around them, as it were.

attach to crumbling portraits and statues have complicated associations—
sometimes with more than one individual, sometimes with ugly events,
sometimes with changes in status or the "lineage" instantaneously created
by adoption.[29] Even if we do not probe that deeply, we can catch Juvenal
playing games with convention. For example, while the Senecan exam-
ples are generic and the Ciceronian fully personalized, Juvenal blends the
specific with the general, conjuring one large, impossibly decorated and
crowded atrium. His addressees change their identities, and the ancestor
images Juvenal evokes are many and varied (whom does this Ponticus per-
son actually claim as ancestors?[30] is *any* modern-day aristocrat obligated
to live up to *every* Roman leader's example?). This fuzziness makes it
difficult to believe that Juvenal means to earnestly employ the convention
of invoking exemplary ancestors to lecture their descendants. Adding to
the ambiguity in line 8 is the mention of men who held offices to which
modern-day nobles could never aspire: the republican dictators and *mag-
istri equitum* (8) are long gone by Juvenal's day. Their images thus not
only represent certifiably ancient and arguably irrelevant virtues but could
be seen as a distracting reminder of the vastly different political context
in which the *maiores* competed for distinction. A return to this past seems
no more possible than a return to the Augustan model of poetic patron-
age remembered in *Satire* 7. One more sign of distance and alienness: the
images are physically deteriorating. Limbs are broken (4), faces are crum-
bling (5), surfaces are smoke-begrimed (8)—all constituting another insult
to the ancestors.[31] It is a sad museum on display here, a tribute to the past
that looks like it might even be some shameless noble's idea of a joke.

While *Satire* 8 ironizes the concept of decline itself in various ways, it
still presents a case for the idea, focalizing it through the ancestor images.
One of Juvenal's methods is to make these "characters" into spectators of

---

[29]."Kinship-structures [are] good to think with, even better to pretend with" (Henderson, *Figuring
Out Roman Nobility*, 10). Several other observations in this paragraph are indebted to or inspired
by Henderson (29–59).

[30].The name Ponticus is not associated with any republican figure, though it implies some
connection to military success in Pontus (Ferguson, *Prosopography to Juvenal*, 188).

[31].See also *Satire* 7.126–28, where an undeserving aristocrat boasts of the "one-eyed" (*lusca*)
ancestor statue in his house; cf. Alexander, "Juvenal 7.126–28." The image, in retrospect, reads
like the seed of the next poem. On *fumosos* (8), Henderson sees there a marker of venerable age
(*Figuring Out Roman Nobility*, 46); smoky coating on *imagines* is also mentioned at Cic. *Pis.* 1
and Sen. *Ep.* 44.5. Cf. Flower, *Ancestor Masks*, 34: this detail emphasizes "the traditional and
consciously 'antique' character of the *imagines* in . . . the late Republic and early Empire." In
the context of Juvenal Book 3, however, smoke and grime are just as likely to be associated with
degradation: cf. the condition of the texts of Horace and Vergil at the end of *Satire* 7, a final symbol
of the degradation of the *diserti* themselves.

modern depravity. As representations of human beings, the images convey a similar vulnerability (thanks to art's deception) and invite a similar outrage from sympathetic onlookers. Other Roman authors hint that as young nobles make their choice between the virtuous and bad paths, lifelike statues of their ancestors are supervising: for instance, Pliny the Younger (an optimistic foil to his uncle on this point) writes that *imagines* in noble atria "seem silently to encourage young men to praise them" (*adulescentes tacitae laudare adhortari . . . videntur, Ep.* 5.17.6). Sometimes the *imagines* seem to demand apologies or self-defense from their living ancestors (e.g., Cic. *Planc.* 51 and *de Orat.* 2.225). This background illuminates Juvenal's emphasis on crime and vice that takes place right in front of statues of ancestor images.[32] We see that motif in the proem (*coram Lepidis male vivitur*, 9; *luditur alea pernox ante Numantinos*, 10–11), later in the poem when a man's triumphal statue has to witness the forgeries of his son (*te, solitum falsas signare tabellas/in templis quae fecit avus statuamque parentis/ante triumphalem*, 142–44), and then in the egregious example of an adulterous, slumming consul (144–50):

> nocturnus adulter
> tempora Santonico velas adoperta cucullo?
> praeter maiorum cineres atque ossa volucri
> carpento rapitur pinguis Lateranus, et ipse,
> ipse rotam adstringit sufflamine mulio consul,
> nocte quidem, sed Luna videt, sed sidera testes
> intendunt oculos.

[What good does it do if] you cover your head with a Gallic hood when you sneak out for your nighttime adultery? Fat Lateranus flies past the ashes and bones of his ancestors in a speeding carriage, while he himself checks the wheel with the break, a muleteer consul—at night, to be sure, but the moon sees it, and the stars are witnesses, keeping their gaze on him.

The moon and stars are personified as seeing disgrace through the dark; perhaps Juvenal means for us to imagine those "ashes and bones" stirring a bit too, as they "watch" or sense their descendant drive his own chariot to an assignation. The image, and the point, recall the underworld scene near

---

[32] Braund (*Beyond Anger*, 103) notes that the preposition *coram* (9) is typically used with living people rather than objects.

the end of *Satire* 2, where a newly deceased pathic is imagined making his shocking entrance into the company of the shades (2.153–58).

As insulted spectators, and ones without influence at that, the ancestor images invite us to stretch the definition of "human victim" just enough to see them as analogues to the wronged and suffering *diserti* in *Satire* 7. The idea of the suffering statue is another throwback to early Juvenal—the opening of *Satire* 1, where we saw statues in private gardens "reacting" to poetry. The description (*convolsa . . . marmora clamant . . . et ruptae . . . columnae*, 1.12–13) suggests pain, outrage, or just degrading submission to the fate of echoing recited poetry. In this all-important vignette from the angry poems, the feelings of these inanimate objects are in harmony with Juvenal's—indeed, their tortured shouting precedes the similarly tortured author's decision to speak out himself. In *Satire* 8, however, the ancestor images suffer in silence.

The association between real people and replicas of people works in both directions. The joke in *Satire* 7 that a starving poet will be remembered by his skinny statue is a taste of what happens in *Satire* 8. The man who smoothes the skin of his groin with pumice "makes a mockery of his hairy ancestors" (*squalentis traducit avos*, 17). In a reversal of roles, the living man has been smoothed with stone, and in fact in the next line is basically equated to a statue of himself, which Juvenal declares should be smashed (*frangenda . . . imagine*, 18; the "golden line" has an appropriately visual dimension). Meanwhile, the man's ancient counterparts stand before him, shaggy and lifelike observers of his depravity. A similar exchange of characteristics between living man and images can be seen in lines 52 through 55, where the satirist seems already to be visualizing how another boastful noble will be remembered:

> at tu
> nil nisi Cecropides truncoque simillimus Hermae.
> nullo quippe alio vincis discrimine quam quod
> illi marmoreum caput est, tua vivit imago.

But you're nothing but a scion of Cecrops who looks exactly like a mutilated Herm. Indeed you're better than that in no other respect but that its head is made of marble, while your image is alive.

This time, the equation between man and one image, the mutilated Herm that represents the man's shamelessness and inferiority, alludes to another suitable image: the wax *imago* that will represent the man in ceremonies staged by his descendants. In *tua vivit imago* Fredericks reads a hint that the man "is his own death-mask," which underscores the exchange between living man and replica.[33]

The images in Roman houses have counterparts in the provinces, as we see in the satirist's advice to a prospective governor. Juvenal warns this man to show mercy to the exhausted, long-extorted people he will be governing: "pity the depleted provincials: you're looking at the bones of kings emptied of marrow, sucked dry" (*miserere inopum sociorum:/ossa vides rerum vacuis exucta medullis*, 89–90). He is thinking particularly of wealthy provincials who have, among other insults, seen their private art collections plundered by Roman administrators (100–104):

> plena domus tunc omnis, et ingens stabat acervos
> nummorum, Spartana chlamys, conchylia Coa,
> et cum Parrhasii tabulis signisque Myronis
> Phidiacum vivebat ebur, nec non Polycliti
> multus ubique labor, rarae sine Mentore mensae.

> Back then [i.e., before the first wave of corrupt governors came], every house was full—there were huge piles of cash, dyed Spartan cloaks and purple Coan garments; there were paintings by Parrhasius and statues by Myron, and lifelike ivories by Phidias; there were many works of Polyclitus everywhere, and few tables lacked a piece by Mentor.

The marvelous paintings and statues that, as Juvenal puts it, "used to be alive" (*vivebat*) represent the despoiled provincials. Historical accounts of bad governors often feature stolen art. Statues are the first item on the list of taboo temptations in Cicero's letter to his newly re-elected brother (*Q. fr.* 1.1.8), and they feature prominently in the same author's accounts of the crimes of Verres (*Ver.* 4.46–47). But Juvenal's vignette takes the topos to another level, suggesting that the life missing from the provincials' "emptied" bodies once resided in the objects they possessed. These fine lifelike works stood passively on walls, pedestals, and tables as their predators approached; their departure meant the loss of their owners' breath and marrow.

In *Satire* 8, statues, wax *imagines*, and the like suggest disregarded, paralyzed, and silent human beings, watching the parade of modern vice in silent horror. Even if their moral superiority and the legitimacy of the

---

[33] Fredericks, "Rhetoric and Morality," 120.

system that valorizes them is simultaneously being called into question, we cannot ignore their function as focalizers of the poem's moral criticism. The theme of spectatorship is developed further in the climactic section that condemns disgraceful performances by nobles on stage and in the arena. There, Juvenal addresses that noble performer and obscene example extraordinaire, the emperor Nero. He underscores the symbolic role of statues by recommending that Nero adorn his own ancestor statues with awards for and mementos of his stage work. The emperor is imagined cultivating this aristocratic custom only to pervert it (227–30):

> maiorum effigies habeant insignia vocis,
> ante pedes Domiti longum tu pone Thyestae
> syrma vel Antigones seu personam Melanippes,
> et de marmoreo citharam suspende colosso.

> Let your ancestors' statues receive the prizes for your voice; go and put before Domitius's feet your gown of Thyestes or your mask of Antigone or Melanippe, and hang your lyre on your marble colossus.

The pious gesture (at least, with different offerings, it would be pious) represents the ultimate misuse of ancestor images, just as Nero's performances perverted the proper public behavior of a noble. His own stage appearances and those of other nobles also had another degrading effect: they exposed the audience to shame. Juvenal tells us that the *populus* who tolerated such shows showed its "hard face" (*frons durior*, 189). The metaphor of shamelessness as hardness is common enough, but in this context Juvenal's phrase effectively petrifies the people and makes them parallel to the insulted ancestor images.[34]

Humans are dehumanized, and inanimate anthropomorphic objects (at least those that represent victims) are made to suffer as humans do. All this exchange between living humans and imitations helps to breathe life into those images that dominate the opening passage of *Satire* 8. But this life only turns them into more pathetic victims of the reprehensible behavior being narrated in the satire. Despite their exemplary status, they are summoned only to perform as witnesses, like the *diserti*. We may note that Roman nobles *did* have ways of making their dead ancestors

---

[34] Keane, *Figuring Genre*, 35. The metaphor in *frons durior* represents a regrettable deviation from promising beginnings: the individual undergoing education resembles soft clay (7.237–38; see above).

talk—reanimating them in processions at funerals, collecting their sayings in books, even summoning them through ventriloquism to lecture their errant descendants. Cicero's *prosopopoeia* of Appius Claudius Caecus, cited in my first chapter, even doubles up on this device: Appius, himself invoked as a speaking *imago*, in turn invokes for Clodia the line of great *imagines viriles* and their female counterparts that should have deterred her from disgracing her family (*Cael.* 34). Although Juvenal might similarly have allowed righteous *indignatio* to perform loudly and clearly in *Satire* 8, he does not give it so much as a brief quotation.

The satirist himself now stands at a remove from the infectious *indignatio* that colored his earlier poems, but the ancestor images, like the *diserti*, are both his proxies and his victims. They are "ancient" in more than one way, representing not just Juvenal's lost angry mode but the supposed origin of *that* version of satire—the genre's glorious angry past that he constructed in his picture of the fiery Lucilius (1.165–68). Frozen in that lost past, they neatly embody old-fashioned anger—they have not been allowed to "evolve" into restrained irony along with the poet. It would be wrong, however, to conceive their victimhood as pure passivity. The silent suffering of these victims performs a satiric function itself, adding a layer of *indignatio* to a poem spun by an emotionally calmer satirist. Meanwhile, Juvenal's audiences—internal and external—are made to gaze at the images much as if they were listening to exemplary tales, "provid[ing] a . . . ratification of [their] exemplary power."[35] Thus this second installment in Book 3, like the first, makes anger—or a disabled form of it—into a meaningful side show.

In *Satire* 8, the idea of a moral past is not straightforwardly undercut, but mobilized to compete with an alternative perspective on the world. By association, the narrative about satiric change that can be traced in the poem is ambivalent, its terms and criteria dynamic. Even as Juvenal highlights how much his satire has changed, his purpose is clearly not to criticize anger itself; even his partial commitment to the cause of the victimized parties creates a connection with them. And their feelings are a reminder of the way Juvenal's earlier poems responded to injustice and insult. While the satirist may now invite readers to enjoy his commentaries from a less emotional perspective, the discomfort of the victims he

---

[35.]Bartsch, *Mirror of the Self*, 119, writing on exemplary tales and visible *imagines* alike. Bartsch adds that "this stress upon the role of the witness in the production of *virtus* meant that the exemplary quality of a deed was effectively felt to be lost without an audience." Cf. Roller, "Exemplarity in Roman Culture," on the importance of the internal audience in narrated exempla.

describes is not simply a laughing matter. The dilemma the spectacle of *Satire* 8 creates is the question of whether, and how, the past can play a constructive role in the present. Readers can no more dismiss indignation as a passé Juvenalian mode than they can reject other paradigms of behavior. Although the angry satirist has departed the scene, Juvenal is not capable of eliminating his readers' appetite for old-fashioned indignant satire—indeed, his suppression of the indignant mode might even serve to keep that appetite alive.

Sermo and Sirens

In these conditions, the unhappy Naevolus enters the scene. At first glance, his story seems out of place in the book's thematic landscape. If anything, Naevolus seems to have emerged from another literary demimonde: the Rome of Martial's *Epigrams*, where his name appears five times. It is not surprising that Juvenal borrowed the strange and striking name ("Little Wart"); Martial's characters are also associated with themes and jokes that may well have inspired *Satire* 9. Two of Martial's Naevoluses are pathics (3.71, 3.95), and two others are ungenerous to clients (2.46, 4.83). While *Satire* 9 twists some of these elements—making Naevolus a penetrator of men *and* women; making not him but his patron the stingy one—it fleshes out Martial's themes of sex, scandal, hypocrisy, and remuneration. But a closer look reveals more local associations. Naevolus is, in fact, a curious hybrid of the victim characters in the two preceding *Satires*. Like the disgruntled *diserti*, he is having problems with a drying-up field of patrons, facing poverty, and dreaming of a past when things were better. He also seems to aspire to a kind of creative, authorial status, as his complaints are laced with literary allusions to texts from Homer to Plato to Horace. Second, Naevolus's moral lament and his longing for his own better past set up a deliciously preposterous parallel with the moral lament in *Satire* 8. Naevolus is eager to expose the moral hypocrisy of the particularly stingy and unappreciative Virro, who hides his relations with Naevolus and the significant role that the latter has had in his personal prosperity. The prostitute seems to have his finger on the pulse of the corrupt society described in *Satires* 7 and 8.

If the theme of *Satire* 9 is not such a novelty in Book 3, the dialogue form represents a meaningful deviation. After keeping his suffering characters silent for two poems, Juvenal is now allowing the voice of indignation to speak, and that for a full two-thirds of the poem. *Sermo* has become a conversation after all. This new character is not just an object on view but a speaking agent who makes us listen to him. In this way he could not be more different from Martial's character in 1.97, a pleader who only speaks when others are sure to drown him out. Martial urges this reticent fellow to put himself on the line: "Hey, everyone's gone silent: say something, Naevolus!" (*ecce, tacent omnes: Naevole, dic aliquid*, 1.97.4). But the epigram ends there; it is Juvenal who turns "Naevolus" into a speaker who stands out in the book's crowd of silent victims.

Naevolus's angry speech from a position of abjection links him to the early Juvenal and his best-known proxy, the downtrodden *cliens* Umbricius.[36] Ironically, it was Naevolus's frank speech that kept him silenced by modern scholars for so long: before the late twentieth century, *Satire* 9 was frequently left out of editions of Juvenal. Things changed with the explosion of ancient sex and gender studies and, equally important, the development of satiric persona theory. Scholars now listen to Naevolus as a figure with generic significance, an embodiment of satiric obscenity and indignation. Both the portrait painted by the satirist in his opening address to Naevolus and the latter's own words present him as unsavory and unreasonable. Even the conventional physical marks of boorishness, *rusticitas*, seem to be all over Naevolus in the portrait that the satirist paints: "your face is grave, you have a forest of untreated hair, there's no sheen in your skin . . . your shins are neglected and rough with bristling hair" (*vultus gravis, horrida siccae/silva comae, nullus tota nitor in cute . . . sed fruticante pilo neglecta et squalida crura*, 12–15).[37] His appearance contrasts with his previous reputation as "a clever dining companion with biting jokes, fierce with urban wit" (*conviva ioco mordente facetus/et salibus vehemens intra pomeria natis*, 10–11).

For Braund, this portrait is only the first indication that Naevolus is meant to represent the abrasive and ridiculous qualities of the angry satiric mode. As the poem continues, Naevolus adopts an air of moral superiority and philosophical dignity. At the same time, he describes his profession in graphically obscene ways, employing overly free speech (*licentia*), and makes bizarre literary allusions that reveal his pretension and degrade his source-texts. He also complains bitterly and hyperbolically about his financial straits, expressing not-so-modest wishes for compensation (27–31, 137–47). For Braund, these are all moral and aesthetic strikes

---

[36.]Bellandi, "Naevolus cliens," examines and compares the two characters as variations on a type.
[37.]Braund, *Beyond Anger*, 150, 157–60; cf. Mason, "Is Juvenal a Classic?," 101.

against Naevolus. In turn, the prostitute's complaints shine a more flattering light on the sly satirist, whose verbal encouragement just lets Naevolus hang himself. The dialogue form allows the satirist to sound more coyly "Horatian"—think of *Satires* 1.9 and 2.4—than aggressively "Juvenalian." Of course this ironist has his own moral flaws: he too acts superior, and, although Naevolus begs him to keep his disclosures secret, he has obviously betrayed them (fictionally) by writing this poem. But from his position of apparent rhetorical control, he may be encouraging his external audience to do a moral reading of Naevolus's style in this "allegory of the procedure of satire."[38]

An "amoral option" also exists for a metaliterary reading of the dialogue. The prominence of Naevolus recalls the way Horace farms out the work of mockery and moralizing to other characters in his second book.[39] Satire is enriched when marginal voices, such as the slave Davus, participate. In this spirit, Plaza suggests, Naevolus is constructed as the "underground self" of the real satirist, unsavory yet capable of "put[ting] up a fight worthy of a fellow satirist." For Uden, too, he represents a satiric voice, one of many in a climate that invites "satirizing" by anyone who has something to gain from accusing others.[40] These readings imply—justifiably, I believe—that Naevolus's performance is too deeply rooted in the traditions of blame poetry to be simply a satiric target. As Rosen has shown, Naevolus's complaints about poverty, his obscenity, and his prurient interest in exposure of vice (as opposed to moral reform) recall blame figures all the way back to archaic Greece.[41] Also like a satirist, Naevolus thrives on the existence of vice, albeit in a more direct and mechanical fashion than the poet who writes down what he sees. Even his disreputable profession does not undermine his authority as a satirist figure, since satire has no stable moral agenda.[42] Thus the entire poem might be seen as dramatizing an enduring aspect of satire itself, not so much setting the two speakers in opposition as suggesting that they are two sides of the same coin.

[38.] Braund, *Beyond Anger*, 142: "our reaction to Naevolus is guided by the speaker's unsympathetic attitude to him . . . [the ironic tone is] a clear signal from Juvenal that we should not sympathise" with his interlocutor. Cf. Braund, "*Libertas* or *Licentia*," 424–26.

[39.] See Keane, *Figuring Genre*, 116–19.

[40.] Plaza, *Function of Humour*, 166; cf. Uden, *Invisible Satirist*, 74–85.

[41.] The remainder of this paragraph condenses the argument of Rosen, *Making Mockery*, 210–35.

[42.] On the odd analogy between satire and prostitution suggested here, see Rosen and Keane, "Greco-Roman Satirical Poetry," 394.

These differing approaches to interpreting the generic markers Naevolus carries may be synthesized in a reading of this character's role within Book 3. While recognizing the stylistic and even the moral differences between Naevolus and his interlocutor, we can also appreciate the former's satiric heritage. To these objectives we should add a clearer understanding of how Naevolus and his story of change into the program of Book 3 and the trajectory of Juvenal's oeuvre.

Naevolus embodies change in his physical condition. Just as his very name evokes physical affliction, he is from the start drawn as a suffering body, like the degraded victims of *Satires* 7 and 8. His deteriorating condition and vigor are at once symptoms of his current difficulties and threats to his livelihood as a prostitute. Even his mental anguish has physical manifestations (he looks "grave . . . with a furrowed brow, like defeated Marsyas," *tristis . . . fronte obducta ceu Marsya victus*, 1–2). His troubles have given him a sorrowful face, unkempt hair, dull skin, stubbly legs, a wasted look (12–17). But the satirist remembers a neater, more stylish Naevolus, defined by his wit rather than his physical characteristics. Completing the body-oriented frame, the climax of the poem is an absurd Horatian lament for lost youth (126–29):

> festinat enim decurrere velox
> flosculus angustae miseraeque breuissima uitae
> portio; dum bibimus, dum serta, unguenta, puellas
> poscimus, obrepit non intellecta senectus.

> You see, that all too brief little bloom of my cramped and wretched life is swiftly passing away; even as we drink and call for garlands and perfumes and girls, old age stealthily creeps up.

Naevolus's imitation of the "old" Horace makes an appropriate cap to his laments, as it combines his literary pretentions, self-pity, and despair for his changing body.[43]

[43.] At numerous points in *Satire* 9, Juvenal evokes his famous predecessor "performing" old age (albeit after his satiric phase). Naevolus's incongruously fanciful thought and diction recall Hor. *C.* 1.11.7–8 (*dum loquimur, fugit invida/aetas*), *C.* 2.5.13–14 (*currit enim ferox/ aetas*), and *C.* 2.11.5–10 (*fugit retro/ levis iuventas et decor . . . non semper idem floribus est honor vernis*). There are also echoes of Horace's protests to Maecenas and Florus at the end of his lyric career: *Ep.* 1.1.4 (*non eadem est aetas, non mens*) and *Ep.* 2.2.55–57 (*singula de nobis anni praedantur euntes;/ eripuere iocos, venerem, conuiuia, ludum;/tendunt extorquere poemata*).

With these afflictions, Naevolus makes an appropriate successor to the other victims of Book 3. But his body is not only defined by deterioration; another story is told in its wrinkles and hair. Some of the features that Naevolus exhibits in the opening passage of the satire—the grave expression, the shaggy head, the hairy limbs—recall certain victims in a more positive characterization. The ancestors in *Satire* 8 are celebrated for their shaggy and severe look—like Roman *maiores* in many literary sources. Making a famous contrast, Cicero's *prosopopoeia* of Appius introduces the talking ghost as "one of those bearded men, not with that modern 'beard-let' that [Clodia] finds charming, but that old shaggy kind that we see in statues and portraits from the old days" (*aliquis . . . ex barbatis illis non hac barbula, qua ista delectatur, sed illa horrida, quam in statuis antiquis atque imaginibus videmus, Cael.* 33). Likewise, in Juvenal *Satire* 8, it is good to be hairy (*squalens*, 17), not to use pumice, and—at least implicitly—to have a *vultus gravis* instead of the festive expression of a libertine. Thus, as Naevolus falls out of his groomed socialite role, he oddly approximates a rough Roman ancestor. His "old" self may have been groomed and decadent, the epitome of modernity, but his situation has *turned* him into something that looks old and out of place.

His appearance at the opening of *Satire* 9 thus seems, humorously, to follow naturally on the end of *Satire* 8. In that poem Juvenal ended his lecture advising his Roman addressee to accept that playing the ancestry card will ultimately lead him back to Romulus's ragtag crew of immigrants: "the first ancestor of your family, whoever he was, was either a herdsman or something I don't want to name" (*maiorum primus, quisquis fuit ille, tuorum/aut pastor fuit aut illud quod dicere nolo*, 274–75). The last part of the last line is particularly suggestive as a transition to the next poem, or even a prompt for it. Perhaps the ancestor conjured by *illud quod dicere nolo* is represented by the strange figure (of "unspeakable" profession) who next walks onto Juvenal's satiric scene. Moreover, just before this tantalizing ending, the satirist has mentioned a significant mythological figure as another hypothetical base ancestor: Thersites, the paradigmatic social critic (269–71). Having ended this poem with a vague gesture to unknown base or scurrilous ancestors, Juvenal immediately provides a colorfully drawn character to fill that role in the shaggy figure who burns with rage and longs for his old powers.

In his complaints, as just noted, Naevolus resembles the late-career Horace—one satiric "ancestor." But his looks suggest both the early Juvenal and—still more "ancient"—the generic father figure whom he claims to follow.[44] The Roman convention of referring to ancestors as shaggy extends to literary forebears: the Saturnian meter, the *Annals* of Ennius, and a number of republican orators are all figured in this way.[45] Moreover, in Juvenal's lifetime, there was a visual reminder of the nostalgic cachet of literal shagginess in Hadrian's adoption of a beard;[46] such contrived "authenticity" could have served as another model for Juvenal's portrait of his angry has-been. Naevolus's physical traits make him appear connected to an idealized and unattainable past. This continues the pattern developed in *Satires* 7 and 8, in which the victims of society resemble antique curiosities. Combining the ideas of literary tradition and genealogy, Naevolus looks as awkward and out of place as the *diserti* and ancestor images did in juxtaposition with the "new" satirist. In this light, the book begins to look more and more like an exploration not just of the idea of change but also of the mixed consequences of veneration of the past.

The prostitute in fact rather exaggerates his "ancient" status, adopting an air of old-fashioned frugality when he makes his absurd prayer near the poem's end. His household gods are small and modest, as are his bits of incense and garlands; the grain he sprinkles at the altar is an offering associated with the humble beginnings of Roman religious practice (*o parvi nostrique Lares, quos ture minuto/aut farre et tenui soleo exorare corona*, 137–38; cf. Ov. *Fast.* 3.3.284; Cato *Agr.* 134.1).[47] As if anticipating Juvenal's advice to offer simple sacrifices and humble prayers at the end of *Satire* 10, Naevolus seems to be reaching for prosperity through an affected, old-fashioned rite. We are left to speculate about the outcome of his attempt to renew himself.

In contrast to the disembodied voice that represents "Juvenal"—which has its aesthetic advantages—Naevolus is a horrid spectacle, an extreme

---

[44.]Persius also interweaves the ideas of age and antiquity in a literary-historical framework; see Keane, *Figuring Genre*, 125–27.

[45.]See, e.g., Hor. *Ep.* 2.1.157–58 (*horridus ille/ defluxit numerus Saturnius*), Ov. *Tr.* 2.259 (*nihil est hirsutius [Annalibus]*), and Quint. *Inst.* 12.10.10 on a list of republican orators who, representing the taste of their times, practiced *horrida genera dicendi*.

[46.]On Hadrian's beard and the style he inspired, see Hardie, "Juvenal, Domitian, and Hadrian," 118 n. 8; Anderson, "Juvenal: Evidence on 117–28"; and Zanker, *Mask of Socrates*, 198–266. I thank Judith Evans-Grubbs for suggesting the connection to me. Courtney remarks that in *Satire* 4 Juvenal erroneously regards the beard, a current "fashion," as "a symbol of pristine virtue" (*Satires*, 31).

[47.]I thank Kim Bowes for pointing out the affected traditionalism of Naevolus's offerings.

version of the early Juvenal (shouting, scribbling, burning) and his visible proxies.[48] At the same time, he is not purely a negative exemplum advertising the folly of angry satire. He clearly reaps benefits that his counterparts in *Satires* 7 and 8 do not; victimhood has come a long way since the book began. Naevolus is allowed, even encouraged, to enjoy the therapy of transgressive speech. Even his noted resemblance to Marsyas may be read as representing a kind of power. A statue of the doomed satyr stood in the Roman Forum near the praetor's tribunal, a default symbol of civic authority and supervision who at the same time strikes a carefree pose.[49] The fact that Naevolus enjoys *libertas* in the service of certain traditional social values in *Satire* 9 means he may imitate both sides of Marsyas, the establishment symbol and the rogue. It could even be a mutually beneficial move that Juvenal (in the fiction of the poem) betrays his interlocutor's confidence by recording this dialogue as a text. Juvenal may be using him for *materia*, but Naevolus has had an opportunity to ventilate. As dubious as his credentials may seem through a moral lens, Naevolus still proves to be a meaningful ancestor for the satirist and for any Roman who would admire free-speaking satire.

He even gets the last word in the book, without any follow-up ironizing from his interlocutor. After uttering his last-ditch prayer for the "necessities" (really luxury goods) he needs to live, Naevolus bitterly attributes his failure to the malice of heaven: "whenever I call on Fortune, she applies wax borrowed from that ship that escaped the Sicilian songs thanks to its deaf oarsmen" (*cum pro me Fortuna vocatur,/adfixit ceras illa de nave petitas/quae Siculos cantus effugit remige surdo*, 148–50). Fortune blocks her ears like Odysseus's crew sailing past the Sirens. It is possible to see in this passage one last sign of Naevolus's unrealistic expectations, and—in the Homeric allusion—a final sign of his pretension.[50] But lurking within that is also the traditional abjection of the mocking poet, and—in the Homeric allusion—a suggestion that Naevolus proudly identifies himself as a blame poet. That is because the Sirens to whom Naevolus likens himself are singers who cause harm, just as satirists are said to

---

[48.]Naevolus is a "master-image" that develops the theme of the "disfigurement" of Roman *virtus* from *Satire* 8 (Henderson, *Figuring Out Roman Nobility*, 96).

[49.]On the symbolism of the statue, see Serv. *A.* 3.20 and 4.58. At *S.* 1.6.120, Horace remarks that he is never obligated to rise early and "report to Marsyas" (*obeundus Marsya*; cf. Porphyrio's gloss). Because provincial towns with the *ius Italicum* received copies of this statue, Gowers (*Horace: Satires Book 1*, 247) suggests that Horace's Marsyas "might . . . be considered a mascot of satirical *libertas*."

[50.]Braund, *Beyond Anger*, 156.

cause pain and their iambographer ancestors allegedly drove their victims to suicide.[51]

The Sirens allusion should also remind us, however, that Naevolus has had the special privilege of voicing his indignation, and that for our part, we have been listening all along. Perhaps that is because the Sirens' song works by being appealing—by singing what people like Odysseus want to hear. In Book 1, Juvenal's reader is trained to attend to and enjoy the angry complaints of the abject persona. While Book 3 trains the same reader to enjoy a different Juvenal, it also produces regular reminders of the old mode, compelling in its own way, in the low but steady hum of indignation in *Satires* 7 and 8. As the bubbling rage of society's victims is kept on view and in check, a reader's taste for that rage may continue to be cultivated. Some readers may even find themselves missing the angry Juvenal. And as Juvenal reminds Naevolus, Rome is not running out of reprobates (130–33); the stimuli for angry satire remain.

It was claimed in *Satire* 1, after all, that anger is part of satire's heritage—that it made the satire of Lucilius great; that it is heroic; that it makes a difference. Seneca argues otherwise, but Seneca—while his influence enriches and complicates Juvenal's engagement with *indignatio*—is not the father of Juvenal's genre. If Juvenal leaves anger behind, then, he is doing something different than embracing Senecan ethics. He is abandoning a characteristic that he had claimed was fundamental to his genre. Old-fashioned perhaps—morally suspect perhaps—but part of satire's beginnings. And in Roman culture especially, one does not just reject beginnings.

Thus the Juvenal of Book 3, the "transitional" book, manages to have it both ways. These three poems are not simply a demonstration of how far the satirist has come. All the holding back that is represented in the restrained sermons of *Satires* 7 and 8 is balanced by the chafing, indignant characters glimpsed in those poems and finally by the more successful Naevolus in 9. Readers who have taken all this in have to decide whether to appreciate Juvenal's experiments in more indirect mockery and philosophical stances—taking what we could call a "progressive" view—or to adopt a "nostalgic" view, prompted by some of the moral commentary in the poems and by their memory of how satisfying *indignatio* could be. While the former view is echoed in some critical assessments, the latter

---

[51.]Rosen, *Making Mockery*, 228.

has support in satire's overall nostalgic posture and its championing of its origins in republican outspokenness, *libertas*. The changes that Juvenal works in Book 3 greatly enrich the genre; new and different satire becomes part of satire's history. But even the progress to a more refined future can be accompanied by a sense of loss.

CHAPTER 4 | Considering Tranquility

BEFORE SATIRE SCHOLARS IDENTIFIED multiple Juvenalian personae, they were talking about two Juvenals. The second, "mellower" one, who sounded "unechte" to Ribbeck, emerges at the beginning of Book 4 and produces "quieter . . . more philosophical, more ironic, more urbane" verse than we have seen previously.[1] The musings about the drawbacks of power and wealth that open *Satire* 10 suggest a new, more contemplative persona. This seems to be confirmed when Juvenal goes on to cite an ancient moral authority on the folly of human aspirations, the "laughing philosopher" Democritus (28–35):

> iamne igitur laudas quod de sapientibus alter
> ridebat, quotiens a limine moverat unum
> protuleratque pedem, flebat contrarius auctor?
> sed facilis cuivis rigidi censura cachinni;
> mirandum est unde ille oculis suffecerit umor.
> perpetuo risu pulmonem agitare solebat
> Democritus, quamquam non essent urbibus illis
> praetextae, trabeae, fasces, lectica, tribunal.

Now do you approve of the way one of the pair of philosophers used to laugh every time he set foot off his threshold, while the authority of the opposite disposition would weep? But the censure [consisting] of a harsh laugh is easy for anyone; it's just a wonder how the other guy could keep his eyes supplied with tears. Democritus used to shake his

---

[1.]"Mellower" is Highet's term (*Juvenal the Satirist*, 138); the longer quotation is from Singleton, "Juvenal's Fifteenth Satire," 198.

sides with constant laughter, even though cities in his day didn't have purple-bordered togas, equestrians' robes, rods of office, sedan chairs, and tribunals.

The contrast made in lines 28 through 32 was a well-worn literary motif by Juvenal's day: the first thinker, Democritus of Abdera, is said to have laughed at life, while the other, Heraclitus of Ephesus, was the "weeping philosopher."[2] In this admired frontspiece of his most beloved and most imitated poem,[3] Juvenal focuses on Democritus as the example to learn from (47–53):

> tum quoque materiam risus invenit ad omnis
> occursus hominum, cuius prudentia monstrat
> summos posse viros et magna exempla daturos
> vervecum in patria crassoque sub aere nasci.
> ridebat curas nec non et gaudia volgi,
> interdum et lacrimas, cum Fortunae ipse minaci
> mandaret laqueum mediumque ostenderet unguem.

Even back then, he found cause for laughter in all human goings-on—a case of sound thinking that demonstrates great men and fine examples can indeed be born in the land of muttonheads, where the air is dull. Democritus used to laugh at the mob's worries and joys alike, and even at their tears, all the while telling Fortune to hang herself and flipping her the middle finger.

To generations of readers and scholars, the Democritus passage has looked like a signal of Juvenal's own new worldview and approach to satire. There are certainly textual clues that suggest a self-referential agenda. First, Juvenal explicitly imagines the philosopher being transported from his own time to contemporary Rome to observe the ridiculous display of folly at the opening of the *ludi Romani* (36–46). Democritus is employed as a fresh and defamiliarizing lens through which the satirist and his readers can view the familiar procession of magistrates and their retinues. As

---

[2] The opposition could not have been staged or cultivated by the two philosophers, as the traditional *floruit* for Heraclitus is ca. 500 B.C.E. and Democritus's birth about forty years later. Their pairing was a Hellenistic invention. See Halliwell, *Greek Laughter*, 345.

[3] The poem has proved to have a uniquely "*transferable* seriousness" (Hooley, *Roman Satire*, 123–24), leading to imitations such as Johnson's *The Vanity of Human Wishes* (see Hooley, "Imperial Satire Reiterated," 355–57).

Horace had transported Democritus to an artistically degraded Roman the-
ater (*Ep.* 2.1.194–200) and Seneca had planted Hieronymus of Rhodes in
front of a magistrate's angry theatrics (*Ira* 1.19.3), now Juvenal appro-
priates the Abderite's vision—insightful even for a "muttonhead" from
Thrace. Second, Juvenal likens the object of Democritus's gaze to the
stuff of satire, recalling in lines 47–48 the *quidquid agunt homines* epi-
gram from *Satire* 1.[4] The material is the same, but the scribbling *iratus* is
replaced with a philosopher of unruffled and amused demeanor. Finally,
in the closing passage Juvenal declares that "the one and only path to the
tranquil life undoubtedly lies through virtue" (*semita certe/tranquillae per
virtutem patet unica vitae*, 363–64). He may be nodding to Democritus's
book on how to achieve "tranquility" (Greek *euthumia*).[5] A fourth clue can
be seen where Juvenal gives the brush-off to Fortune in the poem's last
two lines, seeming to mimic the image of Democritus giving *Fortuna* the
finger (52).

So, too, in the rest of *Satire* 10, many readers have found suggestions of
a "Democritean" emotional perspective. There is the systematic mockery
of all human ambitions: people who pray for success in politics, oratory,
or military conquest, or who wish for long life or beauty, are courting
an unhappy fate. The orderly treatment gives the impression of contem-
plative calm.[6] There is the fact that *Satire* 10 touches less on humanity's
vices and failings (potential causes for anger) than on the pure folly of
action. Juvenal's moral arguments are conventional, his illustrations the
stuff of moral and rhetorical education, his commentary reminiscent of
philosophical literature from Cicero to Seneca.[7] These elements convinced

---

[4] Compare *quidquid agunt homines, votum timor ira voluptas/gaudia discursus, nostri farrago
libelli est* (1.85–86) to *tum quoque materiam risus invenit ad omnis/occursus hominum* (10.47–48)
and *ridebat curas nec non et gaudia volgi/ interdum et lacrimas* (10.51–52). The list of Roman
politicians' trappings (10.35) also fits this pattern; see Keane, "Theatre, Spectacle, and Satirist,"
14. Cf. Hendrickson, "*Satura Tota Nostra Est*," 55, and Plaza, *Function of Humour*, 34–35 (where
10.31, *sed facilis cuivis . . .*, is called a "positive counterpart" to *difficile est saturam non scribere*
at 1.30). The term *materia* (10.47) is sometimes used to refer to literary subject matter (e.g., Cic.
Inv. 1.5.17, *Off.* 1.5.16, *Q. fr.* 1.2.1, *Att.* 2.12.13; Hor. *Ars* 38), though of course it can also denote
objects of mockery (e.g., *materiam iocorum*, Juv. 3.147).
[5] On Democritus's lost *On Cheerfulness (Peri Euthumias)*, see DK 68 [55] B 2c-4 (=Diels,
Fragmente der Vorsokratiker, 2:132–33). The philosopher is cited for these views at Sen. *Ira*
2.10.5 and *Tranq.* 2.3, 13.1, and 15.2. Cf. Courtney, *Satires*, 450, on other relevant Democritean
fragments.
[6] De Decker (*Juvenalis declamans*, 84) notes the comparative orderliness of the poem's structure
and use of exempla.
[7] On the satirist's exempla and correspondences with declamation, see Van der Poel, "Use of
Exempla." On parallels for the poem's theme and specific reflections in Cicero and Seneca, see
Rebert, "Literary Influence of Cicero," and Dick, "Seneca and Juvenal 10."

Anderson that "*ratio* (4) . . . governs the insights of the satirist, like the *prudentia* (48) which defines Democritus' character," and that "Democritean" tendencies could be seen in the rest of Book 4: in *Satires* 11 and 12, "the satirist clearly speaks with the voice of *ratio*," with subjects that once prompted anger now becoming "vehicle[s] for . . . Democritean *cachinnus*."[8] Assessments like these support the larger narrative of Juvenal's gradual rejection of anger.

But a little prodding produces significant cracks in this neat interpretation of Book 4, *Satire* 10, and the Democritus vignette itself. For one thing, if Juvenal is criticizing Heraclitus's tears, this is not necessarily the same as rejecting anger. If it were, there would still be another problem: we would be looking at the anger-rejecting persona not as the artificial construction that it is but as a commentator somehow outside the drama of satire, judging the earlier persona along with us. Yet the new satiric persona is surely no less a part of the satiric fiction than its angry counterpart. To appreciate this, it is helpful to consider the unique take of Bellandi on the "two Juvenals." Eschewing persona theory entirely, Bellandi offers a mirror image of persona studies' conclusions: Juvenal's early indignation reflects his special and authentic approach to satire, while the Democritean attitude represents a conventional mask, a concession to the precedent of earlier satirists and more recent moralists. Furthermore, Juvenal only partially succeeds in his attempt to perform this new "ethic of indifference," occasionally letting indignation slip through.[9] For all its biographizing flaws, Bellandi's approach has two very important merits. First, it urges us to view a Democritean persona—if we believe in its existence—as something artificial (albeit by means of an unsound contrast; even if Juvenal felt personally compelled to write "angry" satire, he still needed a mask to do it). Second, Bellandi's reading points up the difference between what we may call a prescriptive programmatic statement and a descriptive one. Even the most explicit declaration of program does not automatically equal execution of that program. It is important for Juvenal's readers to

---

[8.]Anderson, "Programs of Later Books," 157 (=*Essays*, 289). Also on *Satire* 10, see Bartsch, "Persius, Juvenal, and Stoicism," 236 ("the entire Satire . . . is a singularly consistent representation of views found in . . . Seneca"—a figure who is incidentally killed off, so to speak, in the opening lines), and Dick, "Seneca and Juvenal 10," 243 (the "philosophy" of the concluding *mens sana* passage "is Democritean, Seneca, Juvenalian, humanistic"). On the rest of the book, see also Anderson, "Anger in Juvenal," 194 (=*Essays*, 360). Braund adds that "Democritean *tranquillitas* is mentioned explicitly as the goal of life [at the end of 10] and the same is implied in *Satires* 11 and 12" (*Beyond Anger*, 184)

[9.]Bellandi, *Etica diatribica* (especially 66–101).

come to the "post-Democritean" part of Book 4 without having made premature conclusions about its style.

The seductive Siren that is the laughing philosopher (with the attitude tendentiously described as "easy for anyone," *facilis cuivis*, 31) can all too easily keep us from noticing the text's complex ideas and tensions, even from asking basic questions.[10] Is the nonverbal laughter represented in the Democritus vignette an appropriate symbol of literary satire? (The most obvious precedent, Persius's *cachinno* at 1.12, is only a prelude to dazzlingly intricate poetry.) Does the Democritean perspective demonstrably operate throughout all three poems? Certainly, if we equate "Democritus" roughly with "humor" or "mockery" (sidestepping the nuanced definition of Democritean humor reconstructed by Halliwell),[11] we can comfortably answer yes to both questions. As evidence, scholars cite the famous Juvenalian quips that decorate *Satire* 10: the description of the conversion of Sejanus's statues into "little pitchers, basins, saucepans, and chamber-pots" (64), the identification of the people's interests as "bread and circuses" (81), the quotation of an unfortunate verse of Cicero's on his consulship (122), and the exhortation to the doomed Hannibal to go off and "make boys happy by becoming a declamation" (167).[12] *Satires* 11 and 12 have similar moments. But irreverent quips, bathos, and grotesque defamiliarization are nothing new in Juvenal; they are not evidence of a specifically Democritean program. Nor do we have real evidence for the "rationality" or "tranquility" of either Book 4 or *Satire* 10. In fact, when scholars concentrate on cultural themes instead of persona in reading *Satire* 10, they have tended to characterize the poem as dark, unnerving, disturbing, and extremist.[13] I hope to show that there is an inherent incompatibility between the perspective represented at 10.28–53 and the execution of the rest of *Satire* 10, and that this and the two subsequent poems perform something very different than simple "illustration of program."

The laughing Democritus is not so much a symbol for Juvenal as a spectacle. Neither admiring nor antagonistic, Juvenal objectifies Democritus in

---

[10.]This problem is recognized by Walker ("Juvenal's Later Books," 36) and Iddeng ("Juvenal, Satire, and Persona," 122–24).

[11.]See Halliwell, *Greek Laughter*, 343–71.

[12.]For surveys of these "Democritean" qualities in *Satire* 10, see Eichholz, "Art of Juvenal," and Lawall, "*Exempla* and Theme."

[13.]Nussbaum finds the humor of *Satire* 10 "not precisely funny," but "dark" and akin to what she calls "Stoic laughter" in its rejection of earthly goods ("Stoic Laughter," 102–3). Cf. Uden, *Invisible Satirist*, 159-69. (I was fortunate to encounter Uden's work before its publication and in the midst of my own work on *Satire* 10; it will be clear that my analysis is in lockstep with his on certain points.)

order to begin an exploration of his real utility to a Roman satirist. Under the neat and organized surface of *Satire* 10 is ambivalence, immoderation, and disruption—with regard to Roman social values and the idea of prayer, to begin with.[14] Juvenal also undermines the very idea of detached mockery once he has appeared to champion it. If we are open to these possibilities, *Satire* 10 and Book 4 become not just better illuminated but much more interesting to read.

Democritus on Display

What does it mean for Juvenal to call Democritus an exemplum (49) at the beginning of a long examination of exempla? And what might Democritus have in common with the assorted historical and mythical characters that Juvenal presents throughout *Satire* 10? For one thing, the philosopher is being remembered as an outsized figure. This is typical for ancient philosophers; many are included in Valerius Maximus's nine-book catalog *Memorable Deeds and Sayings*, and among them is Democritus, remembered for his extraordinary dedication to study and his self-mastery (8.7.ext.4, 8.14.ext.2). But Juvenal is clearly highlighting other attributes in his caricature. In the pieces of the portrait that bookend lines 28 through 52 of *Satire* 10, the Abderite is colorfully drawn in the acts of stepping over his threshold, shaking his sides with laughter, and giving the finger to Fortune. This is a social critic that Juvenal wants his readers to observe and critique in turn, not just a lens that transmits the spectacle of society to them.[15]

Juvenal stresses that Democritus found cause for laughter in *all* human occupations (*omnis/occursus hominum*, 47–48). As portrayed here, the philosopher is a very reductive interpreter. This idea is not Juvenal's invention: it is also manifested in the pseudepigraphica of Hippocrates that concern Democritus, an instructive source. *Letters* 10 through 17 concern the author's journey to Abdera, whose troubled populace has asked him to cure Democritus of his evident madness—manifested in constant laughter

---

[14]Fishelov compellingly argues that our interpretation of the satire "should be less bound to the aphorism-like form of the concluding lines and more open to Juvenal's exuberant mind; less committed to the reconstruction of a coherent 'philosophical' argument and more sensitive to the dynamics of the text-continuum and its effects on the reader" ("Vanity of Reader's Wishes," 372).

[15]For a reading of the passage within theatrical discourse in the *Satires*, including a comparison with the Horatian model, see Keane, "Theatre, Spectacle, and Satirist," 269–73.

"at everything, large and small."[16] Confronting Democritus, "Hippocrates" expresses deep moral concern about the interpretation of all human affairs—good and bad, joyful and tragic—as material for laughter. His letters emphasize how disturbing this perspective can seem to observers. When rehearsing for his meeting with Democritus, he imagines himself saying "when people are sick, being killed, dead, besieged, subject to any evil, everything that happens to them is matter for laughter for you" (*Ep.* 14).[17] At their meeting, he develops this point (*Ep.* 17.4):

'ἢ οὐκ οἴει ἄτοπός γε εἶναι γελῶν ἀνθρώπου θάνατον ἢ νοῦσον ἢ παρακοπὴν ἢ μανίην ἢ μελαγχολίην ἢ σφαγὴν ἢ ἄλλο τι χέρειον ἢ τοὔμπαλιν γάμους ἢ πανηγύριας ἢ τεκνογονίην ἢ μυστήρια ἢ ἀρχὰς καὶ τιμὰ ἢ ἄλλο τι ὅλως ἀγαθόν; καὶ γὰρ ἃ δέον οἰκτείρειν γελῇς καὶ ἐφ᾽ οἷσιν ἥδεσθαι χρή, καταγελᾷς τούτων, ὥστε μήτε ἀγαθὸν μήτε κακὸν παρά σοι διακεκρίσθαι.' "

"Don't you think you are outlandish to laugh at a man's death or illness, or delusion, or madness, or melancholy, murder, or something still worse, or again at marriages, feasts, births, initiations, offices and honors, or anything else wholly good? Things that demand grief you laugh at, and when things should bring happiness you laugh at them. There is no distinction between good and bad with you."[18]

"Hippocrates" dwells on the alarming sight of an antisocial and unproductive Democritus and on the impression of amorality that his laughter gives. Democritus is a paradox: immoderate as he appears, his life's work adds up to the promotion of *ratio*. The divide between Democritus's image as a madman and the wisdom he actually possesses—a divide that Halliwell argues was basically caused by the philosopher's own methods[19]—is the main theme of this series of letters. The Abderite eventually demonstrates his deep wisdom to "Hippocrates," after being confronted about its off-putting manifestation. This paradoxical Democritus, who is more

---

[16.]Hp. *Ep.* 10.321. The Democritus letters can only be roughly dated to the late Hellenistic or early imperial periods; see Smith, *Hippocrates: Pseudepigraphic Writings*, 20–29.

[17.]"Δημόκριτε, καὶ νοσέοντος καὶ κτεινομένου καὶ τεθνεῶτος καὶ πολιορκουμένου καὶ παντὸς ἐμπίπτοντος κακοῦ ἕκαστον τῶν πρησσομένων ὕλη σοι γέλωτος ὑπόκειται." I use Smith's translation (*Hippocrates: Pseudepigraphic Writings*, 67).

[18.]Smith, *Hippocrates: Pseudepigraphic Writings*, 79.

[19.]Halliwell, *Greek Laughter*, 360–64.

than meets the eye (if the eye is observing the laugher), is essential to the program of *Satire* 10.

It is easy to overlook the abrasive and unnerving qualities of Democritus if we write another important character out of Juvenal's vignette—the "other guy," who wept at all human affairs (28–30, 32). Heraclitus of Ephesus's writings addressed a wide range of ethical and physical topics, yet he is everywhere plugged into the "opposites" topos as a symbol of unrelenting melancholy. The double caricature, though artificial and ahistorical, had a life of its own in antiquity and its reception.[20] The key meanings of the topos, in Juvenal and elsewhere, are that the two figures are defined by one another, that they each represent an extreme attitude, and that both their attitudes are technically justifiable by the conditions of human life. In other words, there is much more to the conventional representation of this pair than an exposure of a "wrong" attitude and selection of the "right" one. Juvenal's question for the reader is "do you not approve of Democritus and Heraclitus, those wise men, of whom one laughed whenever he set foot out of doors, and the other wept?" (28–30).[21] *Quod . . . ridebat* and *quod . . . flebat* parallel one another; the satirist neither immediately approves of nor immediately dismisses either "philosophy."

This equivocation characterizes many other instances of the Democritus-Heraclitus topos. The philosophers come across as two sides of the same coin—a reflection of their ironic interdependence as symbols in literary tradition. Seneca invokes the two in this way at *Ira* 2.10.5, while arguing the irrationality of anger. Heraclitus pitied and wept at everything he saw, while Democritus could not take a single thing seriously; the Stoic's conclusion is "what room is there here for anger, if everything calls

---

[20.]The relevant Senecan passages are discussed below. Other caricatures of the pair include the quotation from Sotion at Stob. 3.20.53; *AP* 9.148 (discussed in the next paragraph); Lucian *Vit. Auct.* 13–14; Robert Burton's *Anatomy of Melancholy* (1621); the painting by the Baroque artist Hendrick ter Brugghen; and the similar Bramante work on this book's cover. Cf. Lutz, "Democritus and Heraclitus." Seneca, like Juvenal, refers specifically to the passions of the crowd as Democritus's target (*Tranq.* 15.2: *omnia vulgi vitia non invisa nobis, sed ridicula videantur*). This is not a purely Stoic perspective: Democritus was a favorite of Cynics, including in Juvenal's day; see Uden, *Invisible Satirist*, 160. Democritus's prescription for *euthumia* may have become associated with *gelōs* and satiric mockery, and contrasted with a caricature of Heraclitus, by mocking diatribists (see Lutz, "Democritus and Heraclitus," 311). Finally, much ancient testimony about the two men actually undermines the "laughing/weeping" dichotomy; Halliwell's extensive discussion (see n. 11 above) shows how poorly the caricatures fit the other evidence. Cf. Kaster and Nussbaum, *Lucius Annaeus Seneca*, 112–13 n. 156, and Wright, "Ferox Virtus," 170–71 (where it is noted that Heraclitus stands out among pre-Hellenistic philosophers for his staunch criticism of anger as a purposeless passion).

[21.]Translation by Eichholz ("Art of Juvenal," 65).

either for laughter or tears?" (*ubi istic irae locus est? aut ridenda omnia aut flenda sunt*).[22] Seneca uses the caricature to highlight two analogous alternatives to anger, not emotional stances that should be judged relative to one another.

A poetic version of this point can be seen in poem 9.148 of the *Greek Anthology*, where—as in Juvenal—the two philosophers are resurrected to observe contemporary life (1–4):

> τὸν βίον, Ἡράκλειτε, πολὺ πλέον, ἤπερ ὅτ᾽ ἔζης,
> δάκρυε· νῦν ὁ βίος ἔστ᾽ ἐλεεινότερος.
> τὸν βίον ἄρτι γέλα, Δημόκριτε, τὸ πλέον ἢ πρίν·
> νῦν ὁ βίος πάντων ἐστὶ γελοιότερος.

> Heraclitus, weep at life much more than you did while alive, for now life is more pitiable. Democritus, laugh at life more than before, for now life is more laughable than anything.

The emotional responses of both philosophers are both equally justified and equally strange, as the poet concludes: "looking upon the two of you, I'm uncertain as to how I can weep with the one, and how I can laugh with the other," (εἰς ὑμέας δὲ καὶ αὐτὸς ὁρῶν τὸ μεταξὺ μεριμνῶ/ πῶς ἅμα σοὶ κλαύσω, πῶς ἅμα σοὶ γελάσω, 5–6). The poem illustrates the true point of the Democritus-Heraclitus topos: that the troubles of humankind are real, that laughter and tears are the most extreme possible emotional reactions to these troubles, and that both these reactions are at once understandable and troubling.[23]

Some ancient treatments, to be sure, express a preference for Democritus's laughter. The Hippocrates of the pseudepigraphica explains (*Ep.* 17.5–10) that in the end, Democritus presented him with an irrefutable self-defense (though one can look in vain for the logic in his argument). Plutarch employs Democritus as a weapon in polemic against Stoic and Epicurean views; the Abderite seems to be an all-purpose tool.[24] Seneca,

---

[22.]Translation by Cooper and Procopé (*Seneca*, 50).

[23.]*AP* 9.148 "does not merely juxtapose the mentalities of these contrasting figures but intimates that they are easily yet perplexingly reversible." Much like at Juv. 10.30, incidentally, "the lack of a connective particle between the first two couplets accentuates the opposition: look one way, it gestures, and see things in this light; look the other, and the reverse is seemingly just as compelling. The choice is undecidable" (Halliwell, "Greek Laughter," 124–25). Lucian also emphasizes the symmetry between the two men and dismisses both philosophers as equally ridiculous (*Vit. Auct.* 13–14).

[24.]Hershbell, "Plutarch and Democritus," 98–103.

when elaborating on the goal of *tranquillitas* that the "real" Democritus promoted, argues, "let us imitate Democritus rather than Heraclitus . . . it is more civilized to laugh at life than to lament it" (*Democritum potius imitemur quam Heraclitum . . . humanius est deridere vitam quam deplorare, Tranq.* 15.2). This is generally understood to be Juvenal's view of the pair, since the satirist makes Democritus his primary focus and praises his *prudentia*. But this interpretation requires us to overlook the equivocal judgment Juvenal makes on Democritus and Heraclitus when he first introduces them: he begins by contemplating both, then stages his choice of model.[25] This may be because the pair of lines in question is difficult to understand: "but the censure [consisting] of a harsh laugh is easy for anyone; it's just a wonder how the other guy could keep his eyes supplied with tears" (*sed facilis cuivis rigidi censura cachinni;/mirandum est unde ille oculis suffecerit umor*, 31–32). Commentary after commentary is silent on the precise senses of *facilis cuivis* and *mirandum est*.[26] But the sense of the couplet as a whole seems much closer to that of the Greek epigram than that of the *On Tranquility* passage. Like the poet, Juvenal admits that a Heraclitus would find plenty of *materia lacrimarum* in this world. That he calls the Democritean *cachinnus* "easy" does not mean that it is more natural, more justified, or "easier" on onlookers, but that it requires less effort—and perhaps that it *feels* better. Meanwhile, he gives the other side a hearing, albeit a brief one.

In sum, the philosophers vignette does not introduce a "right" and a "wrong" thinker but instead introduces a particular perspective on the "chosen" thinker of the two—whose popular image is as likely to alarm as to charm onlookers. Juvenal and his ancient audience must have been aware of a more complex version of Democritus and his philosophical aims, a version that survived both in fragments of Democritus's work and in other testimonia. Yet with one stroke, the satirist produces the caricature and absorbs Democritus into the exemplary discourse of *Satire* 10. This seems to be an invitation to look critically at this Democritus, and even to consider him as fallible, like the other exempla that fill the rest of the poem. In all those other cases, the satirist's task is to point out that *magna*

---

[25] Eichholz briefly acknowledges this in "Art of Juvenal," 65: "are we to weep . . . with Heraclitus, or [laugh] with Democritus? The answer is that it is legitimate to do either, but easier by far to laugh." But he concludes that ("needless to say") Juvenal chooses to align himself with Democritus. It is also rare to see scholars acknowledging a "Heraclitean" perspective in any of the vignettes, but see Lawall, "*Exempla* and Theme," and Romano, *Irony in Juvenal*, 159.

[26] Campana (*Iuvenalis Satira X*, 102–4), like many previous commentators, focuses on the meaning of *cachinnus*.

exempla are not always what they seem. In this case, Democritus's fallibility would affect his suitability as a model for satire, especially *this* satire. This is the point of the spectacle we are given: we are meant to look at it, revisit it, and keep asking whether and how it is relevant to the matters under discussion.

Beyond Laughter

The traditional approach to exempla in Roman moral writing, historiography, and rhetoric is incompatible with Democritean reductiveness—or, more accurately, the reductiveness of the "laughing Democritus." Exempla were valued as shared cultural capital, endowed with individual meanings, and preserved for contemplation in new contexts—in short, they represented a kind of specialized language within Roman moral discourse. As such, they were valued for their diversity and complexity. Even the exemplary history of Valerius Maximus, for all its resemblance to a catalog, demonstrates sensitivity to these qualities. Its very structure acknowledges that the same qualities or vices are best illustrated by many different exempla and suggests further that Roman and foreign ("external") exempla may have very different political or moral implications.[27] Irony is appreciated as well: Valerius Maximus recognizes that Hannibal eventually failed as a world-conqueror, that Alexander was doomed to die young, that Xerxes retreated to Persia with his tail between his legs, that the beauty and virtue of Lucretia and Verginia led to their deaths.[28] In a pose superficially analogous to that of Juvenal in *Satire* 10, Valerius Maximus claims to be living in an era of *tranquillitas* (thanks to Tiberius's sound rule) and looking back at a history of turmoil (8.13.pref.). Yet his professed contentment does not preclude engagement or nuanced evaluation. This makes it easier to see that Juvenal, despite his satiric, ironic perspective, takes a more or less conventional view on his chosen historical and mythical exempla.

Consequently, the juxtaposition of a laughing Democritus and an extended examination of traditional exempla represents a clash of

---

[27.]Valerius Maximus's organizational scheme is analyzed in Bloomer, *Valerius Maximus*; Lucarelli, *Exemplarische Vergangenheit*; and Skidmore, *Practical Ethics*.

[28.]Sample citations from Valerius Maximus on Hannibal: 1.7.ext.1 (on divine signs of his impending failure) and 9.8.ext.1 (on his rash decision-making). On Alexander: 1.7.ext.2 and 1.8.ext.10 (on warnings about his vulnerability). On Xerxes: 1.6.ext.1a (on a divine sign that he would become like a *fugax animal*). On the *pudicitia* (but implicitly also the beauty) of Lucretia and Verginia: 6.1.1–2.

programs. The language of exemplarity would not mean anything to a philosopher who views all human goings-on as an undifferentiated mass of absurdity, responding to it with a wordless laugh. The *cachinnus* does not exemplify the capacity or motivation to distinguish between things, the basic ability that the satirist praises and claims is scarce (specifically referring to the distinction between good and bad; 2–3). For his part, while Juvenal does use his catalog of doomed politicians, orators, conquerors, old fathers, and young beauties to promote one point—that ambition and success are perilous things—he needs each story to be understood on its own terms, not just sucked down a homogenizing drain.

This is a reasonable expectation to bring to the work of a satirist who was trained to perform *suasoriae* and other set speeches, and who possessed an extensive toolkit of rhetorical techniques—*Satire* 10 being recognized as outstanding proof.[29] Exempla are among these tools: a speaker needed to be able to choose and interpret useful exempla from literature and history, and Juvenal's chosen figures are in many cases identical to the moral exempla paraded in "serious" literature: epic, historiography, biography, moral essays, and the like.[30] Moreover, the skills developed in this practice added up to the very opposite of Democritean withdrawal. The intended purpose of the ubiquitous rhetorical training of the imperial period was to serve society's institutions, by inculcating core values in future elites and by helping them learn to engage in the relationships and negotiations that could define their adult lives.[31] The opposition in worldview between mainstream rhetoric and Democritean rejection of

---

[29.]Most recently, Hooley, "Rhetoric and Satire," 407–8 points to the numerous pithy *sententiae* that end vignettes and the tight structure built around multiple illustrations of the main theme. The poem's resemblance to a standard thesis, or "(treatment of a) general question," is analyzed in Walker, "Moralizing Discourse," 64–70. For a brief rhetorical "anatomy" of *Satire* 10, see Tengström, *Study of Tenth Satire*, 8–15; cf. de Decker, *Iuvenalis declamans*, 103–25. At the same time, de Decker (108–10) suspects Juvenal's extensive catalog would have displeased Seneca the Elder, who thought it excessive to comb the earth (*longe arcessere, Con.* 7.5.13) for exempla to illustrate a single theme.

[30.]On exempla in declamation, see the survey in Van der Poel, "Use of Exempla." Quintilian devotes some space to recommendations on effective use of exempla (*Inst.* 5.11) and notes that students also learn through imitation to produce their own moralizing aphorisms and vignettes (1.9).

[31.]As the core activity of the rhetorical schools, declamation is recognized to have been a critical vehicle of acculturation to elite society and to the role of advocate and *paterfamilias*. See, e.g., Bloomer, "Schooling in Persona"; Kaster, "Controlling Reason"; Gunderson, *Declamation, Paternity, and Identity*; and Connolly, *State of Speech*, 237–61. Quintilian stresses that the themes of school exercises should be as true-to-life as possible because the orator's skills will be employed in real-life situations (*Inst.* 2.10.4–9). On Juvenal' *suasoria* to Sulla recalled in *Satire* 1, Henderson writes: "[in performing declamations about generations-old subjects] each new pupil must feel afresh what it is like to hold the world at gunpoint" ("Pump Up the Volume," 25=*Writing Down Rome*, 269).

society has no better illustration than *Lesser Declamation* 283 attributed to Quintilian, in which an orator explains his disowning of a son who has become a Cynic.[32] Also antithetical to the Democritean *cachinnus*, and equally critical in the orator's arsenal, were emotional manipulation and the expression of sympathy.[33] The satirist and his contemporaries were conditioned to respond emotionally to the stuff of their own rhetorical education and of the professional declaimers' repertoire.

All of this points to the defining conundrum of *Satire* 10: the work of this poem could not be conducted under the Democritean model presented in its long proem. The difference can be seen not only between nonverbal laughter and rhetoric, or between unconcerned dismissal and moral interpretation, but also in the perspectives that generate these two agendas. Juvenal's satire requires and is enriched by a cultural memory that the laughing philosopher either does not share or does not acknowledge. This difference, and the other tensions just identified, must have been perceptible to the poem's original audience.

We can learn something about author and audience expectations—or at least affectations—regarding emotional responses to exempla from Valerius Maximus, who regularly covers first Roman, then foreign, examples of each idea or attribute. Speaking about variety in general, the author asserts that it is both pleasing (1.6.ext.pref.) and instructive (5.6.ext.5).[34] But what does he have to say about the role of closeness and distance in the use of exempla to teach? An ideal exemplum, Valerius Maximus writes, will be like a painting that affects the reader's mind even if its subject is old (5.4.ext.1). There is reason to believe, however, that the author of *Memorable Deeds and Sayings* has other reasons to look to the past and other cultures. In the lengthy but oblique digression on Sejanus, a figure evidently too recent and too upsetting even to merit an official entry as an exemplum, Valerius Maximus declares that he will gladly move on to

---

[32] The orator father opens sarcastically: "no doubt, we who frequent the forum and safeguard the dignity of the republic are fools" (*scilicet nos stulti qui forum celebramus, qui rei publicae dignitatem tuemur*, Quint. *Decl.* 283.1). This depends on *celebramus, qui* being the correct text; see Shackleton Bailey, *Quintilian: The Lesser Declamations*, 308.

[33] As Bloomer argues ("Schooling in Persona"), the student of rhetoric is trained to adopt and speak from his imaginary clients' perspectives, though not to imagine them as his equals; there is a difference between true fellow-feeling and the ability to express or garner sympathy. Still, as Quintilian makes perfectly clear (*Inst.* 6.2.2–6), the audience of a declamation expects to feel something, and it is the speaker's job to make this happen. According to Juvenal, even the most shallow and social-climbing father expected to hear convincing passion when his son belted out a *suasoria* to Hannibal, and the rhetoric teacher himself despaired when his students failed to be excited by their exercises (7.158–64).

[34] Cf. Skidmore, *Practical Ethics*, 83–92.

foreign cases of *dicta improba et facta scelerata*, because he can relate these "with calmer emotions" (*tranquilliore adfectu*, 9.11.ext.1). As contrived as this claim reads, it is evidence that the writer is (or thinks he should pretend to be) more touched by historically or culturally "closer" exempla than by remote ones. Juvenal, for his part, exploits both this notion and the idea that ancient exempla become relevant if they are vividly narrated. The result is another great irony: the satirist uses the tools of moral tradition and rhetoric to show that the appeal of laughter has its limits.

Democritus in Rome?

The series of vignettes in *Satire* 10 must be read with awareness that Democritus did not share the satirist's (and his audience's) feeling of identification with and cultural ownership of these stories. Juvenal makes this clear enough in the proem, highlighting another "extreme" attribute of Democritus: the philosopher comes from another world. This idea is more developed than it is in, for example, the passage from Horace's epistle to Augustus cited earlier. As Juvenal notes, "cities in [Democritus's] day didn't have purple-bordered togas, equestrians' robes, rods of office, sedan chairs, and tribunals" (*non essent urbibus illis/praetextae, trabeae, fasces, lectica, tribunal*, 34–35). The opening of the *Ludi Romani* (the *pompa circensis*) is in the following lines focalized through Democritus's eyes, dismantled into absurd and meaningless pieces. But line 35 does not just denote generic "modern" or even "Roman" sights to contrast with the philosopher's personal experience. These are specifically the trappings of Roman politics, and signify true and threatening power in the world of the *Satires* (e.g., the *lectica* containing a criminal who threatens the satirist's safety at 1.158–61). Democritus, the fifth-century B.C.E. Thracian, would have recognized the story of Milo of Croton that is briefly mentioned in the proem, but he did not know of Nero's victims, Sejanus, Cicero, Demosthenes, Hannibal, or Alexander, the exempla Juvenal covers in lines 15 through 174.[35]

[35.]Milo the athlete, alluded to in lines 10–11, died in the act of trying to split an oak tree; see Strabo 6.1.12. In 15–18, Juvenal mentions C. Cassius Longinus, Seneca, and Plautius Lateranus, all casualties of Nero's response to the Pisonian conspiracy: the first man was banished (Tac. *Ann.* 16.9.1, Pomponius *Dig.* 1.2.2.51), the second forced to commit suicide (Tac. *Ann.* 15.60–63), and the third executed (Tac. *Ann.* 15.60). These men died only around the beginning of Juvenal's life; their treatment in the *Annals* would have made them seem even more recent.

Democritus would have no investment in such episodes as culturally or morally meaningful. But *Satire* 10 would not exist if the opposite were not true for Juvenal and his contemporaries. This is most strikingly obvious in the case of the first story treated after the Democritus section, also the poem's best-known passage (56–113). Sejanus, praetorian prefect under Tiberius until he was charged with conspiracy, lived and died a generation before the Neronian figures already mentioned. But from Juvenal's perspective his story was hot off the press, told with dramatic suspense in the fourth and fifth books of Tacitus's *Annals*. Interestingly, the end of Sejanus's career also represents the starting point of Valerius Maximus's own backward-looking work, as is indicated in the Sejanian digression near the end of the last book. Two generations later, Tacitus's account surely helped Juvenal make Sejanus seem relevant in his day, even as his story was transforming into an "old" exemplum.[36] Sejanus is the perfect example of someone who learned all too well that *fasces* and the like could indeed affect his life.[37] A contemporary of Juvenal could hardly miss this. It is particularly significant that the story of Sejanus's spectacular fall heads up Juvenal's catalog: a reader might get the impression that the sermon from here on will concern itself with Roman examples, including the raw, the recent, and the political. One familiar with imperial-era "doublespeak" might even read Sejanus as an exportable cipher functioning in a more contemporary story.[38] After the invocation of the detached and apolitical Democritus, the circumstances of Sejanus's career and fall could appear especially frightening and immediate. For Valerius Maximus, the closeness of this example of a *factum sceleratum* is occasion for an explosion of emotion, which can only be eased by a retreat into external exempla.

As if confirming that he has access to plenty of fresh and disturbing material, Juvenal also ends his catalog with a Tacitean exemplum, creeping forward in time to boot. In lines 329 through 345, closing the section on ill-fated physical beauty, Juvenal tells the story of Gaius Silius, husband for a few hours to the empress Messalina and doomed to execution.

[36.]The Sejanus books of Tacitus's *Annals* certainly predated Juvenal's composition of his fourth book, if not earlier books (an argument for the latter chronology is made in Syme, "Juvenal, Pliny, Tacitus," 277; cf. 266–69).

[37.]Sejanus appears in Seneca's writings, but mainly as a symbol of abusive power (see his *Consolation for Marcia*). At *Ep.* 55.3, however, he also represents the risks of great wealth.

[38.]Imperial authors sometimes employed earlier stories as code to comment on contemporary affairs. See Bartsch, *Actors in the Audience*, 93, arguing for one example in Juvenal: the mention of the Neronian Tigellinus at 1.155. As Kirk Freudenburg suggests *per litteras*, the "fallen statue" theme in Juvenal's story of Sejanus might evoke the praise of Domitian's grand equestrian statue in Stat. *Silv.* 1.1.

This tale is told in *Annals* 11, where Tacitus (disingenuously) expresses disbelief that such a thing ever happened and embarrassment at having to relate it (11.27). For Juvenal, however, the story of Silius is neither unbelievable nor trivial but a valid illustration of his moral theme. It is also multivalent, and thus more sensitive a subject than a simple story of ill-fated beauty might be. Silius might be cited as a case of beauty leading to doom (*formonsissimus . . . miser extinguendus*, 331–32), but if we call a spade a spade, this is also a political drama—the illicit marriage of a consul-elect to the emperor's wife during the emperor's absence from Rome could hardly *not* be. Such was the thinking of members of the emperor's household, according to Tacitus (*Ann.* 11.28). Thus Silius actually brings the satire back to the topic of destructive ambition (in this case not entirely his will, Juvenal implies throughout). At the same time, his story picks up the theme of beauty that briefly surfaced in the Sejanus passage, where the crowd marveled at the prefect's ruined body (or perhaps his statues; see below): "what lips the man had! What a face! (*quae labra, quis illi/vultus erat!*, 67–68).[39] The two Tacitean bookends mirror one another, and just as the first follows on a vignette of Democritus, the second leads into a Democritean prescription, the recommendation of *tranquillitas*. Both stories certainly seem to illustrate everything a Cynic (or even just a cynic) would cite in an argument for nonparticipation in society's institutions. But Democritus, as Juvenal has made plain, would not share the uncomfortably close—and surely more conflicted—imperial Roman perspective of the satirist and his audience. If the philosopher could have laughed at these hideous stories, it would surely be because he was unfamiliar with their context. Thus he is even better off than the poor who, Juvenal notes at the beginning of the poem, have little to fear from the emperor's men ("it's rare for a soldier to storm a garret," *rarus venit in cenacula miles*, 18).

Though it is often cited for its irreverent perspective, Juvenal's account of Sejanus would better be called disturbing. The satirist could have taken the same tack as Valerius Maximus, addressing the ambitious prefect as a madman ("fiercer than the monstrousness of the savage barbarian world," *efferatae barbariae immanitate truculentior*, 9.11.ext.4) and asking him rhetorical questions about his expectations for himself and his aims for the empire. Instead, he chooses to relate the man's downfall from a frighteningly close-up view. Although Juvenal initially defamiliarizes the human

---

[39.]Because of these connections between the stories, I am reluctant to agree with Nappa that Juvenal's Silius account lacks the political dimension of Tacitus's ("Unfortunate Marriage of Silius," 199).

subject by replacing him with a statue, this hardly results in a humorous cast to the story (10.58–63):

> descendunt statuae restemque secuntur,
> ipsas deinde rotas bigarum inpacta securis
> caedit et inmeritis franguntur crura caballis.
> iam strident ignes, iam follibus atque caminis
> ardet adoratum populo caput et crepat ingens
> Seianus . . .

Statues fall, following the rope; then the ax smashes even the chariot wheels and cuts them down, and the legs of the guiltless nags are smashed. Now the flames hiss, now amid the bellows and furnace, that head that was the darling of the people burns and crackles, the great Seianus . . .

The close-up view of the fires that destroyed Sejanus's numerous statues dramatizes Sejanus's entrapment and punishment. Is this a strategy for taking the tragedy out of the story and identifying the comedy within? Or is it actually a subtler technique of confusing innuendo, wherein the satirist shifts back and forth between reference to inanimate objects and a flesh-and-blood man? Considering the quasi-human qualities of statues in previous *Satires*, experienced readers of Juvenal should be flinching. Sejanus's name is delayed, of course, and when it appears it is applied to the statue and not the man; perhaps this downplays the horror somewhat. A reader could relax into seeing that burned and broken-down object as a mere statue, and enjoy the famous deflating line about its conversion into common household objects (64). But surely the opposite effect is produced a few lines later with Juvenal's reverse move, this more macabre spectacle: "Sejanus is being dragged along by the hook for all to see!" (*Seianus ducitur unco/spectandus*, 66–67). There is no mistaking *this* for anything but a mutilated human body. It seems impossible, then, to label any part of the account as unambiguous comedy.[40]

The story Juvenal tells also undermines the idea of the emotionally detached observer. Imperial-era readers already knew that in an event like the fall of Sejanus, spectators become objects of scrutiny.[41] Juvenal plays up this point. A substantial digression, which does not cleanly illustrate the

---

[40] Keane, "Historian and Satirist," 420–23.
[41] Bartsch, *Actors in the Audience*, 1–35.

ostensible point about ambition, seems to have the function of demonstrating that people observing cataclysmic events do not always respond freely or genuinely. In the beginning, the satirist writes, just *reacting* to the fall of Sejanus was a delicate business (66–89):

> Seianus ducitur unco
> spectandus, gaudent omnes. 'quae labra, quis illi
> vultus erat! numquam, si quid mihi credis, amavi
> hunc hominem. sed quo cecidit sub crimine? quisnam
> delator, quibus indicibus, quo teste probauit?'   70
> 'nil horum; verbosa et grandis epistula venit
> a Capreis.' 'bene habet, nil plus interrogo.' sed quid
> turba Remi? sequitur fortunam, ut semper, et odit
> damnatos. idem populus, si Nortia Tusco
> favisset, si oppressa foret secura senectus   75
> principis, hac ipsa Seianum diceret hora
> Augustum. iam pridem, ex quo suffragia nulli
> vendimus, effudit curas; nam qui dabat olim
> imperium, fasces, legiones, omnia, nunc se
> continet atque duas tantum res anxius optat,   80
> panem et circenses. 'perituros audio multos.'
> 'nil dubium, magna est fornacula.' 'pallidulus mi
> Bruttidius meus ad Martis fuit obvius aram;
> quam timeo, victus ne poenas exigat Aiax
> ut male defensus. curramus praecipites et,   85
> dum iacet in ripa, calcemus Caesaris hostem.
> sed videant servi, ne quis neget et pavidum in ius
> cervice obstricta dominum trahat.' hi sermones
> tunc de Seiano, secreta haec murmura volgi.

Sejanus is being dragged along by the hook for all to see; all are rejoicing. "What lips the man had! What a face! If you ask me, I never liked the guy. But under what charge did he fall? Who was the informer? What evidence and witnesses made the case?" "None of that; a wordy and weighty letter came from Capreae." "OK, say no more." But what does Remus's mob do? It follows fortune, as always, and hates the condemned. That same populace would have been hailing Sejanus as Augustus that very moment if the Etruscan [Sejanus] had had the support of his goddess of Fortune, if the aged emperor had been smothered in a careless moment. Long ago, once we stopped selling votes, the people let their cares go; so it is that that same body that once gave out commands, offices, legions, and the rest now limits itself to yearning for two things alone: bread and circuses. "I hear many will die." "No doubt, the furnace is big." "My Bruttidius was a bit pale when I saw him at the altar of Mars; I'm afraid that 'defeated Ajax' will seek vengeance for his being so poorly protected. So let's rush down and kick Caesar's foe while he's lying down—and make sure the slaves see, so none can deny it and get his master dragged by the neck into judgment." These were the things being said about Sejanus then, the private murmurs of the mob.

Time and time again, the famous tag *panem et circenses* (81) has been extracted from its context and taken as an elitist complaint about popular taste. Yet surely what Juvenal is narrating here is the *management* of popular inclinations under different governments—quite a different thing from the people's disposition.[42] Indeed, throughout the quoted passage, where Juvenal seems to include among the fickle *populus* those people who are important enough to have to self-monitor under the gaze of power, we can see a drastic method of social control in action. Genuine political passions have been replaced with new, performed ones. The spectacle of Sejanus's *damnatio* was created for a purpose and forced on the Roman people. In turn, the *turba Remi* that "hates the condemned" (73–74) is reacting to *fortuna* and calculating. This is made obvious in the initial emotional response of the public, which shows a combination of gut reaction and fearful self-censorship, an authentic-looking ambivalence: "what a figure he cut! . . . mind you, I never liked him . . . but is this whole thing fair?" The people even employ code to speak about Caesar, the "defeated Ajax" (84) who will be looking for parties to blame for the near coup and prompting the crowd to demonstrate its allegiance (85–88).[43]

This is not the kind of scenario that the reincarnated Democritus needs to worry about, but it is closer to home for Juvenal's contemporaries, if only just because Tacitus's own account is so fresh. Freudenburg even likens it to the dilemma of the imperial satirist.[44] In this way the idea of a free and authentic response to human events, especially one along the

---

[42] Keane, *Figuring Genre*, 36–37.

[43] Cf. Romano, *Irony in Juvenal*, 161: "To the irony of [Sejanus's] destiny, Juvenal adds another one, the irony of self-betrayal in the dialogue of the people." Like many others, Romano takes Juvenal to be criticizing the weakness of the *turba*.

[44] The people's public "reinvention" of themselves echoes satire's adaptation to political change (Freudenburg, *Satires of Rome*, 11–13).

lines of Democritus's irrepressible cackle, is problematized in the context of the real world. "Easy" laughter would be quite out of reach for imperial-era readers of satire. Thus the first vignette of the main sermon does much more than illustrate the proposition "political power is risky"; as if addressing those who understand imperial politics, it shows that there is no such thing as a safe bystander.

Demolition and Reinvention

Although at this point Juvenal begins to travel back in history from the Julio-Claudian era in the search for exempla, he continues to tell stories in which his contemporaries have a heavy investment. The subject of eloquence in political speech is a prime example. Cicero and Demosthenes, though not the cultural property of Democritus, were giants from Juvenal's perspective. To take up these examples of dangerous eloquence, Juvenal begins by reporting the typical schoolboy's prayer: "he starts praying and keeps on praying through the spring holidays for the eloquence and fame of Demosthenes or Cicero" (*eloquium ac famam Demosthenis aut Ciceronis/incipit optare et totis quinquatribus optat*, 114–15). This opening conveys how these "ancient" models were defined by their importance to the educational mentality of the imperial era, right down to the dreams of a small schoolboy (116–17). The topic of great orators was a favorite in rhetorical exercises, not just because Cicero and his kind offered great stylistic examples to follow but because—and Cicero is the prime example— their careers embodied the kind of ethical path that declamation tended to examine. Cicero's story of powerful speech leading to danger and death was close to home for imperial declaimers and students—if not because their lives were on the line, at least because they were conscious of the fact that their particular rhetorical niche was a product of the post-Ciceronian world.[45] As a sort of poetic declaimer, Juvenal can claim to share this perspective. (Then, too, as a satirist who began his career claiming to wrestle with a choice between writing and safety, he may be tendentiously asserting a personal connection with the orators).

Like the declaimers trained to construct arguments in response to questions like "should Cicero beg Antony's pardon?" (Sen. *Suas.* 6) and

---

[45.]Kaster, "Becoming 'CICERO' "; see also Wilson, "Your Writings or Life"; Gunderson, *Declamation, Paternity, and Identity*, 79–87; and Roller, "*Color*-Blindness." Demosthenes and Cicero—a logical enough set of exemplary twins, as Plutarch and others recognized—are cited as examples of "death by eloquence" at Quint. *Decl.* 268.20.

"if it will win him mercy from Antony, should Cicero burn his writings?" (*Suas.* 7; cf. Quintilian *Inst.* 3.8.46), Juvenal weighs the value of the orator's political commitment and literary achievement against that of his life. But the satirist breaks with tradition, taking the position that Seneca suggests was always avoided (*Suas.* 7.10):[46] he advocates self-censorship and mediocrity as a route to safety. A "Democritean" *suasoria* to Cicero would even steer the great orator toward his lesser talent, verse writing. If his speeches had been this bad, Juvenal quips, Cicero "could have made light of Antony's hired swords" (*Antoni gladios potuit contemnere si sic/omnia dixisset*, 123–24). The Democritean solution would un-write the history of Roman oratory by taking Cicero out of the equation. It would replace serious, engaged speech (the famous *Philippics*) with powerless and laughable verses (*ridenda poemata*, 124).[47] It would shut down Cicero's true talent, urge him to oppose his nature in the name of self-preservation. With Demosthenes, we can infer, his recommendations would be no less drastic: forget about becoming the impressive example of the son who outdoes his father (cf. V. Max. 3.4.ext.2), abandon your education in rhetoric, and go to train at the family forge instead (129–32). Both Cicero and his Greek counterpart Demosthenes chose a risky career, but their choice was a part of history—a part that a Democritus would be just as happy to erase.

While Juvenal pretends to give his historical subjects "advice" that illustrates the drastic Democritean vision, he speaks from a position that is distinct from and patently incompatible with it. The satirist continually shows us just how deep his cultural roots go, and particularly how his culture has mined history—recent and ancient, Roman and non-Roman—for moral exempla. The more readily the satirist's audience accepts these stories as familiar currency (notwithstanding their nontraditional cast here), the more obvious the divide between Democritus and themselves should be. The same continues to be true as Juvenal turns to the subject of imperial conquest, and some of the figures who were literally responsible for creating the history that shaped his experience. Uden has observed that in *Satire* 10 Juvenal puts on display, and pulls to pieces, some cherished Roman ideals—distinction in politics, the exercise of *libertas*, military glory.[48] In fact, it is not just the values of the empire that the satire breaks down; it is the very stories that supported the articulation and exploration of those

---

[46] Cf. Gunderson, *Declamation, Paternity, and Identity*, 82.

[47] Also on the contrast between Cicero's poetic and oratorical abilities, see Sen. *Con.* 3 pr. 8.

[48] Uden, *Invisible Satirist*, 152-9, analyzing the Cynic παραχάραξις ("debasement") enacted in the poem.

values, not to mention steered history itself all the way up to Juvenal's time. Without these outsized figures and their achievements, intended or not, there would be no history, no rhetoric, no tradition of moral discourse that interpreted and remembered their examples.

This idea is underscored by the order of Juvenal's exempla: we can observe a distinct chronological regression, an unusual pattern in exemplary discourse.[49] Backward through the great ages of Roman expansion we go, back through the Hellenization of the Mediterranean world, back to the crucial twists of history that ignited the Athenian Golden Age. Hannibal, Alexander, and Xerxes are all held up as conquerors who failed sooner or later in their thirst to break down boundaries. The Democritean vision ignores or even denies the fact of their extraordinary legacies; it boxes them up, as symbolized in the diminishing images of Hannibal weighed on a scale (147–48), Alexander confined in his sarcophagus (172), and Xerxes struggling home in a single ship (185). The satirist who constructs the poetic *suasoriae* to these historical figures warns them of impending doom. But he is fooling no one; he knows how much his culture needs these figures to march to their fates. His sarcastic directive to Hannibal points to the important role the Carthaginian will play in Roman experience and identity, not just immediately but in the era of the rhetorical schools: "go ahead, madman, streak through the harsh Alps and make boys happy by becoming a declamation" (*i, demens, et saevas curre per Alpes/ ut pueris placeas et declamatio fias*, 166–67). As with the life story of Cicero, the satirist and his readers know perfectly well where this will— and should—end up: in the language of the empire's students and public speakers. And with his arrival at the expedition of Xerxes, Juvenal has finally hit on an event that preceded Democritus's lifetime and could have shaped the Thracian philosopher's entire life and worldview. The detachment of the mocking figure appears in even starker relief.

It would be like the real Democritus to scoff at world conquerors, but that does not mean that Juvenal's hypothesized Democritean take is entirely logical and sound. By ancient historical and rhetorical accounts, the conquerors—like the orators in the previous section—were following their inborn nature. What the satirist's Democritean vision advocates is suppression of that nature—the drive that made the world feel like a prison or a sickness to Alexander (168–70), and that made the naturally

---

[49.]Valerius Maximus often orders the stories in each of his subsections chronologically. His intention may be to suggest that there is a "cyclical dimension to exemplary discourse: deeds generate other deeds" (Roller, "Exemplarity in Roman Culture," 6).

greedy *barbarus* Xerxes pull out all the stops in his desire to reach Greece (175–84). There is patent irony in the scenario of a philosopher who followed his own nature (to the point of notoriety) suggesting that other men should not. Moreover, to impress his view upon these men, the laughing philosopher would have to disregard their real power, in a violation of the rules of rhetoric. As the declaimers knew, it was necessary to address kings with discretion and praise, especially when advising them against a course they desired. It could be risky to refer to their human limitations. That goes even for *suasoriae* to long-dead kings, which of course constitute practice for the real thing; this is why Cestius dwells on the matter of the proper approach in a *suasoria* to Alexander (Sen. *Suas.* 1.5). The satirist, for his part, would understand the problems inherent in laying into three conquerors like a Democritus. Still, the most compelling reason for him to stand apart from Democritean laughter is that, if imitated and followed to its logical conclusions, it would prevent a poem like *Satire* 10 from ever seeing the light of day. The rhetorical and cultural architecture of the poem is that deep and substantial.

So far, Juvenal has been able to illustrate the inherent problems of Democritean laughter by feigning a demolition of history and culture, from his own present back down to the Persian Wars—the one episode in the list that would have influenced Democritus's own experience. The satirist now takes up a different approach to testing the limits of the untroubled *cachinnus:* an examination of more universal human troubles. The lengthy section that criticizes prayers for long life ("*da spatium vitae, multos da, Iuppiter, annos,*" 188) begins not with old exempla but old people. Here Juvenal employs the same close-up technique that made the Sejanus passage particularly discomfiting. Grotesque, mundane, and tragic, the description of the typical old man seems the oddest target for laughter in the whole poem.[50] The figure that Juvenal begins to examine is an example of suffering in old age, not of foolish ambition; moreover, he is nameless and generic, so that his experience is no less connected to Democritus than to Juvenal.[51] (Juvenal will display himself as a wrinkled old man at 11.203; as chapter 5 will discuss further, senectitude becomes part of his persona.) The point is that "all old men look the same" (*una*

[50.]This and the passage on beauty are the sections Lawall, "*Exempla* and Theme," labels as relentlessly "Heraclitean."

[51.]On this unique aspect of the old age section, see Jones, *Juvenal,* 57: "the anonymity [of the man described in 188–239, before Greek epic exempla appear] seems strongly to intensify the content of the paragraph—the anonymity and sameness of old people, their lack of identity and memory."

senum facies, 198), and Juvenal very explicitly explains what he means by that: a dramatically altered face, wrinkled skin, trembling limbs and voice, hairless head, a baby's dripping nose, toothlessness (191–200). The same is true, he implies, for the old man's feelings: he loses pleasure in food, wine, sex, and music, and even loses the ability to communicate (203–16). Making things worse is the host of diseases that "dances about [the *senex*] in a throng" (*circumsilit agmine facto*, 218), assaulting one body part after another and leading to helplessness and dependence on others. The old man's state is both infantile and inhuman: he is like a baby bird that needs to be fed by hand (229–32). Finally, when the mind is affected by age, a man's entire awareness of his family, friends, and obligations slips away, resulting in a classic inheritance catastrophe when he leaves his entire estate to a mistress (232–39).

Throughout, the satirist probes the elderly body and deteriorating mind up close, creating for his audience the same "disgusting" (*gravis*) spectacle that the man's own family and hangers-on cannot endure (201–2). His descriptive technique is familiar from the other *Satires*, but it is especially striking here, after grand historical *exempla* have dominated the poem so far. In this case we are observing a particularly curious blend of influences on the satirist. To be sure, old age and related themes—death, inheritance, family disputes—are common in the declamatory exercises, and declaimers exploited the topos of old age and its sorrows when speaking on behalf of elderly parties. Fathers in distress who disown their sons, parents who experience neglect from their children, others who must bury their children—these unfortunate characters, experiencing "the worst things that could happen to a family," populate the declamations of Seneca the Elder and pseudo-Quintilian.[52] But the traditional rhetorical exercises did not prompt the speaker to survey an old man's body and describe its failing parts from hairless head to withered penis (205). For all the dead, dying, and mutilated bodies of old men that populate the declamations, there is hardly any age-specific description focusing on the mundane physical plight of the old man; words and ideas seem to matter most.[53] In other

[52] Bloomer, "Roman Declamation," 305 (at the same time recognizing that the plots of the exercises are more concerned with politics than suffering). From the long list of examples involving disowning of sons by fathers, some highlights are Sen. *Con.* 1.1 (which also features an aging father in need) and 2.4 (involving an accusation of insanity, and the favoring of a bastard child), and Quint. *Decl.* 256 (insanity and filicide), 283 (rebellion by the Cynic son), 322 (patricide and accusations of political plotting), and 330 (the dilemma of estranged parents).

[53] On the tragic *pathos* cultivated in declamation, see Van Mal-Maeder, *Fiction des declamations;* on mutilation, fathers, and sons, see Gunderson, *Declamation, Paternity, and Identity*, 59–89. In the *Lesser Declamations* there are, for example, victims of parricide and beating whose death or

literature, too, positive accounts of old age emphasize the rhetorical and moral authority of the *senex* (cf. chapter 5). In contrast, Juvenal's catalog of the old man's woes strips his subject of dignity.

There is, however, a plausible source for the images Juvenal spins here, and it is one that Democritus ought to recognize. When Juvenal finally invokes named exempla (as he identifies the greatest tragedy to beset old age, the death of one's children), he looks back as far as he could, to the old men of Homer (246–70). Though Nestor, Peleus, Laertes, and Priam inhabit the world of epic and are noted for siring heroic sons, they are all depicted in Homer with one or other of the vulnerabilities that Juvenal also highlights. Each is shown weighted down with sad experience, anxious for sons at war, neglected and frail, or pitifully straining to summon up lost strength.[54] By evoking some of the most heart-rending moments in epic, first obliquely with his generic *senex* and then explicitly with his catalog of grieving fathers, Juvenal makes us consider whether Homer's world, with its extremes of grandeur and grief, is an appropriate target for an uncaring *cachinnus*. What he highlights are visual and emotional horrors—frankly, perfect *materia lacrimarum* for a Heraclitus, who would understand that we are all in this together.

As if to underscore the point that this subject is not inherently comic, Juvenal summons up the rhetoric of his angry *Satires* in a curious fashion. The list of old men's diseases, he claims, is harder to relate than "the number of Oppia's lovers, the patients that Dr. Themison killed off in one autumn" (*quot amaverit Oppia moechos,/quot Themison aegros autumn occiderit uno*, 220–21), and several other equally scandalous and mock-epic catalogs.[55] But in the climax of this list about lists, Juvenal declares, "I could sooner rattle off all the villas owned by that guy whose clippers made my beard rasp when I was a young man" (*percurram citius*

---

wounds are nevertheless not described in any age-specific way (*Decl.* 299, 314.20, 372.7), and a father accused of dementia whose response, far from illustrating the condition, demonstrates that the accusation is false (*Decl.* 349). Seneca the Elder also tends to be brief in physical description; see, e.g., the simply *squalidus* old man at *Con.* 1.1.19.

[54.] At *Il.* 1.254–59 and 11.670–95, Nestor claims that in his long life he has seen generations die (including all eleven of his brothers) and his own strength wane; at *Od.* 3.111–12 he expresses grief for Antilochus. Peleus, though absent from the action, is conjured as a vulnerable and grieving old father at *Il.* 24.486–502; Achilles elaborates on the contrast between Peleus's former good fortune and his imminent loss at 534–42. Priam is scrawny, trembling, and fearing a shameful death and desecration at *Il.* 22.71–76; cf. his pitiful arming scene at Verg. *A.* 2.507–25. Laertes is seen living in shameful (though self-sufficient) neglect at *Od.* 15.352–57 and 24.226–55. Finally, Romano (*Irony in Juvenal*, 165) and Courtney (*Satires*, 476) see an echo of *Il.* 9.323–24 in the baby bird simile Juvenal uses to describe the old man being fed (229–32).

[55.] Jones, *Juvenal*, 100–101.

quot villas possideat nunc/quo tondente gravis iuveni mihi barba sonabat,
225–26). We know this barber-cum-millionaire from *Satire* 1: line 10.226
is identical to 1.25. What is the purpose of the allusion? Does Juvenal's
recollection of one of his original stimuli to satire mean that the angry sati-
rist still resides somewhere in our speaker? Or has the satirist just decided
that his hyperbolic rhetoric is better applied to the tragic case of the sick
old man? Either way, the satirist is pulling out his big rhetorical gun to
describe these particular human calamities. The Democritean *cachinnus*, a
nonverbal dismissal, is the very opposite of such hyperbolic rhetoric. Both
may be extreme responses, but in this case, the former would seem to be
the one that is out of place.

Drawing on the universally shared territories of ordinary experience
and epic, Juvenal has surrounded the laughing Democritus with sad every-
day reality on the one hand, and sad epic exempla on the other. He thus
closes the gap that initially existed between his satiric material and the
Democritean *cachinnus*. If we are meant to be imagining the philosopher
still laughing away (as is treated as a given in most readings), the anti-
social nature of his laughter should be more starkly apparent than ever.
That laughter is also clearly very different from the complex verbal satire
Juvenal practices, which depends so heavily on literary borrowing, per-
suasion, and modulation of tone. This is the perfect occasion for Juvenal
to rush back through history to Roman examples of long-lived men (*fes-
tino ad nostros*, 273), in particular the fates of Marius and Pompey (276–
88).[56] The Roman satirist takes full possession of the topic with which his
imperial-era audience should also feel a connection. His treatment implies
that history, with all its variety, offers numerous lenses through which we
may understand the phenomenon of suffering, and in distinct and nuanced
ways. For while the first parts of the section on old age highlights physical
deterioration and bereavement, there is a new angle in the Roman sec-
tion: Juvenal expresses pity for Marius and Pompey for outliving what
he claims are their greatest political hours.[57] This is the kind of variety

---

[56] This follows a brief *praeteritio* mentioning the aged Mithridates and Croesus (273–75). Packaged
within the Marius and Pompey passage are additional references (for contrast) to Lentulus,
Cethegus, and Catiline.

[57] As Courtney (*Satires*, 453) notes, Juvenal's account of Marius's career at 276–82 could be
interpreted as claiming—inaccurately—that Marius died in exile and violence. But if we read it
next to the lines on Pompey, which suggest that Pompey would have had a more beautiful corpse
if he had died during the height of his power (283–88), it seems that Juvenal is mainly trying to
connect senescence with loss of political power.

(*ubertas*) that Valerius Maximus finds inspiring in examples of virtue (5.6 ext.5); it is just as instructive in catalogs of misfortune.

Roman life and history, Juvenal goes on to show, also offer good examples of ill-fated beauty. The horrific cases of Lucretia and Verginia (293–95) are enshrined in Roman historiography and other literature.[58] Roman stories again coincide with "the worst thing that could happen to a family . . . the worst things that children could suffer."[59] Hippolytus and Bellerophon (cited at 324–28) are the mythic predecessors of the beautiful victims of Nero (306–9) and Messalina (329–45). It is with his final and most extended exemplum of doomed beauty that Juvenal returns completely to the imperial Roman perspective with which he began his catalog. The account of Gaius Silius's dilemma and eventual death is first introduced as a *suasoria* that the poem's reader might perform: "choose what course you'll urge on that man whom Caesar's wife has resolved to marry" (*elige quidnam/suadendum esse putes cui nubere Caesaris uxor/ destinat*, 329–31). The exercise would be familiar, although the particular case is especially difficult, with *no* available course offering safety: "if you [Silius] aren't willing to indulge [Messalina's wish], you'll have to die before nightfall; if you do commit this crime, there'll be a short delay" before Claudius learns the truth and retaliates (*ni parere velis, pereundum erit ante lucernas;/si scelus admittas, dabitur mora parvula*, 339–40). Silius must go to his death—incidentally, just like the empress and emperor who will soon fall like dominoes. Tacitus's incredible story here becomes an allegory for the helplessness of humanity.[60] All of this, Juvenal suggests, has been brought to you by Roman imperial history.

Democritus's wordless laughter is, to say the least, oddly applied to this series of unsettling stories. Even satire laced with mockery of social and political institutions represents far greater humanity and complexity. *Satire* 10 has inspected the caricature of the laughing philosopher for what it is—a limited and unusable model—and shown the way toward a more complex digestion of human history and experience using the tools of culture. While the satirist has tried to use these tools to distinguish between real goods and their opposites (*dinoscere vera bona atque illis multum diversa*, 2–3), the laughing Democritus does not do that kind of work. This

[58.]Cf. V. Max. 6.1.1–2, Liv. 1.57.6–59.3 and 3.44–48.5; cf. Sen. *Con.* 1.5.3, [Quint] *Decl.* 3.11, and Sen. *Oct.* 297–303.

[59.]Bloomer, "Roman Declamation," 305.

[60.]Keane, "Historian and Satirist," 423–25.

magnum exemplum has turned out to be the most problematic, and arguably the most appalling, of the entire collection.

At the very end of the poem, however, Juvenal rehabilitates the philosopher as a satiric ancestor. He does this by moving away from the incomplete and unusable caricature of the "laughing philosopher" introduced in the poem's opening, and toward a fuller, more accurate, and more nuanced representation of the atomist's ideas on ethics. For the *peroratio* of *Satire* 10 offers, instead of additional Cynic "debasement," a positive prescription. This is the section outlining what would be a reasonable and safe prayer to present to the gods. Mockery is not absent, of course—here we find the famous image of a prayer made "at little shrines with the sacred little innards and sausages of a pure-white piglet" (*sacellis/exta et candiduli divina tomacula porci*, 354–55)—but the actual terms of the prayer are described with striking seriousness. The passage is the source of one of Juvenal's most celebrated "serious" *sententiae*, the recommendation to ask for a "sound mind in a sound body" (*mens sana in corpore sano*, 356), and the rest is of a piece with this (357–60):

> fortem posce animum mortis terrore carentem,
> qui spatium vitae extremum inter munera ponat
> naturae, qui ferre queat quoscumque dolores,
> nesciat irasci, cupiat nihil . . .

> Ask for a brave heart that has no fear of death, that reckons a long life to be among the least of Nature's gifts, that can bear any sorrows you can think of, that doesn't know how to get angry, that desires nothing . . .

Besides being put in straight ethical terms, this recommendation on prayer sends an important message about the condition of the poem's audience and implicitly about the satirist himself: namely, that no one can automatically become a Democritus, untroubled by life's misfortunes. Even anger evidently still lurks nearby, threatening to trap the one who is not armed against it. The state of *tranquillitas* that could afford this perspective takes much work to achieve; as Juvenal notes, the means of getting there is the exercise of *virtus* (364). And by ending with a prayer, Juvenal steers the theme of wish fulfillment into a new context, in which a constant state of desire is a *good* thing.[61]

[61.] The recommended prayer makes a contrasting bookend to the list of perceived goods at the opening of *Satire* 10, which included *argenti vascula puri* (19). These were objects of Naevolus's closing prayer (9.141 contains the same three words in the same metrical *sedes*).

This all looks very serious at the end of a poem that has depicted plenty of human experiences in a mocking light, and that began by expressing at least some approval of laughter. But the recommendation on prayer is still integrated with the rest of the poem. The link is Democritus himself. Juvenal does not name the philosopher here, but evidence about Democritus's writings and ideas confirms that he concerned himself with just what the satirist is describing here. The caricature of him laughing unconcerned represents a small part of that, and represents it misleadingly. Over the course of the poem, Juvenal has taken us on a journey from that caricature—superficially representing a satiric position—to the real Democritus, the one who advised good cheer, tranquility, and a balanced approach to human problems. Seneca and other philosophers who wrote after Democritus were fully familiar with this more accurate picture. In the satire, it is the two versions of the philosopher that have turned out to be the *verum bonum* (3) and something quite different; the poem has made the distinction between the two. Cognizant of the difference between caricature and reality, Juvenal has been neither unequivocally embracing nor condemning Democritean laughter all along; instead, he has rolled out his parade of sobering exempla as a way of gradually appropriating a more complex Democritus.

This is not to say that our satirist merges with his ancient model. A huge divide still separates them. But Juvenal has declared his interest in exploring his material through the lens that the philosopher and his admirers offer. The consideration of a viable model for the path to *tranquillitas* at the end of *Satire* 10 is only a beginning. It does not establish the satirist himself as *tranquillus* in the poem or the book, any more than the caricature of Democritus in the opening passage does. But it is still programmatic in that it initiates Juvenal's foray into the subject of tranquility, an investigation that steers the course of the rest of Book 4. Satire in this phase of Juvenal's career becomes more focused on the satirist figure, more inward-looking, more "personal." Following instructions from the Senecan treatment of *tranquillitas* (and more generally from Seneca's recommendations on positive self-transformation),[62] Juvenal makes himself the subject of the journey. The result is more pushing of the boundaries of what satire can do. Having just learned that it is difficult to write culturally

---

[62] Edwards ("Self-Scrutiny and Self-Transformation," 36) contextualizes Seneca's *Letters* in "a larger turn in the first and second centuries CE toward interiorization."

meaningful satire as a laughing nihilist, we will now see whether it is possible to write "tranquil satire."

The Senecan Model

As Seneca's *On Anger* helps us understand the operation of anger in Juvenal's early books, so his dialogue on *tranquillitas* can shed light on the satiric program initiated at the end of *Satire* 10. It has been argued that Juvenal took inspiration from *On Tranquility* to construct the elusive persona of his seventh *Satire*,[63] but the influence of this Senecan work seems much more present in Book 4. It is not just that *Satire* 10 mentions *tranquillitas* explicitly; the book itself also introduces a prominent authorial "I," an appropriate vehicle for dramatizing ideas from the Senecan discussion. *On Tranquility* explores the complicated condition of unease that is the opposite of tranquility and explicitly describes the path away from it.[64]

As we have already seen, the standard double caricature of the laughing Democritus and the weeping Heraclitus is misleading. According to Seneca, there is nothing simple about either tranquility or its opposite; neither can be summed up so quickly. One telling aspect of Seneca's dialogue is that the philosopher and his ailing interlocutor have difficulty putting a name to the condition that is tranquility's opposite. As Harris notes, while "un-tranquility" is best diagnosed in modern terms as depression, there is no question that the lack of an ancient term posed a challenge for those who wrote about it.[65] In Seneca, metaphors abound, especially the usual metaphor of sickness and in particular here seasickness (contrasted with the more intense affliction caused by a storm: Serenus says *non tempestate vexor sed nausea*, 1.17). Serenus seems a bit embarrassed by his elusive problem, saying that he is aware of being "neither sick nor well" (*nec aegroto nec valeo*, 1.2). And Seneca takes up this point when he speaks, saying that one problem with this condition is that people fancy themselves to be suffering more than they actually are—almost implying that Serenus would be right to feel sheepish about his discontentedness.

But the complexity of Serenus's condition and the fact that his friend undertakes to heal him all the same suggest that the problem is meant to be taken seriously and approached with care. This man is not trapped in a

---

[63.]Hardie, "Condition of Letters," 151–60; cf. chapter 3, n. 10.
[64.]See André, "Sénèque"; Griffin, *Seneca*, 321–27; Motto and Clark, "Serenity and Tension"; and Costa, *Seneca: Four Dialogues*, 186–98.
[65.]Harris, *Restraining Rage*, 17–18; cf. Toohey, *Melancholy, Love, and Time*, 155 and 326 n. 40.

weeping Heraclitean mode, in need of levity or distance. He has earnestly been trying to find contentment in his everyday pursuits, both private and public, and failing. He even knows already that there is such a thing as tranquility, and he desires it—he enthusiastically uses the word twice in his speech (1.11, 1.17). Where he has gone wrong is in his strategies for seeking it. As we all have both Democritus and Heraclitus in us, so the irritable Serenus is not unaware of the possibility of adopting a tranquil attitude; he is simply unable to attain it. This is partly because he misunderstands the recipe for *tranquillitas*. He evidently thinks it will make him "free from care in public and private matters" (*expers publicae privataeque curae*, 1.11), when as it turns out it can *only* be achieved through "dedicated and constant care" (*intenta et adsidua cura*, 17.12). It is no wonder that his own experiments fail, and that he must ask Seneca to "deem me worthy to owe my tranquility to you" (*dignum me putes qui tibi tranquillitatem debeam*, 1.17).

Serenus already has a vocabulary, ideas, and philosophical learning to work with. These things are just not working to make him content. Because he cannot even sum up his problem with a name, he gives examples of situations that reveal his "mental infirmity" (*animi . . . infirmitas*, 1.4). Sometimes Serenus enthusiastically and eloquently praises the simple lifestyle, but glimpses or visions of luxury tempt him to feel discontent with his own choices (1.5–9). He begins to resemble the confused Horace of *Satire* 2.7, who (claims the slave Davus, 22–37) is uncommitted in his moralizing, shuttles discontendedly between town and country, and craves social approval in spite of himself. Sometimes Serenus vows to follow the examples of philosophers in his public affairs, but ordinary challenges easily perturb him and send him homeward looking for isolation and freedom from care (1.10–11). Once home, however, thoughts of noble exemplars whet his ambition to go back out into the world and make a difference (1.12). Even in his writing, he resolves to stay on topic and hold modest ambitions for his reception, but then he gets carried away with lofty thoughts, as if not speaking in his own voice (*ore iam non meo*, 1.14). Serenus makes what he considers noble resolutions and then cannot keep them. He vows to be happy with circumstances that begin to seem inferior when he imagines alternatives.

As we have seen, even diagnosing Serenus's problem is a process, requiring illustration and metaphorizing on the part of both patient and philosopher-interlocutor. Likewise, the road to tranquility is long and difficult, as is indicated by Serenus's failure to hold on to the mental condition that he believes will free him from discontent. Healing will come from different strategies, and first of all from recognition that there are wrong paths and pitfalls. The road also happens to be quite compelling to read about, as the wandering description of Serenus's trials and errors in their different private and public context shows. The struggles that come with depression, discontent, and emptiness are far more interesting than either the endless weeping or the "easy cackle" initially ascribed to Heraclitus and Democritus.[66]

Seneca offers a more complex solution. He immediately picks up on Serenus's claim to have sought *tranquillitas* and on the fact, obvious from his friend's account, that there are plenty of wrong ways to look for this blessed state. His intended audience is not wise men but "the imperfect, the mediocre, the not quite sound" (*imperfectos et mediocres et male sanos*, 11.1)—implying, despite the contrast with the *sapiens*, that these may include many who like Serenus have already done some work on themselves. He examines the recommendations of the philosopher Athenodorus at length (3–4). The latter proclaimed that tranquility could be achieved through withdrawal from public affairs and whittling down one's pursuits and friends to a small and stress-free collection. This is a solution that Serenus has already attempted to apply—disappointments, challenges, and irritations in his public career make him resolve to "confine his life within its own walls" (*intra parietes suos vitam coercere*, 1.11). And it has not worked because the forum, with its promise of fame and other rewards, always calls Serenus back.

Seneca explains at length that the ideal path involves more moderate withdrawal and continued involvement in rewarding affairs both public and private—especially where such pursuits are balanced in a way appropriate to the personality of the sufferer. He writes that one can find tranquility not through a universal formula but through one designed to match one's character and talents. In a nutshell, "self-shaping and the self-conscious management of the relationship between self and others are crucial to achieving tranquility."[67] But the self must be the first object of study. While one ought to examine the potential tasks at hand (6.3–4) and potential friends (7), even before that it is necessary to aim for self-knowledge (6.1–2).

This is not so different, after all, from the solution that Juvenal recommends at the end of *Satire* 10. The satirist declares that the *vita tranquilla*

[66.] Seneca recognizes the difficulty of "getting to goodness" (Inwood, *Reading Seneca*, 271–301).
[67.] Inwood, *Reading Seneca*, 144.

may be reached one way: through *virtus*. By praying for the right mental qualities, one can become equipped for this path (356–62). Again, this suggestion runs counter to the argument, presented throughout the poem, that there is no single answer for those who seek happiness.[68] The *Satire* thus ends on a note of playful indeterminacy, even undermining itself. In another sense, however, Juvenal's proposition is self-evidently complex. *Virtus* is no simple solution. As writers from Lucilius on know (1196– 1208 W; cf. Cicero's *Tusc.* 5), it takes some labor to define and act out. Juvenal's recommendation, if scrutinized in its moral-philosophical and literary context, is no simpler than Seneca's methodical description of the steps to *tranquillitas*.

Moreover, the two authors' recommendations are related. *Virtus* is a manifestation of self-knowledge, in that it can refer to one's excellence in a chosen field. It may even designate literary achievement, and so becomes an especially loaded term at this point in Juvenal's career. In Horace *Satire* 2.3, the converted Stoic Damasippus accuses the poet of laziness. Having brought a bundle of Greek books to his country estate, Horace stalls when he puts pen to paper. Damasippus warns that he will be criticized for shirking the art at which he excels (*virtute relicta. . . contemnere miser*, 13–14), and so should either keep writing or quit once and for all: "whatever you've accomplished in a better time of life, give it up with equanimity" (*quidquid vita meliore parasti /ponendum aequo animo*, 15–16). In this poem, one of a series in which he is criticized, marginalized, or erased from the scene of *sermo*, Horace portrays himself as confronting a crisis over the state of his writing—or, as Damasippus calls it, his *virtus*. The entire second book of *Satires* plays with the theme of Horace's ambivalent retirement, showing him withdrawing from his satiric career even as he is obviously behind the scenes composing the book. The relationship between *sermo* and autobiography, concretized in the votive tablet analogy at 2.1.32–34, is highlighted in a novel way in this book that features an author figure relinquishing his *auctoritas*.[69]

Virtus is one's chosen field of excellence, a field that Horace portrays as elusive in *Satires* Book 2. It is also what Juvenal identifies as the prerequisite for *tranquillitas*, and both are heavily dependent on self-knowledge. It makes sense that Juvenalian satire becomes more personal at this point. But can satire come from a tranquil man? What exactly would "tranquil

---

[68]·Cf. Fishelov, "Vanity of Reader's Wishes."

[69]·Keane, *Figuring Genre*, 114–20.

satiric rhetoric" sound like? This may sound like a paradox, but it will seem more plausible if we look for a satiric *plot* that "thinks with" tranquility. To bring this about, as Seneca implies, Juvenal must become the most visible he has ever been—even if this ultimately reveals the artificiality of satiric "identities."

The Satirist behind Closed Doors

In *Satires* 11 and 12, Juvenal makes his most vivid appearance since *Satire* 1. He performs not only as the "I" that delivers satire but as a person with a body, a house, and a fairly ordinary social identity. The first poem presents a social portrait of the satirist, living in a house and engaging in a ritual of friendship by inviting his addressee to dinner. In the next, we again observe him engaged in domestic rituals, even relating to more than one friend. *Satire* 12 portrays the poet's sacrifices of thanks upon the safe return of a friend, Catullus, from sea; but it is addressed to another man, Corvinus. The personal and domestic themes of these poems combine to create a striking new kind of performed authenticity in Juvenalian satire. We should wonder why the poet is even making these unparalleled appearances.

The performances of this more visible and socially connected satirist figure make an odd epilogue to the ambitious, panoramic *Satire* 10. Following the grand lecture on prayer, Juvenal produces what appear to be modest examples of two poetic subgenres: the invitation to a simple meal (11) and the *prosphonetikon* to a returning traveler (12). As I have noted, this new concentration on domestic and social rituals has been read as a reflection of the satirist's tranquil persona. But conventional exteriors and predictable gestures to well-worn moral topics (such as the connection between diet and moral character) can be misleading. Even poems crafted around recognized subgenres tend to have a complex social, ideological, and metapoetic texture that belies the simple generic label.[70] In terms of their internal structure, too, *Satires* 11 and 12 are a surprise after the opening of the book. *Satire* 10 is long and well organized, with subjects ranging across history, myth, and contemporary life; it is followed by two shorter texts of noticeably uneven structure. These formal shifts beg to be

---

[70] See Cairns, *Generic Composition*, 74–75 and 18–23; cf. the readings of specific invitation poems in Gowers, *Loaded Table*, 220–79. Juvenal 12 has many surprises for the reader expecting the usual elements of the *prosphonetikon*; see Smith, "Greed and Sacrifice."

investigated rather than quickly explained as variations on a "tranquil" or epistolary theme.

Juvenal's remarkable presence as a character in *Satires* 11 and 12 is easy to miss if we concentrate on identifying dominant diatribe themes (friendship, the simple lifestyle, sacrifice) or on listening for clues about the rhetorical persona. But by putting himself on display, Juvenal is responding to his own recommendation at the end of *Satire* 10. Thus the unity of Book 4 derives not from a consistent demonstration of the poet's tranquility but from the drama that it stages. Juvenal introduces himself in the flesh—quite literally, with an image of his "wrinkled skin drink[ing] the spring sunshine" near the end of the middle poem (*nostra bibat vernum contracta cuticula solem*, 11.203). Our satirist figure is evidently aging. This retrospectively gives an extra edge to the picture of grievous old age in *Satire* 10—perhaps that "generic" satire veered closer to the "personal" than we realized on first reading. Now, in Juvenal's reference to his own body, there is a more explicit invitation to connect what we are reading to his advancing age. In response, we should not just call Book 4 "the work of an ageing man,"[71] but recognize that the satirist has handed us this clue as an interpretive framework, one that is relevant to his domestic, personal, and social themes. Juvenal asks his addressees to look at him and learn. "Spend an evening in my dining room and see how well I live up to my own moralizing," he tells Persicus in *Satire* 11. To Corvinus in 12: "look at how I honor an absent friend, both in public and in private." Juvenal's external audience is receiving the same summons; in addition, we can inspect Juvenal's interactions with the internal addressees.

The dramatic structure of both poems underscores their personal nature, their similar personal plots. *Satire* 11 begins with a general diatribe and shifts to a private dramatic scenario; the next poem does the reverse, allowing the pair to be viewed together as forming a chiasmus.[72] In both cases, however, the setting for the second part is the satirist's house. What does being at home—or, to put it more accurately, *going* home—mean for Juvenal's satiric work? First, it links him to numerous literary models in which a domestic setting is relevant to theme and genre. The house of Evander described by Vergil in *Aeneid* 8, to which Juvenal compares his

---

[71.]Highet, *Juvenal the Satirist*, 123; Highet calls Juvenal and his guest Persicus in *Satire* 11 "two old gentlemen" (132). Cf. Courtney's comment that the sunbathing Juvenal proposes to do at 11.203 "was thought good for the health, especially of old men, as Juvenal now was" (*Satires*, 514–15).

[72.]See Bellandi, *Etica diatribica*, 6 n. 12.

own (11.60–63), is—like Vergil's poem—humble but fit for demigods.[73] The letters of Seneca that center on villas employ topography and domestic space as tools for moral discourse.[74] Literary homes are the setting for dramas, for friendships and other social interactions, and for recitals; so Juvenal caps his invitation to Persicus with the promise of some Homer and Vergil with dinner (179–82). In the domestic social occasions that Martial conjures, poetry recitals are standard fare; private houses are the setting of continued social and literary performance.[75] Persius ends his book of *Satires* with an epistolary "retreat" poem, a highly allusive and metaliterary valediction.[76] This dramatized withdrawal is of course only a relocation; the satirist does not escape his genre but continues to reinvent it in a new place.

Before Persius, Horace made the domestic retreat an element of the satirist figure's story, and the case of his Sabine villa is especially illuminating. In *Satire* 2.6, Horace claims to be retreating from the disturbances of urban life to a private sanctuary filled with friends, a situation that is both a throwback to the world of Lucilian satire (cf. 2.1.71–74) and a long-awaited boon attained through his literary work and association with Maecenas (2.6.1). In this house (also the setting for the Saturnalian 2.3 and 2.7), Horace's satire changes: contributing to the atmosphere of equality, Horace relinquishes satiric authority to the rest of the company and ethically themed *sermo* "arises" (*sermo oritur*, 2.6.71)—including the tale of the two mice told by Cervius. We are encouraged to see this as organic satire, which reduces a compliant Horace to the role of audience member and oblique target.[77] Thus the poem establishes and plays with connections between place, authority, and generic program; the house is represented as the inspiration for the text. This gives a foretaste of Horace's later *Epistles*, which, in conjunction with a (claimed) retreat from public

---

[73.]Evander also makes a rich alter ego for the epic poet; see Gransden, *Aeneid Book VIII*, 24–29, and Drew, *Allegory of the Aeneid*, 32–39. As Edwards notes ("Self-Scrutiny and Self-Transformation," 29–30), Seneca approvingly quotes Evander's injunction to Aeneas to "fashion" (*finge*) himself into someone worthy of Hercules (Verg. *A.* 8.364–65, quoted at Sen. *Ep.* 31.11).

[74.]Henderson, *Morals and Villas*; cf. O'Sullivan, "Mind in Motion."

[75.]On the numerous relevant poems by Martial, see Colton, "Dinner Invitation" and "Echoes of Martial."

[76.]See Hooley, *Knotted Thong*, 154–74; Malamud, "Out of Circulation," 61; Henderson, "Persius' Didactic Satire," 135–36 (=*Writing Down Rome*, 241–42); and Freudenburg, *Satires of Rome*, 205–6.

[77.]For the interpretation of the mouse fable as a jab at Horace, see Leach, "Horace's Sabine Topography," 285–87; Frischer, "La Villa ercolanese," 224–26; and Oliensis, *Rhetoric of Authority*, 50.

arenas, thematize the poet's "authentic" definition and expression of self. All of these models offer Juvenal images of domestic settings that are as dynamic as the streets of Rome.

Outside-In Satire

In *Satire* 11, we follow Juvenal from a public setting to a private one. This "retirement" translates into an adjustment of satiric technique, though not a quieting of the satiric voice. The first section of the poem (lines 1–55) mocks gourmands who fall into bankruptcy. This generic diatribe stands out from the personal invitation that follows (56–208).[78] Between the sections are thematic connections but also a visible seam in the shift in dramatic setting. The first section conjures the public, urban environment. Juvenal describes the shameless gluttons searching the markets for expensive delicacies, hiring themselves as gladiators, selling their property, and ultimately fleeing Rome in debt. Horace does something similar in the epistolary mode (cf. the passage about wastrels at *Ep.* 1.18.21–36), so we need not infer that Juvenal is out patrolling the streets again; still, the public nature of his vision should be noted. The downward spiral of the reckless spenders takes place as if in public view, with a series of vignettes emphasizing their shamelessness. Squandered inheritances are devoured for all to see (*ventrem fenoris atque/argenti gravis et pecorum agrorumque capacem*, 40–41). Creditors watch their loans "consumed" on the spot (*pecunia . . . coram dominis consumitur*, 46–47). Even in their hasty exile the gourmands are visible, marked not by blushes of shame (*sanguinis in facie non haeret gutta*, 54) but by sorrow at missing the upcoming races (52–53).

Juvenal also makes reference to a public critical voice: that of the *vulgus* that judges and mocks the doomed. "What gets a bigger cackle from the crowd than an Apicius in the poorhouse?" (*quid enim maiore cachinno/excipitur volgi quam pauper Apicius?*, 2–3). The *cachinnus* has reappeared, but this peformance of mockery comes from the crowd, not from a single and special authority figure. The crowd's judgment is heard

---

[78.]See Adamietz, *Untersuchungen zur Juvenal*, 121 ("statt eines anonymen einfachen Mahles . . . hat Juvenal die Version des eigenen Mahles gewählt"). Jones notes that the delayed personal address is unparalleled in Juvenal, and the switch from diatribe to address is "designed to leave the audience wondering about the connection. The introduction is, then, a factor influencing the audience's receptiveness to what follows and demands close inspection" ("Persona and the Addressee," 161; cf. *Juvenal*, 142).

in "every party, bathhouse, stopping place and theater" (*omnis/convictus, thermae, stationes, omne theatrum*, 3–4). In these public haunts, all convenient transmitters of information and sound, mockery is multiplied and legitimized. But Juvenal's own relationship to it is complex. On the one hand, he essentially repackages the crowd's mockery in textual form: the entire first section is rhetorically constructed as a paraphrase and elaboration of the thinking of other people (*habetur*, 1; cf. *nomen*, 22; *famam*, 23; *vocantur*, 178). Yet Juvenal also takes a critical stance on this mockery, noting a double standard in practice. People refrain from laughing at big spending among the comfortably rich, while zestfully mocking those who lose their fortunes to their vice (21–23; cf. 176–78). With the emphasis on this detail, Juvenal can resist being entirely associated with the "satiric" approach of the crowd to the behavior of gourmands. In this way he suggests a certain detachment from this particular ethical problem, and in turn strengthens some scholars' impression that his persona is morally and emotionally moderate.[79] The opening section certainly lacks the scathing tone of comments about greedy or selfish diners in Book 1, such as Virro in *Satire* 5.

But do such markers of mood or attitude tell the whole story? Just as telling is the way the poem brings us to envision the satirist behind the words at all. The first person is not introduced until lines 23 and 24; the invitation and mention of an addressee (56) are yet to come. The satirist has so far been invisible and intangible, and is treating a conventional topic as old as moral criticism itself.[80] This generic feel is certainly not unprecedented—there was nothing personal about the opening of *Satire* 10, for example—but in this new context, it seems to be part of a playful drama of self-revelation. As he sets about improving on the inconsistent moral criticism of the *vulgus*, chiding the gourmands in his own way, Juvenal cites the Delphic maxim "know thyself" (γνῶθι σεαυτόν, 27). Authenticity will turn out to be relevant to the satirist, too. Juvenal's readers are to be involved in this self-revelation, as if in a game. Even the Delphic quip is a hook for properly curious readers: Juvenal applies it to a most banal scenario. "One should know one's own means . . . even when buying fish" (*noscenda est mensura sui . . . etiam cum piscis emetur*, 35–36). Concern about fish size could set us thinking about an earlier poem. Is this a wink,

---

[79.] See., e.g., Weisinger, "Irony and Moderation"; cf. Bellandi, *Etica diatribica*, 80–83.

[80.] On the various diatribe themes related to luxurious living, see Oltramare, *Origins de la diatribe*, 49–52.

meant to get us seeing connections to an old Juvenal in this curious new one?

With the formal beginning of the dinner invitation and the satirist's self-insertion into the picture, the questions should not stop. Who is this "I," the host and owner of a farm? Once he makes himself more visible, ironically, his proud announcement of a homegrown meal starts to look much like an imitation of someone else's. Bellandi's argument, summarized earlier, that we are seeing Juvenal don an unfamiliar and awkward mask has much to do with the literary memories in the poem. In *Epistle* 1.5, Horace invites Torquatus to dine; like Juvenal, he avoids the crowd and recommends that guest and host be themselves.[81] And the simple, authentic dinner has an older context in Horace's *Satires*. On the one hand, in the context of Juvenal's *Satires*, the Horatian allusion is novel enough to make it look as though we have a strikingly new persona. On the other hand, it is a persona that brings its own baggage with it. Even the revelation that Juvenal's food is supplied by his own farm ought to remind us of the more complicated story behind Horace's *modus agri*. In that case, Horace's identity as the country lord was a gift, not something he possessed naturally. Character, too, can be performed. So when Juvenal plays the modest, homebody host, is he really a virtuous "Evander" (as he claims at 60–63)—or a Thersites donning Achilles's armor (as he implies some people are, at 30–31)? And although his dinner guests can do with a recitation of Homer and Vergil by an unpolished slave ("what does it matter what voice recites verses like these?," *quid refert, tales versus qua voce legantur?*, 181), satire should be another matter; it is I-poetry.

The meal, of course, is supposed to be the "I" here. By playing along with the premise, we can gain insight into the satirist's character. As Horace would agree, a private social event is a good occasion for commencing a self-conscious self-redefinition. In his description of the meal to come, the satirist plays up the idea of authenticity—especially that of the food itself, but by extension his own as well. The ingredients of the dinner, he promises, will all come from his own Tiburtine farm. There will be a tender kid, still clinging to its mother, asparagus picked by his bailiff's wife, and other carefully picked and preserved fruits (65–76). The eggs are personified: they will be served alongside *their* mothers (70–71), as if implicitly to prove their origins. The wine, too, is homegrown (147–53, 159–61). Even the slaves who serve it were born on Juvenal's estate, and they prove it by

---

[81.]On the self-revelatory theme of the *Epistle*, see Putnam, "Horace to Torquatus."

speaking Latin and visibly daydreaming of home (152–53). The description of one rustic slave boy, shy and uncharacteristically groomed for the party, pining for his hut (152–54), evokes the country-loving Horace of the *Satires*; even this is a kind of stamp of generic authenticity on Juvenal's meal.

Authenticity and artificiality (or imitation) constitute one significantly fragile dichotomy; another is inside and outside. Juvenal's private meal is not invisible to the rest of the world, as is suggested when he imagines a "haughty dinner guest" invading his home and scorning the fare (*ergo superbum/convivam caveo, qui me sibi comparat et res/despicit exiguas*, 129–31). And a collection of dinner ingredients that is so calculatedly pure is, if not necessarily vulnerable, necessarily defined by what it is not.[82] In large part the value of the items served derives from the comparanda and foils against which Juvenal defines them, so that images of decadent alternatives permeate the description of the dinner. In this sense, the poetic invitation has it both ways whereas the "real" meal cannot: the text serves up both simple and decadent, ancient and contemporary, approved and forbidden fare. The pattern of negation begins when the poet initially describes his meal as "equipped by no markets" (*nullis ornata macellis*, 64) in a pointed reference to the contrasting lifestyle of the gourmands.

For less tangible inspiration, Juvenal has the model of the virtuous Roman past, in which even a meal like his own represented the utmost luxury (77–119). By itself, the idealizing description of the ancient customs complements and enriches the description of Juvenal's dinner. But the juxtaposition does not amount to an invocation of the past as a static, validating model for the present. Instead, the vignettes of the past add up to a story about change and influence. The old-time soldier who came upon fine goblets amid booty from a sacked city would convert them into striking decorations for his armor (100–110). The anecdote is telling: material wealth, and the appetites it fosters, find an insidious way even into the lifestyle of the naive and virtuous. Jupiter's statues changed from earthenware to gold (116), and the families who casually ate porridge from Etruscan bowls (108) were the ancestors of those who now require massive and elaborate dining tables to stimulate their taste buds (120–31). The luxury wares that the gourmands hocked for food in the first section are reappearing elsewhere, as if acknowledging a law of conservation of poetic matter.

---

[82]Gowers, *Loaded Table*, 201.

The account of the virtuous past also serves as a transition into another extended, complicating description: that of the luxurious modern-day banquet that he refuses to host. In fact, nearly three-quarters of the description of the meal (131–71) consists of negations—depictions of the extravagant dishes and outlandish entertainments that will *not* be found at the poet's home. There will be no ivory tables, Juvenal vows; no exotic game or elaborate performances by a carver, no erotic Spanish dancing that would titillate the most jaded guests. In effect, he uses these images to construct his *cena* just as he imagines the ancient, rugged soldier using silver goblets to deck out his weapons of war. Although the soldier did not make or even covet them, the images of Mars, the she-wolf, and the twins could make an emotional impression on his enemy at the moment of death (*perituro . . . hosti*, 107). In the same way, the satirist's vicarious use of other people's lifestyles adds color and complexity to his invitation poem.

Satire 11 treats its audiences, internal and external, to images of forbidden luxury and pleasure. This poetic strategy evokes the Senecan model that is said to lurk behind the poems of Juvenal's fourth book, although not quite in the way that the persona studies imply. We will recall that in *On Tranquility*, Serenus confesses to being prone to distracting flights of the imagination—about the quiet of home, the promise of glory in the forum, great thoughts that he longs to put into writing (1.11–13). The very first scenario of discontent that Serenus describes, however, is his susceptibility to fantasies of luxury and pomp even as he strives to live frugally. Images of beautiful slaves, houses glittering with precious stones, and diners surrounded by lavish feasts plague him (1.4–9). Serenus admits further that "none of these things changes me, yet none of them does not shake me up" (*nihil horum me mutat, nihil tamen non concutit*, 1.9). In other words, images of the kind that haunt him are troubling even to one who can resist them consciously. This aspect of his condition makes Juvenal's style of invitation, an elaborate series of comparisons and visualizations, seem potentially upsetting to his own addressee. Persicus may indeed be especially vulnerable. The invitation may be a tease, designed to hint that the poet's evocatively named friend has tastes on the luxurious side (cf. the nudge at line 162, *forsitan expectes . . .*).[83] Even if Persicus were more like Serenus, of course, he would still hypothetically be susceptible to temptation. His host is walking a fine line by giving him such an

---

[83.]Jones ("Persona and the Addressee"; cf. *Juvenal*, 142) argues that Juvenal makes Persicus the indirect target of the poem. It is tempting to see an echo of Horace's *Persicos odi . . . apparatus* (*C.* 1.38.1).

elaborately descriptive text, in which the positive and negative elements are interdependent.

At any rate, Persicus is getting more than a simple meal and a little epic recital. He is exploited: having been invited to inspect his host's lifestyle, he finds himself in the spotlight. His possible decadent tastes are not his only vulnerable area. Thanks to his host, and despite appearances, Persicus's busy and anxious life is following him all the way to the dining room. Juvenal urges his addressee to put aside his worries about finances, clients, wife, household, and associates (183–92). This is a commonplace of the invitation genre.[84] Horace ends his poem for Torquatus with laughing encouragement: use the back door to give the slip to the client in your atrium, and come to my place (*Ep.* 1.5.30–31). But in Juvenal, the list of Persicus's troubles seems to aim at the opposite effect. It is essentially a *praeteritio*, raising the specter of the guest's various troubles. This fits the pattern of negation that we have seen in the construction of the dinner itself. The very items that Persicus is supposed to leave "out there" are put to use in the text, and the addressee thus becomes an emotional participant whether he wants to or not. Especially manipulative is a vision of another arrival elsewhere: Persicus's wife coming home with a suspiciously damp, rumpled, and flushed appearance (186–89):

> nec, prima si luce egressa reverti
> nocte solet, tacito bilem tibi contrahat uxor
> umida suspectis referens multicia rugis
> vexatasque comas et voltum auremque calentem.

> . . . and don't let your wife's behavior produce silent rage in you, if she tends to leave home at dawn and return at night, sporting damp underthings along with suspicious wrinkles, tousled hair, and a flushed face and ears.

This is not just a needling depiction of evidence for the wife's brash adultery.[85] It is also a needling depiction of her husband's typical bilious and silent response to this evidently common sight (187). If Persicus misses that explicit reference, perhaps he will notice that the vision of his wife's

---

[84] Cf. Hor. *Ep.* 1.5.9–10; on other parallels, see Adamietz, *Untersuchungen zur Juvenal*, 156 n. 82, and Braund, *Beyond Anger*, 186–87.
[85] So Smith ("Greed and Sacrifice," 291) describes the passage, comparing it to the treatment of Corvinus in *Satire* 12; cf. Courtney, *Satires*, 491: "186–9 could never be addressed to [an actual friend]."

body is stamped with hints of his own rage, like a mirror, what with the wrinkles in her clothes, her "vexed" hair, her hot face. Juvenal re-enacts the encounter itself, ensuring that his addressee will access his customary anger—that unpleasant feeling that he was supposed to leave on the other side of the doorstep, like Torquatus escaping out the back of his house. The fact that this vignette also conjures a memory of Juvenal's longest poem, the sixth *Satire*, is another reminder of the "old" satirist. Even now he is willing to make jokes about adultery at the husband's expense.[86]

Juvenal's private meal is infused with images and problems from "out there." The point of entry for all of this external material is the entrance to his house itself. "Put down whatever is upsetting you in front of my doorstep," the satirist tells Persicus as he rattles off his friend's problems (*protinus ante meum quidquid dolet exue limen*). Couched in the goading catalog of troubles, this already sounds slightly disingenuous. But the reference to Juvenal's *limen* is especially suggestive. After all, this is the vantage point from which the laughing Democritus drew his *materia risus* (10.29). The doorstep is not an isolating boundary but by definition the mocking figure's point of contact with the outside. Throughout *Satire* 11, Juvenal has been drawing on outside material for his dinner—using the crowd's gossip and images of culinary paragons and villains. And now Persicus is approaching the threshold, bringing with him a treasure trove to dump easily within the satirist's range of vision. This addressee would probably not call his creator a certified *tranquillus*.

The backhanded invitation in line 190 is one punch line of the poem. A second one follows as Juvenal puts the finishing touches on the temporal and geographical setting of his dinner. It is confirmed that we are not in some distant country retreat but in Rome, within earshot of the lively *vulgus* pictured at the poem's opening.[87] The Megalesia holiday is underway, the whole city is at the races, and the excited cries and groans of the crowd reach the poet's ear (197–98). Like the earlier descriptions of food and furnishings that will not be present at the dinner, the ten-line vignette of the races is vivid with colors, movements, and interactions.[88] Like Martial's Saturnalian Book 11, *Satire* 11 has a holiday setting. Its internal drama is removed from the festivities, but just as the Saturnalia holiday pursues

---

[86.] See Bellandi, *Etica diatribica*, 72–73 n. 110, for the remark that Persicus's bile now substitutes entirely for the satirist's.

[87.] The only other hint that we are not in the country is the reference to the slave boy's homesickness (152–53); as Highet notes (*Juvenal the Satirist*, 279 n. 2), many readers have been misled as to the setting.

[88.] Bellandi, *Etica diatribica*, 74 n. 116.

Horace in *Satire* 2.3, the distant holiday becomes part of Juvenal's dinner. Horace's *Epistle* 1.5 is another relevant model: there, the private space and authentic performances of self of Horace and his guest are made possible by an impending holiday, Caesar's birthday (9–11). The Horatian *cena* is essentially defined by a backdrop that is much more public and political.[89] In the Juvenalian case, the satirist is quite willing to let the holiday in: his eager ears are the metaphorical *limen* that gives him access to more satiric material outside his home. This constitutes a variation on Senecan metaphors of games, courts, elections, and other activities of public life, used in "articulating relationships within the self."[90] Because Juvenal is defining *his* self more literally in relation to the outside, he seems to be engaging in both resistance and connection.

With this image comes a memory of Umbricius's permanent withdrawal from Rome in *Satire* 3, a move that I have argued amounts to only a temporary separation from satiric exchange. Juvenal finds his own way to have it both ways. From inside his city home, he keeps his ears, eyes, and imagination open to what is "out there." The image of the circus, paired with the opening snapshot of public gossip, makes a busy and emotionally rich border for the satirist's poetic house—one that he reaches out and touches. In the metapoetic lexicon of Juvenal's satire, the interior of the house is neither sterile ground for satire nor a site of tranquility. It is a new setting where the drama of satire happens, much like Horace's pretended retirement in *Satires* Book 2. It is a place for reflection on his own satiric abilities and tendencies, as well as a vantage point from which he can choose to keep engaging the feelings of his audience. Although gritty street satire may be a thing of the satirist's past, the action is not over.

Reclaiming a Legacy

Juvenal probes further into the possibilities of satiric friendship with *Satire* 12. While some scholars insist that an observable theme—"Friendship True and False"[91] gives the poem coherence, most acknowledge its formal oddities, including multiple characters and settings and a dramatic shift

---

[89] On Juvenal's expansion of the Horatian scenario, see Adamietz, *Untersuchungen zur Juvenal*, 156.
[90] Edwards, "Self-Scrutiny and Self-Transformation," 36.
[91] See Ramage, "Juvenal, Satire 12," and more recently Stramaglia, *Giovenale*, 229–33. For Ronnick ("Form and Meaning") the unifying theme is more abstract (bonds of various kinds); for Highet (*Juvenal the Satirist*, 136) it is greed.

from one narrative subject (the return of a friend from sea) to another (the societal blight of legacy-hunting).[92] Only Uden's reading highlights the poem's apparent disjointedness as central to its satiric agenda: the reader is compelled to see connections between practices as superficially different as sacrifice and legacy-hunting.[93] But there is still a satirist figure to be considered—one who puts himself at the center of this tour. After *Satire* 11, we should be primed to look for a story about him. First, then, we can note that this poem reverses the diptych pattern of the previous one: the spotlight falls first on the satirist's actions, later on general social ills. As in 11, however, we begin out in public—indeed, we learn where we are before we know why we are there. On this special day, Juvenal is at the turf altar on the Capitoline, with Corvinus as his witness, sacrificing to Juno, Minerva, and Jupiter (3–9). Only fifteen lines in do we learn his present purpose: he is making a thank-offering for the miraculous return of Catullus from stormy seas.

Like its predecessor, *Satire* 12 puts in the foreground the relationship between public self-presentation and private behavior; it also reactivates the authenticity theme. Viewed through this lens, the poem appears to offer different kinds of evidence about the character of the speaking satirist who commands our attention from the beginning (*mihi*, 1). First comes a "public" display of symbols of Juvenal's character (1–16); after the storm narrative Juvenal points to his private behavior so that we may compare it with his public performance (83–91), and finally comes a description of the kind of insincere, extravagant behavior that the poet condemns—the machinations of legacy-hunters (93–130). In the first two passages, the presence of Corvinus functions as test and guarantee of Juvenal's sincerity. But such a concerted effort at proof is bound to have other effects. For one thing, images of decadent and dishonest lifestyles cannot but color this text about the poet's supposed purity of practice and intentions. Moreover, on the level of rhetorical delivery, as he pursues his topic Juvenal seems to transform into a scathing satirist again. This furthers the hints made in *Satire* 11 that domestic satire is not equivalent to tranquility. Although this poem's ostensible purpose is to display the satirist's piety, affection, and joy, this is only half the story of his true nature. Juvenal's *virtus* again turns out to be the work that he has been doing in various forms since his

---

[92.] Helmbold calls *Satire* 12 "largely unsuccessful" ("Juvenal's Twelfth Satire," 22); Courtney calls it "slack" and "Juvenal's weakest" (*Satires*, 518). Henke, "Elefanten, Tochtermörder und Erbschleicher," 202–3 cites other criticisms.

[93.] Uden, *Invisible Satirist*, 176—202.

first book: attack and criticism. And in this case, *indignatio* looks to be resurfacing.

In the Capitoline scene, Juvenal describes his sacrificial victims as if he knows them personally; they were all raised on his farm, like the ingredients of his dinner in *Satire* 11. The young calf (7–9) is a slightly older analogue of the kid at 11.65–69.[94] Although the satirist lacks the material means (*res ampla domi*, 10) for a lavish sacrifice, he compensates with offerings that reflect his own nature. This includes, appropriately for this poet, plenty of items that recall other literary texts—within a poem already dotted with literary names (Corvinus, Catullus, Pacuvius)—and with vivid descriptions of the animals proceeding to the altar.[95] Even the long narrative of Catullus's ordeal at sea, which seems at first to interrupt the description of the first sacrifice (17–82), may be read as an element of the thank-offering. The account is as vivid as the conventional "poetic storm" (*omnia fiunt/talia, tam graviter si quando poetica surgit/tempestas*, 22–24), a gesture to the expert imitation of epic noise that opened *Satire* 1.

The storm narrative is also Juvenal's textual version of the votive tablets that shipwrecked sailors hang in temples (26–29):

> . . . dira quidem sed cognita multis
> et quam votiva testantur fana tabella
> plurima: pictores quis nescit ab Iside pasci?
> accidit et nostro similis fortuna Catullo.

> [The fate of shipwreck is] terrible indeed, though known to plenty of people, as many a shrine full of votive tablets attests; who doesn't know that painters make their living from Isis? A similar fate befell my friend Catullus.

This image is not just a gratuitous sideswipe at shipwreck victims or the artists whom they employ; it is a key to understanding the function of the storm narrative within the poem. By highlighting the practice of representation of sea-storms, first in textual (*poetica tempestas*) and then in material form, Juvenal detaches his account from Catullus's actual experiences and advertises it as his own version of the event.[96] The poet standing in the

---

[94.]Cf. Smith, "Greed and Sacrifice," 288.

[95.]The satirist's sacrificial victims recall passages from Vergil (*G.* 3.232, 2.146–48) and Horace (*C.* 4.2.53–60). On the particularly Augustan flavor of this poem (and the previous one) as relevant to Hadrian's self-presentation, see Uden, *Invisible Satirist*, 178—86.

[96.]At the end of the account, too, Juvenal briefly pictures the now-safe sailors babbling their story (*gaudent . . . garrula securi narrare pericula nautae*, 81–82).

temple is our window into what happened "out there." The votive tablet analogy has two particularly interesting effects. First, it evokes the analogy that Horace made between Lucilius's autobiographical poetry and votive tablets (*S.* 2.1.30–34), and so prepares us for satire even in this "authentic" poem of thanks. Second, in the context of a poem that describes a sacrifice, it encourages us to read the content of the storm narrative as if it were present at the scene, displayed by the altar.

Juvenal's narrative votive tablet is not entirely of a piece with the home-grown lambs and calf that he is offering to the Capitoline gods. For one thing, the account of the storm is not entirely kind to Catullus. True, the merchant made the crucial decision to throw his cargo overboard in hopes of lightening his load; this might be interpreted as a valorous, even Stoic move.[97] But the praise for Catullus's actions is undercut with mockery. He is a dealer in luxury goods, so already in a vulnerable position with the satirist, who has mocked the consumers of such goods in *Satire* 11 and many other poems, and even pauses to rant against fools who undergo the dangers of seafaring (57–59).[98] The decision to dump the cargo reminds Juvenal of the trapped beaver who chews off his valuable testicles rather than let the hunter get them (34–36). Thus Catullus is implied to have lost his manhood along with his goods—an idea that is later echoed in the image of him cutting down the ship's mast (54).[99]

Moreover, Catullus's loss of his goods is painted in luxurious detail; the poet catalogs the cargo as it tumbles overboard (37–47). The "whole lot" (*cuncta*) includes "the finest objects" (*pulcherrima*): purple clothing "fit for soft Maecenases," fabrics made from the wool of sheep that are "naturally" dyed with gold from Spanish rivers, silver platters, a huge mixing bowl, baskets, plates, and goblets. This textual, almost ecphrastic, tribute to the goods undercuts the sentiment that Juvenal tacks onto the end of the catalog ("what other man, in what part of the world, would dare to prefer his life to his silver, his safety to his property?," *quis nunc alius, qua mundi parte quis audet/argento praeferre caput rebusque salutem?*, 48–49). It is difficult to imagine that this part of the tale would comfort the traumatized merchant, who will, so to speak, see his goods one last time in the satirist's account of their loss. As he does with the hocked property in *Satire*

[97.]Adamietz, "Juvenals 12. Satire," 240–41.

[98.]Here, too, Juvenal is trotting out a common theme of diatribe; see Oltramare, *Origins de la diatribe*, 63.

[99.]Larmour, "Lightening the Load."

11, Juvenal retrieves and uses these goods for his poem, this time hanging their image in the temple.

In exploiting Catullus's adventure, Juvenal has conflated his own two identities of friend and satirist. The latter seems to emerge from the miniature drama of the temple scene. At the close of the account, however, Juvenal appears eager to emphasize his role as friend again, reviving the authenticity theme and expanding it in a new direction. In two swift dactylic lines (87–88), the poet returns to his home to begin his second round of thank-offerings. Although the reading audience was already privy to the ceremony performed at the Capitoline temple, this change of venue is highlighted so as to emphasize the essentially sacred privacy of the satirist's home. Juvenal means to show us, as in *Satire* 11, that what goes on inside his house matches what he presents on the outside. For his "own Jove" and Lares, Juvenal has put out garlands, incense, branches, and lamps (87–92). The sparkling contents of the house are as vividly evoked, and as authentic-looking, as the dishes served in the previous poem. Underneath the decorations we once again see Juvenal's door (here a *ianua*, 91), looking like an emblem of the correlation between his public and private gestures. This might make a nice closing image for the poem, to balance the opening scene of public sacrifice.

As it happens, however, the symmetry and the silence are broken, when the poet anticipates a suspicious response to the proceedings from his addressee. Juvenal has invited Corvinus to observe his sacrifices, but now that he is conscious of being watched, he addresses this unspoken question: Are his efforts genuine, or aimed at securing a place in Catullus's will? (93–95). This makes Corvinus into a spectator of the satirist's speech as well as his actions, for there follows a nearly thirty-line tirade against legacy-hunters that finishes off the poem. Catullus already has heirs, Juvenal points out; it is the rich and childless who attract unscrupulous *captatores*. The latter vie with one another to show their devotion by offering increasingly preposterous sacrifices when their patrons fall ill. So goes the "satire in miniature":[100] we are first shown temples full of votive tablets like the poet's own, then hecatombs, elephants, and even human offerings—slaves and modern-day Iphigenias. The extravagant sacrifices are piled up with poetic gusto, much as Catullus's wares were serially and almost majestically ejected from his ship. Although Juvenal's overall treatment of legacy-hunting shares some elements with light treatments of

---

[100.]Ramage, "Juvenal, Satire 12," 233.

this conventional theme, the amplification in the sacrificial imagery also suggests a resurgence of his former *indignatio*.[101] This is a surprising turn of events in the hushed interior of the satirist's house.

It is true that there is a visible difference between the satirist's offerings on behalf of Catullus—modest and from the heart—and the overdone performances of the unscrupulous legacy-hunters. But this is not the only point of contrast around which the poem evolves. Having begun his poem with a prayer of thanks, the satirist concludes with a curse against the most excessive and shameless of the *captatores*. Pacuvius may live as long as Nestor and be wealthy as Nero with a mountain of ill-gotten gold, but "let him love no one and be loved by no one!" (*vivat Pacuvius quaeso vel Nestora totum,/possideat quantum rapuit Nero, montibus aurum/exaequet, nec amet quemquam nec ametur ab ullo*, 128–30). As a final comment on friendship, these words have a decent literary pedigree: Cicero's *Laelius* imagines the misery of living in luxury while neither loving nor being loved.[102] From another angle, there is the recent model of Statius *Silvae* 1.3, a poem that ends with a wish for Manilius Vopiscus to live more years than Nestor, so he can fully enjoy the luxurious and peaceful villa that Statius has been praising.[103] In this way, then, the *Satire* leaves a final impression that friendship is its main theme. But what of the satirist himself, his rhetorical style, and his state of mind at the end of this "tranquil" book? The curse is not tranquil retreat or even mockery, but interventional, magical speech, the potent ancestor of satire itself. There is no tranquility here, although there are ironic gestures to the prayers surveyed in *Satire* 10.[104] On the other hand, as one nineteenth-century commentator put it, this "side-blow" against legacy-hunters is the closest Juvenal seems to come to true satire in this poem.[105]

Why does the topic of *captatores* absorb the satirist's attention at this juncture, diverting his poem about Catullus to an end that puzzles and

---

[101] On the tone, see Henke, "Elefanten, Tochtermörder und Erbschleicher," 217; cf. Smith, "Greed and Sacrifice," 297–98. For similar sketches of *captatores*, see Mart. 6.63, 10.19(18), 10.97, 11.44, and 12.90 (cf. Colton, "Echoes of Martial," 168–72), and Petr. 116–17, 124.2–125, and 141.

[102] Cic. *Amic.* 52: *qui velit, ut neque diligat quemquam nec ipse ab ullo diligatur, circumfluere omnibus copiis atque in omnium rerum abundantia vivere?* Cf. Ramage "Juvenal, Satire 12," 235–37.

[103] Stat. *Silv.* 1.3.108–10. Vopiscus's Tiburtine villa seems far more luxurious than Juvenal's own, but according to Statius, it is perfect for his brand of the contemplative life (90–93).

[104] Walker, "Moralizing Discourse," 101: the prayer for vengeance turns out to be "true prayer" in the satirist's eyes, despite the implication at the end of *Satire* 10.

[105] Macleane, *Juvenalis et Persii Satirae*, 277.

even—in Henke's intriguing wording—angers scholars?[106] How does this diatribe take over the poem, upsetting the perfect triptych created by the public sacrifice, the narrative "votive tablet," and the private ceremony? However we answer the question, and however we attempt to stitch the poem's two main sections together by noting thematic echoes, the account of *Satire* 12 as a performance of tranquility cannot stand. The drama that unfolds here may suggest an intrusion by a critical Corvinus that derails the poem from its intended course. Alternatively, we may imagine that Juvenal has led both addressee and reader through the public and then private rituals only to trap us in a performance of his old *virtus*, invective. In the larger context of Book 4, too, there are some thematic connections to note: certainly the *captatores*, like the characters in *Satire* 10, practice a selfish piety and are punished in their own way. And as in 11, the portrait of a generic vice stands as a counterpart to Juvenal's own behavior at home. But this static assessment is challenged by the dramatic reading that centers on the curious satirist figure. This is no detached figure like the laughing Democritus but an active character who responds to his environment in a more engaged and creative way. The surroundings of his own home stimulate him to wax satiric, not tranquil.

As for the subject of the satirist's final rant in Book 4, a closing review of earlier examples helps to explain Juvenal's use of the theme at this point. Persius's richly metapoetic swan song, *Satire* 6, features the satirist in the pose of a rich man teasing his greedy heir by vowing to enjoy his wealth in the present. That authorial role represents a novel use of the legacy-hunting theme that also appears in Horace's second book of *Satires* (2.5). Persius is parading his poetic stores and refusing to send his carefully crafted text into the world as a commodity; Horace, for his part, uses his impoverished Ulysses to satirically dramatize the choices available to a former "outsider" like himself in post-Actian Rome.[107] Before Juvenal, then, legacy-hunting is a theme of the late satiric career. Moreover, Juvenal has re-enacted Persius's concluding attack in *Satire* 6—"satire pure" emerging from the "massive feint" of the epistolary setting.[108] The Neronian poet's

---

[106] On "der Zorn der Literarkritiker . . . gegen die 12. Satire," see Henke, "Elefanten, Tochtermörder und Erbschleicher," 203.

[107] On both texts, see Osgood, "Introduction," 5–10; Freudenburg, *Satires of Rome*, 99 and 195–208; and other relevant discussions of Persius in n. 76 above. Woods ("Hunting Literary Legacies," 19) calls the *captatio* theme in Horace S. 2.5 "the ideal metaphor for the artist's struggle to create a place for himself in literary history."

[108] Hooley, *Knotted Thong*, 171. The victims of the *Satire* turn out to be "the greedy heir and the reader [who has fallen for Persius's contented epistolary pose]."

strange version of the epistolary persona highlights the cross-pollination between satire and epistle, a relationship that destabilizes the conventional images of the individual genres. In turn, Persius's "epistle" helps us to read Horace's *Epistles* more perceptively—not as demonstrations of authorial tranquility but as works that scrutinize and play with the concept of performed relaxation. A rhetorical and generic source of inspiration in Book 4, the "Democritean" epistolary persona of Horace is itself an illusion. With this poetic patrimony in tow, Juvenal's "tranquil" book is bound to be anything but.

CHAPTER 5 | The *Praegrandis Senex*

BOOK 4 USED FRIENDSHIP as a framework and a subject; what comes next makes a fitting sequel. Juvenal appears to be taking on the role of frank adviser in *Satire* 13, his sights on a man named Calvinus who has been defrauded of a loan. In an unsettling parody of the *consolatio* genre, the satirist rebukes Calvinus for his unseemly anger.[1] A quick survey of the poem's opening turns up a number of the "Doug Piranha" techniques cited at the opening of chapter 3. On the microscopic level, there is litotes and overdone metaphor: Calvinus's financial means are "not slight," his recent loss "not rare" in human experience (6–8); yet, having been "buried" by "fortune's heap," he "burns" with rage (8–14). These rhetorical nuts and bolts are part of a larger ironic tapestry in the satirist's mock *consolatio*, which within the first few lines develops into criticism and mockery of Calvinus for his emotional overreaction. We might imagine the addressee feeling like a victim, lured by an initial expectation of sympathy only to find himself the satiric target of this misleadingly friendly "Doug."

Juvenal's twist on the *consolatio* taps into a delicate aspect of ancient friendship. For Roman writers, the business of consolation can involve tough love and tension.[2] So do the duties of friendship between men; frank

---

[1] See Pryor, "Juvenal's False Consolation"; Fredericks, "Calvinus in Thirteenth Satire"; Edmunds, "Juvenal's Thirteenth Satire"; Morford, "Juvenal's Thirteenth Satire"; Adamietz, "Juvenals 13. Gedicht"; and Braund, "Passion Unconsoled."

[2] Seneca *Ep.* 99, addressed to Lucilius but recapitulating Seneca's *consolatio* to a grieving Marullus, is an example. Wilson ("Subjugation of Grief," 66) calls the *Epistle* "a non-consolatory consolation" that is grounded in Seneca's earnest Stoic principles (challenging the Epicurean Metrodorus's teachings on grief) but takes extra liberties because it is "quoting" a *consolatio* delivered to someone other than the addressee (perhaps even a fictional person). Social competition also made its way into *consolationes*; see Wilcox, "Sympathetic Rivals."

speech can be not just a prerogative, but a requirement, of true *amicitia*.[3] This means that friends face other fears and challenges besides the possibility of false affection highlighted at the end of Book 4. *Libertas* between friends, notionally a good thing, could hurt; by the same token, *libertas* might look like friendship, but not be. We have seen Juvenal exploit these possibilities in *Satires* 5 and 6, and again in 11, where his invitation to Persicus contains a share of abuse. Now in *Satire* 13, the emotional theme of the ironic *consolatio* sets the stage for more satiric manipulation. This time there is a very special dramatic setting. We glean not just that the satirist is an adviser to his addressee but that they are both old men. This detail, which has played into interpretation of the entire fifth book, requires some deeper consideration and contextualization.

Rethinking the Grand Narrative

Prior analyses of Book 5 may be the best illustration of the difficulties entailed in the rhetorical approach to Juvenal's personae. In a word, the book is very hard to characterize with any single descriptor, including an "emotional" label. There are mellow notes in these poems, and even some unprecedented meditation on positive moral ideals. Juvenal praises what we might call the "civilized emotions" of paternal concern and fellow feeling in *Satires* 14 and 15.[4] Accordingly, some have tentatively diagnosed the mindset of the new persona as "calmer and more detached," and as possessing "a measure of the *tranquillitas* advocated by Seneca and the Democritean satirist [*sic*],"[5] But some scholars have been more struck by the harshness of the address to Calvinus or the satirist's extreme pronouncements on human nature, characterizing his tone as cynical, harsh, disenchanted, and disillusioned.[6] Finally, still others have highlighted

---

[3] For more on frank speech between friends, see Sen. *Ep.* 3, Cic. *Amic.* 25–26, Plu. *How to Tell a Flatterer from a Friend*, and the Epicurean sources discussed in Armstrong, "Be Angry and Sin Not." Juvenal, of course, does not justify his harsh speech with philosophical principles; he dismisses strict philosophical doctrine as a life guide at 13.120–23.

[4] For the argument that *humanitas*, rather than misanthropy, is Juvenal's new guiding principle, see Corn, "Persona in Fifth Book" (especially 112), and cf. the discussion of *Satire* 15 in this chapter.

[5] See, respectively, Braund, *Beyond Anger*, 194–95 (actually proffering several different labels: calm detachment, cynicism, and *humanitas*), and Anderson, "Anger in Juvenal," 190 (=*Essays*, 356).

[6] See Braund's labels (previous note) and cf. Walker's comparison of this persona to the harshly laughing Democritus ("Moralizing Discourse," esp. 112 and 130). Ficca calls him an "osservatore ormai disincantato e disilluso" (*Giovenale Satira XIII*, 9; cf. 12). Lindo surveys contradictory descriptions of the trajectory ("Evolution of Later Books," 17).

inconsistencies in tone that they regard as definitive—as evidence of two competing personae or satiric worldviews.[7]

The cause of both the emotional theme of analyses of Book 5 and the ambivalence of those analyses is surely the emotional *subject matter* of the book's opening poem. Juvenal's command to Calvinus to let go of his anger has been a focal point not just in discussions of Book 5 but in broader assessments of "late Juvenal." To see the poet who made his debut embracing *indignatio* now explicitly make fun of the mindset of righteous rage is, if not a surprise, an irresistible invitation to compare past and present. While in *Satire* 1 he reveled in the physiological symptoms of anger and even evoked "frankness" or "simplicity," *simplicitas*, with reverence (1.153), in *Satire* 13 he treats the burning Calvinus with apparent scorn and assures him that his *simplicitas* is the butt of public mockery (13.33).[8] No wonder that—Ribbeck's theory of a "false Juvenal" aside—the poem is the most frequently cited next to *Satire* 10 in overviews of "late Juvenal."[9] Indeed, the negative, ironizing perspective on anger in 13 seems to draw a line between early and later *Satires* even more explicitly than the vignette of Democritus in *Satire* 10. It makes sense that *Satire* 13 became "a touchstone for the criteria to be followed in the interpretation of Juvenal."[10]

It is critical, however, that this touchstone not be treated as a sort of authentic commentary on the passions or on Juvenal's career trajectory. The satirist does not come to "reject" the emotion that was so central to his early *Satires*; he is still performing, not reflecting on his text from the outside. To start understanding this performance better, we may work from Braund's careful characterization of Juvenal's early and late work, respectively: "an engagement with the passion of anger . . . followed by a critique of that engagement."[11] The description fits as long as we understand that the "critique" is still a kind of "engagement with anger" itself. After all, anger has not been a recent issue in the *Satires*, something that demands

---

[7.]See Corn, "Persona in Fifth Book" (arguing that *Satires* 13 and 16 feature an "ironic" persona, 14 and 15 an "indignant" one); Bellandi, *Etica diatribica*, 66–101 (Juvenal shows discomfort with the "Democritean" mask he adopts); and Fredericks, "Juvenal's Fifteenth Satire," 189 (*Satire* 15 models "two possible reactions to evil in the world, outrage and astonishment . . . and cynical worldly wisdom").

[8.]For more on the mockery of *simplicitas* in 73, cf. Pryor, "Juvenal's False Consolation," 172–73, and Braund, "Passion Unconsoled," 72.

[9.]See Ficca, *Giovenale Satira XIII*, 9; Anderson, "Programs of Later Books," 150 (=*Essays*, 282) and "Anger," 174–95 (=*Essays*, 340–61); Fredericks, "Calvinus," 225; and Adameitz, "Juvenals 13. Gedicht," 469–70.

[10.]Courtney, *Satires*, 533.

[11.]Braund, "Passion Unconsoled," 87–88.

a reaction from the satirist now. It is Juvenal himself who raises the topic in *Satire* 13.[12] Although his approach is now colored by anger-control discourse, the last thing we should think is that the author is holding passions themselves at an ironic distance.

The Satiric *Senex* and the Emotional Plot

The opening of *Satire* 13 highlights two linked subjects: anger (and, more precisely, the need for anger control) and life experience, represented in the claims that Calvinus is at an advanced age (a *senior* of sixty; 17, 33). The latter topic has played its own part in the emotionally themed characterizations of Juvenal's latest *Satires*. By establishing Calvinus's birth year and age, Juvenal provides us with a terminus post quem for Book 5,[13] and allows us to infer that he, too, is an old man by now. He certainly claims the right to call Calvinus *senior bulla dignissime*, "an old man who ought to be wearing a child's amulet" (33); this sounds like an address to a coeval. A useful comparison text is Plutarch's treatise *Whether an Old Man Should Engage in Public Affairs*, which begins by underscoring that not just the addressee Euphanes but also the author has reached the age in question, as if to make the advice seem more acceptable.[14] We may also look back to Juvenal's mentions of old age in Book 4—first a catalog of old men's woes, then a glimpse of the wrinkled satirist.[15] Juvenal is feeding the theme of senectitude into his work as if to suggest a framework for reading.

In fact, assumptions and expectations about old man's satire have visibly colored assessments of Juvenal's changing style; here, then, is another area where we will benefit from acknowledging how these expectations are cultivated. The emergence of a "late" Juvenal invites generalizing

---

[12.]Keane, "*Persona* and Satiric Career," 116.

[13.]Coffey, *Roman Satire*, 120; Syme even speculates that Juvenal is actually revealing his own birth year ("Juvenal, Pliny, Tacitus," 259–60, and *Tacitus*, 775). Cf. Courtney, *Satires*, 1–2 (warning that the consul Fonteius named in 17 could refer to the years 58, 59, or 67).

[14.]In Plu. *Mor.* 783b, note the first person plurals: "our avoidance of political struggles and our infirmities" (αἱ πρὸς τοὺς πολιτικοὺς ἀγῶνας ἀποκνήσεις καὶ μαλακίαι); cf. 783c "I think myself obligated to discuss the things that I ponder continually in my own mind with you" (οἴομαι δεῖν ἃ πρὸς ἐμαυτὸν ἑκάστοτε λογίζομαι καὶ πρὸς σὲ διελθεῖν). The special relevance of works like this one that feature a strong "I" (cf. the discussion of Cicero below) is the main reason I pass over Plutarch's biographies, although these contribute to ancient discourse about old age.

[15.]*Satire* 12 also culminates in a curse on the *captator* that wishes him loneliness as he grows as old as Nestor (128–30), echoing an enduring literary formula (see, e.g., Stat. *Silv.* 1.3.110 and Mart. 11.56.13) but also the tragic picture of Nestor in *Satire* 10.

narratives about the poet's changing attitude to satire and to life. First, consider an example of careful description from Duff: The satires in the last two books are really letters . . . there is no dialogue and little dramatization. The style is . . . much less abrupt and elliptical [than that of Books 1–3]. The sentences are longer and more complicated; there is far more repetition. Nor is the contrast less striking, when we consider [the poems'] substance. . . . They are moral essays.[16]

Duff does resist attributing the different character of the later *Satires* primarily to advancing age.[17] But in other cases, the awareness that the poet was aging clearly has more influence on assessments of the poetry. A rough theory of senescent satiric style emerges, together with some negative judgments on it. Longer, more complicated sentences are interpreted as signs of loquacity; lack of topical subject matter reflects social withdrawal, even bitterness; and abstract moral musings are taken to indicate decreasing vigor and increasing reliance on books for ideas.[18] Perhaps the most damning summary of his declining powers—or declining will?—is the comment that he came to treat satire as "a routine."[19] In these evaluations, we can discern an underlying assumption "that the composition of good satire is dependent upon a presumed vitality of youth."[20] Even the compliment Highet pays to the satirist regarding the last book is colored by specific expectations: "Book III was weaker. Book IV was mellower. But as we reach . . . Book V, we are surprised to hear the old lion roaring away with a new access of vigor."[21] Even this observation underscores the idea that this descendant of the "old lion" is simply *old*.

The views Juvenal expresses in his later work also feed into these expectations. Ficca's claim that Juvenal modified his indignant tone to fit a "more ironic vision of the world and of evil"[22] comes close to merging poetic style with personal views. There is a hint that with age comes moderation of moral perspective. If we bring this belief to a reading of the later

---

[16.]Duff, *Iuvenalis Saturae XIV*, xxix–xxx. Cf. Courtney (*Satires*, 18) on the "more meditative approach" reflected in subject matter and style.

[17.]Similarly careful are Walker, "Moralizing Discourse," 32–39, and Lindo, "Evolution of Later Satires."

[18.]Lupus (*Vindiciae Iuvenalianae*, 21–22) sees *senilis loquacitas* in the late *Satires*; cf. Friedländer, *Juvenalis Saturarum libri V*, 95–96. On similar criticisms by Friedländer and others, see introduction, n. 18. Highet (*Juvenal the Satirist*, 138–39) interprets the decline in topical references as a sign that a disappointed Juvenal was turning away from the outside world to "live in the world of memory and of abstract thought" (139). Cf. Romano's diagnosis (*Irony in Juvenal*, 179).

[19.]Townend, "Literary Substrata to Juvenal," 159.

[20.]Walker, "Moralizing Discourse," 35.

[21.]Highet, *Juvenal the Satirist*, 138.

[22.]Ficca, *Giovenale Satira XIII*, 9.

Satires, we will certainly find what looks like supporting evidence. But it makes little sense to approach this kind of reading as detective work—to assume that we are looking for signs of a process external to the text, rather than a story being written into the text. In fact, if we wish to understand how Juvenal's late work qualifies as "old man's satire," we will do better to listen to how the *senex* himself, the poet, defines that term.

Juvenal cannot have been oblivious to the way readers of poetry project expectations on the text, including expectations connected to the poet's age. Imitations of famous poets produced throughout the imperial period, such as the faked *juvenilia* of Vergil, reflected common notions of what the "stamp of a youthful and untrained mind" *should* look like (in a word, "primitive").[23] Although such imitators obviously had less opportunity to construct the "late phases" of famous poets' careers, perhaps they could still have imagined a loose analogue for the opposite of *juvenilia*, the work that postdates an author's mature peak. If the crude idea of *juvenilia* as "primitive" is any indication, the phenomenon of *senilia* might have been imagined in the same groping terms we see in modern critics' assessments of late Juvenal. I mean to suggest not that any of our *Satires* might be the work of imitators, but that Juvenal might be milking expectations and stereotypes in these prolix, "diffuse," and moralistic poems, as a sort of game.[24]

In fact, we need not resort to imagination to reconstruct ancient expectations about old age or maturity, at least when it comes to the late Juvenal's moral and rhetorical tone. In Hellenistic and Roman discourse about the passions, maturity in years tends to be associated with management of emotions.[25] Inasmuch as proper handling and performance of emotions could be a tool of normative morality and hence of "civilization" by a certain definition, this was a learned skill, seldom found in the young.[26] Older men were often expected to demonstrate emotional stability and an inclination to didacticism. According to Plutarch, such a difference shows especially in speech: one can expect to see less arrogance, and more mildness, in the λόγοι (encompassing various genres of speech) of someone

---

[23.]Peirano, *Rhetoric of Roman Fake*, 85–86.

[24.]Peirano argues that imitations were composed to be recognized by learned readers *as* clever imitations (*Rhetoric of Roman Fake*; e.g., 200–204 on the *Ciris*).

[25.]Fitzgerald, "Introduction," 15; Wright, "Plutarch on Moral Progress," surveys the theme in Plutarch. Hanson ("Your Mother Nursed You," 187) cites Galen's comments about anger in this vein at *De plac. Hipp. et Plat.* 5.7.74–82 (Kühn, *Galeni opera*, 499–502).

[26.]See Kaster, *Emotion, Restraint, and Community*, for discussion of the dimensions of subtle but highly "civilized" emotions (such as *verecundia*; 13–27).

who has made moral progress.[27] Moralists did not have a monopoly on these concepts; progress to emotional maturity makes a powerful literary plot. At the very beginning of Greek literary tradition, Achilles is shown moving from isolating rage to a more socially integrated position (incidentally, with help from an old man's perspective). Closer to Juvenal's era, one Greek romance also begins with the young hero's rage and sends him on a journey toward greater self-control.[28]

In this discussion it is important not to oversimplify old age, real or fictitious, or to conflate it with maturity in other senses. But, interestingly, criticism of Juvenal's late work has itself straddled the line between seeing the older poet as "mature" and seeing him as descending into some sort of poetic senility. Viewed en masse, descriptions of Books 4 and 5 almost seem to be having their cake and eating it too—seeing now mellowness and moral authority, now lack of restraint and bitterness. These differences do not have to do with the fact that different stages ("maturity" vs. "old age") are being represented or perceived in the late *Satires*; rather, they are a reflection of the unstable characterization of the *senex* in ancient stereotyping. Not all "older men" are equal, at least not in ancient literature. This makes Juvenal's transformation into satiric *senex* a humorously easy task, as there are so many ways he can meet expectations. The same fact also underlies the drama in the book's first poem.

Old Men and *Sermo*

Satire 13 features not one old man but two, and their differences create the occasion for the poem itself. The satiric speaker makes himself out to be worldly-wise and self-controlled. His addressee Calvinus, the vehicle for Juvenal's "relativizing" of anger,[29] is trapped in a different *senex* stereotype. Though he may be striving to be the textbook righteous revenge seeker of Aristotle and aristocratic Roman ethics, the satirist likens him to another Aristotelian portrait. In *Rhetoric* 2.13, Aristotle describes the character of the πρεσβύτερος (cf. Juvenal's *senior*) in his rhetorical guidelines

---

[27.]Plu. *Mor.* 78e–80e (from *How One May Become Aware of His Progress in Virtue*); these signs are considered among other evidence of moral progress in Wright, "Plutarch on Moral Progress," 142. Seneca constructs a definition of elderly wisdom (his own and others') in *Epistles* 12, 26, and 30.

[28.]On the *Iliad*, see Most, "Anger and Pity." In Chariton's *Chaereas and Callirhoe*, the hero's destructive anger is "a key narrative impulse" (Scourfield, "Anger and Gender," 165).

[29.]"Ritorna il lessico epodico-fisiologico dell'ira, ma non riferito, questa volta, alla persona del poeta, e quindi, in qualche misura, relativizzato" (Cucchiarelli, *Satira e il poeta*, 215).

on appealing to different types of audiences. Among other things, old men are diffident, miserly, cowardly, small-minded, self-praising, shameless, fixated on talking about the past rather than living in hope for the future, calculating rather than moral (1389b13–1390a23). They are prone to sudden, but ineffectual, flare-ups of anger (οἱ θυμοὶ ὀξεῖς μὲν ἀσθενεῖς δέ εἰσιν, 1390a11), and they are complainers (ὀδυρτικοί εἰσι, 1390a21–22). Aristotle provides biological and social reasons for all these characteristics, but his main purpose is descriptive.

Another rhetorically relevant analogue is *Ars Poetica* 169–76, the longest section of Horace's instructions on depicting different age groups in drama. A typical *senex* is surrounded by troubles (*incommoda*, 169—the same word Juvenal uses in lecturing Calvinus about coping skills, 13.21). As in Aristotle, the dramatic *senex* is supposed to be "sluggish in hoping, idle, fearful for the future, cantankerous, complaining, praising the old days when he was a boy" (*spe lentus, iners, pavidusque futuri,/difficilis, querulus, laudator temporis acti/se puero*, 172–74).[30] Amusingly, this sounds not unlike Highet's reconstruction of Juvenal's overall life and character: the poet had a "peculiar personality, harsh and cruel yet timid and evasive, indignant about the past, withdrawn from the present, despairing of the future, lonely and defeated, furious at first and gradually growing resigned in pessimism."[31] But it is certainly Calvinus—"Baldy?"[32]—who is made out to be the *senex querulus* in *Satire* 13. Although the fact that he shows "grief" over lost money becomes fodder for Juvenal's parodic *consolatio*,[33] from another perspective Calvinus is simply conforming to expectations of a discontented old man.

Querulousness and cantankerousness, suggests Aristotle, are linked to fits of (feeble, but still felt) anger. So Seneca, aiming to give a medical explanation for anger even as he judges it, states that old men are *difficiles et queruli* due to their dry constitutions (*Ira* 2.19.4). General weakness of body also makes the elderly prone to anger (along with the sick and the

---

[30.]For point-by-point comparison of the Aristotle and Horace passages, see Rudd, *Horace: Epistles II*, 177–78. I am using Rudd's preferred readings *spe lentus* and *pavidusque*—admittedly, some parallels would fall away otherwise, though the passage would also make less sense—and some of his translations. Braund, "Passion Unconsoled," 78, sees in Juvenal's portrayal of Calvinus "the irate and irascible old man of New Comedy." Cokayne (*Experiencing Old Age*, 75–90) collects ancient sources characterizing old people as pessimistic, quarrelsome, irritable, loquacious, avaricious, and cowardly.

[31.]Highet, *Juvenal the Satirist*, 41.

[32.]Calvinus is an attested cognomen (Ferguson, *Prosopography*, 44); like so many names in Juvenal, it also appears in Martial (attached to a mediocre poet; 7.90.3–4).

[33.]Pryor, "Juvenal's False Consolation," 167–68.

very young; *invalidum omne natura querulum est*, 1.13.5). And in old age, the fact of approaching death thrusts the *senex* into a kind of cycle of reciprocal emotion. Our evidence about ancient wills implies that the negative feelings of *senes* were felt or at least imagined even in death, when their wills came under scrutiny. "Wills are, most obviously, expressions of emotion," for they give the impression of judgment on the living, and can generate unpleasant feelings among them in turn.[34] Considering this social reality along with the literary and rhetorical sources on old age, it is possible to see the *senex* as a regular focal point of disgust, fear, amusement, and ire—sometimes all at once.

However we are to imagine Calvinus's usual condition, I suspect that Juvenal is both exploiting the conventional idea that old men are anger-prone and tapping into a related (and unfair) one: that anger is particularly unattractive on an old and weak person. This is not quite morally based criticism along the lines of Seneca's; it has more in common with comedy in its exploitation of ethical stereotypes. By specifying that Calvinus is a *senex*, Juvenal gives his audience an image to which to attach his references to the man's pain (his *dolor* and *vulnus*, 12; his inner burning and biliousness, 11, 14–15, 143). Accompanying this is a soundtrack of impotent cries: Calvinus groans (*gemitus*, 11), invokes *fides* (31–33), cries out to the gods (36–37 and 112–19), pounds his chest and face (127–29), and utters the highly un-Stoic complaint "but revenge is a good thing, sweeter than life itself" ("*at vindicta bonum vita iucundius ipsa*," 180).[35] This performance is clearly contributing to the public ridicule that Juvenal insists Calvinus is incurring: "aren't you aware of the laughter your naiveté raises in the crowd?" (*nescis/quem tua simplicitas risum vulgo moveat . . . ?*, 34–35). With this, the earlier rhetorical question "what do you think is people's opinion on this recent 'evil deed,' this 'crime of broken faith'?" (*quid sentire putas homines, Calvine, recenti/de scelere et fidei violatae crimine?*, 5–6) takes on a new and harsher sense: the answer is that they're all laughing.[36]

---

[34]Champlin, *Final Judgments*, 8, continuing with: "fundamentally, and implicitly, [wills] offer a simple index of likes and dislikes. . . . Seldom do the actual documents that survive at any length omit some overt indication of the testator's feelings. Hope, fear, anger, doubt, delight, satisfaction, and disappointment . . . can visibly tumble over each other in the succeeding paragraphs of a single will." No wonder that wills could in turn make people feel anger and other emotions.

[35]Cf. the *iratus* at Sen. *Ira* 2.32.1 (discussed in chapter 1). Juvenal also compares Calvinus to a woman in his lust for revenge (191–92), much as Seneca essentially genders Marullus's grief for his son as feminine: *diceretur molliter ferre* (*Ep.* 99.1; cf. Wilson, "Subjugation of Grief," 60).

[36]Ficca, *Giovenale Satira XIII*, 43, infers that the inflated terms *scelus* and *fidei violatae crimen* echo the distressed Calvinus's language; elsewhere in the poem Juvenal uses more modest terms for this case of fraud (e.g., *res modica*, 143) and reserves *scelera* and *crimina* for extreme offenses.

Behind the symptoms are other faults, connected to his addressee's anger, that Juvenal revels in exposing. The epithet *senior bulla dignissime* evokes a commonplace that old age is a second childhood—one that Juvenal has already injected into his elaborate description of the pathetic *senex*.[37] The wrinkles, wobbling, baldness, runny nose, and toothlessness of the old man (10.193–200) are not his only childlike qualities. Here, the fleshed-out character of Calvinus can do what the generic *senex* in *Satire* 10—otherwise self-focused and quiet—could not. What Juvenal insinuates is that Calvinus possesses a kind of childishness of vision, being far too old-fashioned about the past and morality. Where the satirist is a cynic, Calvinus is an idealist. His *simplicitas* is implied to entail a black-and-white view of oaths and divine justice: "you demand that a man not perjure himself, and that he think there's some power in temples and bloody altars" (*exigis a quoquam ne peieret et putet ullis/esse aliquod numen templis araeque rubenti*, 36–37). The stereotype of the backward old man meshes conveniently with another, that of the superstitious man— one that Uden notes is painted with equal vividness in this poem and in Plutarch's *On Superstition*.[38] Calvinus fuels his anger with desperate theological certainty. In short, old Calvinus represents the "old days" themselves—except that Juvenal also rewrites those, scathingly, suggesting that they were both laughably backward and always on the brink of transformation into depravity. Young men respected their elders, even if the former possessed bigger stores of berries and acorns (54–59). The gods had not yet begun having festive banquets complete with attractive cupbearers, or devising the tortures of the underworld (42–52). But today, the discovery of an honest man is considered a miracle, even a terrifying prodigy (60– 70).[39] Yet Calvinus, like Seneca's stricken Marullus, behaves as if he were unaware of the ubiquity of misfortune and wrongdoing (16–18).[40]

[37.]The *Satire* 10 passage has been mined for the stereotypes it reflects; see Parkin, *Old Age*, 81–86, and Cokayne, *Experiencing Old Age*, 16. For discussion of this and other literary references to the notion of *senes* as children, see Parkin, "Elderly Children," and cf. Seneca's hint to Marullus at Sen. *Ep*. 99.10.

[38.]Uden, "Invisibility of Juvenal," 260–69; this and the next paragraph draw on Uden's reading of Juvenal's "objectionable, even alarming" antireligion stance (265).

[39.]The satirist "must be on the side of civilization," concludes Singleton ("Juvenal VI.1–20," 164) in a survey of Juvenalian and other disparaging ancient depictions of the "Golden Age." Cf. Anderson, "Programs of Later Books," 150 (=*Essays*, 282). Jones (*Juvenal*, 115) stops short of concluding that the satirist aligns himself with modern civilization here, but he does see a "secular sensibility" (112).

[40.]Cf. Seneca's question to Marullus: "What can happen that's unbelievable or novel?" (*quid incredibile, quid novum evenit?*, *Ep*. 99.22).

Although he indulges Calvinus with a vision of his enemy's future heaven-sent punishment (174–249), Juvenal seems to identify with an atheistic view that is the opposite extreme from Calvinus's religious morality and credulity. For Plutarch, these two types are really two sides of the same coin—something like the caricatures of Democritus and Heraclitus. The effect in the *Satire* is unnerving, as it rules out a moderate view on the subject of religion. But it seems to be part of the satirist's representation of himself as disinclined to anger in any circumstances. His description of how the world *really* works, which occupies the bulk of the poem, has a playful and jaded rather than emotionally troubled tone. There is the spirited speech of the brazen perjurer (92–105) who is "acting a mime" (110) to make a fool of Calvinus. There is the battering of Calvinus, called a "precious pet" (*delicias*, 140), with the argument that his loss is minor compared with the everyday sufferings of his fellow humans (135–61). Juvenal's mimicry of Calvinus's moans and groans is implicitly good for a laugh, as is the catalog of so-called marvels that are strictly speaking ordinary phenomena (162–73) and the caricature of the guilt-ridden and superstitious criminal seeing divine vengeance everywhere he looks (211–40).

Juvenal's criticisms, then, are concerned mainly with appearances and worldly wisdom rather than with the moral problems anger creates for individuals or communities. Indeed, the importance of anger itself diminishes as the poem concentrates increasingly on unveiling the true, depraved state of humanity. We are not seeing a tranquil man showing an unenlightened one the problems with the passions, but a cynical man berating an unrealistically principled one—and paint him as an old fool to boot. This suggests a competition between peers who exhibit both similarities and differences. Not all old men are alike—neither in their bodies, contrary to Juvenal's sweeping claim *una senum facies* (10.198),[41] nor in their personalities. But both men in *Satire* 13 could reasonably be called *difficilis*, and their clash viewed as inevitable in this light. The Juvenalian persona that rejects Calvinus's religious naiveté and emotionality stakes his own claim as a right-thinking *senex*. While he may not exhibit a serene wisdom, he certainly insists on appropriating certain prerogatives associated with the wise Roman elder.

Juvenal's most relevant forebear in this regard may be Cato the Elder, already an on-and-off model for the moralizing satirist,[42] but a particularly

---

[41.]Cokayne points out that Juvenal's claim was not espoused by, for example, the artists who have left us many and varied portraits of *senes* (*Experiencing Old Age*, 25–29).

[42.]Anderson discusses the relevance of the figure of Cato, qua moralist and orator, to Juvenal's satire generally; see "Juvenal and Quintilian," 86–89 (=*Essays*, 481–84). Corn ("Persona in Fifth

interesting model for his last book. Cicero used Cato to speak for old age in a way that blends not just eloquence and social criticism but also a kind of cheerful belligerence—perhaps captured in the term *animosus* that Cato applies to healthy and brave old age (*Sen.* 20.72). In the dialogue named for him, he explicitly rejects the comic stereotype of the weak old man as seizing on *bad* old men's qualities. "[These characters] are gullible, forgetful, and unkempt—vices that belong not to old age itself, but to old age that is indolent, idle, and slothful" (*credulos obliviosus dissolutos, quae vitia sunt non senectutis, sed inertis ignavae somniculosae senectuti, Sen.* 11.36; cf. 18.65). His speech responds to Scipio's remark that he seems to defy common assumptions about *senes* (2.4; cf. 1.3).[43] Cato is happy to help overturn younger men's expectations. But he also takes advantage of the question to deliver a more full-blown sermon that includes not just advice for a long and happy life but also plenty of moral criticism aimed at the young and foolish (6.20, 11.36, and 12.39–41). All this, we should infer, is the most proper use of mature eloquence, moral certainty, experience, and learning.[44] In some regards, Juvenal can be seen aiming for the authority of a Cato, reaching for exempla in ancient history and across the inhabited world (38–70, 162–73). Granted, Juvenal's rhetorical moves are often patently comic, but his smugness is not so different from Cato's.[45]

Among the many pieces of wisdom Cato has to offer is that a *senex* is especially *admirabilis* if he bears grief well (as Fabius Maximus did at his son's death; 4.12). Juvenal's Calvinus is no such wonder of elderly fortitude but the opposite kind of wonder, a man who "grieves" for his money but should know better. Of course, the man who is catching him out in this has not faced such a test—at least, he offers no testimony about himself that could serve as a contrast or a model. The *senex*-satirist is all adviser and censor, and no victim of fate. This fact disrupts what might otherwise look like a peer relationship that makes a good foundation for

---

Book," 43) associates the Catonian model with Book 5 in particular, and asserts that this persona sounds "banal" in the second century C.E. (its ideas less convincing even than when articulated by Quintilian a generation earlier).

[43] This chapter cites Powell's text of *On Old Age* (*Cicero: Cato Maior*). For another example of the "old man full of surprises," cf. Plin. *Ep.* 3.1 on the daily routine of old Spurinna (see discussion below).

[44] At *Sen.* 4, Cato remembers his own youthful surprise at the vigor of Q. Fabius Maximus and enumerates the qualities the latter exhibited, including rich conversation, valuable *sententiae*, good memory, and broad learning. Strikingly, Cicero makes the old Cato a lover of literature (1.3, 17.59); on his probable rationale, see Powell, *Cicero: Cato Maior*, 19–21 and *ad loc.*

[45] Powell remarks that both Cato and Cicero were fond of talking "*de suis virtutibus*" (Cicero's expression at *Sen.* 10.31; *Cicero: Cato Maior*, 166). This is another subject that interested Plutarch (see *On Praising Oneself Inoffensively* and n. 67 below).

frank advice. *Satire* 13 does not gesture to "us" and "our common experience" even in the generic way that, for example, Plutarch's treatise for Euphanes does. Juvenal therefore does not join Calvinus in the spotlight as fellow *senex* so much as insinuate he possesses an old man's authority, so he can concentrate on the task of criticism. In this respect he is different from Seneca, who—as Wilson points out—has a way of playing the fellow sick man even in his "non-consolatory" consolations.[46] In earnest cases of anger management between friends or social peers, some advisers take a moderate view of anger, allowing that it is sometimes justified while still aiming to tamp down its disruptive symptoms.[47] But Juvenal is eager to stigmatize Calvinus's deluded "righteous" anger, and less interested in his moral correction. In this he is aided by the stereotype of the old man whose emotions are unseemly and highly visible.

Despite the poem's implication that Juvenal is Calvinus's coeval, there is an inequality between them that governs the entire lecture: this is a case of unidirectional, provocative speech, false *sermo*, like those we saw playing out in Books 1 and 2. This time, anger is not just entirely embodied in the internal audience but explicitly mocked by the satirist. For Calvinus, who must already think numerous *incommoda* are swirling around him, Juvenal's mockery must only be adding to his woes. According to Braund, Juvenal does plant "evidence" that Calvinus is responding angrily to this malicious false *consolatio*, as if in real time.[48] If so, this is just another way that the satirist aims "to 'control' the reaction of Calvinus" to his misfortune.[49] Indeed, since Juvenal invented Calvinus, he can do what he likes with him—scripting not just his original emotional processing of the fraud but his discomfort and anger at the satirist's words. This could last all the way to the end of the poem, where the final *phantasia* of divine punishment mocks Calvinus's desire even as it mimes satiric justice.[50]

[46.]Wilson, "Subjugation of Grief," 49.

[47.]An interesting postclassical comparandum is the interaction of medieval aristocrats studied in Barton, "Zealous Anger." Lords who jostled with one another for power needed to use anger to assert themselves and negotiate their relationships; for this purpose, they (and their audiences) maintained a special definition of "good," legitimate anger that bolstered rather than erased authority. In this context, the recognition of a "good" anger comes from Christian theology; see Barton 155–59, and cf. Little, "Anger in Monastic Curses," 12. Little quotes August *C. D.* 9.5 as an early articulation of the idea that a pious man's anger is just if it aims to correct a wrongdoer.

[48.]See Braund, "Passion Unconsoled," 81–84, on the ways Juvenal seems to represent Calvinus getting more agitated.

[49.]Ficca, *Giovenale Satira XIII*, 10.

[50.]On Juvenal's agenda of "satirical justice" in the final vision of the wrongdoer's torment, see Edmunds, "Juvenal's Thirteenth Satire," 73; cf. Keane, *Figuring Genre*, 96.

It should not surprise us that when Juvenal takes an interest in anger control, it concerns someone else's anger. Satire, despite some claims of Horace and Persius, must be directed outward; Juvenal is no Achilles or Chaereas being challenged to ascend to emotional maturity. Nor does he take this opportunity to meditate on the condition he shares with Calvinus. Instead, like many an ancient *senex*, he appropriates the right to lecture others. This is a fine joke, since he has been doing this since long before he had the excuse of age. Now he grows into the role of satirist as if it had been waiting for him at the end of his life.

Nestor *Redivivus*

In retrospect, Umbricius, who claimed to be in *prima et recta senectus* (3.26) as he performed his own satire, looks like a taste of things to come from the poet himself. In his last book, Juvenal still has an appetite for satire's games—and new justification for engaging in them. As if he has established his persona of seasoned *senex* by putting Calvinus in his place, Juvenal moves on to embrace the "wise adviser" role more vigorously (and droningly) in *Satire* 14. The poem channels conservative voices on childrearing, ranging from Cato the Elder (as Plutarch memorializes him) to Plutarch himself (in *On the Education of Children*).[51] The conventionality of Juvenal's representations of childhood and education, combined with the length of the poem, explains why critics have seen a decline in Juvenal's satiric powers in this stage of his career. Literary and particularly philosophical influence is more visible than ever; hence scholars' impressions that the poet was by now relying on the "experience" of books rather than personal observations. But another likely reason for the "bookish" impression Book 5 gives off is that Juvenal's pose of the authoritative and wise elder itself draws on many literary sources. These include a range of treatments that imagine the public and intellectual role of the *senex*—and in both charitable and uncharitable ways.

An old man's sphere of influence may be limited, but old age surely suits one whose version of "public life" is doing satire. At the same time, there is something potentially transgressive in this enduring "routine" of Juvenal's old age (to gesture to Townend's critical use of the term).[52] In

---

[51.]See Keane, "Philosophy into Satire," 35–36, for other relevant citations from Horace, Cicero, and the Stoics.

[52.]Juvenal "exhausted his most fruitful vein of literary exploitation" by Book 5, where "satire becomes a routine" (Townend, "Literary Substrata," 159).

the ancient sources, the authority of the elderly is a tenuous thing, at risk of being dismissed with mockery.[53] Plutarch and other authors imply that the *senex* must train his energy on private affairs or risk being seen as stepping out of line. The principle that for old men, an active and orderly life is appropriate but "industry is too late, and ambition unseemly" underlies Pliny's praise for old Spurinna's vigorous but socially unobtrusive daily routine.[54] In Pliny's eyes, Spurinna hits the mark by alternating between walks, baths, family interaction, reading, and writing of lyrics—all "trifles" (*parva*) that seem less trifling when practiced so gracefully (*Ep.* 3.1.3). Juvenal's social criticism, in contrast, might have struck Pliny as crossing the line between the "becoming" (*honestum*, 3.1.12) and the offensive.

An older source, Cicero, has become newly relevant to Juvenal in this book. This happens on two levels. First, Cicero's late work models the way an author writes toward the end of his life, for even though Cicero's demise was not a natural one, he did explore new topics in his last years. This adumbrates a model for a "final" career phase that includes self-conscious and philosophically themed writing, and even some (less self-conscious) revision of positions.[55] (One change, it is worth noting, is the expression in the *Tusculan Disputations* of the belief that the passions are destructive— not a possibility that troubled the younger orator.)[56] Second, as acknowledged earlier, the dialogue on old age featuring Cato the Elder is among

---

[53.]See Parkin, *Old Age*, esp. 242, and Cokayne, *Experiencing Old Age*, 91–111. Cicero's Cato half justifies old men's difficult disposition this way: "they believe themselves to be scorned, despised, and mocked" (*contemni se putant, despici, inludi, Sen.* 18.65).

[54.]*senibus placida omnia et ordinata conveniunt, quibus industria sera turpis ambitio est* (*Ep.* 3.1.2). Pliny explains that Spurinna had held offices and engaged in state affairs "as long as it became him" (*quoad honestum fuit,* 3.1.12). For more on Spurinna as a model of the ideal retirement, see Gibson and Morello, *Reading the Letters*, 115–23. Seneca, writing on the long career of old Sextus Turrannius, concludes that old men hold on to their public roles longer than they should, for their desire to remain included blinds them to the decline in their abilities (*Brev. Vit.* 20.2–5; cf. Cokayne, "Age and Aristocratic Self-Identity," 215).

[55.]While Gibson and Steele ("Indistinct Literary Careers," 123–25) find no evidence of a purposeful "career trajectory" in the last part of Cicero's oeuvre, they note that Cicero "did find new ways of structuring, and promoting, his writing." In his worsening political circumstances, Cicero may have concluded that he would not get to play the grand old man, or play him for long; this would have motivated many aspects of his favorable portrait of Cato in this role. See Powell, *Cicero: Cato Maior*, 3: even if Cicero "felt the exact opposite of all the favorable sentiments about old age which he makes Cato utter in the dialogue," he probably wished to employ a figure of undisputed authority and a positive outlook to represent *senectus.* Cf. MacKendrick and Singh, *Philosophical Books of Cicero*, 210–11. Undoubtedly, writing under such circumstances generates "persona issues," and some of the surprising details of the portrait of Cato must stem from Cicero's identification with his spokesman; see Powell, *Cicero: Cato Maior*, 17–22; Jones, "Cicero's Accuracy of Characterization," 308–12; and Novak, "Old Man and C."

[56.]On Cicero's change of position on the passions, visible at *Tusc.* 4.55, see Graver, *Cicero on the Emotions*, xii–xv and 168, and Harris, *Restraining Rage*, 111 and 211 (cf. chapter 1, n. 24).

the most extensive discussions from antiquity on this subject. As we will see, the portrait Cicero paints of respectable old age can at times be profitably compared and contrasted with the persona in *Satire* 14.

But no one influence dominates this ambitious poem. There is something almost hubristic about the satirist's agenda—the tracing of the development of vice itself through the generations.[57] Fittingly, the satire becomes a kind of retrospective on the satiric tradition itself—particularly through the conventional topic of avarice, which dominates the last two-thirds of the poem.[58] As the satirist rolls out one catalog after another of foodstuffs, household objects, garments, and luxury wares—the trappings of troubled mortal life—he symbolically represents all the baggage he is taking into this poem. The actual "teaching" that Juvenal pretends to be doing is ambitious, too. Uden regards it as one of the satirist's provocative, extremist moves: an attempt to construct ethical education as an entirely domestic, insular process, with schools and philosophers excluded and only Juvenal's own discourse supplementing parental influence.[59] Amid the other literary play here, there is a strong taste of Catonian educational conservatism, recalling the "real" Cato and Plutarch's biography even more than the Ciceronian version.[60] Viewed from another angle, too, Juvenal's "teaching" aims high: the satirist is setting out to school not children but their parents. In one way, this suggests that he is identifying with the generation that does the teaching—another mark of age and authority. In another way, though, he transcends even that role, abstracting the problem of ethical teaching beyond the present configuration of fathers and sons. His interest is a timeless phenomenon: "so Nature decrees it: examples of vice set at home corrupt us sooner and more swiftly, since they enter our minds on high authority" (*sic natura iubet: velocius et citius nos/corrumpunt vitiorum exempla domestica, magnis/cum subeant animos auctoribus*, 14.31–33). This "long view," including all past and future generations, echoes the early, ambitious assertion of Juvenal's that he will write about everything that people have done since Deucalion (1.81–86).

The rhetorical and moral power grab is ironically suited to a poem that is so concerned with greed. Avarice conquers everyone, even against their will (107–8); the satirist, too, seems to want his poem to contain everything. By not just covering a broad range of human experience but

---

[57.] On the grand scope of *Satire* 14, see Keane, *Figuring Genre*, 134–35.

[58.] On the theme of *avaritia*, see Bellandi, "Struttura della Satira 14."

[59.] Uden, "Invisibility of Juvenal," 197–210.

[60.] See Plu. *Cat. Mai.* 20.

conjuring a long and broad literary tradition, he acts out the moral of his own poem, quite on purpose.[61] Even as he plays the grand old man of satire, he is also taking his place as literary heir, claiming his own "legacy" from the satiric tradition's treatment of greed. Seemingly to remind his readers of the theme's pedigree, in the final lines of *Satire* 14 Juvenal conjures an image of a man so greedy that even the riches of Croesus or Narcissus would not sate him (316–30). This is reminiscent of the ending of Persius's sixth *Satire*, where the poet (simultaneously indulging in his own poetic gorging) challenges his greedy heir to fix the size of the "pile" that would satisfy him (6.75–80). Always thinking bigger, Juvenal turns this pile into entire treasuries.

This poem, the third-longest in Juvenal's entire corpus, is an extended victory lap following the dismissal of the weak Calvinus. Juvenal is alone now in his *senex* persona. That does not mean, however, that we cannot ask what gives him the right to go on so long. With plenty of meditation on *avaritia* and its consequences already behind him, spread through so many vignettes in earlier poems, this lengthy sermon pushes the envelope. Just in terms of his choice of subject and the duration of the treatment, Juvenal is straddling the line between a valued elder and an insufferable drone; no surprise, then, that some modern critics characterize his later style as weak and prolix, and connect this to his age.[62] The same connection between ineffectual verbosity and old age is made in some ancient discussions of decorum among the elderly. It is implied that while *senes* might have serious conversation (*sermo*) to offer, they are also prone to compulsive "idle chatting" (*loquacitas*).[63] Terence appears to milk this stereotype in his speeches for *senes*.[64] As with many details of the stereotype of the *senex*, the distinction between useful *sermo* and laughable or irritating *loquacitas* may not be easy to pin down.

Those sources that see age as enhancing rhetorical prowess still acknowledge that the aging orator is only considered wise and useful if he adopts the right persona and manner. Cicero's Cato is one example: "In fact, the

---

[61.] As the satirist says, *avaritia* is the one vice that parents force on their children (107–8), and this all-enveloping vice turns the poem itself into an outsized monster (Keane, "Philosophy into Satire," 36–41).

[62.] See n. 18 above and cf. Mayor, *Thirteen Satires of Juvenal*, 247: "The effect [of Juvenal's performance in *Satire* 13] is marred by verbosity. The aged poet forgets the caution: *manum de tabula* [sc. *scire tollere*]."

[63.] Cokayne, *Experiencing Old Age*, 81; there are signs of old age in Theophrastus's garrulous man (*Char.* 3.1–2).

[64.] Maltby, "Linguistic Characterization."

resonant quality in the voice somehow gains brilliance in old age. . . . But still, it is a quiet and relaxed style of speech that best suits an old man; and coming from an eloquent elder, elegant and gentle speech wins a hearing for itself on its own" (*omnino canorum illud in voce splendescit etiam nescioquo pacto in senectute. . . . sed tamen est decorus seni sermo quietus et remissus, facitque per sepse sibi audientiam diserti senis compta et mitis oratio, Sen.* 9.28).[65] Notice the warning couched in praise of the ideal, similar to Pliny's praise for Spurinna's daily routine. On the one hand, Cato is combating a negative stereotype, the expectation that speech loses power with age or is even best suppressed. On the other hand, he is indicating that there is room for an older orator to go wrong. More explicit advice can be found in Plutarch: an older speaker must avoid undignified moves, such as frequently jumping up to the speaker's platform, relentlessly restricting the expression of younger men, and refusing to accept defeat (*Mor.* 794c–795d). Though he nods respectfully to some cases of successful theatrics (Appius Claudius Caecus, Solon), Plutarch cautions aging speakers to tighten the reins on their expression, especially in public. This will put them in a solid position to serve as wise "Nestors" when strife flares up among younger statesmen (795b–c).

Quintilian too weighs in (*Inst.* 11.1.31–32): just as younger men may be able to get away with sporting brilliant purple clothing, they can safely experiment with oratory that is "full and elevated and bold and florid" (*plenum et erectum et audax et praecultum*), even "adventurous" (*periclitantia*), whereas older men are better off sticking to the "compressed and mild and polished" (*pressum et mite et limatum*) style. The advantage for old men is that audiences will tolerate "dry, cautious, and clipped" (*siccum et sollicitum et contractum*) speech from them but would see the same style in a young man's speech as an affectation. Quintilian's terms all have particular associations in the history of rhetoric, but most important for our purposes is the demarcation of kinds of speech that are more and less acceptable from *senes*. It is difficult to put chickens and eggs in order here. The "rules" might be a strategy for offsetting a perceived natural tendency of old men to emotion or loquaciousness. Alternatively, notions of propriety could reflect rhetoricians' *observation* of a shift toward dry and compressed speech in older men. Cicero, quoted by Quintilian, rather obscured the cause-and-effect relationship when he said his speech had

---

[65.]I have borrowed from Powell's translation (*Cicero: Cato Maior*, 162).

begun to "grow gray" (*Cicero . . . dicit orationem suam coepisse canescere*, 11.1.31).

Plutarch gives old men credit for being less subject to strong passions in the political arena (788f). But he imagines other pitfalls for the older speaker who is not careful. He stresses that an old man, in his rightful role of adviser to the young, should not abuse and shame them in public (795b). In *Satire* 13, Juvenal avoids this particular error by attacking a peer. In 14, he begins to flirt with transgression, schooling fathers of young children and, increasingly as the poem moves on, berating the maturing children themselves. He channels the authority of an uber-elder—even a Cato, in the digression about the rise of greed (164–88). He employs *libertas* to address bad fathers directly in a rebuke that is much longer (210–55) than his analogous frank speech to the cruel Virro back in *Satire* 5 (107–13). Following that, Juvenal's account of the absurd lengths to which greedy men go for gain attacks the children who have grown into copies of their parents (implied to have been killed off; see 244–55). All of this can only be so appealing to the hypothetical fathers and sons who hear what Juvenal has to say. Juvenal is identifying ills of the present, future, and past, giving all generations a share in the blame. Again, ambitious.

This multipronged attack, the curse on the houses of both *maiores* and *minores*, is reminiscent of one literary old man in particular: Nestor, and particularly the Nestor of the *Iliad*. The first appearance of this character establishes his perspective as a man who has seen multiple generations come and go (1.250–52) and who finds increasing cause for lament as the years pass. Forthright and eloquent,[66] Nestor commands respect but often delivers abuse. In that first speech to the assembled Achaean chiefs, where the question of relative honors is being disputed, the message of the old man's life narrative is that to him, all the men he sees around him look the same (1.259–72). In a way, he is indifferent to the ways Agamemnon and his junior Achilles insist on distinguishing themselves from one another, though he is smart enough to offer distinct titles to each (Achilles the demigod is "the stronger," καρτερός, but King Agamemnon is "better," φέρτερος; 1.280–81). This is the kind of balancing act that ensured Nestor's reputation as a wise and politic adviser to younger men in the later literature. Cicero's Cato includes him in his list of effective elderly advisers—in fact, he cites him specifically as a model in the practice of proudly advertising

---

[66.]For Nestor's "sweet" speaking style, described in the same terms used for the Muses' utterances, see *Il.* 1.248–49.

one's own good qualities (*Sen.* 10.31; cf. Plu. *Mor.* 789e–90a). Nestor does, of course, reserve plenty of praise for *tempus actum se puero*, including his own career as a younger man. His contemporaries were "the strongest of mortal men," and their foes in battle were the "strongest" too.[67]

Plutarch ranks Homer's Nestor among tactically savvy speakers when it comes to making peace and advising younger men (*Mor.* 795b), and the social world of the *Iliad* clearly grants Nestor a highly respected status and important social function even when his advice is flawed.[68] But the comic potential of the old king's self-congratulatory and lengthy performances was not overlooked by other authors; it is hard not to detect a jaded wink when, eight centuries after the *Iliad*, Ovid has Achilles address Nestor as "eloquent old man, wisdom of our age" (*o facunde senex, aevi pruden-tia nostri, Met.* 12.178). Juvenal, I would argue, borrows from Nestor his sweeping vision of humanity and his long-windedness, but he does not sit-uate himself in a social environment that works to preserve respect for his perspective. In effect, the speaker of *Satire* 14 has no social environment at all (late in the poem, the aside "if anyone should ask me," *si quis me con-sulat*, 317, only reminds us that no one has). He is a voice aiming his criti-cism at everyone around him, casting all living generations as an exhibit of moral decline. The shipwrecked merchant at 295–302 gets no more and no less respect than the father who taught him to be greedy. There is room for both audiences (or as many age groups as this poem sweeps into its scope) to take offense. Juvenal may be advocating "mildness" in example-setting at home (*mitem animum et mores . . . aequos*, 15), but it is hard to say that his own lecture exemplifies the "mild" *style* recommended by Quintilian (*mite, Inst.* 11.1.31). In a sense, by its mere breadth and duration, the rhe-torical assault undermines its own exhortations to restraint.

Our rhetorical sources, and Plutarch most vividly, make it sound as though an old speaker needs to take pains to avoid arousing resentment or laughter; there are hints that an old man's audience will be justified in disrespecting him or getting angry if he ignores decorum.[69] Old men's

---

[67.]*Il.* 1.266–67; cf. 7.124–60, 11.670–762, and 23.629–45. By the time Plutarch was writing his essay *On Praising Oneself Inoffensively*, it was only natural to cite not just Nestor but also Cato *and* Cicero as exemplars in self-praise (*Mor.* 540f, 544 c–d and f).

[68.]Roisman ("Nestor the Good Counsellor," 17) argues that despite some bad or rejected advice, Nestor still functions as the model of the "good counsellor" in the *Iliad*; that quality is about something bigger than the *results* of his advice—that is, "preserving social solidarity."

[69.]For example, by rushing into controversy, the old man will "undo the young men's respect for him and . . . instill in them the habit and custom of disobedience and disregard for his advice" (ἀποχαλινοῦντα τὴν πρὸς αὐτὸν αἰδῶ τῶν νέων . . . μελέτην ἐμποιοῦντα καὶ συνήθειαν ἀπειθείας καὶ δυσηκοΐας, 794c–d).

speech should work at calming their juniors' passions (*Mor.* 795a, b), not fuel them. (Presumably, they should also think twice about taunting other πρεσβύτεροι who may be sensitive.) Juvenal's seeming carelessness implies that he is comfortable playing the ire-inducing or laughable old man in his audience's eyes. His *senex* persona has Nestor's sometimes-comic irritations without his aura of decorum and savvy. As he characterizes humanity's problems, he shows little concern for the feelings or the future authority of younger men.

This is one way, then, that this poem continues and enriches the emotional plot of the *Satires*. Another way has to do with its representation of vice. *Satire* 14 implicitly condemns excessive passions. For passions and vices go hand in hand; the satirist puts it this way when he is digging into the subject of avarice ("the cause of most crimes is wicked desire"; *fere scelerum causae . . . saeva cupido*, 173–75). More generally, passions certainly lurk behind all the bad examples—gambling, luxury, cruelty— set in the first part of the poem. Another culprit, also seen in the early *Satires*, is the deficiency of socially beneficial emotions (*reverentia legum, metus, pudor*, 177–78). These two connected causes are well represented at 14.15–24:

> mitem animum et mores modicis erroribus aequos
> praecipit atque animas servorum et corpora nostra
> materia constare putat paribusque elementis,
> an saevire docet Rutilus, qui gaudet acerbo
> plagarum strepitu et nullam Sirena flagellis
> conparat, Antiphates trepidi laris ac Polyphemus,
> tunc felix, quotiens aliquis tortore vocato
> uritur ardenti duo propter lintea ferro?
> quid suadet iuveni laetus stridore catenae,
> quem mire adficiunt inscripta, ergastula, carcer?

Is Rutilus teaching a child to have a gentle heart and a fair attitude toward small mistakes, is he being taught that slaves' lives are made of the same stuff and parts as our own bodies, or instead to become a savage, when he takes pleasure in the harsh crashing of blows and thinks no Siren can match the sound of whips, being the Antiphates or Polyphemus of his frightened household, and who is happy whenever the torturer's been called in and somebody's being scorched by burning iron on account of a couple of lost towels? What is he instilling in the young man when he rejoices in the grating sound of chains, when he's incredibly aroused by brands, workhouses, jails?

This picture, complete with sounds, is highly reminiscent of Seneca's creative representation of anger (*Ira* 3.3.6):

Ne quem fallat tamquam aliquo tempore, aliquo loco profutura, ostendenda est rabies eius effrenata et attonita apparatusque illi reddendus est suus, eculei et fidiculae et ergastula et cruces et circumdati defossis corporibus ignes et cadavera quoque trahens uncus, varia vinculorum genera, varia poenarum, lacerationes membrorum, inscriptiones frontis et bestiarum immanium caveae: inter haec instrumenta conlocetur ira dirum quiddam atque horridum stridens, omnibus per quae furit taetrior.

Lest anyone be fooled into thinking that rage can be beneficial at some time or place, we should reveal it in its unbridled senselessness; we should give it back its equipment—racks, cords, workhouses, crosses, fires set around bodies staked in the ground, the hook dragging even dead bodies, many kinds of fetters and punishments, mangling of limbs, letters carved in foreheads, and pens of savage beasts; among these tools let us picture anger sitting, hissing in a terrible and frightening manner, more hideous than all the instruments through which it shows its fury.

Seneca's *On Anger* also touches on fathers, sons, and the mechanisms of moral tradition. The Stoic advises fathers on cultivating anger control in children (*Ira* 2.19–21). But he has to spend much more space schooling adults; he even implies, with one anecdote about a precocious boy, that children are capable of recognizing parental error (2.21.10). That makes a good illustration of Seneca's interest in angry parental behavior per se, not just because it may victimize children directly. But in Juvenal 14 there is no child philosopher to staunch the spread of destructive passions with an astute criticism of his father. Juvenal's children are only equipped to imitate.[70] Thanks to this force of nature, as the satirist sees it, passions and their related vices will continue to spread. What is more, material success (a result of greed) leads to more greed (*crescit amore nummi quantum ipsa*

---

[70] Juvenal implies that parents have no right to angrily discipline their children if they themselves have inspired the misbehavior. Children could certainly be targets of parental anger, as Seneca recognizes. Although the Stoic uses the analogy of the forgiving father in *On Mercy* (chapters 14–15), this is a wishful metaphor; it reads as much like an exhortation to fathers as to his addressee the *pater patriae*.

pecunia crevit, 139); wealth that is gained through risk generates more pleasure, boldness, ambition, worry, and fear (*gaudia, temeritas*, and *spes* in 270–78; cf. *cura* and *metus* in 303). Vice and its concomitant passions grow within single lifetimes as well as across the generations.

The only exception in this cycle is anger. Although the vignette just quoted criticizes "inherited" anger as a spur to cruelty, it may also be said that Juvenal makes *ira* a special case in this poem, albeit briefly. Specifically, Juvenal acknowledges a constructive, legitimate, and indeed institutionalized form of *ira* in the responses of censors and (briefly well-functioning?) parents to bad behavior. A wicked son might "one day do something that merits the censor's anger . . ." and cause his father to strike him from his will in a rage (*si quid dignum censoris fecerit ira/quandoque . . . corripies nimirum et castigabis acerbo/clamore ac post haec tabulas mutare parabis*, 50–55). This gesture to a kind of "establishment anger" that is not at odds with the satirist's own critical project is another piece of evidence for our reassessment of how the late Juvenal regards *ira* (the next poem will offer a great deal more).

Meanwhile, *Satire* 14 attacks plenty of other passions. In one way, this Juvenal can be seen as a new-and-improved Nestor: he is no "ancient" but has centuries of civilization shoring up his self-appointment as critic. He feels he is witnessing the degradation of humanity into a subhuman condition. This generates a fascinating thematic play. As one illustration of how tradition works, Juvenal points to various animals who feed their young in order to show them what and how to eat (73–85). Next to the human fathers who care more about the appearance or size of their homes (59–67, 86–95), the animals in Juvenal's examples look highly civilized. Eagles and vultures pass on their practical knowledge to their chicks, and although this involves hunting other animals and eating carrion, the whole process comes across as purposeful, dispassionate, and orderly. These animals are only touched by human corruption in that they feed on a byproduct of human injustices (the corpses of convicts; *crucibus . . . relictis*, 77). Things are very different with the eaters of corpses that we see in the next *Satire*, and indeed with the bad human exemplars that fill *Satire* 14. Fathers even forcibly teach their children to be greedy, hastening the decline of humanity. Here Juvenal appears to be revising the claim in *Satire* 1 that vice had reached its peak—that "our descendants will do and desire the same things as us" (*eadem facient cupientque minores*, 1.148). As the seasoned satirist sees it, while stork, vulture, and eagle chicks grow up to duplicate their parents, today's men are outdoing their fathers in greed.

Behind the illusory material success that can be had from a military career, pleading, commerce, and other careers (192–207) can be seen a quantifiable downward spiral, as well as more dehumanizing imagery. Juvenal launches into a lecture to fathers who harangue their sons to pursue wealth. A greedy and ambitious son will become like a horse ignoring his driver's reins (*totas effundit habenas/curriculo*, 230–31); Juvenal is remapping the Platonic metaphor to concentrate all the negative animal imagery on the son, who will grow up to kill his wife and father.[71] The son then becomes even less recognizable as human when he transforms from horse into raging fire (244–45). Next, he returns to animal form: a lion in a cage, threatening to destroy the trainer who reared him (*trepidum . . . magistrum/in cavea magno fremitus leo tollet alumnus*, 246–47). The father does not hold on to this human status for long, since in the son's eyes he is living too long, to a "deerlike" old age (251, alluding to a common belief about this animal).[72]. But it is the lion, significantly situated in an unnatural habitat in contrast to the birds described earlier, that represents outsized and destructive passions. A feral generation has been spawned, and the cycle will continue.

The disintegration of humanity's civilized nature is also visible as the last third of the poem begins. The famous "games" analogy for human lives lived in pursuit of profit (256–64) makes unbridled human passion out to be a spectacle. Even as Juvenal calls men's doings *humana negotia*, he makes them into objects of display, Others—or perhaps beasts. Orestes and Ajax, both tragic figures, are remembered as examples of madness (284–87); we might recall that these two characters were beset with animal visions that underscored the bestial nature of their madness. When the poem comes to an end with Juvenal's speculation about how much wealth would be enough for the greedy, he indicates that the human appetite now surpasses even the most extreme limits: all the wealth of Croesus, Persian kings, or the freedman Narcissus would not suffice (327–31). The implication is that people have lost the ability to appreciate not just the soundness of limits imposed by human institutions like the law but the limits prescribed by nature. The noble tag "nature never says one thing and wisdom another" (*numquam aliud natura, aliud sapientia dicit*, 321) is irrelevant, for no one is listening to this nature anyway. The more damaging aspects of *natura*—animal passions, physiologies that push us toward destructive

---

[71.]Lines 241–43, which some editors delete as spurious, elaborate the "sown men" myth of Thebes, providing another glimpse of humanity's animal nature.

[72.]See Plin. *Nat.* 8.50.119.

feelings, and of course our imitative inclinations—have already done their work.[73]

The old satirist who has been spinning this story, meanwhile, makes himself out to be the sole torchbearer for civilized humanity, the ideal that ought to keep people from murdering their family members, creating private worlds of wealth and pleasure, defying nature's limits, and so on. His imagined audience is not the irrelevant addressee Fuscinus, who is as indistinct as his name,[74] but the endless series of generations that have failed to carry the torch along with him. For now, he restricts the expression of his old man's bitterness to the enormous length and scope of his sermon. In the next poem, where he turns his eyes to an even worse moral world, this breadth and scope shrink dramatically—though the emotional energy and content of his satire does the opposite.

Not Your Father's *Ira*

Of all Juvenal's later poems, *Satire* 15 tests the potential of emotion as theme and satiric mode in the most intriguing ways. It takes its audience to a kind of wilderness, physical and emotional, and offers a variable and confusing authorial voice as guide. The satirist narrates a frenzied act of cannibalism perpetrated in a brawl between two Egyptian villages—an act motivated, as he claims, by *ira* above all (131, 169). The entire violent narrative employs familiar anger-related terms and imagery, and the Egyptians' behavior is made out to be a perversion of humanity's true purpose—to unite and to cultivate fellow feeling. On the surface, then, the poem seems to condemn destructive passions; for persona scholars, it therefore marks the total repudiation of the emotion that colored the early *Satires*.[75] Yet if this was Juvenal's emotional agenda, we might wonder why he chose a subject that at times seems to bring out the angry orator in him again. There is little sign of the view, expressed in *Satire* 13, that one should just brush off the enormity and diversity of human criminality. Musing on the Egyptian practice of worshiping animals, he

---

[73] Seneca explains different types of anger with reference to *natura*, though in a more variable and individualized sense: a *natura* ("constitution") that is hot or moist or dry can bring about sharp or short-lived or severe anger (*Ira* 2.19–20). On the thematic coherence of *Satire* 14 around *natura*, see Corn, "Thus Nature Ordains."

[74] Ferguson, *Prosopography*, 98.

[75] For examples, see n. 5 above and cf. Anderson, "Anger in Juvenal," 191–92 (=*Essays*, 357–58), and Cucchiarelli, *Satira e il poeta*, 215 ("È chiaro quanto ormai sia lontano il Giovenale indignatio, aggressive, delle prime satire"); cf. Harris, *Restraining Rage*, 226.

sarcastically exclaims, "oh, these pious people!" (*o sanctas gentes*, 10); he also compares the cannibals unfavorably to (other) barbarians and beasts (124–25, 159–64; cf. Cic. *Inv.* 1.103). Such elements, along with flashes of humor, have been read variously as signs of renewed *indignatio*, irony, and cynicism.[76]

If we expect more consistency of a satirist in a single poem, we might remind ourselves that the topic of cannibalism normally inspires a mixture of feelings. Kaster asserts that more than any other transgression, the notion of cannibalism generates "reflexive disgust": "there is nothing like the *fastidium* caused by the prospect of eating human flesh."[77] But their gut reaction did not stop many ancient authors from exploring the topic; even in their most damning portrayals of the act, they use wordplay and creative imagery to describe it, creating a kind of subgenre we could call "cannibalism humor." Even moralistic treatments seem compelled to exploit the dark ironies of the practice in neat wordplay: Valerius Maximus, no poet, writes that even people facing starvation under siege should not "nourish their own insides *with* their own insides [i.e., their children and relatives]" (*viscera sua visceribus suis aleret*,7.6.ext.3). The way that Ovid and Seneca handle the stories of Tereus and Thyestes plays on the same imagery.[78] Ironically, the satiric treatment of cannibalism that is most often cited as a source for Juvenal, Petronius *Satyricon* 141, is fairly straight in its presentation; the speaker earnestly defends the practice, and the absurdity of this generates humor.[79] Finally, a rhetorical treatment of the topic, the pseudo-Quintilianic *Greater Declamation* 12, makes it seem that painfully creative rhetoric just comes with the territory. The speaker, accusing a man of causing an outbreak of cannibalism during a famine, laments (to give just one excruciating example) that his dead relatives will not be fully laid to rest until those who ate their bodies are dead and buried (2).

[76.] Scholars who see Juvenal returning to *indignatio*, albeit with ambivalence or a parodic intent, include Bellandi (*Etica diatribica*, 97–99); Corn ("Persona in Fifth Book," 65–101); Stramaglia (*Giovenale*, 293–95); and Coffey (*Roman Satire*, 135: despite appearances in *Satire* 15 of the "restrained irony characteristic of Juvenal's later work . . . the introduction and narrative revert to the explosive violence of his earlier manner"). Somewhat more hesitant is Ficca (*Giovenale Satira XIII*, 10–11); cf. Singleton, "Juvenal's Fifteenth Satire," especially 198–99.

[77.] Kaster, *Emotion, Restraint, and Community*, 110 (quoting the famous instructions of Eumolpus at Petr. 141). *Fastidium* at cannibalism is an example of a visceral (or, as Kaster puts it, "centered in the stomach . . . or in the eyes," 112) disgust at an incident that is ethically disturbing.

[78.] See, e.g., Gildenhard and Zissos, "Barbarian Variations" (on Ovid's Tereus), and Meltzer, "Dark Wit" (on Seneca's Thyestes). Both characters had tragic and comic faces in Greek drama; Dobrov, "Tragic and Comic Tereus," identifies elements of tragic parody in Aristophanes's comic Tereus.

[79.] There are noncomic precedents for Eumolpus's defense of cannibalism; see Rankin ("Eating People Is Right").

Indeed, as I will discuss further later, it may be said that the most emotionally high-pitched moments in this speech are also the moments that come closest to humor; they highlight cannibalism's perversities with nauseated fascination. No wonder, then, that Juvenal concocts as a label for unrepentant Egyptian cannibalism "hungry hatred" (*ieiunum odium*, 51), or declares forgivingly of people who have been driven by famine to eat their dead that they were "even prepared to eat their own bodies" (*esse parati/ et sua [membra]*, 102–3).[80]

In the grand scheme of things, then, Juvenal's inconsistent tone is not so strange; it is the content that merits investigation, if we are to understand *Satire* 15 in its immediate context. What does this poem mean to our satirist at this point in his career? One clue may lie in the rhetorical question that serves as an opening: "Who does not know, Volusius Bithynicus, what sorts of monsters mad Egypt worships?" *quis nescit, Volusi Bithynice, qualia demens/Aegyptos portenta colat?*, 1–2). Since this question is modeled superficially on one in Cicero's *Tusculan Disputations*, we could infer that Juvenal means to evoke Cicero qua philosopher, to give another dimension to his *senex* persona. But Juvenal's gesture to Egypt is made in a very different spirit from Cicero's; he is not being *that* old man.[81]

On the other hand, *Satire* 15 does complement and continue the thematic program of *Satire* 14 in some regards. From an account of chronological decline, Juvenal shifts to a similarly schematic comparison of civilized and barbarian ideals, and the irrational, animal qualities of superficially civilized people in 14 foreshadow the true subhumanity of the people attacked in *Satire* 15. Looking for context farther afield in the *Satires*, there is a memory of Juvenal's early career in the focus on Egypt. The first offensive individual he described in great detail, and one saw fit to summon up again later in the same book, was Crispinus the Egyptian. If an old man becomes a child again, perhaps an old satirist returns to his roots—with a little more ambition, for he has abandoned the offenses of one man to tell of the crimes of an entire people (15.31). This idea has been expressed in a biographizing version: Highet senses a personal hatred for Egypt and Egyptians driving the poem.[82] He is thinking not just of Crispinus but of the claim in the ancient biography that the aged

---

[80.]Unlike in the Valerius Maximus passage, this *sua* does not refer to family members but makes a contrast with *[membra] aliena* in line 102.

[81.]Cf. Cic. *Tusc.* 5.78, where Cicero goes on to praise Egyptian protection of their sacred animals as a manifestation of *virtus*, and see Keane, "Philosophy into Satire," 44–48.

[82.]Highet, *Juvenal the Satirist*, 152; cf. 29.

satirist was given an undesirable military post in a remote part of Egypt as a punishment for offensive verses.[83] Though commonly discredited due to its impossible chronology,[84] the story is interesting for our purposes: was it fueled by this certifiably late poem that implies Juvenal has been an eyewitness to Egyptian practices? ("[these people are depraved] as far as I myself have observed," *quantum ipse notavi*, 45).[85] This kind of virtual exile *would* have been a nightmare for an octogenarian who had expressed hatred even for provincials he saw as civilized. At any rate, for the poem's persona, the horrors of Egypt are real, and details of Juvenal's past satiric "life" are evoked to make a meaningful background.

Here as in *Satires* 13 and 14, the ambivalent status of the *senex* in ancient society is pertinent. If the previous two poems dramatized, in unique ways, the potentially alienating qualities of a *senex* who is also a practicing satirist, 15 seems to dramatize the alienation and marginalization of the *senex* himself.[86] More to the point, it dramatizes the way that the perspective of the *senex* is dictated by this marginal status. This is shown through both literal and metaphorical means. The book opened with an address to a peer whose character was relatively fleshed out; now, the satirist is addressing a cipher of an addressee, without an identifiable perspective. His moral targets, meanwhile, are "Others" in both cultural and rhetorical senses; this is not advice between *amici*. Cultural alienation is a concomitant condition: Juvenal has apparently seen Egyptian behavior in action (*quantum ipse notavi*), so that throughout the Egyptian narrative he gives the impression of an unhappy expatriate trapped in another world, like the exiled Ovid. In his eyes, the spectacular tale of cannibalistic fury may look like a

---

[83.]"Although he was in his eighties, [for seeming to attack an imperial favorite in *Satire* 7] he was pushed out of the city and sent to hold a prefecture of a cohort occupying the furthest region of Egypt. This was seen as the proper kind of punishment, since it fit the light and frivolous nature of the crime. And then within a very short time, due to vexation and boredom, he died" (*quamquam octogenarius urbe summotus est missusque ad praefecturam cohortis in extremam partem Aegypti tendentis. id supplicii genus placuit, ut levi atque ioculari delicto par esset. verum intra brevissimum tempus angore et taedio periit, Vita Iuvenalis* lines 17–21). It is hard to tell what the biographer thinks about the nonfrivolous result of the frivolous punishment. Cf. the scholiast's brief vita in Wessner, *Scholia in Iuvenalem vetustiora*, 2.

[84.]For theories that Juvenal visited Egypt for reasons other than exile, see Cizek, "Juvénal et Certains Problèmes," and Syme, "*Patria* of Juvenal," 6.

[85.]Juvenal also provides a date for the cannibalism incident (127 C.E.) by naming the consular year (*nuper consule Iunco*, 27).

[86.]"Marginality" and "marginalization" are frequently used terms in studies of the life of elderly people in antiquity; see Parkin, *Old Age*, 239–72; Cokayne, "Age and Aristocratic Self-Identity"; and Harlow and Laurence, *Growing Up*, 118. Giardina's examination of the theme of old age in Juvenal ("Vari tipi di satira," 41–46) emphasizes the vulnerable status of old men in the glare of satiric criticism.

perversion of a Roman beast hunt, a spectacle of violence and victory that would often have concluded with a public feast (on animal flesh).[87] And, in fact, many analyses of the poem conclude that Juvenal intends for his comments about Roman "civilization" to ring hollow—in other words, that he is taking *Romanitas* down in one fell swoop along with barbarian *feritas*.[88] In this light, the satirist appears uncomfortably positioned outside of his culture as well as the culture he is attacking.

Juvenal's condemnation of the cannibalism incident also shows him to be in an outsider's position regarding something that was previously part of his own turf. I refer not to cannibalism itself but to the anger that the Egyptian villagers supposedly displayed when attacking their hapless neighbor. *Ira* used to be the satirist's sphere, after all. Even within Book 5, Juvenal has not repudiated the emotion in any deep, moral-philosophical sense. In *Satire* 13, despite his Senecan strategies, the attack he launches on anger is not based on concern for Calvinus's moral state but emphasizes the foolish impression he makes when in the grip of ineffectual anger. In 14, as I have noted, *ira* is—albeit briefly—awarded a special status among the passions, for although it takes harmful forms, it is also a privilege of (responsible) censors and parents. In other words, Juvenal there associates anger with (theoretically) constructive social forces and institutions. These are all reasons to rethink the notion that *Satire* 15 furthers a programmatic rejection of *indignatio*.

The many forms and contexts of the passions continue to be a central interest. Like some of its predecessors, *Satire* 15 is an emotionally *big* poem. But it uniquely shows *ira* in action in a strange setting, almost inaccessible to the intellect—untranslatable. We also learn that other people have feelings too, and they are anything but one-dimensional. The audience of an outrageous tale of this kind can react with rage—or laughter (*bilum aut risum*, 15). Later, the nameless god who looks down on humanity in its degraded state feels amusement *and* hatred at once (*deus quicumque aspexit, ridet et odit*, 71). As these telling scenes illustrate, judgment can be an emotionally complex task. Again, a case of cannibalism poses particular problems, since its very improbability might arouse laughter or amazement (*miranda quidem . . . gesta*, 27–28), while its content, tragic

---

[87] Kyle, *Spectacles of Death*, 187–94.
[88] Juvenal's "tirade against [Egyptians] is a tissue of hysterical racism, stupid morbidity, and smug self-congratulation," writes McKim ("Philosophers and Cannibals," 58) on the way to exposing the poem's subtler criticisms of Roman civilization. Anderson similarly concludes that Juvenal means to discredit his own persona ("Juvenal Satire 15").

in nature, is likely to arouse tears and pity, like a play (30–32).[89] Juvenal insists on viewing emotions in their particular *contexts*, even if he does not fully theorize or evaluate them. With this complicated emotional texture, the poem amounts to far more than an attack on *ira*.

Indeed, from the beginning, an entirely different attack is advertised: namely, Juvenal denounces Egyptian religion, which purportedly makes gods out of animals and even vegetables (2–12). From religious devotion—or perhaps xenophobia on a small scale?—comes hatred, *odium*, between villages with different cults (33–38, 51). When this feeling is activated in a violent brawl during a religious festival, Juvenal sees *ira* and its affiliated feelings (e.g., *rabies*, 126). These are names the satirist gives to the impulse to commit murder and cannibalism. (The act itself is mentioned as early as line 13, to underscore the perversity of animal worship, and it is evoked again in the coda, 171–74.) Whether his lexical choices are entirely accurate, colored by his own interest in anger, or in fact a complete misdiagnosis of ritual fervor (as Powell thinks),[90] it is vital to acknowledge that in his capacity as spectator, Juvenal can only diagnose from the outside. His fellow Roman Calvinus might have been easy to read as an *iratus*, but these barbarians are arguably less so.

In sum, it is the satirist who weaves *ira* into this story about religion and cannibalism. Yet anger itself is not the target. It is specifically anger that blurs into cannibalism that is so offensive; Juvenal's climactic conclusion is this: "in the minds of [the offending villagers], anger and hunger are equal and alike" (*in quorum mente pares sunt/et similes ira atque fames*, 130–31). This passage, in fact, comes at a critical moment in the poem, capping the sensational account of the Egyptian event and preceding the *peroratio* on human nature. It is echoed near the very end of the poem when Juvenal again accuses the villagers of a perverse *ira* that merged with hunger: they "couldn't satisfy their anger by killing someone" (*quorum non sufficit irae/occidisse aliquem*, 169–70), but saw his body as food (*crediderint genus esse cibi*, 171). These claims about the misunderstanding and misapplication of *ira* are just about as absurd as the alleged offense. The cannibals supposedly ate in a hateful frenzy, but "hunger" is hardly the right word for it. And Juvenal makes this outlandish charge, I contend, because his real aim is to condemn what he sees as the Egyptian

---

[89] Juvenal calls the story he is about to tell "more terrible than all tragic plays put together" (*cunctis graviora cothurnis*, 30–32). The Vascones, who were driven to cannibalism in order to survive a siege, aroused pity in their enemies and the gods (103–4).

[90] Powell, "What Juvenal Saw."

construction of *ira*—one that mixes the emotion with other elements like bad religion and drunkenness and directs it toward the act of cannibalism. The satirist seems concerned only with the misapplication of *ira* in a disgusting act. He is doing the work of civilization by maintaining that such things should be distinguished.[91]

Juvenal imagines that a philosopher like Pythagoras could not grapple with the phenomenon of cannibalism (171–74), but the fact is that plenty of ancient authors took an interest in such tales, finding them perfectly good narrative frameworks for meditation on the principles of civilization and order. Studies of *Satire* 15 duly cite Valerius Maximus, who includes two stories of famine that led to cannibalism in his collection of *exempla* about "dire straits" (*necessitas*, 7.6.ext.2, 3). Valerius Maximus performs a swift moral *krisis* on both cases: oppressed as they were, the people of Numantia and Calagurris, under siege by Roman forces, should have chosen death over the consumption of their loved ones.[92] Far more elaborate, more morally complex, and with a different purpose—but very useful background for our reading of Juvenal 15—is the twelfth of the *Greater Declamations* attributed to Quintilian. While the collection is almost definitely not Quintilian's work and may postdate Juvenal by decades or centuries,[93] it can certainly illuminate the way our rhetorically trained satirist handles his topic. The case is the kind of conundrum that Roman declaimers loved: it puts broken taboos on lurid display and inspects their most painful consequences. The accused had been appointed to fetch a supply of grain during a famine in his town, but was delayed in his return. He is now being prosecuted for causing an outbreak of cannibalism during his absence. The accuser himself partook in the eating of corpses. The speech is thus a fascinatingly macabre first-person account of the experience woven into a moral and legal attack on the imaginary defendant.

[91.]On discrimination as one job of satire and social institutions, see Bogel, *Difference Satire Makes*, and cf. Keane, *Figuring Genre*, 68–71, for the argument that *Satire* 15 is (deliberately) only partially successful at this.

[92.]In the first passage, on the Numantines under siege by Scipio, Valerius asserts that "there is no excuse of necessity in this case, for since they had the option of dying, it wasn't necessary to stay alive the way they did" (*nulla est in his necessitatis excusatio: nam quibus mori licuit, sic vivere necesse non fuit*). The second example passes the same judgment on the choice of the men of Calagurris, but with longer and more colorful commentary on its perversity.

[93.]Arguments on this collection's authorship and date are summarized in Sussman, *Major Declamations*, vii–x. Most recently, Stramaglia, who performs a full rhetorical analysis of the speech, settles on the second century (*Quintiliano*, 27–28). I use Stramaglia's section numbers in my citations.

For emotional variety, this speech rivals Ovid.[94] On the one hand, the accuser clearly feels, and milks, "reflexive disgust" over the very notion of cannibalism. Yet this is no outside judge but one who admits to having eaten his own deceased family members. The more horrific he makes the episode out to be—at his own expense, morally speaking—the stronger his case against the man who allowed it to happen. At the same time, as prosecutor he duly strives to arouse rage at the defendant and pity for the survivors and their victims. To do this, he must infuse even the viscerally repellent vignettes of cannibalism with the "civilized," "good" emotions of pity, affection, and grief, along with the unfortunately dominant emotion of fear (of starvation); all of these somehow continue to operate during the account, signaled by a word or image embedded in horrific details. For example, it is implied that funerals should be attended in the spirit of mourning, not greed (9.4, 27.2), that the sick should not fear their own caregivers and have to beg for proper burial or even for a natural death (10.1), and that childbirth should be a prelude to maternal love, not to a bona fide tragic meal (27.4). By recognizing the proper places of all these feelings, this speaker manages to maintain his claim to civilized human status even as he professes the barbarity of his acts. (He also remembers wishing that he could harvest acorns and berries like his primitive ancestors, or even that instead of a man he could be a beast, unfazed by meals of human flesh; 5.2, 8.5). He maintains his image as a civilized person by maintaining his grasp on the wide spectrum of emotions that make him human, despite everything. But even the perversion in which he has participated does not cause him to *confuse* one emotion with another.

Compared with Juvenal's cannibalistic villagers with their misapplied *ira*, this sad character is a torchbearer for *humanitas* in that he recognizes, and dictates, a range of emotions that fit different aspects of a complicated situation. For his part, the satirist can play the civilized person (from an arguably more secure position than the declamation's speaker) by putting names to the feelings he claims to have seen in action. The late date of our example from the *Declamations* aside, there surely is a rhetorical background to Juvenal's humane framing of the topic. The satirist's language and imagery, which Bellandi sees as part of his "philosophical filter,"[95] would be perfectly at home in declamation. His digression on cases of

---

[94.]On the speaker's "emotional creativity" and exploitation of literary themes in creating his role, see Hömke, "Declaimer's One-Man Show," 249–50; Stramaglia, *Quintiliano*, 25–27; and Sussman, *Major Declamations*, iv and 252–53.
[95.]Bellandi, *Etica diatribica*, 98.

cannibalism in famine is studded with references to a variety of human feelings. As in the *Declamation*, we glimpse the perpetrators in despair, and their equally piteous victims, now shades, forgiving them (100–106). Juvenal even asserts that the Roman forces whose long siege led to cannibalism among the Vascones of Calagurris felt pity (*hostibus ipsis . . . miserantibus*, 100–101). This does not represent the moral view of Valerius Maximus, as we have seen. Yet the satirist is confident in attributing a softer view to the Roman forces, the gods, and the unlucky dead (106), all because they are all capable of feeling pity. In making this choice he does not just heighten the criticism of Egyptian savagery but commends a kind of moral relativism, making a nuanced emotional outlook look like a mark of civilization. The poem's conclusion emphasizes the sin of cannibalism, not the impropriety of passions: it is the former that is imagined to shock Pythagoras, and Pythagoreans appear not to have been absolutists on the matter of the passions.[96]

Pity, in its delicate navigation of moral conflict, apparently represents the most civilized emotion of all: beginning the poem's climactic evaluation of human nature, Juvenal calls the ability to soften and weep at other people's misfortunes the "noblest aspect of our sensibility" (*pars optima sensus*, 133). More to the point, "what good person . . . believes anyone else's troubles to be unconnected to himself?" (*quis enim bonus . . . ulla aliena sibi credit mala?*, 140–42). In this seeming emotional jumble, we can identify a governing principle: emotional sophistication, consisting in the ability to properly name and apply a range of feelings even when they are troubling, is the fulfillment of humanity's purpose. The numerous first-person plural forms Juvenal uses throughout this passage help him to act out and enforce this principle.[97] And even a scholiast joins in the prescribing of emotions, explaining the case of the Vascones as an example "that should make you feel sadness, not horror" (*quod doleas, non horreas*).[98]

In this light, what is the role of *ira* in civilization, as distinguished from its alleged role in the Egyptians' (elective) cannibalism? There are, as I have noted, civilized contexts for *ira*—particularly, in the regulation of morality. Another such context is identified in the *Declamation*. In his very

---

[96.] While Kalimtzis calls the Pythagoreans "pioneers" in the area of restraint of passions (*Taming Anger*, 28), Thom finds a "wide spectrum" of attitudes among followers of Pythagoreanism in the Hellenistic period ("Passions in Neopythagorean Writings").

[97.] *nostri*, 133; *gemimus*, 138; *nos*, 142; *traximus*, 146; *nobis . . . nos*, 149; *nostris*, 153.

[98.] Wessner, *Scholia in Iuvenalem vetustiora*, 230.

first sentence the accuser asserts that he is positively choking on material for *indignatio* (*me indignandi causae . . . strangulent*, 1.1). But this feeling is also the *solution* to his unbearable grief and guilt: performed *indignatio* is the legal expression of his pain, and might accomplish something constructive, as it can be applied in a prosecution "for harm done to the state" (*rei publicae laesae [actio]*; pref.).[99] In a startling opening flourish that is strangely reminiscent of a line in *Satire* 15, the speaker in his opening paragraph recollects his feelings upon the delinquent agent's return to the city: he himself was both hungry and angry (*et esurirem et irascerer*, 1.4),[100] so he could well have torn that man apart for food at once, since he had already crossed that ethical line. Of course he and his fellow citizens did not take this "Egyptian" step, being entirely fixated on the newly arrived grain (2.1), but the anger clearly remains. It can now be contained and packaged in forensic rhetoric, and held up to represent the proper response (as he sees it) of civilized people to the entire story. This anger will bind speaker to audience: the former is milking his rage *and* horror *and* pity *and* grief *and* guilt; the latter should be encouraged to let anger and other strong feelings spring up in them in the present. In this form *ira* can be called "establishment anger," the kind with which the old satirist has already begun to ally himself (cf. *censoris ira*, 14.50).

One more comparison case of "establishment anger" addressing a form of anger represented as uncivilized makes illuminating background for the *Satire*. In 41 C.E., the emperor Claudius wrote a letter to the Alexandrians that has partially survived on papyrus. Addressing the nagging conflict between the city's Greeks and Jews, Claudius criticizes their "destructive anger" (ὀλέθριον ὀργὴν) toward one another and threatens a display of "relentless" and "just" anger (ὀργὴν ἀμεταμέλητον . . . ὀργὴν δίκαιαν). That Claudius had a reputation as being prone to excessive rage is less important for present purposes than the fact that he saw fit to call his emotion and the Alexandrians' by the same name, while spinning them in different ways.[101] The Alexandrians are destructive in their anger, the emperor righteous and—going by the overall tone of the long letter—benevolent in his. We may note other occasions when writers "split" anger in order to claim the right to rage while denying it to others. From classical Greek

---

[99.]On this charge, see Bonner, *Roman Declamation*, 97–98.
[100.]Stramaglia (*Quintiliano*, 95) notes the parallel with Juvenal and also cites Seneca's comparison of the two conditions at *Ira* 3.4.3.
[101.]*P. Lond.* Vi. 1912, printed as document 370 in Smallwood, *Documents Illustrating Principates*, 101 (see lines 77–82). Harris gives attention to the letter in his discussion of the "angry ruler" topos (*Restraining Rage*, 250). On Claudius, see n. 103 below.

authors' portrayal of transgressive women as ruled by their passions, to early Christian theologians' criticism of sinners, to accounts of peasant uprisings in premodern Europe, we can see two kinds of anger being defined side by side: one objectified as illegitimate, the other aligned with authority and held to be legitimate, even noble.[102]

Juvenal may be engaged in similar rhetorical work, preserving anger so that not just his "civilized" culture, but he himself as satirist, can continue to own anger even as he nears the end of his career and life. The models for this satiric project could have included the example of Claudius's anger, which had become a theme in historiography and philosophy. That emperor was not just a sort of perpetual *senex* (due equally to his late acquisition of power and his lifelong disabilities) but one who recognized that anger was a trademark of his rule. From his position of power, Claudius both acknowledged his anger's dangerousness and defended it as just.[103]

The satirist of Book 5, despite his critical representation of *ira* and other passions, has not relinquished anger as a tool of satire and civilization alike. This analysis of the satirist's persona and perspective is further supported by the last part of *Satire* 15 (131–71). In the eyes of numerous scholars, this is the point where Juvenal cements his critical attitude toward *ira* by praising the feelings that unite, rather than divide, people. First comes a Stoic-flavored account of humanity's creation and special purpose, next a small catalog of the everyday occasions (prosecutions, funerals) that make normal people feel sympathy and sadness, then another narrative that focuses on the building of human communities around common needs, and finally a despairing comparison of bad human acts with the comparatively decent behavior of animals. The same themes and terms appear in many summaries of the passage: Juvenal "exposes [the ugliness of the Egyptians' crime] from the perspective of Stoic humanitarianism. . . . In other words, while he utterly condemns Egypt, he preaches a positive creed." "Juvenal goes beyond the incident of Egyptian cannibalism . . . and delivers a protreptic argument for *humanitas*." In *Satire* 15 more than

---

[102.]On these cases, see first Harris ("Rage of Women," 138), who notes that for Greek men "appropriating anger for themselves was . . . a matter of strengthening men's social and sexual control." (I borrow the phrase "right to rage" from the last sentence of Harris's essay.) Cf. the early Christian theologians' distinction in Little, "Anger in Monastic Curses," 12 (n. 47 above), and Freedman, "Peasant Anger."

[103.]"Aware of his [fits of] anger and [general tendency to] resentment, he excused both in an edict and he distinguished between them, promising that his fits of anger would be brief and harmless, and his harboring of resentment not without cause" (*irae atque iracundiae conscius sibi, utramque excusavit edicto distinxitque, pollicitus alteram quidem brevem et innoxiam, alteram non iniustam fore*, Suet. *Claud.* 38.1).

anywhere else, "the satirist is concerned, not just with the condemnation of vice, but with the assertion of positive values."[104]

This refrain that Juvenal balances his attack on the cannibals with an articulation and praise of positive values is inspired, if not consciously in all cases, by a particular theory of satire. The idea that any given satiric poem must attack a single vice, and praise the "opposite" virtue, is a creation of Dryden's that Griffin notes is the most-quoted of all his theoretical assertions, and "lay[s] the cornerstone for all subsequent theories of satire's artfulness and its moral purpose." The twentieth-century version of this theory was equally influential.[105] But is it right to ascribe it to an ancient poet? Even Dryden notes that Juvenal does not faithfully adhere to this bipartite, balanced formula;[106] from the beginning, he appears to have other satiric theories in mind. As for *Satire* 15, as I have shown, it is not so easy to pin down the "vice" under attack,[107] while the lengthy meditation on *humanitas* is simply unparalleled in the rest of the *Satires* in its positive foundations and emotional appeal. Indeed, various aspects of the poem's subject matter and rhetoric led at least one nineteenth-century scholar to single it out as a forgery—this critic, at least, was not inspired to look for Dryden in Juvenal.[108] So, too, when we discuss the (relatively) positive turn *Satire* 15 takes, it is best to take an approach that does not route us back to Dryden's theory.

The *humanitas* passage should be appreciated as a more dynamic element of the poem, and specifically as the (staged and calculated) *reaction* of the satirist to the terrible event he has been dissecting. If the passage has seemed unusual and tacked on to some readers, that is because up until now Juvenal has provided very little "humanistic" commentary on the Egyptian incident. The digression on peoples who were driven to cannibalism in dire straits is the exception; elsewhere, we see criticism of cannibalism (and animal worship, and luxury, and so on), but the moral

---

[104.]The quotes are from Anderson, "Programs of Later Books," 151 (=*Essays*, 283); Fredericks, "Juvenal's Fifteenth Satire," 175; and Singleton, "Juvenal's Fifteenth Satire," 198.

[105.]Griffin, *Satire*, 19–20. Griffin contextualizes Dryden's claim in its immediate polemical context and later (28) does the same with its equally influential twentieth-century descendant (Randolph, "Structural Design of Satire").

[106.]Griffin, *Satire*, 23–24.

[107.]Powell, otherwise unconcerned with satiric theory, still makes this interesting concluding remark: "*Satire* 15 does not work very well because the vice around which Juvenal structures his attack is . . . a special case, recalcitrant to the sort of generalization that he would put it to" ("What Juvenal Saw," 189).

[108.]Kempf, *De satira quinta decima;* for discussion of this work, see Highet, *Juvenal the Satirist*, 286 n. 9. Highet, for his part, believes that Juvenal gradually took on the role of "a positive teacher" in *Satire* 8 (*Juvenal the Satirist*, 104–5).

foundations of that criticism are not articulated. If Juvenal has been keeping the "Stoic-humanitarian" account of his species up his sleeve all this time, he has hidden it well. Now, it emerges from this almost entirely negative picture as a response to a crisis.

We can identify the crisis as not simply the horror of the Egyptian incident but the confusion of feelings that Juvenal pinpoints at that climactic point I have already discussed, *in quorum mente pares sunt/et similes ira atque fames* (130–31). It is immediately after those words, in the same line, that the "Stoic-humanitarian" account begins. The confusion of *ira* and *fames* drives the satirist to rethink everything he knows about human nature. And Deucalion and Pyrrha, once his first *homines* of interest, will not do—Juvenal must go back to the playbook of the *mundi conditor* (147–48). This is the foundation of his positive description of human nature. We can read this not as an injection of some preexisting theory of satire that Juvenal has barely acknowledged throughout his career but as the staged production of a sort of theory—moral, biological, *and* satiric— as a reaction. Experiencing dire circumstances of his own, our satirist is forced to innovate. The result may superficially conform to a satiric theory, but it is not driven *by* that theory.

In this light, Juvenal's professed *humanitas* does not so much appear to balance, or demolish, the *ira* that he has condemned in the Egyptians as to contribute to his own construction of an emotional toolkit for civilization—which includes the appropriation of "civilized *ira*." Claiming *humanitas* (in the end, this concept is illustrated rather than given a name) gives Juvenal's critical posture more credibility, as has his alliance with other vehicles of "civilization," such as education (106–12) and armies that show pity in the very act of conquering (100–101). Even those Roman soldiers approach godlike understanding, if in witnessing desperate attempts at survival, they share the forgiving attitude that "[all] humans and gods" rightly adopt (*hominum . . . deorum*, 103). This unsurprisingly comes across as cultural chauvinism, with Juvenal and his people showing all manner of civilized emotions and the Egyptians none.

To this end, the satirist even appropriates and reinvents the supposed defining element of the Egyptian religion: worship of animals. The poem had opened with a list of the *portenta* (2) worshiped as gods in Egypt— preposterous pseudo-gods. The particular strangeness of the first few examples—crocodile, ibis, ape—conveniently reflects the strangeness of the people who revere them. But when Juvenal turns his attention to the theme of human deviation from the ideal of *humanitas*, animals reappear in the form of—not gods, strictly speaking, but good *exempla* that make humanity look "animal" by comparison (159–64):

> sed iam serpentum maior concordia. parcit
> cognatis maculis similis fera. quando leoni
> fortior eripuit vitam leo? quo nemore umquam
> expiravit aper maioris dentibus apri?
> Indica tigris agit rabida cum tigride pacem
> perpetuam, saevis inter se convenit ursis.

> But these days there's greater harmony among serpents [than people].
> A beast spares its spotted relations, due to their like appearance. When
> has a stronger lion ever taken a weaker lion's life? In what meadow has
> a boar ever perished by the teeth of a bigger boar? Indian tigers keep
> lasting peace with one another despite their fierceness, and there is a
> pact between savage bears.

The animal-human dichotomy is turned on its head—something we might conclude was foreshadowed in *Satire* 14. Animals were said to feed on human corpses but only in the name of survival and when they were made available by other humans (14.77). As the satirist argues in 15, it is humans who show "beastliness" (*feritas*, 32), and conversely, beasts deserve to be looked up to as examples of fellow feeling.[109] Juvenal has appropriated the animal world for his own cultural agenda: the definition of appropriate emotions. For all his expressions of marginality, he comes out looking like someone with an interest in promoting the culture that made him.

On Reading the End, or "You and What Army?"

The partially preserved sixteenth *Satire*, which probably marked the end of the original book, is an enigma.[110] After the chronologically,

---

[109.]Fredericks, "Juvenal's Fifteenth Satire," 187: the play between the story of human *feritas* and the praise of *humanitas* is a "humorous contradiction . . . cynical and paradoxical." A similar irony has been identified at the poem's end, where Juvenal uses Pythagoras the vegetarian as a moral authority, "align[ing] him not with Roman but with Egyptian values." He thus "closes the supposed gap between barbarism and civilization" (McKim, "Philosophers and Cannibals," 69–70).
[110.]If Book 5 was meant to roughly parallel the others in length, this should have been the last poem. The original manuscript's "tail," constituting one or more quires, is believed to have been lost early in its transmission. On the history of the question, see Parker, "Manuscripts," 148–49, and Stramaglia, *Giovenale*, 292–93.

geographically, and philosophically expansive *Satire* 15, it makes a strange coda: sixty lines, ending in the middle of a sentence, cataloging legal privileges enjoyed by soldiers and the contrasting restrictions on ordinary civilians. Is this a manifestation of satire's resistance to closure,[111] mapped onto an entire career? Or are we being presented with a unique conception of closure that we must work to understand? To end with a mundane treatment of military matters is a far cry from, say, the Vergilian ascent to epic—alternatively, it could be meant as a clever parody of that model.[112] This is just one example of how expectations and imagination can either confuse or inspire our efforts to understand Juvenal's last performance. In the end, we cannot be sure whether and how Juvenal might have been trying to acknowledge this poem as his last appearance. But an interesting story can be found in what he is taken to be saying: as we consider the poem, it will be worth spotlighting the (albeit tiny) body of scholarship concerned with *Satire* 16, for it exposes basic and unresolved questions about satire and the character of the satirist.

In thematic terms, this poem could be said to satisfy various imaginable requirements for a fitting literary finale: it reinforces, combines, and innovates. While the topic of soldiers' rights is in itself unusual, the theme of civilian resentment against soldiers is seen earlier in Juvenal and in other imperial literature.[113] *Satire* 16 also revisits other broad issues that permeate previous *Satires*, including the poems of Book 5 with their emphasis on "crime and punishment and the courts . . . money and gain and greed."[114] Delivered by a speaker who is himself cast from a familiar Juvenalian mold—a civilian who resents the greater privileges enjoyed by soldiers—*Satire* 16 becomes a catalog of injustices from the civilian's perspective. The addressee, Gallius, appears to share the status of the satirist who "enumerat[es] the rewards of a military career, blessed by fortune" (*numerare . . . felicis praemia . . . militiae*, 1–2). The two appear to experience the conventional conditions for *indignatio*. As Juvenal explains, soldiers are safe from assault by civilians, and even—far from representing law and order—enjoy pummeling helpless civilians with impunity (7–12).[115] Their military courts are guaranteed to disappoint and terrorize

---

[111.]Griffin, *Satire*, 95–114.

[112.]I owe the latter idea to Susanna Braund (*per litteras*).

[113.]Umbricius recalls being stomped on by a careless soldier's boot (3.248). For more bullying and/or oafish soldiers, see Persius 3.77–85 and 5.189–91 and Apul. *Met.* 9.39–42. Cf. Clark, "Fragmentary Justice," 116 nn. 10 and 12.

[114.]Braund, *Beyond Anger*, 196.

[115.]Keane, *Figuring Genre*, 71.

any civilian who brings a charge against a soldier: the judges, sympathetic to their peer, make an intimidating spectacle with their hobnailed boots and muscles. "The entire cohort is your personal enemy" (*tota cohors . . . est inimica*, 20). Meanwhile, the civilian, lacking loyal advocates of his own, is effectively silenced by the hostile environment and the dearth of honesty in the world (25–34). This colorful scene, in which the civilian is still bleeding from his wounds and his soldier adversaries giving him a second, legal humiliation, simultaneously recalls the vulnerability of Umbricius bullied in the streets and Calvinus mocked in court.

In short, we are looking at a resurrection of Juvenal's favorite topics in a new form: the unusual rhetorical scenario of a catalog of soldiers' privileges. The rest of the fragment provides more evidence that justice is unfairly distributed. If an ordinary *togatus* is subjected to property violation and fraud (apparently inevitable in this depraved world), he is restricted to the inefficient civilian courts (36–47). Now, instead of a bleeding face and thuggish judges, he endures endless delays of his trial in the "sticky sand of the forum" (*lenta . . . fori . . . harena*, 47). The image of the arena turns the civilian litigant into an unwilling and resourceless gladiator—or an arena victim, contrasting with "those whom arms protect and sword-belt encircles" (*illis quos arma tegunt et balteus ambit*, 48). And in the final lines of the fragment, Juvenal is apparently beginning to discuss soldiers' special control over their own property: only a soldier may make a will while his father is living (51–57).[116] It has been suggested that these lines were only the beginning of a longer treatment of financial matters;[117] the financial straits experienced by unfortunate *togati* may have been colorfully documented as in *Satires* 1, 3, 5, 7, and 9. As usual, the satiric protagonist's purse and belly are as vulnerable as his body.

Another aspect of the poem in which we might hope to find closure is emotional color and persona. Assessments have varied. One scholar hears a "resentful tone [that] brings us back to early Juvenal . . . [perhaps] an intentional touch if he was writing what he meant to be his last complete poem."[118] All these complaints about society are framed by insistent and repeated wonder at the soldier's good fortune, as if the speaker were a deluded straw man in a philosophical diatribe, clinging to his belief that someone else's grass is greener.[119] Yet the substance

---

[116.] On this theme, see also Clark, "Fragmentary Justice."
[117.] Highet, *Juvenal the Satirist*, 288 n. 6.
[118.] Hooley, *Roman Satire*, 129.
[119.] Keane, "Philosophy into Satire," 48–51.

of Juvenal's complaints aside, rhetorical expressions of *indignatio* are hardly to be found—for instance, the opening question ("who can enumerate the rewards . . .?) is not of the same angry species as "will I always just have to listen?" Indeed, since the catalog of injustices is framed as sarcastic praise of the military life, persona scholars imagine we are listening to an ironist or cynic.[120] A third option is to read this as a "combination" persona, mixing "Juvenal's earlier aggression with his later irony."[121] Each one of these interpretations points to a different way emotional closure might be staged. Juvenal is returning to his angry roots. Or he is demonstrating how well he has mastered his "late" style. Or, finally, he is having it all, making the most of this last performance. Without stable criteria for defining the proper emotional endpoint of this book or of Juvenal's career, we may only try out different notions of "proper."

One more approach is to ask whether *Satire* 16 continues the series of "old man's satires," listening not merely for tone but for signs of a character behind the words. In fact, the stereotypical condition of the *senex* has a certain relevance to the subject at hand. As Courtney puts it, *Satire* 16 is "an interesting document of the alienation of the *togati* (8) or the *pagani* (33) from the army" as the latter's duties evolved to fit the empire's peacetime needs.[122] If civilians in general felt alienated from the army, for an old man the situation would have been doubly difficult; this could be what Juvenal is dramatizing. He sees soldiers as an imposing assembly of muscles and arms: boots and big calves, hobnails and protective gear (14, 24–25, 48). No match for a soldier physically, a *senex* was also denied the soldier's legal privileges—unless, of course, he himself had chosen the same career long ago. Our satirist might have noted his current ineligibility in a missing line(s) in the opening, giving more sense to our extant line 3 ("[would that?] the camp gate would take me in, a trembling novice," *me pavidum excipiat tironem porta*).[123] It is too late for this. And while the optimistic Plutarch claims that old men lack their younger counterparts' susceptibility to envy (*Mor.* 787c), Aristotle and Horace, as we have seen, portray old men as habitual complainers. We have seen a relevant

---

[120.]Anderson calls the satirist's manner in 16 "urbane" and "smiling" (see "Programs of Later Books," 151 (=*Essays*, 283); cf. Romano, *Irony in Juvenal*, 197. Braund cautiously concludes that Book 5 "is unified by its . . . superior and cynical speaker" (*Beyond Anger*, 196).

[121.]Courtney, *Satires*, 613.

[122.]Courtney, *Satires*, 613; cf. Gérard, *Juvénal*, 340–41.

[123.]Clausen's text hypothesizes a lacuna between 2 and 3.

performance from Umbricius—delivered, as he claimed, in *prima senectus* and saturated with envy and resentment.

The difference between young(er) soldiers and old men is emphasized in the last section of our text of *Satire* 16. Because they can make their wills while their fathers are living, soldiers have control over their own earnings (51–54), yet another privilege that makes civilians look comparatively hamstrung—this time by *patria potestas*. But Juvenal highlights an interesting detail: the consequences for a soldier's father. "Although now wobbly [with age], the father strives to win [his son's] legacy" (*quamvis iàm tremulus captat pater*, 56). Ordinary *captatio* is bad enough; this double perversion represents a victory of the military son over aged father. Juvenal appears to pity the latter. Might he even have been posing as a soldier's frustrated father in the original poem, exploring this particular victim's perspective? That would have made a sad (and funny) joke after *Satire* 14, where we saw avaricious fathers urging their sons to seek gainful work, such as a career in the military: a soldier could earn the post of senior centurion by his sixtieth year (197–98). The soldiers of *Satire* 16 seem to be doing well along the way, too. But even if Juvenal is not speaking in the character of a soldier's unlucky father, he is certainly speaking against a group that can be broadly marked "young," and from a position of powerlessness familiar to the stereotypical *senex*.

Knowing the identity or role of the addressee Gallius might help us reconstruct the dramatic scenario, but this shadowy figure is marked only as a fellow suffering civilian.[124] A most interesting speculation is made by the poem's most ambitious and creative critic, Schnur, who took the text's damaged state as a challenge to write the rest of it himself. Schnur's jokingly titled "Newly Discovered Fragment," a Latin composition first published in 1969, supplies a fictional frame by ending the poem with a nudge to Gallius: if he has a son who is mentally slow but strong, he should be urged to join the army (169–72).[125] This final jab at the army is also a way of clearly marking Juvenal and his addressee as members of the older generation, watching their juniors begin profitable careers. Schnur may have read this detail into the *Satire* after reflecting on the experience and authority Juvenal projects in *Satires* 13 and 14.

There is much more food for thought in Schnur's reconstruction, and much of relevance to the current discussion. Both technically impressive

---

[124.]While the hypothesized soldier is first addressed as "you," the unlucky civilian becomes the "you" in line 24, and Juvenal and his addressee are "we" at 28 and 47.

[125.]Schnur, "Iuvenalis Saturae XVI fragmentum," 215.

and playful, these 113 lines are a fascinating document of the reception of Juvenal.[126] While Highet only outlines a "big catalogue-poem" resembling *Satires* 3, 6, and 10, showing his belief in an ambitious finale,[127] Schnur actually creates one. The satirist's running complaint about military privileges is spun into a survey of big "Roman themes": patronage (soldiers do not need the protections of the system that humiliates civilians, 68–72); the empire's ethnic and cultural diversity (Italians having gone soft, the army teems with foreign men and tongues, 99–135); and dynastic politics (the army has the power to proclaim an emperor, 136–55). Schnur's composition becomes a grand (if quite economical) finale, complete with personal revelations and recapitulation of Juvenal's greatest hits. The hapless civilian client is described as "eloquent" and "expert at writing satires" (*facundus . . . saturas . . . scribere doctus*, 70)—a wink to the reader of the real *Satires* and possibly also an echo of Martial's epithet for (our?) Juvenal (7.91.1). There is a playful gesture to the slender evidence from the lost "Juvenal inscription" at Aquinum in the claim that the poet learned about military life firsthand as tribune in the First Dalmatian Cohort (96–98).[128] In the passage on the un-Roman provinces, Ovid is apostrophized as a "pitiable poet, so similar to me in your fate" (*miserande poeta/tam similis fato nobis*, 119–20)—hinting at the ancient *Life*'s claim that Juvenal was sent to Egypt as a punishment for his writings. And in a final reference to a perennial satiric theme, Schnur's closing line summarizes the soldier's lot as "never lack[ing] a legacy-hunter or ample funds" (*captator numquam deerit nec copia nummum*, 173). Juvenal is thus allowed to echo Persius and close off his oeuvre with a gesture to *captatio*.

In Schnur's composition, Juvenal's mysterious biography is (at least partially) illuminated, and his last poem is recast as polished, full in scope, and appropriately self-conscious for a poetic swan song. Besides the autobiographical gestures, there are allusions to other Juvenalian lines; the first *Satire* with its prominent *ego* and backstory is recalled by *ipse . . . iuvenis* (96–97; cf. 1.25, *iuveni mihi*). Schnur has given the Juvenalian corpus both continuity and closure. In the present discussion, the thematic breadth of this reconstruction is as significant as his reconstruction of a plausible satiric persona. Schnur would seem to agree with other scholars

---

[126.] See translation and comments in Winkler, "Media Age," 538–41. As Winkler notes, Schnur employs some phrases and imagery from Juvenal's other poems.
[127.] Highet, *Juvenal the Satirist*, 158–59, and the detailed reconstruction at 288–89 n. 6.
[128.] On the recorded text of the inscription, which is actually not substantial enough to make our poet a military tribune, see Courtney, *Satires*, 2–5.

concerning the wider social relevance of the military topic, for he extends the complaints about local justice into a more sweeping lament. His Juvenal becomes an explicit commentator on the consequences of empire: dilution of *Romanitas*, diversification in culture and language, and increasing political strife and uncertainty. His Juvenal, it would seem, knows that the "soldier emperor" phenomenon will develop and the empire will fragment. He may also know that for a long time he will be viewed as the final spokesman for his civilization, stationed at the boundary between "Silver" Latin and what lies beyond.

"End of the empire" thinking also colors scholarly assessments of the real *Satire* 16: in this context, too, the poet comes to stand for bigger things. With its precise complaints about military privilege, this poem is often cited as a source on specific legal, social, and political developments of the imperial period. At this time the Roman army, now virtually made up of career soldiers and increasingly segregated from the civilian population, was having its legal and financial needs better served. As Schnur's fragment also emphasizes, even outside of times of crisis such as civil war, the army was seen as closely attached to the seat of imperial power— certainly under the military-friendly Adoptive emperors.[129] In this general picture some see the satirist's motive for writing this poem: the attack on the army is also an attack on policies of the current administration and dynasty. Enhancements made to soldiers' rights (such as the flexible inheritance law) by Nerva and his successors "aroused the satirist's ire."[130] Hadrian, under whose role the poem was composed, is being criticized as unfairly attentive to soldiers' rights.[131]

But is this what we expect from Juvenal? Although complaints about misbehaving soldiers may be conventional, the political criticism as it is described above sounds far from trivial (even if a one-man attack on the army evokes Monty Python once again). Stramaglia entertains the possibility that the satirist carried out this attack because he had "little to lose" at this point in his life.[132] Could Juvenal be testing the truth of his own quip in *Satire* 10 that "it's rare for soldiers to storm [an ordinary citizen's] garret" (*rarus venit in cenacula miles*, 10.18)? Doubtlessly, few would venture to

---

[129] See especially Gérard, *Juvénal*, 340–41. Cf. Courtney, *Satires*, 613: the alienation mentioned above "has been regarded by some scholars as a main cause of [the empire's] decline and fall."
[130] Clark, "Fragmentary Justice," 120.
[131] Gérard, *Juvénal*, 341. Cf. Courtney, *Satires*, 613: Juvenal "seems to criticize Hadrian directly" (cf. 616 on line 15). Durry, "Juvénal et les prétoriens," reads the poem's references to soldiers as particularly relevant to the praetorians in Rome.
[132] Stramaglia, *Giovenale*, 295; the ellipsis that follows ends the book.

imagine such a dramatic outcome for the satirist, but even Highet pauses to wonder if the criticism of the *milites* themselves and their powerful patron might have had an ill effect: Was this "striking, though slightly dangerous, peroration . . . unofficially censored, after all?"[133] While such questions about the political impact of *Satire* 16 and the text's fate are insoluble, for the present study it is significant that scholars describe this poem as something quite different than what has come before. The point is not just that the project seems to have a "slightly dangerous" character; it is that this is unprecedented in Juvenal.

In the (albeit scant) scholarly commentary, we see the onetime attacker of the dead transform into a critic of contemporary policy and power. It is an ironic reception for a poem that describes the army as an intimidating presence. The old satirist is invested not just with renewed resentment and aggression but with courage. The intricate "art of safe criticism" in his early work is replaced with blunt indictment of a sort that had been markedly absent in satire since Lucilius. Scholars may not have his agenda right, of course, and their promotion of Juvenal to fearless speaker of truth to power—not to mention historian and prophet—may be an entirely unconscious move. But it is the satirist's inadvertent doing, his final, unprogrammed legacy. Juvenal is firmly contextualized in imperial history, the climax and closure of his career merged with the empire's own apex and coming fall, before he slips away for good.

[133.]Highet, *Juvenal the Satirist*, 159, shortly after arguing that the text's damage could not have been caused by censorship. Contrastingly, Waters concludes that it was only the accession of Hadrian that made Juvenal feel safe writing satire at all—while also asserting that in the *Satires* there is "careful avoidance of contemporary issues, of imperial affairs, and of comment regarding policy in the post-Domitianic period" ("Juvenal and Trajan, 76").

| Conclusion

JUVENAL WAS FATED TO be remembered mainly for his beginning, and in a retrospective framework. His first *Satire* announces major changes in the genre and looks back on the tradition that precedes it. His first book includes meditations on recent history, which has encouraged Juvenal's readers to do the same when they read him—packaging him alongside other authors who wrote during this "good" dynasty but who used the "bad" ones for material. In a line of poets who style themselves as "successors," he is the last. He is even a successor (less strictly speaking, generically) to his older contemporary Martial. The epigrammatist, a precious if enigmatic contemporary source on Juvenal, fixes for posterity an image of the satirist in his early years, beginning as Martial is acting out his own ending (*Ep.* 12.18). Juxtaposed with the older poet's reclaimed provincial life (late sleeping, casual clothing) is the urban grind (the *salutatio* in a sweaty toga) that still imprisons the younger. But place and social activity are not the only points of contrast; the two men's life cycles are out of sync. Martial is retiring, Juvenal fully engaged with the life of the imperial capital. He is imagined, fittingly, as living the life that his first book of *Satires* depicts—or (if publication is still a decade away) as soaking up the material that will go into it.[1]

If Juvenal had had a successor like himself, a new satirist following in the post-Lucilian tradition and duly producing a capsule-history-of-satire-in-satire, how might this writer have portrayed his predecessor? One

---

[1] In the Martial poem "Juvenal is imagined trapped in the Rome of his own first book" Uden, *Invisible Satirist*, 224, taking this as evidence that Book 1 had been published by 102).

possibility is a portrait like this one of Lucilius, from Horace's second book of *Satires* (Hor. *S.* 2.1.30–34):

> ille velut fidis arcana sodalibus olim
> credebat libris, neque si male cesserat usquam
> decurrens alio, neque si bene; quo fit ut omnis
> votiva pateat veluti descripta tabella
> vita senis.

> In his time, he used to entrust his secrets to his books, as if to trusty comrades, never running off anywhere else whether things had gone badly or well; as a result, the old man's entire life lies open and visible, as if inscribed on a votive tablet.

This passage expresses, through several themes, Horace's ambivalent stance toward his republican predecessor. The analogy with a votive tablet, a crude kind of "art," subtly renews Horace's earlier criticisms of Lucilius's writing style as undisciplined, unselfconscious, and unpolished.[2] The detail in *senis* may be meant to underscore this suggestion, considering some of the associations the term carries: garrulousness, stubbornness, and unseemly noncooperation with nature's prescriptions.

At the same time—and with consequences for posterity's view of Lucilius—Horace conveys admiration for his predecessor. He was not just a babbling old *senex* but the grand old man of satire—greater than Horace, as the latter goes on to declare (74–75). This portrait is presented on an occasion when Horace could be said to be reaching for a kind of senior status himself. He is doing his own "running on" (cf. *decurrens* at 32) into a second book of *Satires*, and even as he begins, he claims that some critics see him as slack and rambling (2–4).[3] Then, too, there might be a note of envy in Horace's portrayal of the republican-era satirist sharing his feelings and experiences so unselfconsciously. His successors will become increasingly less self-revealing, at least in their programmatic remarks (Persius whispers into a ditch, and Juvenal is brief at best on his education and influences).

---

[2] Harrison, "Confessions of Lucilius." Cf. Anderson, "Ironic Preambles," 39: Horace means that "Lucilius . . . treated his poems like a diary, drawing no distinction, exercising no artistic restraint regardless of the character of a situation, good or bad."

[3] Harrison, "Confessions of Lucilius," 47–48, reads a second sense in *decurrens*—"running on, spouting off"—in keeping with Horace's previous criticisms of Lucilian profuseness; cf. 49–51.

Horace's claim that Lucilian satire reads like autobiography gets at another key theme of the tradition, one with particular relevance to Juvenal. On the face of it, Horace seems to be voicing a common ancient view of first-person literature.[4] Ancient authors wrote of their predecessors as people with personal histories; some—with varying regard for historical fact—even filled in perceived gaps with inventions of their own. A genre that went informally by the name of *sermo*, "chat," would especially seem to be inviting interpretation as authentic, subliterary self-expression.[5] Lucilius has been identified as the first Roman poet who devoted himself to this kind of writing, creating "objective representations through subjective observations."[6] Horace's votive tablet passage is an homage to that, whatever else it implies along the way. And yet there is an interested, tendentious dimension to what Horace says in this detail as the others. It is not just that the characterization of Lucilius's *Satires* as containing the poet's "entire life" oversimplifies and exaggerates (surely deliberately and playfully).[7] More important, Horace's wording suggests that Lucilius's autobiographical mode may not have been a conscious strategy, but is revealed in reading. The revelation of his "entire life" in the *Satires* is not necessarily the *purpose* of his practice but a *result* (*quo fit ut omnis . . . pateat . . . vita senis*). In contrast, Horace certainly writes "autobiographical" passages, but he picks and chooses the revelations and occasions.[8] Another contrast can be seen in an echo of the Lucilius passage later in *Satire* 2.1, where Horace declares his intention to continue writing satire: "whatever the *color* of my *vita*, I will write" (*quisquis erit vitae scribam color*, 60). This portrays the ups and downs of Horace's life as circumstances of his writing, not the stuff of it. But what Horace says about Lucilius is that someone—or is it only the clever Horace?—can read his work and *see* the man's life laid out plainly. Lucilius is being portrayed as an accidental diarist.

As we have seen, Juvenal claims a particular connection with Lucilius. He is certainly more like him than his predecessors were in one significant sense: just as Lucilius wrote only satire, and evidently over the last

---

[4.]Mayer, "Persona (I) Problems" (on this passage, see 73–75).
[5.]Lucilius 1085 W: *de me ista foris sermonibus differs*; 1086 W: *maledicendo in multis sermonibus differs*); cf. Horace 1.4.48, *sermo merus, Ep.* 2.2.60, etc.
[6.]Haß, *Lucilius*, 12.
[7.]Freudenburg, "Horatius Anceps," 273–76.
[8.]For more on the parallels Horace suggests with Lucilius, see Harrison, "Confessions of Lucilius," 43–44. Cf. Freudenburg, "Horatius Anceps," 276: Horace, after pretending to capture Lucilius neatly, "pattern[s] his life in new terms of his own."

few decades of his life, Juvenal too concentrated on satire until he wrote no more. Might he have taken inspiration from the portrait of Lucilius in Horace—even thrusting himself into the place that Horace would not fill—in the construction of his own poetry and persona? Juvenal could become a "new Lucilius" by reinventing Horace's interpretation as a deliberate program; by creating the impression of a full life, with its good and bad parts, across his satire. Experience, aging, and other changes are suggested by gestures of many kinds: the energetic outburst of the angry "I"; the friendships, conflicts, and dialogues; the self-portraits in domestic settings (complete with reference to wrinkles and relaxation); and the "conversation" with a peer about the benefits of long life experience.

The attitudes and feelings Juvenal expresses, in connection with his choice of satiric subjects (bad wives, barbaric Egyptians), have certainly been read as displaying how "things had gone badly or well" during his life. But the underlying reason for this reception is that Juvenal begins by rewriting the satirist's job description. Like Horace and Persius, Juvenal appoints himself homilist on human behavior, but he is the first to play up the specifically emotional imperative behind this work. His creation of a reactive model for satire reinvigorates even the genre's most traditional topics, making them seem "personal." And the satirist figure need not be front and center at all times to create this effect; it arises from the smallest rhetorical gestures, starting with the first person forms in *Satire* 1.1. Juvenal thus initiates his readers' detective work. This is not to say that our work is less valuable than we thought, but that it should done in a different spirit, with attention to all the ways the satirist tells us about himself. Rhetorical analysis can yield descriptions of satiric personae. But we also need to take more impressionistic soundings of the poems, listen more attentively to the fictions the poet presents, and especially consider *what* he chooses to write about at every turn. These are expressions of what satire can and should be attacking, musing about, mocking—as well as how best to do these things. The products of this play are both substantial and fascinating. Even our damaged text shows that Juvenal was, at the end of his career, "running out of time, not of invention."[9] Ultimately he earned not just the label *senex* but also the title *inventor.*

In satire's capacious "stuffed platter," every authorial choice is meaningful. Juvenal adds another menu of choices to this medley when he reinvents satire as emotional engagement with the world. But in the beginning,

---

[9.]Hooley, *Roman Satire*, 129.

significantly, he does not make it look as though the satirist has much choice in this regard. His satire—and, in his tendentious telling, the whole history of satire—is born in a noisy, provocative landscape that programs *indignatio*, especially for a satirist who is rooted to the ground in the *quadrivium*. We learn that satire is reactive, and that it uses and represents common human passions (*votum timor ira voluptas/gaudia discursus*). Emotion—even if it is not always *ira*, and even if the initial claim only applies to the (first) *libellus*—is worked into the generic formula that easily. The loud voice that leads us into the text and makes these claims about satire is very compelling. It is no wonder that the first book has so greatly influenced the reception of Juvenal, leading scholars to ask not *whether* the later books express feelings but *which* feelings they express. It requires only a few more poems and passages—the dialogue with Naevolus, the comparison of Democritus and Heraclitus, the criticisms of Calvinus and the Egyptians—to create the impression of a refrain, and an overarching framework that validates the emotional interpretation of satire. The most lasting result of this work is the fostering of a satiric connoisseurship among postclassical authors and critics, and an enduring habit of "typing" examples of the genre.

Just as Juvenal turns out to be an authority on emotions of all kinds—as the *quidquid agunt homines* couplet would seem to prophesy—his interest in emotion does not stop with his construction of a persona for himself. He fills the *Satires* with faces other than his own—some patently expressive, others that invite his audience to fill in the emotions that seem to fit. These faces become facets of Juvenalian satire: the pained expression of victimhood, the inscrutable mask of indifference or cruelty, the laughing face of tranquility or rage, the tears of the powerless or the morosely contemplative, and the unmoving faces of statues that stand watch over their human counterparts. Satire becomes a representation of the human experience—including personal self-assertion, cultural definition, and all manner of conflicts and crimes—in emotional terms. In this troubled landscape, even the illusion of a controlling perspective is appealing. As readers, we participate in constructing the image of our guide.

BIBLIOGRAPHY

Abrams, M. H. *The Mirror and the Lamp: Romantic Theory and the Critical Tradition.* Oxford: Oxford University Press, 1971.

Adamietz, Joachim. *Untersuchungen zur Juvenal.* Wiesbaden: F. Steiner, 1972.

———. "Juvenals 12. Satire." In *Hommages a Jean Cousin: rencontres avec l'antiquité classique*, 237–48. Paris: Les Belles Lettres, 1983.

———. "Juvenals 13. Gedicht als Satire." *Hermes* 112 (1984): 469–83.

Ahl, Fredrick. "The Art of Safe Criticism in Greece and Rome." *AJP* 105 (1984): 174–208.

Alexander, William Hardy. "Juvenal 7.126–28." *CP* 42 (1947): 123–24.

Allen, Walter. "Ovid's *Cantare* and Cicero's *Cantores Euphorionis*." *TAPA* 103 (1972): 1–14.

Anderson, Graham. "Rhetoric and the Second Sophistic." In Dominik and Hall, *Companion to Roman Rhetoric*, 339–53.

Anderson, Peter. "*Absit Malignus Interpres*: Martial's Preface to Book One of the *Epigrams* and the Construction of Audience Response." In *Emotion, Genre, and Gender in Classical Antiquity*, edited by Dana LaCourse Munteanu, 193–220. London: Bristol Classical Press, 2011.

Anderson, W. S. "Juvenal: Evidence on the Years A.D. 117–28." *CP* 50 (1955): 255–57.

———. "Juvenal and Quintilian." *YCS* 17 (1961): 1–91. Reprinted in Anderson, *Essays*, 396–486.

———. "*Venusina lucerna*: The Horatian Model for Juvenal." *TAPA* 52 (1961): 1–12. Reprinted in Anderson, *Essays*, 103–14.

———. "The Programs of Juvenal's Later Books." *CP* 57 (1962): 145–60. Reprinted in Anderson, *Essays*, 277–92.

———. "The Roman Socrates: Horace and His Satires." In Sullivan, *Satire*, 1–37. Reprinted in Anderson, *Essays*, 13–49.

———. "Anger in Juvenal and Seneca." *California Publications in Classical Philology* 19 (1964): 127–96. Reprinted in Anderson, *Essays*, 293–361.

———. "Roman Satirists and Literary Criticism." *Bucknell Review* 12.3 (1964): 106–13. Reprinted in Anderson, *Essays*, 3–10.

————. "Persius and the Rejection of Society." *Wissenschaftliche Zeitschrift der Wilhelm-Pieck-Universität Rostock, Gesellschafts und Sprachwissenschaftliche Reihe* 15 (1966): 409–16. Reprinted in Anderson, *Essays*, 169–93.

————. "*Lascivia* vs. *ira*: Martial and Juvenal." *CSCA* 3 (1970): 1–34. Reprinted in Anderson, *Essays*, 362–95.

————. *Essays on Roman Satire*. Princeton, NJ: Princeton University Press, 1982.

————. "Ironic Preambles and Satiric Self-Definition in Horace 'Satire' 2.1." *PCP* 19 (1984): 35–42.

————. "Juvenal Satire 15: Cannibals and Culture." *Ramus* 16 (1987): 203–14.

André, Jean-Marie. "Sénèque: 'De brevitate vitae,' 'De constantia sapientis,' 'De tranquillitate animi,' 'De otio.'" *ANRW* 2.36.3 (1989): 1724–78.

Arena, Valentina. "Roman Oratorical Invective." In Dominik and Hall, *Companion to Roman Rhetoric*, 149–60.

Armstrong, David. "'Be Angry and Sin Not': Philodemus versus the Stoics on Natural Bites and Natural Emotions." In Fitzgerald, *Passions and Moral Progress*, 79–121.

————. "*Juvenalis Eques*: A Dissident Voice from the Lower Tier of the Roman Elite." In Braund and Osgood, *Persius and Juvenal*, 59–78.

Baines, Victoria. "Umbricius' *Bellum Civile*: Juvenal, *Satire* 3." *G&R*, 2nd ser., 50 (2003): 220–37.

Barchiesi, Allesandro, and Andrea Cucchiarelli. "Satire and the Poet: The Body as Self-Referential Symbol." In Freudenburg, *Cambridge Companion*, 207–23.

Barton, Richard E. "'Zealous Anger' and the Renegotiation of Aristocratic Relationships in Eleventh- and Twelfth-Century France." In Rosenwein, *Anger's Past*, 153–70.

Bartsch, Shadi. *Actors in the Audience: Theatricality and Doublespeak from Nero to Hadrian*. Cambridge, MA: Harvard University Press, 1994.

————. *The Mirror of the Self: Sexuality, Self-Knowledge, and the Gaze in the Early Roman Empire*. Chicago: University of Chicago Press, 2006.

————. "Senecan Metaphor and Stoic Self-Instruction." In Bartsch and Wray, *Seneca and the Self*, 188–217.

————. "Persius, Juvenal, and Stoicism." In Braund and Osgood, *Persius and Juvenal*, 217–38.

Bartsch, Shadi, and D. Wray, eds. *Seneca and the Self*. Cambridge: Cambridge University Press, 2009.

Battisti, Daniela Grazia. *La retorica della misoginia: La satira sesta di Giovenale*. Verona: Edizioni Ossana, 1996.

Bellandi, Franco. "Naevolus Cliens." *Maia* 26 (1974): 279–99.

————. *Etica diatribica e protesta sociale nelle Satire di Giovenale*. Bologna: Pàtron, 1980.

————. "Sulla struttura della Satira 14 di Giovenale." *Prometheus* 10 (1984): 154–60.

————. *Giovenale: Contro le donne*. Venezio, 1995.

Berlin, James. "Revisionary History: The Dialectical Method." *PRE/TEXT* 8 (1987): 47–61.

Berry, D. H., and Andrew Erskine, eds. *Form and Function in Roman Oratory*. Cambridge: Cambridge University Press, 2010.

Bertman, Stephen S. "Fire Symbolism in Juvenal's First Satire." *CJ* 63 (1968): 265–66.

Bickel, Ernst. *Diatribe in Senecae philosophi fragmenta*. Vol. 1, *Fragmenta de Matrimonio*. Leipzig: Teubner, 1915.

Bloomer, W. Martin. *Valerius Maximus and the Rhetoric of the New Nobility*. Chapel Hill: University of North Carolina Press, 1992.

———. "Schooling in Persona: Imagination and Subordination in Roman Education." *CA* 16 (1997): 57–78.

———. "Roman Declamation: The Elder Seneca and Quintilian." In Dominik and Hall, *Companion to Roman Rhetoric*, 297–306.

Bogel, Fredric V. *The Difference Satire Makes: Rhetoric and Reading from Johnson to Byron*. Ithaca, NY: Cornell University Press, 2001.

Boll, Franz. "Die Anordnung im zweiten Buch von Horaz' Satiren." *Hermes* 48 (1913): 143–45.

Bond, Robin P. "*Urbs Satirica*: The City in Roman Satire with Special Reference to Horace and Juvenal." *Scholia*, n.s., 10 (2001): 77–91.

Bonner, Stanley F. *Roman Declamation in the Late Republic and Early Empire*. Liverpool: University Press of Liverpool, 1949.

———. *Education in Ancient Rome*. Berkeley: University of California Press, 1977.

Braund, S. H. "Juvenal 7.50–52." *Phoenix* 36 (1982): 162–65.

———. *Beyond Anger: A Study of Juvenal's Third Book of Satires*. Cambridge: Cambridge University Press, 1988.

———. "Juvenal—Misogynist or Misogamist?" *JRS* 82 (1992): 71–86.

———. "A Woman's Voice? Laronia's Role in Juvenal Satire 2." In *Women in Antiquity: New Assessments*, edited by Richard Hawley and Barbara Levick, 207–19. London: Routledge, 1995.

Braund, Susanna Morton [=S. H.]. *Juvenal: Satires Book I*. Cambridge: Cambridge University Press, 1996.

———. *The Roman Satirists and Their Masks*. Bristol: Bristol Classical Press, 1996.

———. "Declamation and Contestation in Satire." In Dominik, *Roman Eloquence*, 147–65.

———. "A Passion Unconsoled? Grief and Anger in Juvenal 'Satire' 13." In Braund and Gill, *Passions in Roman Thought*, 68–88.

———. "*Libertas* or *Licentia*? Freedom of Speech and Criticism in Roman Satire." In *Free Speech in Classical Antiquity*, edited by Ineke Sluiter and Ralph Rosen, 409–28. Leiden: Brill, 2004.

———. *Seneca: De Clementia*. Oxford: Oxford University Press, 2009.

Braund, Susanna, and Giles Gilbert. "An ABC of Epic *ira*: Anger, Beasts, and Cannibalism." In Braund and Most, *Ancient Anger*, 250–85.

Braund, Susanna Morton, and Christopher Gill, eds. *The Passions in Roman Thought and Literature*. Cambridge: Cambridge University Press, 1997.

Braund, Susanna, and Glenn W. Most, eds. *Ancient Anger: Perspectives from Homer to Galen*. Cambridge: Cambridge University Press, 2003.

Braund, Susanna, and Josiah Osgood, eds. *A Companion to Persius and Juvenal*. Chichester: Wiley-Blackwell, 2012.

Brinnehl, Elizabeth A. *Medusa's Blood: Lucan, Libya, and the Geography of Anger*. Madison: University of Wisconsin Press, 2010.

Cairns, Francis. *Generic Composition in Greek and Roman Poetry*. Edinburgh: University of Edinburgh Press, 1972.

———. "Some Observations on Propertius 1.1." *CQ*, n.s., 24 (1974): 94–110.

Campana, Pierpaolo. *D. Iunii Iuvenalis Satura X*. Florence: Felice le Monnier, 2004.

Cape, Robert W., Jr. "Persuasive History: Roman Rhetoric and Historiography." In Dominik, *Roman Eloquence*, 212–28.

Carey, Christopher. "Rhetorical Means of Persuasion." In *Persuasion: Greek Rhetoric in Action*, edited by Ian Worthington, 26–45. London: Routledge, 1994.

Caston, Ruth Rothaus. *The Elegiac Passion: Jealousy in Roman Love Elegy*. New York: Oxford University Press, 2012.

Champlin, Edward. *Final Judgments: Duty and Emotion in Roman Wills, 200 B.C.–A.D. 250*. Berkeley: University of California Press, 1991.

Chapman, Graham, John Cleese, Terry Gilliam, Eric Idle, Terry Jones, and Michael Palin, directors and writers. "The Piranha Brothers." Episode 14, Disc 5. *The Complete Monty Python's Flying Circus*. New York: AETV, 2005.

Cizek, Eugen. "Juvenal et Certains Problèmes de son Temps: Les Deux Exils du Poète et Leurs Conséquences." *Hermes* 105 (1977): 80–101.

Clark, Mark E. "Juvenal, *Satire* 16: Fragmentary Justice." *ICS* 13 (1988): 113–25.

Clarke, M. L. "Juvenal 7.150–153." *CP* 63 (1968): 295–96.

Classen, Carl Joachim. "Satire—The Elusive Genre." *SO* 63 (1988): 113–25.

Clay, Diskin. "The Theory of the Literary Persona in Antiquity." *MD* 40 (1998): 9–40.

Cloud, J. D., and S. H. Braund. "Juvenal's Libellus—A Farrago?" *G&R*, 2nd ser., 29 (1982): 77–85.

Coffey, Michael. "The Indignant Satirist." Review of W. S. Anderson, "Anger in Juvenal and Seneca." *CR*, n.s., 15 (1965): 299–301.

———. *Roman Satire*. 2nd ed. Bristol: Bristol Classical Press, 1989.

Cokayne, Karen. *Experiencing Old Age in Ancient Rome*. London: Routledge, 2003.

———. "Age and Aristocratic Self-Identity: Activities for the Elderly." In *Age and Ageing in the Roman Empire*, edited by Mary Harlow and Ray Laurence, 209–20. Portsmouth, RI: Journal of Roman Archaeology, 2007.

Colton, Robert E. "A Dinner Invitation: Juvenal XI, 56–208." *CB* 41 (1965): 39–45.

———. "Echoes of Martial in Juvenal's Twelfth Satire." *Latomus* 31 (1972): 164–73.

Compton, Todd M. *Victim of the Muses: Poet as Scapegoat, Warrior and Hero in Greco-Roman and Indo-European Myth and History*. Cambridge, MA: Center for Hellenic Studies, 2006.

Connery, Brian A., and Kirk Combe, eds. *Theorizing Satire: Essays in Literary Criticism*. New York: St. Martin's Press, 1995.

Connolly, Joy. *The State of Speech: Rhetoric and Political Thought in Ancient Rome*. Princeton, NJ: Princeton University Press, 2007.

———. "Virile Tongues: Rhetoric and Masculinity." In Dominik and Hall, *Companion to Roman Rhetoric*, 83–97.

Cooper, John M., and J. F. Procopé. *Seneca: Moral and Political Essays*. Cambridge: Cambridge University Press, 1995.

Corbeill, Anthony. *Controlling Laughter: Political Humor in the Late Roman Republic*. Princeton, NJ: Princeton University Press, 1996.

Corn, Alan M. "The Persona in the Fifth Book of Juvenal's Satires." PhD diss., Ohio State University, 1975.

———. " 'Thus Nature Ordains': Juvenal's Fourteenth Satire." *ICS* 17 (1992): 309–22.

Costa, C. D. N. *Seneca: Four Dialogues*. Warminster: Aris and Phillips, 1994.

Courtney, Edward. *A Commentary on the Satires of Juvenal*. London: Athlone Press, 1980.

Craig, Christopher. "A Survey of Selected Recent Work on Cicero's Rhetorica and Speeches." In *Brill's Companion to Cicero: Oratory and Rhetoric*, edited by James M. May, 503–31. Leiden: Brill, 2002.

———. "Audience Expectations, Invective, and Proof in Cicero's Judicial Speeches." In *Cicero the Advocate*, edited by Jonathan Powell and Jeremy Paterson, 187–213. Oxford: Oxford University Press, 2004.

———. "Means and Ends of *Indignatio* in Cicero's *Pro Roscio Amerino*." In Berry and Erskine, *Form and Function*, 75–91.

Cucchiarelli, Andrea. *La satira e il poeta: Orazio tra* Epodi *e* Sermones. Pisa: Giardini, 2001.

———. "*Venusina lucerna*: Horace, Callimachus, and Imperial Satire." In Braund and Osgood, *Persius and Juvenal*, 165–89.

Damon, Cynthia. *The Mask of the Parasite: A Pathology of Roman Patronage*. Ann Arbor: University of Michigan Press, 1997.

Davies, Glenys. "Togate Statues and Petrified Orators." In Berry and Erskine, *Form and Function*, 51–72.

de Decker, Josué. *Juvenalis declamans: Étude sur la rhétorique declamatoire dans les Satires de Juvénal*. Ghent: E. van Goethem, 1913.

Dick, Bernard F. "Seneca and Juvenal 10." *HSCP* 73 (1969): 237–46.

Diels, Hermann. *Die Fragmente der Vorsokratiker*. Edited by Walther Kranz. 7th ed. Vol. 2. Berlin: Weidmann, 1954.

Dobrov, Gregory. "The Tragic and the Comic Tereus." *AJP* 114 (1993): 189–234.

Dominik, William J., ed. *Roman Eloquence: Rhetoric and Society in Literature*. London: Routledge, 1997.

———. "Roman Declamation: The Elder Seneca and Quintilian." In Dominik and Hall, *Companion to Roman Rhetoric*, 297–306.

Dominik, William, and Jon Hall, eds. *A Companion to Roman Rhetoric*. Chichester: Wiley-Blackwell, 2007.

Dozier, Curtis. "Poetry, Politics, and Pleasure in Quintilian." In *Aesthetic Value in Classical Antiquity*, edited by Ineke Sluiter and Ralph Rosen, 345–64. Leiden: Brill, 2012.

Drew, D. L. *The Allegory of the Aeneid*. Oxford: Blackwell, 1927.

Duckworth, George E. *The Nature of Roman Comedy: A Study in Popular Entertainment*. 2nd ed. Norman: University of Oklahoma Press, 1994.

Dufallo, Basil. "Appius' Indignation: Gossip, Tradition, and Performance in Republican Rome." *TAPA* 131 (2001): 119–42.

———. *The Ghosts of the Past: Latin Literature, the Dead, and Rome's Transition to a Principate*. Columbus: Ohio State University Press, 2007.

Duff, J. D. *Iuni Iuvenalis Saturae XIV*. New edition, with introduction by Michael Coffey. Cambridge: Cambridge University Press, 1970.

Duret, Luc. "Juvénal replique à Trebatius." *REL* 61 (1983): 201–26.

Durry, Marcel. "Juvénal et les prétoriens." *REL* 13 (1935): 95–106.

Edmunds, Lowell. "Juvenal's Thirteenth Satire." *RhM* 115 (1972): 59–73.

Edwards, Catharine. "Self-Scrutiny and Self-Transformation in Seneca's Letters." *G&R*, 2nd ser., 44 (1997): 23–38.

Eichholz, D. E. "The Art of Juvenal and His Tenth *Satire*." *G&R*, 2nd ser., 3 (1956): 61–69.

Fantham, Elaine. " 'Envy and Fear the Begetter of Hate': Statius' *Thebaid* and the Genesis of Hatred." In Braund and Gill, *Passions in Roman Thought*, 185–212.

———. "The Angry Poet and the Angry Gods: Problems of Theodicy in Lucan's Epic of Defeat." In Braund and Most, *Ancient Anger*, 229–49.

Farrell, Joseph. "Greek Lives and Roman Careers in the Classical Vita Tradition." In *European Literary Careers: The Author from Antiquity to the Renaissance*, edited by Patrick Cheney and Frederick Alfred de Armas, 24–46. Toronto: University of Toronto Press, 2002.

Ferguson, John. *A Prosopography to the Poems of Juvenal*. Brussels: Latomus Revue d' Études Latines, 1987.

Ficca, Flaviana. *D. Giunio Giovenale Satira XIII*. Napoli: Loffredo, 2009.

Fillion-Lahille, Janine. *Le De ira de Sénèque et la philosophie stoïcienne des passions*. Paris: Klincksieck, 1984.

———. "La production littéraire de Sénèque sous les règnes de Caligula et de Claude, sens philosophique et portée politique: Les 'Consolations' et le 'De Ira.' " *ANRW* 2.36.3 (1989): 1606–38.

Fishelov, David. "The Vanity of the Reader's Wishes: Rereading Juvenal's *Satire* 10." *AJP* 111 (1990): 370–82.

Fitzgerald, John T. "The Passions and Moral Progress: An Introduction." In Fitzgerald, *Passions and Moral Progress*, 1–25.

———, ed. *Passions and Moral Progress in Greco-Roman Thought*. Routledge Monographs in Classical Studies. London: Routledge, 2008.

Fjelstad, Per. "Restraint and Emotion in Cicero's 'De Oratore.' " *Philosophy and Rhetoric* 36 (2003): 39–47.

Flower, Harriet. *Ancestor Masks and Aristocratic Power in Roman Culture*. Oxford: Oxford University Press, 1996.

Fox, Matthew, and Niall Livingstone. "Rhetoric and Historiography." In Worthington, *Companion to Greek Rhetoric*, 542–61.

Fraenkel, Eduard. *Horace*. Oxford: Clarendon Press, 1957.

Fredericks, Sigmund C. "Rhetoric and Morality in Juvenal's 8th Satire." *TAPA* 102 (1971): 111–32.

———."Calvinus in Juvenal's Thirteenth Satire." *Arethusa* 4 (1971): 219–31.

———. "Juvenal's Fifteenth Satire." *ICS* 1 (1976): 174–89.

Fredricksmeyer, Hardy C. "An Observation on the Programmatic Satires of Juvenal, Horace, and Persius." *Latomus* 49 (1990): 792–800.

Freedman, Paul. "Peasant Anger in the Late Middle Ages." In Rosenwein, *Anger's Past*, 171–88.

Freudenburg, Kirk. *Satires of Rome: Threatening Poses from Lucilius to Juvenal*. Cambridge: Cambridge University Press, 2001.

———, ed. *The Cambridge Companion to Roman Satire*. Cambridge: Cambridge University Press, 2005.

———. "*Horatius Anceps*: Persona and Self-Revelation in Satire and Song." In *A Companion to Horace*, edited by Gregson Davis, 271–90. Chichester: Wiley-Blackwell, 2010.

Friedländer, Ludwig. *D. Junii Juvenalis Saturarum Libri V*. Leipzig: S. Hirzel, 1895.

———. *Roman Life and Manners under the Early Empire*. Vol. 4, *Appendices and Notes*. Translated by A. B. Gough. London: Routledge; New York: Dutton, 1928.

———. *Essays on Juvenal*. Translated with a preface by J. R. C. Martyn. Amsterdam: Hakkert, 1969.

Frischer, Bernard. "Fu la Villa ercolanese dei Papiri un modello per la Villa Sabina di Orazio?" *Cronache Ercolanesi* 25 (1995): 211–29.

Fruelund Jensen, B. "Crime, Vice, and Retribution in Juvenal's Satires." *C&M* 33 (1981–82): 155–68.

———. "Martyred and Beleaguered Virtue: Juvenal's Portrait of Umbricius." *C&M* 37 (1986): 185–97.

Furneaux, Henry. *The Annals of Tacitus*. 2nd ed. Vol. 1. Oxford: Clarendon Press, 1896.

Gérard, Jean. *Juvénal et la réalité contemporaine*. Paris: Les Belles Lettres, 1976.

Giardina, Rita Cuccioli-Giancarlo. "I vari tipi di satira." In *Senectus: La vecchiaia nel mondo classico*, vol. 2, edited by Umberto Mattioli, 31–52. Bologna: Pàtron, 1995.

Gibson, Roy K., and Ruth Morello. *Reading the Letters of Pliny the Younger: An Introduction*. Cambridge: Cambridge University Press, 2012.

Gibson, Roy, and Catherine Steele. "The Indistinct Literary Careers of Cicero and Pliny the Younger." In Hardie and Moore, *Classical Literary Careers*, 118–37.

Gildenhard, Ingo, and Andrew Zissos. "Barbarian Variations: Tereus, Procne and Philomela in Ovid (Met. 6.412–674) and Beyond." *Dictynna* 4 (2007). Accessed March 30, 2013. http://dictynna.revues.org/150.

Gill, Christopher. "The Emotions in Greco-Roman Philosophy (Introduction Part II)." In Braund and Gill, *Passions in Roman Thought*, 5–15.

———. "Passion as Madness in Roman Poetry." In Braund and Gill, *Passions in Roman Thought*, 213–41.

———. "Reactive and Objective Attitudes: Anger in Virgil's *Aeneid* and Hellenistic Philosophy." In Braund and Most, *Ancient Anger*, 208–28.

Gold, Barbara. "Humor in Juvenal's Sixth Satire: Is It Funny?" In *Laughter Down the Centuries*, vol. 1, edited by Siegfried Jäkel and Asko Timonen, 95–111. Turku: Turun Yliopisto, 1994.

———. " 'The House I Live In Is Not My Own': Women's Bodies in Juvenal's *Satires*." *Arethusa* 31 (1998): 369–86.

———. "Juvenal: The Idea of the Book." In Braund and Osgood, *Persius and Juvenal*, 97–112.

Goldberg, Sander. "Appreciating Aper: The Defence of Modernity in Tacitus' *Dialogus de oratoribus*." *CQ*, n.s., 49 (1999): 224–37.

Goodyear, F. R. D. *Tacitus*. Oxford: Clarendon Press, 1970.

———. *The Annals of Tacitus*. Vol. 1 (*Annals* I.1–54). Cambridge: Cambridge University Press, 1972.

Gowers, Emily. *The Loaded Table: Representations of Food in Roman Literature*. Oxford: Clarendon Press, 1993.

———. "Fragments of Autobiography in Horace Satires 1." *CA* 22 (2003): 55–92.

———. "The Restless Companion: Horace, Satires 1 and 2." In Freudenburg, *Cambridge Companion*, 57–61.

———. *Horace: Satires Book I*. Cambridge: Cambridge University Press, 2012.

Gransden, K. W. *Virgil, Aeneid Book VIII*. Cambridge: Cambridge University Press, 1976.

Grant, Mary. *The Ancient Rhetorical Theories of the Laughable: The Greek Rhetoricians and Cicero*. University of Wisconsin Studies in Language and Literature 21. Madison: University of Wisconsin, 1924.

Graver, Margaret. *Cicero on the Emotions: Tusculan Disputations 3 and 4*. Chicago: University of Chicago Press, 2002.

Griffin, Dustin. *Satire: A Critical Reintroduction*. Lexington: University Press of Kentucky, 1994.

Griffin, Miriam T. *Seneca: A Philosopher in Politics*. Oxford: Clarendon Press, 1976.

Griffith, John G. "The Ending of Juvenal's First Satire and Lucilius Book III." *Hermes* 98 (1970): 56–72.

Gunderson, Erik. *Declamation, Paternity, and Roman Identity: Authority and the Rhetorical Self*. Cambridge: Cambridge University Press, 2003.

Habinek, Thomas. *The Politics of Latin Literature: Writing, Identity, and Empire in Ancient Rome*. Princeton, NJ: Princeton University Press, 1998.

———. *The World of Roman Song: From Ritualized Speech to Social Order*. Baltimore: Johns Hopkins University Press, 2005.

———. "Satire as Aristocratic Play." In Freudenburg, *Cambridge Companion*, 177–91.

Hall, Jon. "Oratorical Delivery and the Emotions: Theory and Practice." In Dominik and Hall, *Companion to Roman Rhetoric*, 218–34.

Halliwell, Stephen. "Greek Laughter and the Problem of the Absurd." *Arion* 13 (2005): 121–46.

———. *Greek Laughter: A Study of Cultural Psychology from Homer to Early Christianity*. Cambridge: Cambridge University Press, 2008.

Hanson, Ann Ellis. "'Your Mother Nursed You with Bile': Anger in Babies and Small Children." In Braund and Most, *Ancient Anger*, 185–207.

Hardie, Alex. "Juvenal and the Condition of Letters: The Seventh Satire." *Papers of the Leeds International Latin Seminar* 6 (1990): 145–209.

———. "Juvenal, Domitian and the Accession of Hadrian (Satire 4)." *BICS* 42 (1997–98): 117–44.

———. "Juvenal, the *Phaedrus*, and the Truth about Rome." *CQ*, n.s., 48 (1998): 234–51.

———. "Name-Repetitions and the Unity of Juvenal's First Book." *Scholia* n.s., 8 (1999): 52–70.

Hardie, Philip, and Helen Moore, eds. *Classical Literary Careers and Their Reception*. Cambridge: Cambridge University Press, 2010.

———. "Introduction: Literary Careers—Classical Models and Their Reception." In Hardie and Moore, *Classical Literary Careers*, 1–16.

Hardy, Ernest. *Decimi Junii Juvenalis Saturae XIII*. London: Macmillan, 1883.

Harlow, Mary, and Ray Laurence, *Growing Up and Growing Old in Ancient Rome: A Life Course Approach*. London: Routledge, 2002.

Harris, William V. *Restraining Rage: The Ideology of Anger in Classical Antiquity*. Cambridge, MA: Harvard University Press, 2001.

———. "The Rage of Women." In Braund and Most, *Ancient Anger*, 121–43.

Harrison, Geoffrey. "The Confessions of Lucilius (Horace *Sat.* 2.1.30–34): A Defense of Autobiographical Satire?" *CA* 6 (1987): 38–52.

Harrison, Stephen. "There and Back Again: Horace's Poetic Career." In Hardie and Moore, *Classical Literary Careers*, 39–58.

Haß, Karin. *Lucilius und der Beginn der Persönlichkeitsdichtung in Rom.* Hermes Einzelschriften 99. Stuttgart: Franz Steiner, 2007.

Heinze, Richard. *Vergil's Epic Technique.* Translated by Hazel Harvey, David Harvey, and Fred Robertson. Berkeley: University of California Press, 1993.

Helfert, Dave. "Unfortunately, Anger Works." *The Blog, Huffington Post*, January 20, 2011. www.huffingtonpost.com/dave-helfert/unfortunately-anger-works_b_810630.html.

Helmbold, W. C. "Juvenal's Twelfth Satire." *CP* 51 (1956): 14–23.

Helmbold, W. C., and E. N. O'Neil. "The Form and Purpose of Juvenal's Seventh *Satire.*" *CP* 54 (1959): 100–108.

Henderson, John G. W. "Satire Writes 'Woman': *Gendersong.*" *PCPS* 35 (1989): 50–80. Revised version in Henderson, *Writing Down Rome*, 173–201.

———. "Persius' Didactic Satire: The Pupil as Teacher." *Ramus* 20 (1991): 123–48. Revised version in Henderson, *Writing Down Rome*, 228–48.

———. "Pump Up the Volume: Juvenal, Satires 1.1–21." *PCPS* 41 (1995): 101–37. Revised version in Henderson, *Writing Down Rome*, 249–73.

———. *Figuring Out Roman Nobility: Juvenal's Eighth* Satire. Exeter: University of Exeter Press, 1997.

———. *Writing Down Rome: Satire, Comedy, and Other Offenses in Latin Poetry.* New York: Oxford University Press, 1999.

———. *Morals and Villas in Seneca's Letters: Places to Dwell.* Cambridge: Cambridge University Press, 2004.

Hendrickson, G. L. "*Satura Tota Nostra Est.*" *CP* 22 (1927): 46–60.

Henke, Rainer. "Elefanten, Tochtermörder und Erbschleicher: Juvenal, Sat. 12, 93–130." *Hermes* 128 (2000): 202–17.

Hershbell, Jackson P. "Plutarch and Democritus." *Quaderni Urbinati di Cultura Classica* 10 (1982): 81–111.

Highet, Gilbert. "The Philosophy of Juvenal." *TAPA* 80 (1949): 254–70.

———. "Juvenal's Bookcase." *AJP* 72 (1951): 369–94.

———. *Juvenal the Satirist.* Oxford: Clarendon Press, 1954.

———. "Masks and Faces in Satire." *Hermes* 102 (1974): 321–37.

Hoffer, Stanley E. "Cicero's 'Stomach': Political Indignation and the Use of Repeated Allusive Expressions in Cicero's Correspondence." In *Ancient Letters: Classical and Late Antique Epistolography*, edited by Ruth Morello and A. D. Morrison, 87–106. Oxford: Oxford University Press, 2007.

Hömke, Nicola. "The Declaimer's One-Man Show: Playing with Roles and Rules in the Pseudo-Quintilian *Declamationes maiores.*" *Rhetorica* 27 (2009): 240–55.

Hoof, Lieve van. "Strategic Differences: Seneca and Plutarch on Controlling Anger." *Mnemosyne*, 4th ser., 60 (2007): 59–86.

Hook, Brian. "Umbricius *Caligatus*: Wordplay in Juvenal 3.322." In *Studies in Latin Literature and Roman History*, vol. 14, edited by Carl Deroux, 365–74. Brussels: Latomus Revue d' Études Latines, 2008.

Hooley, Dan. *The Knotted Thong: Structures of Mimesis in Persius.* Ann Arbor: University of Michigan Press, 1997.

————. "Rhetoric and Satire: Horace, Persius, and Juvenal." In Dominik and Hall, *Companion to Roman Rhetoric*, 396–412.

————. *Roman Satire*. Oxford: Blackwell, 2007.

————. "Imperial Satire Reiterated: Late Antiquity through the Twentieth Century." In Braund and Osgood, *Persius and Juvenal*, 337–62.

Hopkins, David. *Conversing with Antiquity: English Poets and the Classics, from Shakespeare to Pope*. Oxford: Oxford University Press, 2010.

Hutcheon, Linda. *Irony's Edge: The Theory and Politics of Irony*. London: Routledge, 1994.

Hutchinson, G. O. *Latin Literature from Seneca to Juvenal: A Critical Study*. Oxford: Clarendon Press, 1993.

————. *Talking Books: Readings in Hellenistic and Roman Books of Poetry*. Oxford: Oxford University Press, 2008.

Iddeng, Jon W. "Juvenal, Satire and the Persona Theory: Some Critical Remarks." *SO* 75 (2000): 107–29.

Inwood, Brad. *Reading Seneca: Stoic Philosophy at Rome*. Oxford: Clarendon Press, 2005.

Itic, Stéphanie. "Les implications poétiques du terme 'farrago' dans la première 'Satire' de Juvénal." *REL* 84 (2006): 223–38.

Jensen, H. James. *A Glossary of John Dryden's Critical Terms*. Minneapolis: University of Minnesota Press, 1969.

Johnson, W. Ralph. "Male Victimology in Juvenal 6." *Ramus* 25 (1996): 170–86.

Jones, Brian W. *The Emperor Domitian*. London: Routledge, 1992.

Jones, Frederick M. A. "The Persona and the Addressee in Juvenal Satire 11." *Ramus* 19 (1990): 160–68.

————. *Juvenal and the Satiric Genre*. London: Duckworth, 2007.

Jones, Robert Epes. "Cicero's Accuracy of Characterization in His Dialogues." *AJP* 60 (1939): 307–25.

Joshel, Sandra. "Female Desire and the Discourse of Empire: Tacitus's Messalina." *Signs* 21 (1995): 50–82.

Kalimtsis, Kostas. *Taming Anger: The Hellenic Approach to the Limitations of Reason*. London: Bristol Classical Press, 2012.

Kaster, Robert. "Becoming 'CICERO.'" In *Style and Tradition: Studies in Honor of Wendell Clausen*, edited by Peter Knox and Clive Foss, 248–63. Stuttgart: Teubner, 1998.

————. "Controlling Reason: Declamation in Rhetorical Education at Rome." In *Education in Greek and Roman Antiquity*, edited by Yun Lee Too, 317–37. Leiden: Brill, 2001.

————. *Emotion, Restraint, and Community in Ancient Rome*. Oxford: Oxford University Press, 2005.

————. "The Passions." In *A Companion to Latin Literature*, edited by Stephen Harrison, 319–30. Malden, MA: Blackwell, 2005.

Kaster, Robert, and Martha Nussbaum. *Lucius Annaeus Seneca: Anger, Mercy, Revenge*. Chicago: University of Chicago Press, 2010.

Keane, Catherine. "The Critical Contexts of Satiric Discourse." *CML* 22 (2002): 7–31.

————. "Satiric Memories: Autobiography and the Construction of Genre," *CJ* 97 (2002): 215–31.

————. 2003. "Theatre, Spectacle, and the Satirist in Juvenal." *Phoenix* 57 (2003): 257–75.

————. *Figuring Genre in Roman Satire*. Oxford: Oxford University Press, 2006.

————. "Philosophy into Satire: The Program of Juvenal's Fifth Book." *AJP* 128 (2007): 27–57.

————. "Persona and Satiric Career in Juvenal." In Hardie and Moore, *Classical Literary Careers*, 105–17.

————. "Historian and Satirist: Tacitus and Juvenal." In Pagán, *Companion to Tacitus*, 403–27.

Kempf, Karl Friedrich. *De satira quinta decima quae sub Iuvenalis nomine circumfertur*. Berlin: A. G. Schadii, 1843.

Kennerly, Michele. "Getting Carried Away: How Rhetorical Transport Gets Judgment Going." *Rhetoric Society Quarterly* 40 (2010): 269–91.

Kenney, E. J. "Juvenal: Satirist or Rhetorician?" *Latomus* 22 (1963): 704–20.

Ker, James. "Seneca on Self-Examination: Rereading *On Anger* 3.36." In Bartsch and Wray, *Seneca and the Self*, 160–87.

Ker, W. P., ed. *Essays of John Dryden*. Vol. 2. New York: Russell and Russell, 1961.

Kernan, Alvin B. *The Cankered Muse: Satire of the English Renaissance*. New Haven, CT: Yale University Press, 1959.

————. *The Plot of Satire*. New Haven, CT: Yale University Press, 1965.

Knoche, Ulrich. "Eine römische Wurzel lateinischer Persönlichkeitsdichtung." *Neue Jahrbücher für Antike und Deutsche Bildung* 3 (1940): 238–52.

————. "Erlebnis und dichterischer Ausdruck in der lateinischen Poesie." *Gymnasium* 65 (1958): 145–65.

————. *Roman Satire*. Translated by Edwin S. Ramage. Bloomington: Indiana University Press, 1975.

————. "Juvenal's Canons of Social Criticism." Translated by Leofranc Holford-Strevens. In *Persius and Juvenal*, edited by Maria Plaza, 257–77. Oxford Readings in Classical Studies. Oxford: Oxford University Press, 2009.

Knuuttila, Simo. *Emotions in Ancient and Medieval Philosophy*. Oxford: Clarendon Press, 2004.

Konstan, David. "Aristotle on Anger and the Emotions: The Strategies of Status." In Braund and Most, *Ancient Anger*, 99–120.

————. *The Emotions of the Ancient Greeks: Studies in Aristotle and Classical Literature*. Toronto: University of Toronto Press, 2006.

————. "Rhetoric and Emotion." In Worthington, *Companion to Greek Rhetoric*, 411–26.

Kühn, K. G. *Claudii Galeni Opera Omnia*. Vol. 5. Leipzig: C. Cnobloch. Reprint, Hildesheim: Olms, 2001.

Kyle, Donald G. *Spectacles of Death in Ancient Rome*. London: Routledge, 1998.

LaBriolle, Pierre de. "La 7ᵉ satire de Juvénal." *Hum (RES) Cl. de lettres* 7 (1931): 367–74, 419–27.

LaFleur, Richard A. "*Amicus* and *amicitia* in Juvenal." *CB* 51 (1975): 54–58.

————. "Umbricius and Juvenal Three." *Ziva Antika* 26 (1976): 383–431.

————. "*Amicitia* and the Unity of Juvenal's First Book." *ICS* 4 (1979): 158–77.

Larmour, David. "The Incurable Wound of Telephus: Noise, Speech and Silence in Juvenal's *Satire* 1." *Intertexts* 8 (2004): 55–76.

———. "Lightening the Load: Castration, Money and Masculinity in Juvenal, *Satire* 12." *SyllClass* 16 (2005): 139–72.

Lausberg, M. *Untersuchungen zu Senecas Fragmente.* Berlin: De Gruyter, 1970.

Lawall, Gilbert. "*Exempla* and Theme in Juvenal's Tenth Satire." *TAPA* 89 (1958): 25–31.

Leach, Eleanor W. "Horace's Sabine Topography in Lyric and Hexameter Verse." *AJP* 114 (1993): 271–302.

Leeman, A. D. "Structure and Meaning in the Prologues of Tacitus." *Yale Classical Studies Vol. XXIII: Studies in Latin Language and Literature*, edited by Thomas Cole and David Ross, 169–208. Cambridge: Cambridge University Press, 1973.

Leigh, Matthew. "Quintilian on the Emotions (*Institutio Oratoria* 6 Preface and 1–2)." *JRS* 94 (2004): 122–40.

Levene, David. "Pity, Fear, and the Historical Audience: Tacitus on the Fall of Vitellius." In Braund and Gill, *Passions in Roman Thought*, 128–49.

Lindo, Locksley I. "The Evolution of Juvenal's Later Satires." *CP* 69 (1974): 17–27.

Little, Lester K. "Anger in Monastic Curses." In Rosenwein, *Anger's Past*, 9–35.

Lucarelli, Ute. *Exemplarische Vergangenheit: Valerius Maximus und die Konstruktion des sozialen Raumes in der fruhen Kaiserzeit.* Göttingen: Vandenhoeck and Ruprecht, 2007.

Luce, T. J. "Reading and Response in the *Dialogus*." In *Tacitus and the Tacitean Tradition*, edited by T. J. Luce and A. J. Woodman, 11–38. Princeton, NJ: Princeton University Press, 1993.

Luisi, Aldo. *Il rombo e la Vestale. Giovenale*, Satira *IV*. Bari: Edipuglia, 1998.

Lupus, Bernhard. *Vindiciae Iuvenalianae.* Bonn: P. Neusser, 1864.

Lutz, Cora. "Democritus and Heraclitus." *CJ* 49 (1953–54): 309–14.

Mack, Maynard. "The Muse of Satire." *Yale Review* 61 (1951): 80–92.

MacKendrick, Paul, and Karen Lee Singh. *The Philosophical Books of Cicero.* New York: St. Martin's Press, 1989.

Macleane, A. J. *Juvenalis et Persii Satirae.* 2nd ed. London: Whittaker, 1867.

Malamud, Martha. "Out of Circulation? An Essay on Exchange in Persius' Satires." *Ramus* 25 (1996): 39–64.

Maltby, Robert. "Linguistic Characterization of Old Men in Terence." *CP* 74 (1979): 136–47.

Manzella, Simona Manuela. *Decimo Giunio Giovenale Satira III.* Napoli: Liguori, 2011.

Mason, H. A. "Is Juvenal a Classic?" In Sullivan, *Satire*, 93–176.

Mattern-Parkes, Susan P. "Seneca's Treatise 'On Anger' and the Aristocratic Competition for Honor." In *Essays in Honor of Gordon Williams: Twenty-Five Years at Yale*, edited by Elizabeth Tylawsky and Charles Weiss, 177–88. New Haven, CT: Henry R. Schwab, 2001.

Mayer, Roland G. "Persona (I) Problems." *MD* 50 (2003): 55–80.

Mayor, John E. B. *Thirteen Satires of Juvenal.* Vol. 2. London: MacMillan, 1878.

McCabe, Kevin. "'Was Juvenal a Structuralist?' A Look at Anachronisms in Literary Criticism." *G&R*, 2nd ser., 33 (1986): 78–84.

McKim, Richard. "Philosophers and Cannibals: Juvenal's Fifteenth Satire." *Phoenix* 40 (1986): 58–71.

Meltzer, Gary. "Dark Wit and Black Humor in Seneca's Thyestes." *TAPA* 118 (1988): 309–30.

Miller, Paul Allen. "The Bodily Grotesque in Roman Satire: Images of Sterility." *Arethusa* 31 (1998): 257–83.

———. *Subjecting Verses: Latin Love Elegy and the Emergence of the Real*. Princeton, NJ: Princeton University Press, 2004.

———. *Latin Verse Satire: An Anthology and Reader*. London: Routledge, 2005.

———. "Imperial Satire as Saturnalia." In Braund and Osgood, *Persius and Juvenal*, 312–33.

Milnor, Kristina. "Women and Domesticity." In Pagán, *Companion to Tacitus*, 458–75.

Moodie, Erin K. "The Bully as Satirist in Juvenal's Third Satire." *AJP* 133 (2012): 93–115.

Morford, Mark. "Juvenal's Thirteenth Satire." *AJP* 94 (1973): 26–36.

Most, Glenn W. "Anger and Pity in Homer's *Iliad*." In Braund and Most, *Ancient Anger*, 50–75.

Motto, Anna Lydia, and John R. Clark. "*Per iter tenebricosum*: The Mythos of Juvenal 3." *TAPA* 96 (1965): 267–76.

———. "Serenity and Tension in Seneca's *De Tranquillitate Animi*." In *Essays on Seneca*, edited by Michael von Albrecht, 133–54. Studien zur klassischen Philologie Band 79. Frankfurt: Peter Lang, 1993.

Muecke, Frances. "Rome's First 'Satirists': Themes and Genre in Ennius and Lucilius." In Freudenburg, *Cambridge Companion*, 33–47.

Munteanu, Dana L. *Tragic Pathos: Pity and Fear in Greek Philosophy and Tragedy*. Cambridge: Cambridge University Press, 2011.

Nadeau, Yvan. *A Commentary on the Sixth Satire of Juvenal*. Brussels: Éditions Latomus, 2011.

Nappa, Christopher. "*Praetextati Mores*: Juvenal's Second Satire." *Hermes* 126 (1998): 90–108.

———. "The Unfortunate Marriage of Gaius Silius: Tacitus and Juvenal on the Fall of Messalina." In *Latin Historiography and Poetry in the Early Empire: Generic Interactions*, edited by John F. Miller and A. J. Woodman, 189–204. Leiden: Brill, 2010.

Nice, Alex. "The *Persona* of Umbricius and Divination in Juvenal, Satires Three and Six." *Studies in Latin Literature and Roman History*, vol. 11, edited by Carl Deroux, 402–18. Brussels: Latomus Revue d' Études Latines, 2003.

Nisbet, Gideon. "Revoicing Imperial Satire." In Braund and Osgood, *Persius and Juvenal*, 486–512.

Novak, Rachel. "The Old Man and the C: Cicero and the Reception of Cato the Elder in *De Senectute*." Master's thesis, University of St. Andrews, 2007.

Nussbaum, Martha. *The Therapy of Desire: Theory and Practice in Hellenistic Ethics*. Martin Classical Lectures, n.s., vol. 2. Princeton, NJ: Princeton University Press, 1994.

———. *Upheavals of Thought: The Intelligence of Emotions*. Cambridge: Cambridge University Press, 2001.

———. "Stoic Laughter: A Reading of Seneca's *Apocolocyntosis*." In Bartsch and Wray, *Seneca and the Self*, 84–112.

Oliensis, Ellen. "Sons and Lovers: Sexuality and Gender in Virgil's Poetry." In *The Cambridge Companion to Vergil*, edited by Charles Martindale, 294–311. Cambridge: Cambridge University Press, 1997.

———. *Horace and the Rhetoric of Authority*. Cambridge: Cambridge University Press, 1998.

Oltramare, André. *Les origins de la diatribe romaine*. Lausanne: Payot, 1962.

Osgood, Josiah. "Introduction: Persius and Juvenal as Satiric Successors." In Braund and Osgood, *Persius and Juvenal*, 1–16.

O'Sullivan, Timothy. "The Mind in Motion: Walking and Metaphorical Travel in the Roman Villa." *CP* 101 (2006): 133–52.

Pagán, Victoria Emma, ed. *A Companion to Tacitus*. Chichester: Wiley-Blackwell, 2012.

Parker, Holt N. "Manuscripts of Juvenal and Persius." In Braund and Osgood, *Persius and Juvenal*, 137–61.

Parkin, Tim G. *Old Age in the Roman World: A Cultural and Social History*. Baltimore: Johns Hopkins University Press, 2003.

———. "The Elderly Children of Greece and Rome." In *On Old Age: Approaching Death in Antiquity and the Middle Ages*, edited by Christian Krötzl and Katariina Mustakallio, 25–40. Turnhout: Brepols, 2011.

Pasoli, Elio. "La Chiusa della Satira III di Giovenale." *GB* 3 (1975): 319–21.

Peirano, Irene. *The Rhetoric of the Roman Fake: Latin Pseudepigraphica in Context*. Cambridge: Cambridge University Press, 2012.

Pepe, L. "Questioni adrianee. Giovenale e Adriano." *Giornale italiano di filologia* 14 (1961): 163–73.

Plaza, Maria. *The Function of Humour in Roman Verse Satire*. Oxford: Oxford University Press, 2006.

Porter, James E. "*Divisio* as Em-/De-Powering Topic: A Basis for Argument in Rhetoric and Composition." *Rhetoric Review* 8 (1990): 191–205.

———. *Audience and Rhetoric: An Archaeological Composition of the Discourse Community*. Englewood Cliffs, NJ: Prentice-Hall, 1992.

Powell, Barry B. "What Juvenal Saw: Egyptian Religion and Anthropophagy in *Satire 15*." *RhM* 122 (1979): 185–89.

Powell, Jonathan G. F. "The *Farrago* of Juvenal 1.86 Reconsidered." In *Homo Viator: Classical Essays for John Bramble*, edited by Michael Whitby, Philip R. Hardie, and Mary Whitby, 253–58. Bristol: Bristol Classical Press, 1987.

———. *Cicero: Cato Maior de Senectute*. Cambridge: Cambridge University Press, 1988.

———. "Stylistic Registers in Juvenal." In *Aspects of the Language of Latin Poetry*, edited by J. M. Adams and R. G. Mayer, 311–34. Proceedings of the British Academy 93. Oxford: Oxford University Press, 1999.

Pryor, A. D. "Juvenal's False Consolation." *AUMLA* 18 (1962): 167–80.

Putnam, Michael C. J. "Horace to Torquatus: 'Epistle 1.5' and 'Ode 4.7.'" *AJP* 127 (2006): 387–413.

Rabinowitz, Peter. "Truth in Fiction: A Reexamination of Audiences." *Critical Inquiry* 4.1 (1977): 121–41.

Ramage, Edwin S. "Juvenal, Satire 12: On Friendship True and False." *ICS* 3 (1978): 221–37.

———. "Juvenal and the Establishment: Denigration of Predecessor in the 'Satires.'" *ANRW* 2.33.1 (1989): 640–707.

Ramsey, G. G. *Juvenal and Persius*. Cambridge, MA: Harvard University Press, 1918.

Randolph, Mary Claire. "The Structural Design of the Formal Verse Satire." *PQ* 21 (1942): 368–84.

Rankin, H. D. "'Eating People Is Right': Petronius 141 and a TOPOS." *Hermes* 97 (1969): 381–84.

Rebert, Homer Franklin. "The Literary Influence of Cicero on Juvenal." *TAPA* 57 (1926): 181–94.

Ribbeck, Otto. *Der echte und der unechte Juvenal: Eine kritische Untersuchung*. Berlin: I. Guttentag, 1865.

Richlin, Amy. *The Garden of Priapus: Sexuality and Aggression in Roman Humor*. Rev. ed. Oxford: Oxford University Press, 1992.

Riesenweber, Thomas. *Uneigentliches Sprechen und Bildermischung in den Elegien des Properz*. Untersuchungen zur antiken Literatur und Geschichte Band 86. Berlin: De Gruyter, 2007.

Riggsby, Andrew. "Did the Romans Believe in Their Verdicts?" *Rhetorica* 15 (1997): 235–51.

Rimell, Victoria. "The Poor Man's Feast: Juvenal." In Freudenburg, *Companion to Roman Satire*, 81–94.

Roisman, Hannah. "Nestor the Good Counsellor." *CQ*, n.s., 55 (2005): 17–38.

Roller, Matthew. "*Color*-Blindness: Cicero's Death, Declamation, and the Production of History." *CP* 92 (1997): 109–30.

———. "Exemplarity in Roman Culture: The Cases of Horatius Cocles and Cloelia." *CP* 99 (2004): 1–56.

Romano, A. C. *Irony in Juvenal*. Hildesheim: Olms, 1970.

Ronnick, Michele Valerie. "Form and Meaning of Juvenal's Twelfth Satire." *Maia* 45 (1993): 7–10.

Rosen, Ralph. *Making Mockery: The Poetics of Ancient Satire*. Oxford: Oxford University Press, 2007.

———. "Satire in the Republic: From Lucilius to Horace." In Braund and Osgood, *Persius and Juvenal*, 19–40.

Rosen, Ralph, and Victoria Baines. "I Am Whatever You Say I Am: Satiric Program in Juvenal and Eminem." *CML* 22 (2002): 103–27.

Rosen, Ralph, and Catherine C. Keane. "Greco-Roman Satirical Poetry." In *A Companion to Greek and Roman Sexualities*, edited by Thomas K. Hubbard, 381–97. Chichester: Wiley-Blackwell, 2014.

Rosenwein, Barbara, ed. *Anger's Past: The Social Uses of an Emotion in the Middle Ages*. Ithaca, NY: Cornell University Press, 1998.

———. "Worrying about Emotions in History." *American Historical Review* 107 (2002): 821–45.

Rotstein, Andrea. *The Idea of Iambos*. Oxford: Oxford University Press, 2009.

Rudd, Niall. *Lines of Enquiry: Studies in Latin Poetry*. Cambridge: Cambridge University Press, 1976.

———. *The Satires of Horace*. Cambridge: Cambridge University Press, 1966. Reprint, Berkeley: University of California Press, 1982.

———. *Themes in Roman Satire*. Norman: University of Oklahoma Press, 1986.

———. *Horace: Epistles II and Ars Poetica*. Cambridge: Cambridge University Press, 1989.

———. *The Common Spring: Essays on Latin and English Poetry*. Exeter: Bristol Phoenix Press, 2005.

Russell, D. A. "Rhetoric and Criticism." *G&R*, 2nd ser., 14 (1967): 130–44.

Rutherford, Ian. *Canons of Style in the Antonine Age: Idea-Theory in Its Literary Context*. Oxford: Clarendon Press, 1998.

Sarkissian, John. "Appreciating Umbricius: The Prologue (1–20) of Juvenal's Third Satire." *C&M* 41 (1990): 247–58.

Schiesaro, Alessandro. "Passion, Reason, and Knowledge in Seneca's Tragedies." In Braund and Gill, *Passions in Roman Thought*, 89–111.

Schlegel, Catherine M. *Satire and the Threat of Speech in Horace's Satires Book 1*. Madison: University of Wisconsin Press, 2005.

Schmitz, Christine. *Das Satirische in Juvenals Satiren*. Berlin: De Gruyter, 2000.

Schneider, Carl. *Juvenal und Seneca*. PhD diss., University of Würzburg, 1930.

Schnur, Harry C. "Iuvenalis Saturae XVI fragmentum nuperrime repertum." In *Silvae: Festschrift für Ernst Zinn zum 60. Geburtstag*, edited by Michael von Albrecht and Eberhard Heck, 211–15. Tübingen: Niemeyer, 1970.

Scott, Inez G. *The Grand Style in the Satires of Juvenal*. Northampton, MA: Smith College Classical Studies, 1927.

Scourfield, J. H. D. "Anger and Gender in Chariton's *Chaereas and Callirhoe*." In Braund and Most, *Ancient Anger*, 163–84.

Shackleton Bailey, D. R. *Propertiana*. Amsterdam: Hakkert, 1967.

———. *Quintilian: The Lesser Declamations*. 2 vols. Cambridge, MA: Harvard University Press, 2006.

Shero, Lucius R. "The Satirist's Apologia." *University of Wisconsin Studies in Language and Literature* 15 (1922): 148–67.

Singleton, David. "Juvenal VI.1–20, and Some Ancient Attitudes to the Golden Age." *G&R*, 2nd ser., 19 (1972): 151–65.

———. "Juvenal's Fifteenth Satire: A Reading." *G&R*, 2nd ser., 30 (1983): 198–207.

Skidmore, Clive. *Practical Ethics for Roman Gentlemen: The Work of Valerius Maximus*. Exeter: University of Exeter Press, 1996.

Smallwood, E. Mary. *Documents Illustrating the Principates of Gaius, Claudius and Nero*. Cambridge: Cambridge University Press, 1967.

Smith, Warren S. "Husband *vs.* Wife in Juvenal's Sixth Satire." *CW* 73 (1980): 323–32.

———. "Greed and Sacrifice in Juvenal's Twelfth Satire." *TAPA* 119 (1989): 287–98.

———. *Satiric Advice on Women and Marriage: From Plautus to Chaucer*. Ann Arbor: University of Michigan Press, 2005.

Smith, Wesley D. *Hippocrates: Pseudepigraphic Writings*. Leiden: Brill, 1990.

Sogno, Cristiana. "Persius, Juvenal, and the Transformation of Satire in Late Antiquity." In Braund and Osgood, *Persius and Juvenal*, 363–85.

Sorabji, Richard. *Emotion and Peace of Mind: From Stoic Agitation to Christian Temptation*. New York: Oxford University Press, 2000.

Späth, Thomas. "Masculinity and Gender Performance in Tacitus." In Pagán, *Companion to Tacitus*, 429–57.

Staley, Gregory A. "Juvenal's Third Satire: Umbricius' Rome, Vergil's Troy." *MAAR* 45 (2000): 85–98.

Stewart, Roberta. "Domitian and Roman Religion: Juvenal, *Satires* Two and Four." *TAPA* 124 (1994): 309–32.

Stramaglia, Antonio. *[Quintiliano] La città che si cibò dei suoi cadaveri (Declamazioni maggiori, 12)*. Cassino: Edizioni dell'Università degli Studi di Cassino, 2002.

———. *Giovenale, Satire 1, 7, 12, 16: Storia di un poeta*. Bologna: Pàtron, 2008.

Sullivan, J. P., ed. *Satire: Critical Essays on Roman Literature*. London: Routledge and Kegan Paul, 1963.

Sussman, Lewis A. *The Major Declamations Ascribed to Quintilian: A Translation*. Frankfurt: Peter Lang, 1987.

Svarlien, John. "Lucilianus Character." *AJP* 115 (1994): 253–67.

Sweet, David. "Juvenal's *Satire* 4: Poetic Uses of Indirection." *CSCA* 12 (1979): 283–303.

Syme, Ronald. *Tacitus*. Vol. 2. Oxford: Clarendon Press, 1958.

———. "Juvenal, Pliny, Tacitus." *AJP* 100 (1979): 250–78.

———. "The Patria of Juvenal." *CP* 74 (1979): 1–15.

Taylor, Humphrey. "Very Large Majorities Believe Political Discourse Is Angry, Bad-Tempered, and Worse Now Than in the Past." Harris Poll, March 14, 2011. Harris Interactive. www.harrisinteractive.com/NewsRoom/HarrisPolls/tabid/447/mid/1508/articleId/721/ctl/ReadCustom%20Default/Default.aspx.

Tengström, Emin. *A Study of Juvenal's Tenth Satire: Some Structural and Interpretive Problems*. Göteborg: Acta Universitatis Gothoburgensis, 1980.

Thom, Johan C. "The Passions in Neopythagorean Writings." In Fitzgerald, *Passions and Moral Progress*, 67–78.

Tompkins, Jane. "The Reader in History." In *Reader-Response Criticism from Formalism to Poststructuralism*, edited by Jane Tompkins, 201–32. Baltimore: Johns Hopkins University Press, 1980.

Toohey, Peter. *Melancholy, Love, and Time: Boundaries of the Self in Ancient Literature*. Ann Arbor: University of Michigan Press, 2004.

Townend, Gavin B. "The Literary Substrata to Juvenal's Satires." *JRS* 63 (1973): 148–60.

Treggiari, Susan. *Roman Marriage: Iusti Coniuges from the Time of Cicero to the Time of Ulpian*. Oxford: Clarendon Press, 1991.

Uden, James. "The Invisibility of Juvenal." PhD diss., Columbia University, 2011.

———. *The Invisible Satirist: Juvenal and Second-Century Rome*. New York: Oxford University Press, 2014.

Umurhan, Osman. "Poetic Projection in Juvenal's Satires." *Arethusa* 44 (2011): 221–43.

Van Abbema, Laura. "The Autonomy and Influence of Roman Women in the Late First/Early Second Century C.E.: Social History and Gender Discourse." PhD diss., University of Wisconsin, 2008.

Van den Berg, Christopher S. "Imperial Satire and Rhetoric." In Braund and Osgood, *Persius and Juvenal*, 262–82.

Van der Poel, Marc. "The Use of Exempla in Roman Declamation." *Rhetorica* 27 (2009): 332–53.

Van Mal-Maeder, Danielle. *La fiction des déclamations*. Mnemosyne Supplementa 290. Leiden: Brill, 2007.

Van Sickle, John. "The Book-Roll and Some Conventions of the Poetic Book." *Arethusa* 13 (1980): 5–42.

Walker, Bryce. "Moralizing Discourse in Juvenal's Later Books." PhD diss., University of Pennsylvania, 2006.

Walters, Jonathan. "Making a Spectacle: Deviant Men, Invective, and Pleasure." *Arethusa* 31 (1998): 355–67.

Warmington, E. H. *Remains of Old Latin.* Vol. 3, *Lucilius; The Twelve Tables.* Rev. ed. Cambridge, MA: Harvard University Press, 1967.

Waters, Kenneth H. "Juvenal and the Reign of Trajan." *Antichthon* 4 (1970): 62–77.

Webb, Ruth. "Imagination and the Arousal of the Emotions in Greco-Roman Rhetoric." In Braund and Gill, *Passions in Roman Thought*, 112–27.

———. "Rhetoric in the Novel: Sex, Lies, and Sophistic." In Worthington, *Companion to Greek Rhetoric*, 526–41.

Weber, Harold. "Comic Humor and Tragic Spirit: The Augustan Distinction between Horace and Juvenal." *CML* 1 (1981): 275–89.

Weisinger, Kenneth. "Irony and Moderation in Juvenal XI." *CSCA* 5 (1972): 227–40.

Wessner, Paul, ed. *Scholia in Iuvenalem vetustiora.* Stuttgart: Teubner, 1967.

White, Stephen D. "The Politics of Anger." In Rosenwein, *Anger's Past*, 127–52.

Wiesen, David S. "*Classis Numerosa*: Juvenal, *Satire* 7.151." *CQ*, n.s., 21 (1971): 506–508.

———. "Juvenal and the Intellectuals." *Hermes* 101 (1973): 464–83.

Wilcox, Amanda. "Sympathetic Rivals: Consolation in Cicero's Letters." *AJP* 126 (2005): 237–55.

———. "Bad Emperors: Imperial Exemplars in Seneca's *De Ira* Book 3." Paper presented at the annual meeting of the Classical Association of the Middle West and South, Baton Rouge, Louisiana, March 2012.

Williams, Gordon. *Change and Decline: Roman Literature in the Early Empire.* Berkeley: University of California Press, 1978.

Wilson, Marcus. "The Subjugation of Grief in Seneca's *Epistles*." In Braund and Gill, *Passions in Roman Thought*, 48–67.

———. "After the Silence: Tacitus, Suetonius, Juvenal." In *Flavian Rome: Culture, Image, Text*, edited by Anthony J. Boyle and William J. Dominik, 523–42. Leiden: Brill, 2003.

———. "Your Writings or Your Life: Cicero's *Philippics* and Declamation." In *Cicero's Philippics: History, Rhetoric, and Ideology*, edited by Tom Stevenson and Marcus Wilson, 305–34. Auckland: Polygraphia, 2008.

Winkler, Martin M. *The Persona in Three Satires of Juvenal.* Hildesheim: G. Olms, 1983.

———. "The Function of Epic in Juvenal's Satires." In *Studies in Latin Literature and Roman History*, vol. 5, edited by Carl Deroux, 414–43. Brussels: Latomus Revue d' Études Latines, 1989.

———. "Alogia and Emphasis in Juvenal's Fourth Satire." *Ramus* 24 (1995): 59–81.

———. "Persius and Juvenal in the Media Age." In Braund and Osgood, *Persius and Juvenal*, 513–43.

Witke, Charles. *Latin Satire: The Structure of Persuasion.* Leiden: Brill, 1970.

Woodman, A. J. "Juvenal 1 and Horace." *G&R*, 2nd ser., 30 (1983): 81–84.

Woods, Heather A. "Hunting Literary Legacies: *Captatio* in Roman Satire." PhD diss., University of Minnesota, 2012.

Worthington, Ian, ed. *A Companion to Greek Rhetoric*. Chichester: Wiley-Blackwell, 2007.

Wray, David. *Catullus and the Poetics of Roman Manhood*. Cambridge: Cambridge University Press, 2001.

Wright, Maureen Rosemary. "*Ferox Virtus*: Anger in Virgil's *Aeneid*." In Braund and Gill, *Passions in Roman Thought*, 169–84.

Wright, Richard A. "Plutarch on Moral Progress." In Fitzgerald, *Passions and Moral Progress*, 136–50.

Zanker, Graham. "*Enargeia* in the Ancient Criticism of Poetry." *RhM*, n.f., 124 (1981): 297–311.

Zanker, Paul. 1996. *The Mask of Socrates: The Image of the Intellectual in Antiquity*. Berkeley: University of California Press.

Zarini, Vincent. "L'indignation chez Juvénal: Objets et evolutions." In *Stylus: La parole dans ses formes. Mélanges in l'honneur du Professeur Jacqueline Dangel*, edited by Marc Baratin, Carlos Lévy, Régine Utard, and Anne Videau, 445–56. Paris: Classiques Garnier, 2011.

Zetzel, James E. G. "Horace's *Liber Sermonum:* The Structure of Ambiguity." *Arethusa* 13 (1980): 59–77.

INDEX LOCORUM

Note: Citations from Juvenal's *Satires* are simplified for the sections that discuss individual poems in detail (marked in bold). Citations from select prose works are similarly consolidated.

Fasti (Fast.)
3.3.284: 113
Metamorphoses (Met.)
12.178: 187
Tristia (Tr.)
2.259: 113n45

PERSIUS
Satires
1.12: 9, 121
1.103–34: 42n59
1.114–15: 41
1.116–17: 43
3.18: 32n18
3.77–85: 206n113
3.105–6: 44
5.189–91: 206n113
6: 152, 166
6.75–80: 184
PETRONIUS
Satyricon
116–17: 165n101
124.2–125: 165n101
141: 165n101, 193
PHILODEMUS
On Anger (Ir.)
fr. 6: 82n29
PLATO
Philebus (Phlb.)
47e: 31n15
PLINY THE ELDER
Natural History
(Nat. Hist.)
8.50.119: 191n72
10.83.172: 75n13
35.2: 101
PLINY THE YOUNGER
Letters (Ep.)
3.1: 179n43, 185
4.11.4–10: 49n81
5.17.6: 103
6.33.10: 32n21
9.13.4: 32n21
Panegyric (Pan.)
91
48: 53n91, 82n29

PLUTARCH
Life of Cato (Cat. Mai.)
20: 183n60
Moralia (Mor.)
31n14, 125, 169n3, 177–78, 181–82
78e–80e: 174n27
455c: 38n44
455e–f: 82n29
457a: 82n29
462e–f: 38n46
540f: 187n67
544c–f: 187n67
783b: 171n14
787c: 208
788f: 186
789e–90a: 186–87
794c–d: 187n69
794c–795d: 185
795a: 185–88
POMPONIUS
Digest (Dig.)
1.2.2.51: 130n35
PROPERTIUS
Elegies
1.1.28: 38n47

QUINTILIAN
Education of the Orator (Inst.)
1.9: 128n30
2.1.2: 27n4
2.4.15–26: 36n36
2.10.4–9: 128n31
2.17.26–29: 40n50
3.5: 27n4, 70n5
3.8.46: 137
4.1.28: 32n23
4.2.57: 38n45
4.5.6: 40n50
5 pref.: 40n50, 60
5.11: 128n30
6.1: 40n50, 64
6.2: 33n24, 36n38, 40n50, 129n33
6.51: 64n126
7.1: 27n4, 129n33
8.3.1–11: 36n38, 60n114, 65n127
9.2.8: 40n52

GENERAL INDEX

abjection, 75, 108, 114–15
addressee, 102, 195, 150–51, 161, 164, 206, 209
  significant naming of, 71, 175, 192
  victimization of, 23, 62–67, 68–86, 157–59, 168–69, 174–81
adviser, satirist as, 24, 99, 105, 181, 191
  on bearing misfortune, 168–69, 179–80
  on clienthood, 63–67
  on marriage, 68–86
  on prayer, 137, 144
  on writing, 89, 91–92
Agrippina, 71, 77
Alexander, 138–39
ancestry, 98–108, 115, 156, 199
  ancestor images, 100 106, 112
anger
  and community, 14, 15, 178–79, 190
  conditions for defined, 37–39
  conditions for dramatized, 47–49, 52, 57–58, 63–64, 78, 91, 206
  contexts for interpreting, 22–23, 31–35, 47, 115
  as dynamic, 37, 159, 176
  expression of as therapy, 38, 69, 98, 108, 114–15
  as "first" emotion, 22, 40–43, 115
  and humor, 9
  inability to express, 23, 51–52, 63, 66, 104, 107

  Juvenal's changing engagement with, 17–19, 89, 115, 120, 169–71, 192–96, 208
  and old age, 174–81
  pleasures of, 23, 31, 34, 47, 79, 91, 98, 100
  right to anger, 25, 46–47
  and status, 30, 31, 33, 38, 180, 201–202
  symptoms of, 40–41, 57, 64, 67, 82, 159, 168, 170, 176
  and women, 68–86, 176n35, 202n102
  See also indignatio
anger control discourse, 13–14, 30n11, 34, 170–71
  Stoic therapy, 79–83, 85
animals, 81, 152, 162, 199
  as gods. *See* religion: Egyptian
  humans compared with, 127n28, 140, 163, 190–92, 194, 202–5
Appius Claudius Caecus, 32n23, 74, 107, 112, 185
Aristotle, 10, 37n43, 208
audience of satire, 3, 19, 90–91, 108, 115
  ancient audience, 16, 29–31, 37, 53–55, 129–33, 135–39
  ideal narrative audience, 55, 85
  role distinct from addressee's, 23, 55–56, 58
  role similar to addressee's, 86, 151, 154–55, 166

Augustus, 7, 93, 130
authenticity, 5, 120
    thematized in satire, 150–66, 215–16

beards. *See* hair
Bellandi, Franco, 120, 155, 199
biographical readings of Juvenal, 16–17,
    72, 120, 194–95, 210
bodies, suffering, 102–5, 111, 139–42
    violence against, 77–78, 83–86, 206–8
    metaphor of sickness, 97–98, 138,
      146, 180
    See also hunger

cannibalism, 192–205
career, literary, 6–7, 91–98, 210
    satiric careers, 7–8, 17, 166–67
    turning points in Juvenal's, 43, 87–91,
      99, 145, 170–74, 206–12
Cato the Elder, 178–79, 181, 182–83,
    184–85, 186
censor, 45–46, 49–50, 100, 179, 190,
    196, 201
censorship, 212
    self-censorship, 52, 63, 135, 137
children
    and anger, 80, 173, 189
    and parents, 140–41, 181–92, 193,
      196, 209
    and teachers, 96, 98
Cicero, 6–7, 60n113, 121, 136–37
Claudius, 71–72, 75–77, 143, 201–2
consolation, 73, 78, 168–69, 171, 174–80
"cynical" persona, 16, 24–25, 169, 193

Democritus, 24, 117–32, 135–48,
    159, 178
Demosthenes, 136–137
depression, 12n42, 146–48
dialogue, 42, 88–90, 108–16, 172
discomfort of satire's audience, 3, 22–24,
    69, 133, 139, 178
Domitian, 12, 23, 49–53, 82n29, 131n38
drama, 4–5, 119
    actors, 16, 96
    comedy, 175–76, 179, 184

tragedy, 74, 191, 193, 196–97, 199
    See also poets
Dryden, John, 4n9, 9–10, 26, 203

elegy, 7, 13, 74; *See also* poets
emotion, 1–2, 8–16
    and age, 173–74
    and community, 12, 14–15, 196, 199–205
    emotional detachment, 24, 100,
      120–46, 154, 169, 178
    emotional plot, 13, 21–25
    history of ("emotionology"), 14, 22
    infection with, 39–40, 58, 67–86, 189–90
    See also specific emotions
envy, 187, 206–9, 214
epic, 6, 34, 74, 162
    anger in, 13, 40, 80–81
    exempla from, 128, 141–42, 151–52,
      155, 186–87
    mock-epic, 36, 57
    See also poets
exempla, 45, 98–108, 119, 122, 179,
    188–190
    See also ancestors; epic; historical
      subject matter; myth; rhetorical
      education

fear, 11, 39, 76, 190, 199
    as fuel for anger, 58
    as "Golden Age" emotion, 14
    of imperial regime, 135
    and old age, 175–176
    of satiric abuse, 47, 64, 87
    of wives, 70, 83
fearlessness, 4, 51, 132, 144, 212
fire imagery, 40–43, 57, 97
flattery, 51–52, 169n3
forgery. *See* imitation, literary
friendship and the satirist, 24, 53–67,
    150–52, 157–65, 168–69

grief. *See* sorrow
guest satirist. *See* proxy satirist

Hadrian, 113, 162n95, 211, 212n133
hair, 104, 109, 111–13

Hannibal, 121, 129n33, 138
hatred: and cannibalism, 194–97
　　as orator's goal, 30–31, 85
　　and historiography, 32, 49, 53
　　as response to poetry, 26
Heraclitus, 118, 120, 124–26, 141,
　　146–48, 178
Highet, Gilbert, 17, 172, 175, 194, 210,
　　212
historical subject matter, 3, 21, 42, 179,
　　213
　　chronological regression, 93, 99, 136,
　　138
　　See also specific historical figures;
　　exempla; politics
historiography, 32, 74, 96, 128
Horace, 2, 4, 7, 17, 64, 166–67, 181
house of the satirist, 150–67
humanitas, 199, 202–5
humor, 2, 19, 69
　　absent from Juvenal's program, 9
　　cannibalism humor, 193–94
　　See also mockery
hunger, 95–97, 194, 197, 201, 204

iambic poetry, 32, 115
imitation, literary, 4, 5, 24, 118, 209–11
　　forgery, 6, 173, 203
indignatio, 4, 9, 15
　　reappearance in later Juvenal, 161–62,
　　165, 193
　　in satiric plot, 26–67, 68–86
　　strategies for performing, 28, 30–31,
　　99, 141, 192, 201, 208
　　See also anger
"ironic" persona, 16, 19, 88, 110,
　　170n7, 193

jealousy, 13, 75
　　See also envy
joy, 11, 39, 47, 76, 134, 161
　　as target of laughter, 118, 123
　　See also pleasure

Laronia, 46–47, 56
laughter. *See* mockery

libertas, 38, 116, 137
　　between friends, 168–69
　　exercised by Juvenal, 49, 63, 65, 186
　　exercised by reprobates, 47, 114
　　repressed or compromised, 42, 96
love, 77, 165, 199
Lucilius, 2, 4–5, 8, 20, 61, 214–16
　　and anger, 40–44, 64, 97, 115
luxury, 28, 43, 49, 156, 161–64, 183, 188
　　and desire, 114, 147, 157
lyric poetry, 7, 74, 95, 111, 182

Maecenas, 7, 93, 111n43, 152, 163
marriage, 39, 47–48, 68–86
Martial, 6, 58, 63n121, 90n5, 152, 159
masculinity, 29nn5 –6, 70–79, 85
　　priapic stance, 20, 68, 78
Messalina, 71, 75–76, 131, 143
mockery, 3
　　by characters in Juvenal, 44, 88,
　　153–54, 176, 196
　　"laughing philosopher."
　　See Democritus
　　by Juvenal, 18, 24, 163 (*See also*
　　addressee: victimization of)
　　of old men, 187–88
　　See also humor
moral decline, 28, 98–108, 156, 177, 194
morality of satire, 18, 21, 29–30, 58,
　　69, 108–16
myth, 3, 80–82, 84, 127, 143, 204
　　Golden Age, 14–15, 177n39
　　in rhetorical education, 71, 96
　　See also specific mythological figures

Nero, 42, 106, 130–31, 143, 165
Nestor, 186–88, 190
nostalgia for satire's past, 24, 43, 90–91,
　　107, 115–16

obscenity, 3, 7, 32n22, 45, 109–10
old age, 111, 139–41
　　in ancient literature, 172–74, 181–83,
　　184–88, 195, 208–9, 214
　　of satirist, 6, 17, 24–25, 169–212
Ovid, 6, 76, 193, 195, 199, 210

patronage, 56–57, 61–66, 75, 108–16, 210
    satirist's experience of, 16, 20
    literary, 90, 91–98, 102
Persius, 2, 4, 7, 10, 63, 113n44, 181, 210,
    214, 216
persona, satiric, 2, 41, 88–89, 207–8
    allusivity of, 146, 155, 216
    conflicting impressions of, 25, 69,
        169–70, 193–94
    moral characterization of, 35, 70, 154
    need to objectify, 19, 121, 127
persona theory, 16–19, 30, 109, 119–20,
    169
phantasia, 36, 43–45, 65–66, 70, 73–79,
    180
philosophy, 85, 118–19, 144–46, 169n3,
    198, 200
    literary inspiration from, 21, 33–34,
        74, 79–83, 146–50
    philosophical interpretation of Juvenal,
        14–15, 29–30, 72, 115, 169
    See also specific philosophers
Piranha, Doug, 87, 168
pity, 13, 54, 105, 142, 209
    and cannibalism, 197, 199–201, 204
    self–pity, 111
    See also sympathy
pleasure, 11, 39, 71, 75, 157, 190–92
    of audiences, 9–10, 26, 60, 78
    loss of with age, 140
    in others' suffering, 188
Pliny the Younger, 6–7, 50, 52, 63n121
plot, 17, 35, 72–73, 150
    of satiric career, 8, 20, 22–25, 86,
        89–91, 173
poets, 27, 38, 45, 55, 57, 89, 91–98
politics, 118–19, 130–37, 143, 160,
    210–12
    in declamation, 127, 137, 140
    old men and, 171n14, 182n55, 186
    political careers, 6, 91, 102, 142
poverty, 43, 57–58, 63, 72, 91–98, 108–16
    as carefree, 132
    self-induced, 153
progressive view of change, 90, 115–16
prosopopoeia, 32, 74, 107, 112

proxy satirist, 36, 46–47, 56–62, 108–16
Pythagoras, 198, 200, 205n109

religion, 47, 48, 50n83, 75, 197–98
    anti-religious sentiment, 177–78
    curses, 165–66, 171
    Egyptian, 192–94, 203–4
    prayer, 11, 39, 63, 113–14, 119, 122,
        136–45, 149
    sacrifice, 97, 113, 144, 150–51, 161–66
revenge
    and anger, 31n15, 37n43, 53, 174, 176
        (*See also* anger: and status)
    divine, 178
    satire as, 8, 27, 47, 50, 94
    against satirist, 9
rhetoric as entertainment, 12, 15, 30, 37,
    60, 62
    See also audience
rhetorical education
    controversiae and *suasoriae*, 16, 36,
        70–71, 136–40
    Juvenal's evidenced, 5, 36–37, 46, 48,
        119, 128–30, 199–200
    and performance of emotions, 10,
        26–29, 53–55
rhetorical theory
    emotion in, 10–11, 15–16, 19, 29–31,
        53, 60, 64, 129
    on style and age, 184–88
Ribbeck, Otto, 5, 117, 170

satiric theory, 1–2, 4, 17, 203–4
Schnur, Harry, 209–11
self-examination, 146–53
Sejanus, 121, 129–35
Seneca the Younger, 65, 120n8, 130n35,
    160, 169, 180
sermo
    Horace on, 149, 152, 215
    as one-sided, 64, 79, 94, 180, 215
    See also dialogue
shame, 14, 75, 101–2, 141n54, 186
shamelessness, 39, 76, 104–106, 153,
    165, 175
Silius, Gaius, 75, 131–32, 143

Sirens, 114–15, 121, 188
sorrow, 15, 53, 101, 153, 168, 202
    of aging, 111, 140–41, 175–76, 180
    performed in declamation, 199–201
    resistance to, 123, 144
    See also weeping
spectacle, 100–108, 113, 140, 191, 196
    political, 118–19, 122, 133–35
    rhetorical performance as, 23, 56, 85
statues, 55, 94, 114, 121, 131–33
    See also ancestry: ancestor images
story. *See* plot
subject matter and persona, 11, 21, 35, 39,
    45, 73–74, 170
Sulla, 27, 36n35, 79, 128n31
sympathy, 129, 168, 202

Tiberius, 127, 131
tranquility, 24, 92n10, 117–67, 169, 178
Thersites, 112, 155
Trajan, 49n80, 53n91, 91

Umbricius, 56–62, 79, 109, 160, 181,
    206n113, 207, 208–9
variety in satire, 1–3, 8, 37, 41

Varillus, 46, 56
Vergil, 6, 93, 95, 96–97, 155, 173, 206

weeping, 28, 64, 75, 200
    as response to performance, 54, 197
    as response to satire, 9
"weeping philosopher." *See* Heraclitus